"FORTRESS AMERICA" UNDER SIEGE

MARXIST SOCIALISM-COMMUNISM'S WAR ON THE "FREE WORLD"

"The easiest way to take a fortress is from within."

Vladimir Lenin

Marxist-Leninist Totalitarianism

Judeo-Christian Free Democracy

V. Lenin (1870-1924) K. Marx (1818-1883) E.C. Manning (1908-1996) W. Aberhart (1879-1943)

"The wicked shall be turned into hell, and all the nations that forget God."

Psalm 9:17

FRANK CRAWFORD

Disclaimer

The author of this work has quoted the writers of many articles and books. This does not mean that the author endorses or recommends the works of others, though he may speak highly of their research and contributions to the subject at hand. If the author quotes someone, it does not mean that he agrees with all of the author's tenets, statements, or words, whether in the work quoted or any other work of the author. There has been no attempt to alter the meaning of the quotes.

Copyright © 2020 by Frank Crawford
November, 2020
All Rights Reserved
Printed in the United States of America

POLREL_____: Political Philosophy & Religion with Interpretation

ISBN 978-1-7356723-4-2

All Scripture quotations are from the King James 1611 Bible.

No part of this book may be reproduced without the expressed consent of the publisher, except for brief quotes, whether by electronic, photocopying, recording, or information storage and retrieval systems.

Address All Inquiries To:
THE OLD PATHS PUBLICATIONS, Inc.
142 Gold Flume Way
Cleveland, Georgia, U.S.A.

Web: www.theoldpathspublications.com
E-mail: TOP@theoldpathspublications.com

DEDICATION

To The
Faithful and Loving Christian Crawford

My wife, whose prayers and love for God gave me encouragement and faith to take on the challenges of life for 32 years of marriage, and work on this book in retirement as a Bible-believing, freedom-loving Christian. Her father ran for mayor in a Philippine Barangay and lost to a corrupt politician through voting fraud. We both realize that sinful human nature is universal and "eternal vigilance is the price of liberty." Yet, she still loves politics and her favorite Canadian leader is the Hon. Stephen Harper.

This volume is dedicated,
By her affectionate
Husband:
Frank Crawford

ACKNOWLEDGMENTS

A great debt of gratitude is due to Mr. Dennis Snyder of Redlands, Alberta, who provided me with much written material on Mr. Manning and Mr. Aberhart. This information was invaluable and motivated me to do further research and start writing on both of these great men. Special thanks to Dr. and Mrs. D. Williams of *The Old Paths Publications* for offering to help me publish this book. Their assistance made the difference between success and failure in the final product. Miss Cora Gojo's fine work in drawing of the book cover and her expert help in formatting the text and figures were greatly appreciated. My wife, Christian Crawford's words of encouragement and her prayers carried me along the difficult path toward completing this work. A grateful thanks goes to Zuzana Janosova Den Boer who allowed me to publish her experience in Communist Czechoslovakia (Appendix 4). Thanks to Jim Tuovila for supplying much of the material for Canada's Christian Heritage in Appendix 2. A thank you to Evangelist Mark McGaughey for giving me two vintage books on communism that were greatly used as references in this book. I am thankful for my Pastor, Jon Harwood, whose love for Canada and our free democracy motivated me to work that much harder to try and help in some small way my beloved country, Canada, and our friend and neighbor to the south – the United States of America.

FORWARD

The material for this book was provided through a lifetime of experience, the help of a dear Christian friend and many providential workings from the hand of God in realizing the final result, a completed book.

The idea for this book grew slowly out of a lifetime. My younger years were spent in indifference to the fate of my country. My passions and my goals were mostly self-centered, seeking the pleasures of life and not considering the effect on society or others.

When I became a Christian – was saved – on March 24, 1981, my life's goals, values and ambitions changed, from self-centered to Christ-centered as I grew in my faith. Through conversion I saw the world, and my place in it, in a different light. By reading God's Word I saw sin as the plight of the individual personally, and mankind in general; from the degrading of morality to corruption in social institutions, laws and politics. By reference to my younger years I could see my country drifting away from more conservative values to more liberal, permissive and corrupted morals; and it bothered me. I came to see socialism-communism as the root cause of this disintegration. I knew that there was little fear of God in the land, and that would always lead to trouble – God's judgment – down the road. I wanted to try and do something to help, using my experience, Christian conservative values and scientific background to try and make a difference. The only way that I thought of doing this would be to write a book to try and open people's eyes and move them to take action on their part to try and stem the tide of societal decline.

I found two men whose testimonies and life work formed the foundation for this study. They are the late William

Aberhart (1879-1943) and the late Ernest C. Manning (1908-1996), both premiers of the Province of Alberta for eight and twenty-five years respectively. Their conservative values and leadership provide the reader with examples of godly, genuine Christian leaders, which are sorely lacking today in our culture of political correctness and snowflake behavior. Providential circumstances provided me with the right material at the right time to progress in the study of these two men, from their own preaching messages and teachings together with written work about them, in particular Brian Brennan's excellent biography, "The Good Steward: The Ernest C. Manning Story," 2008. Much additional written material came from various sources. Bob Plamondon's "The Truth About Trudeau," (2013) allowed a comparison between the record of E. C. Manning in Alberta and Pierre E. Trudeau in Ottawa. The contrast could not be more striking.

I found the Epoch Times and Calgary Sun newspapers to have the best journalism in reporting without bias concerning day to day events in Canada and Internationally. The Epoch Times "Nine Commentaries on the Communist Party" (2004) and 3 volume "How the Spectre of Communism is Ruling Our World" (2020) to be most informative concerning the changes that have occurred in our country and the Western democracies in general over the last half century. Journalism in The Epoch Times is excellent and informative. The equal cannot be found in the mainstream media. I was thankful to be able to read and use two books from The Rebel Media; Sheila Gunn Reid's "Stop Notley," 2019, and Ezra Levant's "The Libranos," 2019.

This book is not intended to misrepresent or unfairly degrade any individual with whom the writer agrees or disagrees. Most of the comments of those espousing

FORWARD

conservatism or socialism-communism come from their own writings or statements recorded by journalists. Mr. Manning's Christian testimony and conservative political record stands open to scrutiny, offset against Pierre Trudeau's socialist legacy, in this book. The reader is invited to compare and evaluate both men when deciding in what direction this country needs to go in the future.

The beliefs and doctrines of Karl Marx should be carefully examined before embarking on a course of life and career controlled by his philosophy. Many people have accepted his teachings without understanding who this man really was, and the actual historical results of his socio-economic and political doctrines. This book hopefully will help the reader come to an informed decision about Karl Marx and his disciples, and the effects on society of their teachings and political leadership. Canadians should ask themselves, "Is this the man our country needs as its example and guide for the future?

The writer is an older man and has the advantage of having lived through the countercultural revolution of the 1960s, and partaken of some of the restlessness of that generation. He has seen the error of that movement and its negative effects on modern society. He opposed and spoke against Ernest Manning while in university in Calgary. He regrets his youthful folly of those days and wishes to make amends in part by writing this book and setting the record straight.

Hopefully this book will help some reader escape the coming international socialist totalitarian one-world government of the Antichrist portrayed so chillingly in Biblical prophecy. To that end the writer has included the gospel of Jesus Christ in the Appendix of this book to aid those interested in securing their souls against God's sure judgment on sin for each individual person.

TABLE OF CONTENTS

DEDICATION 3
ACKNOWLEDGMENTS 4
FORWARD 5
TABLE OF CONTENTS 8
INTRODUCTION 14
CHAPTER 1 18
THE HON. ERNEST C. MANNING: 18
CHRISTIAN STATESMAN 18
    WHO WAS THIS FELLOW, MANNING? 19
    HUMBLE BEGINNINGS 20
    THE PREACHING OF WILLIAM ABERHART 21
    THE PROPHETIC BIBLE INSTITUTE 22
    ABERHART AND MANNING MOVE INTO POLITICS 23
    E. C. MANNING IN POLITICS 24
    E. C. MANNING'S CHRISTIAN FAITH AND SERVICE 29
    PREMIER SPEAKS AT YOUTH FOR CHRIST RALLY 30
    E. C. MANNING'S EVERYDAY LIFE 31
CHAPTER 2 37
THE HON. ERNEST C. MANNING: 37
A CHAMPION OF THE PEOPLE AND FREE DEMOCRACY 37
    CONTEMPORARY ALBERTA POLITICIANS 38
    ALBERTA GOVERNMENT BUREAUCRATS 41
    UNIVERSITY ACADEMICS 43
    JOURNALISTS AND OTHER WRITERS 45
    CALGARY HERALD NEWSPAPER 48
    SON PRESTON MANNING 51
    MURIEL MANNING & FAMILY 54
    ERNEST C. MANNING 55
CHAPTER 3 81
THE HON. ERNEST C. MANNING: 81
THE PREACHER 81
    MANNING'S PERSONAL CONVERSION TO JESUS CHRIST 82
    MANNING ON TWO IRREFUTABLE CARDINAL TRUTHS .. 82
    MANNING ON GENUINE BIBLE CHRISTIANITY 84
    MANNING ON SIN 86
    MANNING ON THE SUBSTITUTIONAL ATONEMENT OF JESUS CHRIST 89

TABLE OF CONTENTS

    MANNING ON THE CONCERNS OF MODERN SOCIETY 90
    MANNING ON END TIMES GEO-POLITICS 95
    MANNING ON MAN'S FINAL DESTINY[6, #51] 110
    MANNING'S APPEAL 112
CHAPTER 4 114
THE HON. ERNEST C. MANNING'S WARNINGS 114
ON SOCIALISM – COMMUNISM 114
    Vladimir Lenin 114
    1. Destroy a nation's youth; infiltrate and corrupt the education system 124
    2. Gain Control of the Media, thereby taking away Freedom of Speech 147
    3. Deliberately sow strife and division – Marx's "Class Struggle" in society 161
    4. Carry out a program of civil disarmament 169
    5. Undermine faith and confidence in the country's leaders 182
    6. Create civil strife and disorder, and allow it to continue 195
    7. Take power by any means possible through violence, craft and deceit 215
    8. Destroy the fiscal structure through excessive spending and government debt 226
    9. Destroy the moral fabric and character of society 245
CHAPTER 5 261
SOCIALISM – COMMUNISM 261
FULFILLING MANNING'S WARNINGS 261
    WHAT IS COMMUNISM? 268
    1. The abolition of all forms of religion; 282
    Consider Article 17 – 290
    2. The destruction of private property and the abolition of inheritance; 304
    3. Revolution under the leadership of the Communist International (Comintern); 305
    4. Engaging in activities in foreign countries in order to cause strikes, riots, sabotage, bloodshed and civil war; 305
    5. Absolute social and racial equality; add to that gender in 2020; 313
    6. Destruction of all forms of representative or democratic government, including civil liberties, such as freedom of speech, of the press and of assemblage; 319

7. The ultimate objective of world revolution is to establish the dictatorship of the so-called 'proletariat' into a universal Union of Soviet Socialist Republics with its capital in Moscow; 321
8. The achievement of these ends through extreme appeals to "hatred;" 331

CHAPTER 6 336
ALBERTA'S RECENT EXPERIMENTS WITH SOCIALISM 336
Conservative Socialism (1982-1987) 339
A temporary alternative to the Progressive Conservatives 343
NDP Radical Socialism (2015-2019): 344
Rachel Notley 348
Sarah Hoffman (NDP Deputy Premier) 350
Shaye Anderson (NDP MLA) 350
Lou Arab (Rachel Notley's husband) 350
Brian Topp (Original Chief of Staff) 350
Shannon Phillips (Environment Minister) 351
Rod Loyolla (President of Alberta NDP) 352
Graham Mitchell (Chief of Staff in Alberta energy ministry) 353
Colin Piquette (NDP MLA) 353
Dave Mowatt (Ran NDP royalty review) 353
Brian Mason (NDP MLA, former leader) 353
Radical Environmentalism – Federally and Provincially 354
Communism behind Environmentalism and Globalism 362
Communism and globalization 376

CHAPTER 7 390
KARL MARX AND HIS PREDECESSORS, DISCIPLES AND "FELLOW TRAVELERS:" 390
THE DEVIL'S ADVOCATES 390
Bakunin: an anarchist and friend of Karl Marx, said: 393
Karl Marx's personal war with God 395
Friedrich Engels: 402
Eugiene Pottier: 403
Jim Jones: 403
Ella Reeve Bloor: 404
Vladimir Lenin (1870-1924): 404
Sergy Gennadiyevich Nechayev (1847-1882): 408
Joseph Stalin: 410
E. Kardelj: 412
Benito Mussolini: 412

TABLE OF CONTENTS

Adolf Hitler: 412
Reichskommissar Eric Koch: 414
WW II Japanese Rulers: 414
Professor Frederick Schuman: 415
Dallin and Nicolaevsky: 415
Alexander Yakovlev: 415
William Foster: 416
Mao Zedong (1893-1976): 417
Zhou Enlai: 419
'The Party:' 419
Dr. Nguyen Manh Tuong: 423
Communist Party U.S.A.: 423
Western radical left: 424
Bernd Langer: 424
Leibenecht: 424
Saul Alinsky: 425
Herbert Marcuse: 426
Karl Kautsky: 428
Ronald Radosh: 429
Ion Mihai Pacepa: 429
Anonymous author: 430
Lavrentiy Beria: 430
Pierre Elliott Trudeau (1919-2000): 430
Jean Chretien: 431
Hillary Clinton: 432
Barak Obama: 432
Yasser Arafat: 433
Osama bin Laden: 433
Justin Trudeau: 433
M. Stanton Evans: 434
Jiang Zemin: 434
Berdyaev: 435
Deng Xiaoping: 435
Arthur Koestler: 436
Joseph Goebbels: 436
CHAPTER 8 .... **439**
THE LEGACY OF THE HON. WILLIAM ABERHART: **439**
THE VOICE OF REASON **439**

William Aberhart's Prophetic Bible Institute and the False 'Man of Peace' – the Antichrist or Beast of Biblical Prophecy 471
PROPHECY CONCERNING TYRE YET TO BE FULFILLED 478
The Rapture of the Christian Church and the Revealing of the Beast 488

CHAPTER 9 502
THE WAY BACK: 502
A RETURN TO FREE DEMOCRACY 502

"In America, we don't worship government, we worship God." . 503
President Donald Trump 503
THE POLITICAL ISSUES INVOLVED 503
AMERICAN DEMOCRACY WILL BE SAVED OR LOST BY THE AMERICAN VOTER IN NOVEMBER, 2020. 509
THE SPIRITUAL ISSUES INVOLVED 519
SAVED OUT OF SOCIALISM – COMMUNISM 528
MANNING'S ADVICE FOR CONCERNED CANADIANS 532
GOD IS SPEAKING – BUT WILL WE LISTEN? 536

EPILOGUE & PERSONAL TESTIMONY: 543
SOCIALISM-COMMUNISM OR CHRISTIANITY? 543
That is Our Choice 543
MY PERSONAL TESTIMONY FOR WRITING AND COMPILING THIS BOOK 556
APPENDIX 1 562
THE GOSPEL OF JESUS CHRIST 562

By Pastor Travis Alltop & Frank Crawford 562
1. ALL MEN ARE SINNERS, AND THIS INCLUDES YOU. 563
2. YOUR PERSONAL SINS HAVE EARNED YOU A WAGE. 564
3. GOD, IN HIS LOVE AND MERCY, HAS PROVIDED SALVATION FOR YOU. 565
4. YOU CAN BE SAVED AND POSSESS ETERNAL LIFE RIGHT NOW! 568

APPENDIX 2 573
"CANADA'S CHRISTIAN HERITAGE" 573

By Jim Tuovila & Frank Crawford 573
The Dominion of Canada: 573
Thanksgiving Day 574
Canada's National Coat of Arms 575
Canada's Parliament Buildings 576

TABLE OF CONTENTS

The Parliament Building and Peace Tower 579
APPENDIX 3 581
ERNEST C. MANNING 581
RADIO ADDRESS 581
CHICAGO, APRIL 9, 1948 581
   INTRODUCTION 581
   ERNEST MANNING'S TESTIMONY OF SALVATION 582
   GOD'S UNIVERSAL COMMAND 584
   MANKIND'S RESPONSE TO GOD'S COMMAND 586
   MANNING'S ADVICE TO HIS LISTENERS 586
   MANKIND'S REJECTION OF GOD'S COMMAND 588
   ATTITUDE OF THE NATIONS TOWARD GOD 590
   MANNING'S ADVICE ON GOVERNMENT 592
   MANNING CHALLENGES CHRISTIANS 594
   MANNING'S INVITATION TO THE UNSAVED 595
.... 597
APPENDIX 4 598
"I SURVIVED COMMUNISM – 598
ARE YOU READY FOR YOUR TURN?" 598
   - Nikita Khrushchev (1960) 600
   Stage 1:   Polarization – Divide and Conquer 602
   Stage 2:   Destabilization 603
   Stage 3:   Revolution 607
   Life under Communism: 609
   Corruption under Communism: 611
   News Report: Prague, Czechoslovakia 614
APPENDIX 5 615
WILLIAM ABERHART 615
   ERNEST C. MANNING'S MENTOR & BEST FRIEND 615
   Pioneer Reformer 615
   Funeral Service Message 618
   William Aberhart 618
   Dedication Address 625
   William Aberhart Memorial Organ 625
ABOUT THE AUTHOR 630
IN FLANDERS FIELDS 637

INTRODUCTION

Canada and the United States are fighting for their lives in late 2020, on the eve of probably the most important election in U.S. history. "Fortress America," once considered unconquerable, is in mortal danger of defeat by the forces of socialism-communism. The war over the last 50 to 75 years has been fought within both countries borders. Marxism, the teachings and doctrines of the mid-nineteenth century German philosopher, Karl Marx, have displaced the Judeo-Christian foundations of Western democracies, ours included, and threaten to bring us under totalitarian bondage not unlike that envisaged by Adolf Hitler in 1939, at the beginning of WW II. Our democracy is not being defeated by military means just yet, but by infiltration and subversion from within. Our society's values and customs have changed almost overnight. The writer remembers a time when the sanctity of human life and marriage were honored and valued. Today, almost anything goes and those who stand for the old paths are accused of hate crimes. Good has become bad, and bad has become good in society's eyes. This has brought Canada to a precipice which, if passed, will destroy our country and render our children's future intolerable.

Today's media has aided and abetted this decline, by adopting the same Marxist teachings that the present Liberal government and its satellites, the NDP and Bloc, follow. The only viable alternative is the Conservative Party which is struggling to find its soul. Conservative leaders are standing for fiscal conservatism but have abandoned social conservatism out of fear of the voting public and the hostile media gang. Fortunately, there are still a few voices being heard to support traditional values and morality. These sources, namely The Epoch Times, The Calgary Sun and the Rebel Media are quoted

INTRODUCTION

frequently in the chapters following. Good books are still available for people to make intelligent decisions about which kind of leaders will best serve the voting public with integrity and character. Unfortunately, few people read these kinds of books so ignorance of Canadian and American history is on the wane, especially among the younger generation. Fortunately, these books have not been banned, but could be in the future if the current trends are not reversed.

Biblical Christianity has been shut out of the public forum. Socialist ideology arrogantly lifts itself up as the only valid arbiter of modern day society's morals and values. Christians have ceded the battle to Marx's disciples and the future looks dim. The Bible has been taken out of every institution in our society and is considered irrelevant to the discussion of almost every subject dealing with the greatest issues of our day – the right to life of the unborn, capital punishment, gambling, sexual morality, the origin of life, and free speech – to mention only a few.

Alberta is singularly important in having had two provincial premiers, William Aberhart and Ernest C. Manning, who both were Bible-believing Christians and competent politicians at the same time. They led what is termed "God's Government" in Alberta for a period of thirty-three years, from 1935 to 1968 when Mr. Manning retired after twenty-five years as premier. Their terms in office provide a spotlight on leadership that had a clear Christian testimony and motive for public service. Mr. Manning's term in office was described in detail by Brian Brennan (2008) in his excellent biography of the man. In contrast, the opposite kind of leader Pierre Trudeau's legacy was described in the same kind of exposition by Bob Plamondon (2013). Understanding the character and effect on society of these two kinds of leaders is essential for plotting the future course that Canadians and Americans must take for their countries, if their democratic freedoms are to be preserved.

We cannot exclude the Bible from our halls of learning and government. To do so, invites the opposite philosophies to flourish, and that they have done for far too long. Marxism has currently formed the foundation of our society's institutions and it is only a matter time until it shows its true colors, colors that reflect the character of that man and his followers. This book contains a chapter exposing who Karl Marx really was, what he wrote and what his objective was in formulating his socio-economic and political philosophies. The reader is invited to compare Karl Marx with the Lord Jesus Christ as shown in the Christian gospels. The challenge is, which man would you want to follow and give your life for? Again, Ernest Manning and William Aberhart are examples of men who chose to serve Christ. Stalin, Mao, Castro, Chavez, Trudeau and many others chose to follow socialism-communism underlain by Marx's theories. Which bore good fruit? Which saved lives and which took human lives is the evidence of where a "just society" is to be found. This book will provide the evidence for a return to a Judeo-Christian foundation for our Canadian democracy.

The world is entering very perilous times with China on the ascendance and the U.S. beleaguered with racial riots, COVID-19 and anti-free democratic interference in the existing government, all aided and abetted by the mainstream media. The objective is to defeat the incumbent president and bring America under a Marxist-led Democratic Party and President, followed very likely with the extinguishing of freedom in that great republic. America's enemies are watching and waiting to see what will happen, and to take advantage of her at time of

INTRODUCTION

vulnerability and distraction. "Fortress America" is indeed in troubled waters. It is under siege. As Lenin said long ago, "The easiest way to take a fortress is from within."

America relied on God in her beginning. It is time for her to return to her roots. Many Americans profess the Christian faith. However, the evidence of truly committed Christianity is lacking in the country. If totalitarian socialism-communism gains full power in the U.S. many millions of lives will be in peril, young and old, liberals and conservatives, and any who differ with the ruling elites. The only recourse for deliverance is to return to God, return to the genuine Christian faith demonstrated by many godly citizens over the past generations. If Canada and America do not have a revival of individual Christians, and their churches do not experience revival, there is little hope for the continuing freedoms that we and our families presently enjoy. If there is no revival, God's judgment will be meted out in our two countries that are succumbing to totalitarian socialism-communism and the tragic conditions that follow.

This book is a heartfelt attempt to open some people's eyes and perhaps play a small part in helping avert a catastrophe of this kind from happening.

CHAPTER 1

THE HON. ERNEST C. MANNING: CHRISTIAN STATESMAN

"He chose David also his servant, and took him from the sheepfolds: so he fed them according to the integrity of his heart; and guided them by the skillfulness of his hands."
Psalm 78:70, 72

CHAPTER 1: MANNING, CHRISTIAN STATESMAN

"Now and then there comes upon the stage of life, in the theatre of this world, a man who so differs from the rest that he catches the eye and ear at once, and, as long as he moves in the scene, holds the attention of his fellows. When the sable curtain falls, and his part in the drama is over, we who remain to fill the minor roles find time in moments of reflection to ask ourselves: What manner of man was this, and wherein did he differ from others of his kind?" [The Life of General Nathan Bedford Forrest, John Wyeth, 1899]

WHO WAS THIS FELLOW, MANNING?

Many have asked this question. Ernest Charles Manning (1908-1996), in 1935 at 26 years of age, became the youngest Cabinet Minister in the British Commonwealth. In Cabinet from 1935-1943, he then became Premier of Alberta, leading that province from 1943 to 1968, a period of unparalleled growth and prosperity. Mr. Manning retired at 60 years of age having never been defeated in a Provincial Election. On the occasion of his fiftieth birthday the following letter of appreciation was given to him on a formal Provincial Certificate:

> **"Honorable Sir:**
> Upon the occasion of your Fiftieth Birthday, your fellow Citizens of the Province of Alberta desire to convey to you their most sincere congratulations...We are reminded at this time that since 1935, when you became the youngest Minister of the Crown in the Commonwealth, you have devoted Twenty Three continuous years...almost half your lifetime...to the Service of our Province and our People. During these years you have displayed, by precept and by example, the most capable leadership. In the period of your Ministry our Province has grown in Stature, our People have Prospered, and have enjoyed an ever growing measure of Economic Democracy and Social Justice.
>
> In token of our Esteem this Address is presented to you, Honorable Sir, with the Prayer that God will spare you

many more fruitful years in which to serve our Queen, our Province and our People.

Dated at Edmonton, in the Province of Alberta, September 20, 1958."

E. C. Manning's legacy seems to have been almost forgotten. It is timely to review his life and leadership and perhaps learn something of the secret of his success. During his 25 years as Premier, the Government of Alberta was fiscally responsible and notably lacking in scandal and mismanagement. Politicians of all stripes could learn much from the life of E. C. Manning. This tract comes mainly from Ernest C. Manning – A Biographical Sketch, T. Cashman, 1958 and The Good Steward – The Ernest C. Manning Story, B. Brennan, 2008.

HUMBLE BEGINNINGS

His father, George Henry Manning moved from England to Canada at the turn of the century, settling in Carnduff, Saskatchewan where he married his hometown sweetheart, Elizabeth Dickson. Two sons, William and Ernest were born there, and soon after the family moved permanently to a homestead near Rosetown, Saskatchewan. Roy, their third son was born there. Mr. Manning was very industrious and enlarged his farm from 160 to 640 acres. All three boys attended the nearby, one-room Glenpayne School.

Farm life was hard. The family was solidly religious in the Baptist tradition. The boys were assigned their responsibilities, and as teenagers took turns managing the entire operation. Life was not all dull. Ernest, a natural entertainer, played the fiddle in the local dance band, and took great interest in anything mechanical, loving to read "Popular Mechanics." He loved to figure

CHAPTER 1: MANNING, CHRISTIAN STATESMAN

out how things worked and to fix broken equipment. In the 1920s he stripped a Model T Ford down to a knock-off pick up 'truck,' calling it "The Bazoo." He had many exciting experiences in it rocketing around the country roads.

THE PREACHING OF WILLIAM ABERHART

In the fall of 1924, Ernest, ordered a three-tube radio from the Sears-Roebuck of Chicago catalogue. He paid $103 for it from money earned from his harvest work. The radio affected all their lives, but most profoundly, Ernest's. One Sunday afternoon in the fall of 1925 he picked up CFCN in Calgary, and heard William Aberhart broadcasting from the Palace Theatre. Every Sunday at 3 pm, he would be listening to Aberhart's gospel messages. His interest in Mr. Aberhart's teaching grew more intense with each Sunday broadcast.

William Aberhart was a down-to-earth Fundamental Baptist, bedrock strong in all his convictions. He preached that the Bible was ALL the inspired Word of God; every word, every syllable, including the prophecies. And since not all the prophecies were fulfilled in the New Testament, then some prophecies must be moving towards fulfillment in the events of the day.

Aberhart was a gifted teacher of Mathematics and English at Crescent Heights High School in Calgary. His Biblical preaching and teaching talents came through clearly on the radio, and fascinated the young Saskatchewan farm boy. Mr. Manning, Alberta's eighth Premier, says that he became a Christian listening to Aberhart – that he became convinced it was not enough to know ABOUT Christ – that he wanted to know Christ personally. You may read his personal testimony in more detail in Appendix 3. After being saved he made a brief trip by train to meet Mr. Aberhart in Calgary, and "looked in" at the young people's church group consisting of about 200 persons. Muriel Preston, who would later become Ernest's wife, was in the young people's music ministry.

THE PROPHETIC BIBLE INSTITUTE

Back on the farm, Ernest heard of Mr. Aberhart's plan to build a Prophetic Bible Institute on Eighth Avenue in downtown Calgary. Aberhart creatively raised the $65,000 needed to build it. The Institute would be open to young people and would, in effect, be a sort of junior college. Ernest decided he would be a student in the first class in October, 1927, among 35 other youngsters, many of them from the country.

Ernest Manning literally worked his way through college, working on the farm during the summer to pay for the autumn/winter studies at the Institute. In his second and third years he lived with the Aberharts, and became like their son, as they had two daughters. Mr. Aberhart helped Ernest round out his secondary school education. Mrs. Aberhart attempted to put some substance to his thin, wiry frame, with her delicious meals but without much success.

In his last year as a student, Ernest was also on the teaching staff at the Institute. In 1930, Mr. Aberhart asked the 21-year-old Manning to help in the radio broadcast, and from that time on they shared the work. By this time Muriel Preston had become the Institute's permanent organist/pianist, faithfully serving the Lord.

The writer is indebted to Mr. Dennis Snyder of Redlands, Alberta, for providing him with a number of copies of

CHAPTER 1: MANNING, CHRISTIAN STATESMAN

"The Prophetic Voice" bulletins from 1943 to 1948, in which were vintage messages from the Aberhart-Manning era. Many quotations from this material is included in the present work.

ABERHART AND MANNING MOVE INTO POLITICS

William Aberhart's interest in young people was legendary. The students at Crescent Heights lost track of the number of student "companies" Mr. Aberhart organized to buy needed equipment for the school. His brilliant mind made a game of mathematics, and applied that science to life. He told his students, "You must have a standard of values in life; and you must never get your values mixed up." Mr. Manning couldn't have had a better mentor as God led him into His will for his life.

As the 30s Depression ground more deeply into public life Mr. Aberhart agonized over many of his most brilliant students not being able to find work. With all these resources, why couldn't these young people get good jobs? His research led him in 1932 to a book, "The Douglas Theory of Social Credit." He and Mr. Manning discussed the economic problems in light of this book. He rejected the idea of the CCF's "planned economy," which amounted to a Government-controlled economic Socialism. He felt there was nothing basically wrong with the free market economy. The people just needed more purchasing power, and that would come if the "money barons" would loosen up their control of the flow of money into the economy. He began to speak about Social Credit on his broadcasts. Conditions in Alberta were right for his message, and in the 1935 Election he was swept into the Premier's office, and Mr. Manning alongside him was swept into Cabinet at the age of 26. Social Credit had won 55 out of 63 of Alberta's ridings in a landslide.

The next April Ernest Manning married Muriel Preston in the Bible Institute Church in Calgary. William Aberhart gave the bride away to his young Cabinet Minister.

Mr. Aberhart's untimely death on May 23, 1943 deeply affected those who loved and knew him best. Please refer to Appendix 5 to learn more about Mr. Aberhart's life and the deep respect that he earned from those most impacted by his life and ministry.

E. C. MANNING IN POLITICS

Ernest C. Manning had greatness thrust upon him suddenly, and he was able to keep it. He was made Minister of Trade and Industry to a deeply skeptical business and financial community. Mr. Manning became ambassador to this group and was invited to speak everywhere. The 27 year old Minister was pitted against some of the sharpest minds in the province.

Neither aggressive nor defensive he made a favorable impression speaking calmly and clearly. Questions loaded with sarcasm or derision were listened to with complete, searching attention – an attention disarming and disconcerting. Then, without a visible trace of anger, temper or ill-feeling he would produce a calm, lucid answer. Though he knew farm and Bible Institute management, he had no experience in city labor. Yet, his fairness and ability to analyze a problem in clear terms made a good impression. Thus he made Social Credit respectable, and himself respected.

In the Legislature the fledgling Social Credit MLAs were learning to run the government. Out of the confusion E. C. Manning emerged as the floor leader of the party. Cool, calm, fair in debate, willing to listen but always in

CHAPTER 1: MANNING, CHRISTIAN STATESMAN

control – in the opposition cloakrooms nothing but good was heard about Manning.

As the grind continued into 1936, Mr. Manning contracted tuberculosis. He took complete rest at his home, made a remarkable recovery with determination, and was welcomed back to the Legislature in February, 1937.

War broke out in 1939 Mr. Manning responded to his country's call. Not content to sit back he tried to join the Army in 1939. TB scar tissue and a heart valve issue prevented his acceptance. However, he joined the militia, and was assigned to the 49th Battalion as Lt. Manning. He drilled, went on exercises, took summer training and reached the rank of Captain before being forced to give up the military due to the political pressure of becoming Premier of Alberta on June 3, 1943, after the sudden death of a weakened and sickly Premier William Aberhart.

At the same time Pierre Trudeau – the radical socialist, as a member of the "Greatest Generation," the one that defeated the Nazis in war and resolutely stared down the Soviets in the Cold War, took a pass in both battles, noted Stephen Harper. He was against Britain and the Allies. Here are some of his words and actions regarding WW II, and after it, from Bob Plamondon in "The Truth About Trudeau," 2013.

> "Trudeau declared the war to be Imperial, imbecilic and disgusting. "I am not only against conscription, but I'm also against mobilization, against participation, against rearming, against aid to the belligerent. I am against the war. Is that quite clear?" During the war he and a friend paraded around northern Quebec in vintage German military uniforms and helmets."

"FORTRESS AMERICA" UNDER SIEGE

He actively and personally opposed the search for and prosecution of Nazi war criminals in Canada. His political reasons for that are redacted from the 600 page Alti Rodi report (1986).

He was pro-Soviet Union and pro-Fidel Castro's Cuba, and anti-American. Trudeau was a beacon of light to the pacifists – equating moral equivalency to the allies and the communists.

Winston Churchill spoke in the House of Commons in 1941 while the war was raging saying, "There is no room now for the dilettante, for the weakling, for the shirker or the sluggard."

Concerning pacifism which Trudeau promoted unapologetically throughout his lifetime, Ted Byfield wrote:

> "Thirty nations may want peace and disarm, but if one insists upon arming, then the others must either arm as well or submit to annihilation or enslavement. What we must do therefore, and history bears this truth, is observe two principles. First, we must be permanently ready for war. Second, we must be resolved to do everything possible to avert it. **Neglect either one and we're in deep trouble, for the pacifist is every bit as dangerous as the jingoist."** (The Book of Ted, 1998, Lest we forget: the horror of war can cause one, November 19, 1990 Column).

Lt. – General Sir William Dobbie, a veteran of WW I and Governor of Malta during the Malta siege of WW II, wrote the following regarding pacifism:

> "Pacifism in the present state of the world may be little less than a sacrifice of Christian principle to humanitarian sentiment. The Christian attitude must be "Righteousness at any cost," not "Peace at any price," for the best way to preserve peace is to be strong in righteousness." (A Very Present Help, 1945, p. 124).

CHAPTER 1: MANNING, CHRISTIAN STATESMAN

Manning would have concurred with General Dobbie. He offered himself to serve in the military, even before, and after becoming Premier of Alberta. He rose quickly to the rank of Lieutenant in the reserves. Trudeau, though a fighter, did everything he could to support socialism and avoid military service in WW II. When prime minister, Trudeau waged war against the Canadian military, one of the most respected and disciplined fighting forces in the world. He did more damage to our renowned fighting forces than did active combat in war.

> "Our military leaders despised Trudeau for gutting the capacity and the spirit of our fighting forces. "Of all the governments we've had, the one that considered Canada's defense least is the Trudeau government." (Vice Admiral J.C. O'Brien). Jack Granastein, Professor Emeritus of History at York University – "Trudeau was anti-military (and) without a doubt, Pierre Trudeau killed the Canadian Forces." (Bob Plamondon, The Truth About Trudeau, 2013).

E. C. Manning, at 34, was the youngest man in the government, and in the Legislature. Initially, he sought advice from older men in the Cabinet, but the final decision would be his, and the older men went along with his judgment. As Leader, many noted the similarity between his and Mr. Aberhart's voices. But that is where the similarity ended. Their personalities were in so many ways, opposites. Yet, Ernest was loyal to his best friend to the end. Both of them can be credited with helping lift Alberta out of the ravages of the Great Depression.

Manning's defining characteristics as described by his closest colleagues were as follows:

- Preferred peace but would not back away from a fight;

"FORTRESS AMERICA" UNDER SIEGE

- Would not lose his temper under provocation, sometimes saying with a tightened mouth, "Well now, I don't think I would have done it just that way;"
- Was not a talker but a listener – saying, "You can't learn anything when you're talking;"
- Would argue the other side of a question even if he agreed with you;
- Was diplomatic rather than dogmatic;
- Instead of saying, "I'm going," and go, he would say, "I'd like to get there," and usually did;
- Won friends and influenced people by his listening ear, cool perception and sound judgment;
- Was a good administrator and delegator of authority;
- In judging people, trusting; his close associates said, "He doesn't suspect people of being what they CAN be;"
- One minister said, "He's got one of the most analytical minds in the province and has a phenomenal capacity for details. He's got to see the end from the beginning;"
- And, most interesting of all, he had a sense of humor in the midst of politics.

E. C. Manning's ministers ran their departments without interference, but sought his advice because of his penetrating analysis. They were free to discuss things in public which were not yet government policy. No one called him Ernie except his brothers. One minister remarked how a brief with 40 recommendations had been prepared for weeks, all questions were considered and it was then shown to the Premier. He remarked, "I agree with 38 of the sections, but if you do this the end result will be so-and-so. If you do that, the end result will be such-and-such."

The Premier was deeply interested in how things worked, mechanically and otherwise. When he bought a car he wanted to know everything about it. When he toured a new hospital, the Premier would likely spend most of his time in the boiler room, peering at the gauges and asking how they work. Experience in five ministries namely; Provincial Secretary, Trade and

CHAPTER 1: MANNING, CHRISTIAN STATESMAN

Industry, Provincial Treasurer, Mines and Minerals and Attorney General, gave him a detailed knowledge of government. Premier Manning acted also as Alberta's Attorney General from 1955 until his retirement in 1968.

Before Manning talked he knew what he was going to say, and had figured out what peoples' responses would be to what he said. At any official function he was the one who typically made the only clear, coherent and connected one hour speech from a single page of apparently disconnected words on a single sheet of paper.

E. C. MANNING'S CHRISTIAN FAITH AND SERVICE

Mr. Manning left home at age 19 in 1927 to make prophetic Bible teaching his life work. He had no inclination to politics but was swept into government on the merits of William Aberhart's firey political appeals during the Great Depression. He had been saved as a teenager under Mr. Aberhart's preaching and held fundamental Baptist doctrines as did his predecessor. He was motivated by a desire to show people that the Bible offers a guide to life; the present life and the one after, and that the study of the prophecies is a fascinating intellectual pursuit. He was a man of God first of all – and a politician second. Like Mr. Aberhart he had no hesitation to make his Christian faith and beliefs known in all areas of life, both political and civilian. He stated,

> "Your faith had to influence your politics, your business and your religion. And if it did, you ought to say so." (B. Brennan, 2008).

So much for today's timid leaders who skirt around the bush and try to avoid making definite statements on faith-based social conservative values and verities.

"FORTRESS AMERICA" UNDER SIEGE

Magazines called E. C. Manning, "the pole thin Premier who sells oil with the Bible in one hand." When heckled in the early days about mixing religion and politics he would answer without anger that religion is not something that should be taken down from the shelf on Sundays. He would go on to say you can't divorce spiritual values from the things of everyday life, and that a right relationship with God must precede a right relationship with man. While he insisted that religion cannot be kept out of politics, he kept politics out of religion. His Christian sincerity was proven by the consistency of his Bible extension work from 1930, when he began broadcasting with William Aberhart, and onward long after his retirement from politics in 1968. He had a particular fondness for the great evangelist, the Apostle Paul, and used only the KJV Bible.

Following are a few of many examples of Premier Manning's involvement in the spiritual needs of Albertans and all Canadian citizens.

PREMIER SPEAKS AT YOUTH FOR CHRIST RALLY

> Alberta's Premier Manning delivered a stirring challenge to Youth at Calgary's large Youth for Christ rally in Western Canada High Auditorium on Saturday night, September 25th. Mr. Manning pointed the young folk to the one Straight Gate, Jesus Christ, found in Matthew 7:13-14, through which all may pass if they would have everlasting life and a happy and successful journey here below.
>
> "In spite of his many heavy duties as Chief Administrator of the Province, Mr. Manning never fails to grasp an opportunity to preach the Gospel wherever an opening presents itself, and to lend his active support to any and all organizations which he believes are faithfully preaching and teaching the Word of God in these last days."

CHAPTER 1: MANNING, CHRISTIAN STATESMAN

> "Mr. Manning's concern for the spiritual needs of the nation (resulted in) Canada's National Back to the Bible Hour being expanded from coast to coast." (The Prophetic Voice, Vol. 7, No. 3, September, 1948)

For many years Premier Manning conducted regular Sunday services in the City of Edmonton, sometimes three times in one day. He was requested to help a Baptist group in Edmonton on Sundays and the success that followed led to the formation of the Fundamental Baptist Church which then called a full-time pastor. In Calgary, E. C. Manning was asked to help the Prophetic Bible Institute with its Sunday pm broadcasts. He and his wife would travel to Calgary every weekend summer and winter to conduct the broadcast services until 1955 when the pressure of commuting became too great. In 1949, this ministry took the name, "Back to the Bible Hour," with programming that grew to extend across Canada. As costs grew any deficit was born by the Premier out of his own pocket. He became convinced of the value of radio evangelism out of which he himself had been saved. All of his messages ended with an appeal to sinners to repent of their sin and put their faith and trust in Jesus Christ.

E. C. MANNING'S EVERYDAY LIFE

The Premier lived on a 310 acre family dairy farm with a ranch-style house adjoining the Saskatchewan River 11 km. north of Edmonton with his wife, Muriel, and 2 boys, Keith (1940) and Preston (1942). The farm was sold in 1968 when he retired from provincial politics on an annual pension of $12,000.

Ernest C. Manning was an uncomplicated man with simple tastes. On the farm he experimented with raising beef cattle. When his Premier's office was renovated in his absence, many pictures were removed. He asked,

"Where is my bull?" It was only the shorthorn Killearn Max William picture given to him by a friend that he wanted back. He did not drink or smoke, and ate sparingly, except for charcoal steaks that he loved to grill. He remained pole thin, but healthy through into old age. His hi-fi music was confined to opera and he loved playing old-time music on the fiddle as a break.

Traditional, wholesome music lifts the spirit. Mr. Manning had a wholesome spirit. As the saying, reportedly from a German opera house goes:

> "Bach gave us God's Word. Mozart gave us God's laughter. Beethoven gave us God's fire. God gave us music that we might pray without words." (The Epoch Times, "How the Spectre of Communism is Ruling Our World," Desecrating the Arts, Chapter 11, 2020)

The Premier loved the sea and to read about yachting. His only sea voyage was in 1952 when he and Mrs. Manning went to Queen Elizabeth II's Coronation. When on vacation he loved to sit on a deck chair just watching the sea.

He took only one extended holiday in his 25 years as premier; one month to Israel in October, 1964. Mrs. Manning recalled their visit to Israel in her memoirs.

> "The land of Abraham, Isaac and Jacob and, most precious to us, the land where our Savior, Jesus Christ, walked, talked and gave his life for our redemption." (B. Brennan, 2008)

The secret of his personality – was a personality so baffling because it was so uncomplicated. Could another like this great man succeed politically in these times of secular socialist engineering and rampant political correctness? YES! We absolutely need leaders like him

CHAPTER 1: MANNING, CHRISTIAN STATESMAN

in Canada today. If the present trend continues we will end up with an oppressive, statist government just the opposite to that of E. C. Manning's.

E. C. MANNING ON SOCIETY AND GENUINE BIBLE CHRISTIANITY

Ernest Manning stated in the strongest terms possible the only solution that he believed would solve society's problems in his radio address in Chicago in 1948. He went on to spend another twenty years as the Premier of Alberta preaching the same warning message.

> "I have spent a third of my life in legislative halls and the executive offices of government, and I say without hesitation that the problems which stem from human depravity cannot be solved by the laws and efforts of men.
>
> If there is to be a miraculous healing of the mortal wounds from which Christian civilization is dying today, it will not be brought about by governments or by recovery programs, nor by force of arms or iron curtains and atomic bombs. It will come to pass only when men and women profess the Name of Christ, humble themselves before God and prayerfully seek His face in unconditional surrender to His blessed will.
>
> It will come to pass when nations stop making a mockery of their Christian profession and restore the Family Altar to their homes, the Bible to their pulpits, and Jesus Christ to His rightful place in their lives and in the Councils of their land." (Radio Broadcast by E. C. Manning, WMBI and WDLM, Chicago, April 9, 1948 – printed in The Prophetic Voice, vol. 6, no. 11, May, 1948)

The following paragraphs were taken from Ernest Manning's sermons given on the radio broadcast, Canada's National Back to the Bible Hour and reemphasize his conviction that only a return to God and His Word are the solution to society's ills.

> "People are divided into two groups by the way they react to, and seek to deal with, the concerns of our times. <u>One group</u> seeks to deal with them using wholly *secular* or humanistic *(material)* resources – education, political action, economic initiatives, monetary reforms, science, technology, military strength, the control of human behavior by laws and regulations, and so on. They may identify with some form of religion or of a church and participate in religious exercises on Sunday, but on Monday when they go back to their businesses or educational or political activities, they give no evidence that God even exists. No wonder society is in trouble! It gives little thought to the *origin or* reality of SIN.
>
> God created man in His own image, intending that man should live in fellowship with Him in a perpetual paradise free from all care and trouble. *But* Adam and Eve acquired a sin-infected and therefore a sin prone nature when their willful disobedience to the express will of God alienated them from Him and brought about their spiritual death, as God had forewarned. Consequently, their children were born dead spiritually, with sin-infected/sin-prone natures, *and* are prone to evil and corruption and violence. That is why there is no human solution to society's problems. Man cannot change his own nature *and is* unwilling to recognize sin for what it is.
>
> Genuine Bible Christians, <u>the other group</u>, recognize the important role of secular resources, but understand that *the* only *real* solution is the one God has provided through the death and resurrection of Jesus Christ; not mere religion, but genuine spiritual regeneration. The enormity of our sins was such that only by His shedding of His divine blood in atonement was our redemption possible. Through His substitutionary death in our place for our sins, He paid in full the penalty (*Hell*) *divine* justice imposes on wrongdoing (*sin*) of every kind. Today our forgiveness and reconciliation *to God* depends not on our good works, but on our confessing and turning from sin

CHAPTER 1: MANNING, CHRISTIAN STATESMAN

> (*repentance*) and receiving (*by faith*) the resurrected, living Christ as our personal Savior. A supernatural birth then imparts a new nature."
>
> *"Therefore If any man be in Christ, he is a new creature: old things are passed away; behold, all things are become new." (2 Corinthians 5:17).*
>
> "For this reason, genuine Bible Christianity is the greatest force in this world to bring about the transformation of attitude and lifestyle on the part of those who appropriate the salvation of God available in Jesus Christ. Through it spiritual revival has transformed nations."

Premier Manning's goal with a small-c conservative government, and as a genuine Bible-believing Christian, was to show how a society could be established in Alberta on Christian principles that was superior to anything that socialism or communism could produce (Brennan, 2008). He succeeded, leaving a legacy of the superiority of the Judeo-Christian foundation for social stability and a free democracy. Future leaders, can with confidence, emulate his example.

If you wish to see the diametrical opposite to Ernest Manning read Bob Plamondon's literary masterpiece, "The Truth About Trudeau," (2013) detailing the life of the late Fabian Socialist, Pierre Trudeau, Prime Minister of Canada from 1968 to 1984.

And it is this Judeo-Christian foundation that the progressives and Cultural Marxists have largely destroyed in the Western democracies at the time of this writing.

> "May God help the people of this country and the government of this country to wake up to these facts before it is too late."

"FORTRESS AMERICA" UNDER SIEGE

(E. C. Manning, The Face of the Sky – Part 1, 1971 Canada's National Back to the Bible Hour Pamphlet)

Now, in 2020, it is almost too late to stop the long march toward a socialist/communist Canada. Only a miracle of God can deliver us. We are losing the war that followed that won by the "Great Generation," in 1939-1945.

> "Christian men and women should take on the responsibility of seeking out godly leaders and then give them the prayerful and faithful support necessary for them to provide successful leadership in this nation's hour of need. We need such men and women not only at every level of government but in business, in education, in labor organizations, in fact in every facet of community and national life. There is urgent need to act before, as a nation, we pass the point of no return." (E. C. Manning, "It is Written – #3: Wanted, a Man," Back to the Bible Hour vintage message, broadcast on July 5, 2020).

CHAPTER 2

THE HON. ERNEST C. MANNING: A CHAMPION OF THE PEOPLE AND FREE DEMOCRACY

"He that ruleth over men must be just, ruling in the fear of God."

2 Samuel 23:3

"By and large, no provincial leader has ever earned and won more public respect, confidence and admiration than has been sustained over a remarkably long period by Premier Manning." (Brian Brennan, Calgary Herald Tribute, February 21, 1996)

The personal Christian testimony of Ernest C. Manning was affirmed, over and over again, by a wide variety of people, from his own family and those who knew and worked with him for many years, as well as by those who met and interviewed him concerning his political life and his Christian faith. Comments and quotations from some of these people are recorded in this chapter. They are listed with permission of Brian Brennan, author of "The Good Steward: The Ernest C. Manning Story" (2008).

Where pertinent Mr. Manning's testimony is offset against Pierre Elliott Trudeau's to show the vast differences between genuine Christian leadership and radical socialism's legacy. The serious reader should be able to see what kind of leader Canada needs today in light of another Trudeau currently ruling as the Prime Minister of Canada.

CONTEMPORARY ALBERTA POLITICIANS

The Hon. Peter Lougheed [Progressive Conservative Premier: 1971-1986]

> "I've always admired Ernest C. Manning. My government adopted many of the policies he instituted as premier, and subsequent governments have built on those. Anyone wanting to understand how Alberta became what it is today should begin by reading Brennan's biography of the Saskatchewan farmer's son who became this province's longest serving premier."
>
> "If you are looking for real, significant, long-lasting contributions that exist to this day, it was the structure in the oil and gas leasing system developed by Mr. Manning and Mr. Tanner."

Pierre Trudeau was born into privilege and wealth. In 1948 he toured the world. From 1951 to 1961 he was a roving intellectual with no full-time job, living off the inheritance of his father. He never completed his PhD thesis on the Interplay between Marxism and

CHAPTER 2: MANNING: CHAMPION OF THE PEOPLE

Christianity. (Bob Plamondon, The Truth About Trudeau, 2013)

In 2007, 117 academics and other experts were asked by MacLean's Magazine to rate Canada's prime ministers. Trudeau ranked 5th out of 9 who held office for more than one term – in the middle of the pack and way below public opinion surveys. (Ibid) Leftist mainstream media and authors have given Pierre Trudeau and aura of greatness that he absolutely does not deserve. Plamondon's book sets his failed record straight.

Mr. Ray Speaker [Social Credit MLA; & Caucus Secretary: 1964-1966]

He found Manning to be:

> "...a warm, considerate, very open, easy-to-talk-to guy. He didn't rule with an iron fist. He would let the discussion flow until he had a good understanding of what the MLAs were telling him, and then call for a consensus vote. He never told them what they should do – never."

Pierre Trudeau undermined the notion of ministerial accountability and cabinet government federally. His successors have maintained the Trudeau-style grip on power. (Bob Plamondon, The Truth About Trudeau, 2013).

Manning believed in free democracy and non-dictatorial leadership because of his strong Christian faith. Jesus taught His disciples –

> "But Jesus called them unto him, and said, Ye know that the princes of the Gentiles exercise dominion over them, and they that are great exercise authority upon them. But it shall not be so among you: but whosoever will be great among you, let him be your minister. And whosoever will

be chief among you, let him be your servant." (Matthew 20:25-27)

Citizens, whether Christian or non-Christian should never fear having a godly political leader. Brian Brennan describes such a leader in "The Good Steward: The Ernest C. Manning Story, (2008).

Pierre Trudeau illustrates the radical socialist style of leadership. You can contrast his government and Manning's by reading Bob Plamondon's "The Truth About Trudeau," 2013. Had he not been restrained by our Westminster parliamentary democracy who knows where Canada would be today?

> "Issues that came before cabinet were rarely put to a formal vote, and Trudeau always had supremacy to interpret the consensus. He reminded everyone at the table, "It's 18 to 12, and the 12s have it." Power lay with the PM and the hand-picked bureaucrats in the PMO (Prime Minister's Office), thus shifting authority away from Cabinet and Parliament, a clear departure from earlier Prime Minister's policy of making Cabinet their power chamber." (Bob Plamondon, The Truth About Trudeau, 2013).

Mr. Manning governed successfully by:

> "adopting a small-c conservative approach to government with honesty, trust and integrity. People continued to vote for Manning because they trusted him and felt he provided good government. It wasn't because he was Social Credit."

Canada needs today leaders that they can trust. Pierre Trudeau could not be trusted to keep his word or govern with honesty and integrity. His son, Justin, is the same. They both accused their adversaries of having 'frightening and harmful' hidden agendas when, in fact,

CHAPTER 2: MANNING: CHAMPION OF THE PEOPLE

they were the ones who had the real hidden agendas – covert radical socialism. Socialists, by their guilt, transfer their own hidden agendas onto their conservative opponents using the mainstream media as their public platform for propaganda and brainwashing.

Mr. Orvis Kennedy [Social Credit MLA; & Chief Political Organizer]

Manning's provincial government was:

> "a free individual enterprise movement opposed to socialism and all forms of statism."

Trudeau's federal government instituted radical socialist policies.

> The bottom line: Trudeau had little faith in the free democratic system. He kicked corporate Canada in the teeth by taxing capital gains, imposing a costly metric system, repelling foreign investment, giving excessive wage increases to public-sector workers, cutting the legs out from under the energy industry with the NEP, offering huge increases in UI benefits at the expense of employers. With Trudeau in power, Canada was an unattractive investment." (Bob Plamondon, The Truth About Trudeau, 2013).

ALBERTA GOVERNMENT BUREAUCRATS

A former Civil Servant has said that Manning shone the light of his faith over the entire government.

Timothy Byrne [Civil Servant for 29 years; Deputy Minister of Education for 5 years]

> "The bureaucrats, particularly those in senior management, were fully aware of Manning's religious views. Whenever they found themselves dealing with an

issue that might be close to the premier's spiritual heart, they were sensitive to what might be the appropriate responses."

John Barr [Edmonton Journal editorial writer]

On the day Manning formally left office – He cleaned out his office, walked out of the legislature building, and never returned.

> "He had nothing to do with the government after that. He made it very clear he would be gone forever. I can't think of another politician who has done that in recent times."

Trudeau, the radical socialist, came out of retirement to interfere in the affairs of the nation – as an anti-nation builder. The defeat of the Meech Lake and Charlottetown accords were his doing, and they demonstrated his dictatorial mindset. Gordon Robertson, former clerk of the Privy Council, said,

> "Nothing, I think, in Canadian history rivals the irresponsibility Trudeau, a former prime minister, displayed in coming out of retirement to destroy the only prospect of an agreement that would bring Quebec into willing acceptance of the constitution that he himself later admitted was the calculated result of a *coup de force*.
>
> Never before has a former prime minister so actively and decisively thwarted the will of a sitting prime minister (Mulroney), not to mention the Canadian Parliament and the provincial legislatures representing 95% of our citizens. Both accord failures played out in the 1995 Quebec referendum, a horror show for federalists that nearly destroyed the nation Trudeau purported to save with his 1982 patriation of the Constitution."

Radical socialism always take this approach to politics and social policies. It is "get out of my way; I know best

CHAPTER 2: MANNING: CHAMPION OF THE PEOPLE

and I'm going to force you to do my will." It is by its very nature, bullying, and dictatorial.

Ernest Manning, the proponent of free democracy, would have abided by the will of Parliament and the people, even if he disagreed personally. Genuine conservative Christian leadership is NOT dictatorial.

UNIVERSITY ACADEMICS

Don Smith [Professor of Canadian History, U. of C.]

Why no one saw fit to acknowledge his achievements by writing an in-depth biography for so long – 40 years after he retired from provincial politics. It is sad that people fear a genuine Christian while they are willing to put their trust and votes with those who have little or no living faith and Biblical foundation in their lives.

> "I think political historians have been scared off by this religion thing. Manning's politics had such a fundamentalist religious substructure that commentators have found it difficult to divorce the two."

It is vitally important for Canadians to compare E. C. Manning's biography with the life of Pierre Elliot Trudeau, Canada's Prime Minister from 1968 to 1984. The contrast between a genuine Christian statesman and an avowed Marxist socialist statesman and their legacies can be readily compared. Excerpts from Brian Brennan's (2008) and Bob Plamondon's (2013) books will be used often in the present work to draw the stark difference between Manning and Trudeau. Jesus Christ's words remain applicable today.

> "Wherefore by their fruits ye shall know them." (Matthew 7:20)

"FORTRESS AMERICA" UNDER SIEGE

George Melnyk [Professor at U. of C.]

> "For Albertans this book by Brian Brennon is a confirmation of identity: for Canadians a genuine revelation."

Doug Owram [History Professor at U. of A.]

After Manning's retirement in 1968, he wrote:

> "a well-educated voting population exposed to the diversity of secular ideologies[1] in the universities would question the validity of Christian leadership."

Note: Sceptics like this ideologue were many in the 1960s. Pierre Trudeau was one of them.

1. By the 1960s Marxist socialist/communist ideologues had already infiltrated the universities of the Western democracies. Their propaganda now permeates all of our institutions leading to the breakdown of the family and society's morality across-the-board. Pierre Trudeau was the chief instigator of Marxist infiltration in Canada.

Manning proved the validity of the success of godly Christian leadership by his record and example, and nothing can discredit him.

The current writer was a student at the U. of Calgary in 1966 and, in ignorant youthful folly, criticized Manning as:

> "that Bible-thumper in Edmonton."

I criticized him because some of his government policies provided an obstacle for me to live in my sin. That is something missing today in our society. Everything goes, and don't interfere.

CHAPTER 2: MANNING: CHAMPION OF THE PEOPLE

JOURNALISTS AND OTHER WRITERS

Brian Brennan [Herald columnist and author – Author of "The Good Steward: The Ernest C. Manning Story," 2008].

He utilized U. of A. Grad Student, Lydia Semotuk's 38 transcribed 'Manning interviews' tapes (1979-81) in his biography.

In a Herald Tribute on February 21, 1996, wrote: **"Ernest Manning left indelible mark on Alberta"** –

> "Alberta had been extraordinarily well-served by this premier who had moved the province into the modern era with oil-financed education, health and transportation facilities; turning it from a have-not into one of Canada's three most affluent provinces."

Here is the authoritative, documented summation of Pierre Trudeau's legacy on Canada. We could just as well put Justin in the same category today.

> "Trudeau's accomplishments are tarnished by the damage he inflicted on the country. On most major issues – national unity, the economy, government finances, the environment, poverty, immigration, national defense, international relations, foreign aid – Trudeau's record falls far short of the mark. He left deep divisions and scars that remain to be healed." (Bob Plamondon, The Truth About Trudeau, 2013).

Brian Brennan went on to record some of Manning's unique accomplishments and characteristics. His influence on Albertans and the Alberta economy and the trust in free democracy in government are unequalled. They all hinged on his genuine Christian faith.

"FORTRESS AMERICA" UNDER SIEGE

> "This unlettered farm boy from Saskatchewan rose to become the Rocky Marciano of Canadian politics – the heavyweight champ who won every bout and retired undefeated."

> "Mainstream press made only passing reference to the evangelical Christian beliefs that defined him as a human being and also permeated his politics."

> "On the seventh day Ernest Manning preached, and that defined his style and his substance as a political leader."

> "Manning always wore his religion on his sleeve. He never hid the fact that his Christian faith shaped his political ideology."

Manning despised radical socialism and communism as branches of the same unchristian ideological tree. Manning was on record as saying there was a link between radical labor organizations and communism.

Pierre Trudeau knew that his chances for gaining power through a socialist party, the NDP, remained slim, so he joined the Liberals. The NDP are simply, "Liberals in a hurry." Albertans found that out between 2015 and 2019.

> "Trudeau was once an overt enthusiast for the NDP, and embraced many of their causes while prime minister. He was always friendly to the unions. Public union membership doubled during his tenure." (Bob Plamondon, The Truth About Trudeau, 2013).

Two Royal Commissions, appointed by Manning in 1955 and 1968, concluded:

> "all charges against his government were unfounded, and Manning and his ministers were guilty of no wrongdoing. He left government with his head held high and his reputation for honesty intact."

CHAPTER 2: MANNING: CHAMPION OF THE PEOPLE

Thirty-three years of overt Christian leadership, "God's Government," in Alberta ended when Manning retired as premier on September 27, 1968. In 1971, Albertans elected Progressive Conservative Peter Lougheed as Premier of Alberta. From that time onward the Alberta Government has been wholly secular in nature and policy.

Monroe Johnston [Reporter for Toronto Daily Star in 1952 Interview]

Manning spoke candidly and unselfconsciously about his religious beliefs.

> "He has no hesitation in styling himself a fundamentalist who believes in a literal heaven, a literal hell, and literal angels."

He characterized the premier as –

> "a frank, friendly individual."

Tony Cashman [Edmonton broadcast journalist for CJCA Radio & social historian – covered the Alberta Legislature]

Wrote an in-depth profile on Premier Manning for the Social Credit League in 1958. Note: This insight was unprecedented. The writer has used this booklet in compiling Chapter 1.

Cashman was an admirer of Manning and considered it a pity that Albertans never got to know the elusive Premier in an up-close-and-personal way, because he was so busy with legislative duties and his Bible Institute work.

> "They would have seen a decent, straightforward, likeable, honest and essentially uncomplicated man, with

"FORTRESS AMERICA" UNDER SIEGE

> a great sense of humor and a strong sense of right and wrong."

> "He exuded intelligence, radiated integrity, and always enjoyed the greatest respect of everyone in the legislature. You could sense that."

Pierre Trudeau could not claim this respect, either from his contemporaries in Canada or his peers abroad, except for the Soviets, the Communist Chinese and Cuba's Fidel Castro.

By 1978, a senior cabinet minister told journalist Craig Oliver, "the (Trudeau) government had become an essentially corrupt operation." (Bob Plamondon, The Truth About Trudeau, 2013). Sounds like 2020, doesn't it?

CALGARY HERALD NEWSPAPER

A qualified Editorial tribute was given in 1968, at Premier Manning's retirement, when the veteran Social Credit politician retired at the peak of his power after 25 years as premier.

> "Alberta will not seem the same without him."

Manning long considered The Herald "very antagonistic to the government," so he made it his policy not to talk to it.

The paper did a 1963 personality profile on Manning by reporter Doug Sagi, by remotely researching the premier.

> "Probably the most successful provincial premier in Canadian history."

CHAPTER 2: MANNING: CHAMPION OF THE PEOPLE

His political success was due to a willingness to take decisive action whenever a hint of wrongdoing threatened his government. Mr. Sagi failed to recognize God's hand in Manning's success.

Sagi added, "The phantom in the caucus" – The image of complete honesty and integrity was supposed to define the character of the Manning government. The Alberta government reflected the godly character of its leader, something sadly lacking today in our elected representatives on all sides of the political spectrum. A leader with Manning's character could only benefit Canadian society today. But the people don't want one.

> "If you got out of line in your personal or political life, Mr. Manning, at some point, would have something to say to you."

He also noted,

> "The unique walk – still characteristically springy, sonorous nasal voice still timbres on Back to the Bible Hour."

After his retirement, the sceptics chimed – Manning had done a fine job as leader but his party had maintained,

> "old-fashioned complexes in the face of <u>altering social concepts</u>[2] in spheres such as liquor consumption, blue laws and censorship."

2. The effect of Marxist socialist ideology in North American mainstream media & universities was moving in the 1940s to 1960s, and onward. Both Trudeaus were a product of this hedonistic ideology.

Arthur Hailey [Author – interviewed Manning for Maclean's Magazine in October, 1964]

> "Thoughtful and highly intelligent, with a keen and rarely seen sense of humor."

He found no fault in Manning except that he put trust and loyalty in others, perhaps to excess in his personality.

He asked the premier why he still continued his radio preaching when he could have quit without a marked effect on his political success. Manning answered, because Aberhart's radio ministry had –

> "changed the entire course of my life and, for that, I am grateful to God. I want to do what I can to help others in the same way."

He asked Mrs. Manning the same question. She answered,

> "When you have faith in God you want to share it."

Ken MacQueen [Southam News journalist]

Obituary (1996) – Manning possessed an –

> "unblinking faith" in matters spiritual, with "an almost scientific hunger to question, to analyze – to apply – this morality to the temporal world of politics and government."

MacQueen found it hard to imagine, in Manning's Alberta, how the Christian pulpit and secular politics were ever so compatible[3]. Had he known William Aberhart, Manning's mentor, he would have seen the same example.

3. Maybe it was because Manning was a "genuine Bible-believing Christian." Such unashamed leaders are lacking

CHAPTER 2: MANNING: CHAMPION OF THE PEOPLE

today in 2020. The leftist media has made Conservatives scurry to their holes to hide.

Ted Byfield [Journalist and author]

Re: Manning a supremely competent politician who oversaw the transformation of an agricultural province into an industrial powerhouse without allowing any major confrontations between government, labor and industry.

> "That was truly a magnificent achievement. Ernest C. Manning well deserves to be known as the father of modern Alberta."

No such compliments were given Pierre Trudeau in his legacy and at his death, except to say that he was the 'father' of radical socialism that is ravaging our country today.

> "The most telling judgment came at Trudeau's funeral. Only Fidel Castro and Jimmy Carter served as honorary pallbearers. Important world leaders who followed Trudeau did not pay their respects, nor did they express their admiration." (Bob Plamondon, The Truth About Trudeau, p. 61, 2013).

SON PRESTON MANNING

He integrated his Christian faith and his secular political work rather than keeping them in separate compartments. He believed that your faith had to influence your politics, your business, and your religion. And if it did, you were obligated to say so.

Politics took a distant second place to the Christian faith in the Manning household. His father rarely talked about work at the dinner table. Politicians and government people were rarely invited to their home. Manning's phone number was listed in the public directory. His dad rarely refused to take a phone call at home about government business, even from his crankiest or most inebriated constituents, because Albertans needed to have access to their government. It was his Christian duty because –

> "you couldn't write anyone off, because God hadn't written anyone off."

Even non-believers had a kind of reluctant respect for his father's religion and would listen to his Back to the Bible radio program, especially if they felt it would make politicians more ethical or increase their sense of accountability.

Socialism produces 'situation ethics,' which means what you say, how you act and what you don't depend upon a fixed standard of right and wrong, but upon whether it is advantageous to you or not at that time.

> "Prime Minister Justin Trudeau is being investigated for the third time by the ethics commissioner. But even if Trudeau is found guilty – again – nothing earth-shaking will happen. The only person who can remove Trudeau from cabinet for breaking the conflict law is Trudeau himself. He's not going to fire himself." (Calgary Sun editorial, July 10, 2020).

On the day his dad formally left office, Preston said,

> "I met him at the steps (of the Legislature), and he had two boxes of stuff that he took with him. All he had were the two boxes."

His father then hitched a ride home with his twenty-six year old son because he had already turned in the keys to the premier's car.

CHAPTER 2: MANNING: CHAMPION OF THE PEOPLE

For guidance in politics to his son, Preston Manning, he said,

> "Put your hand in the hand of God, and that shall be to you better than a light."

Pierre Trudeau said, "I'm opposed to any political system based on race or religion." (Bob Plamondon, The Truth About Trudeau, 2013). To say that he had to reject God's authority in his own life first.

> *"Righteousness exalteth a nation: but sin is a reproach to any people." (Proverbs 14:34)*

The Manning family declined a state funeral, as he would have done. His legacy, he said, was in the Statutes of Alberta and in the hundred inter-provincial agreements with the federal government. He asked for nothing special and expected no recognition for his achievements. That is the nature of a genuine Christian.

He was mystified by Christian politicians who were reluctant to talk publically about their faith, especially from the 1960s and onward.

> "If you've got a Christian country, why wouldn't you talk about it? You can talk about it in a way that doesn't necessarily offend other people of faith. Why would you go completely in the opposite direction?"

His father was a "master builder" who (beginning with Mr. Aberhart) helped rebuild the Alberta economy after the Great Depression. He laid a modern foundation for Alberta's educational, health care, and social services systems, and established a superb regulatory framework for the oil and gas industry –

> "presiding over the evolution of Alberta from a bearer of grievances to an advocate of solutions."

His last piece of advice to the fellow citizens of the country he loved was the following:

> "Do not let internal discord do to Canada what wars, the depression and hard times were unable to do. Continue to build! Continue to build!"

Pierre Trudeau was the author and originator of discord during his 15 ½ years as Prime Minister. His social policies continue to disrupt our lives.

> "Trudeau left deep divisions and scars that remain to be healed...a legacy of economic mismanagement, regional alienation and international isolation." (Bob Plamondon, The Truth About Trudeau, 2013).

MURIEL MANNING & FAMILY

He always held the view that both God and the people would decide how long he should stay on the job.

> "He had never been dying to be premier and was not married to the job."

When asked to continue to remain in office after 25 years, he stated,

> "Enough is enough. I'm not going to make the mistake of hanging on to office too long. I've done my best. Things are in good shape."

Premier Manning had long loved the sea and had many books on yachting. Yet, he went on only one ocean cruise during his long years in government. Mrs. Manning said,

CHAPTER 2: MANNING: CHAMPION OF THE PEOPLE

> "His infatuation with the sea had been a long, unrequited love affair. To him, an ocean voyage in 1952, to Queen Elizabeth II's Coronation, was the fulfilment of a dream."

His wife was very happy when they later retired to Scottsdale, Arizona, for the winter months, saying,

> "Now in our 80s, we welcomed the freedom, peace and quiet of retirement to a relatively obscure life."

Upon her husband's passing on 19 February, 1996: Mrs. Manning referred to God's Word.

> "He had fought a good fight. He had finished his course."

These words were written through divine inspiration by the great evangelist, the Apostle Paul, in II Timothy 4:8. Paul was probably the greatest Christian missionary of all time, and one of Ernest Manning's favorite Bible characters.

Andrea Manning (granddaughter) said:

> "Grandpa provided a consistent and powerful example of love, patience, integrity, gentleness, wit and incredible wisdom."

ERNEST C. MANNING

A Christian motivation led both William Aberhart and Ernest Manning into politics.

> "I had no desire to go into politics, and I know he (Aberhart) didn't."

A concern for people and a desire to help solve their problems was the reason they ran for office. Entering politics was never Ernest Manning's first choice, but once he made the decision, he stuck by it. He said,

> "I'd just as soon be busy with my Bible work."

Note: He did not lust for political power. Nor was he a **dilettante** like Pierre Trudeau. He finished what he started; and he finished it well.

In his first broadcast as premier in June, 1943, Manning promised the citizens of Alberta –

> "Every decision made by his government would be in the best interests of the people of Alberta as a whole."

He kept this promise faithfully for the next 25 years.

When it came to exploiting the resources in the West, Ernest Manning exercised wisdom when he recognized the need for American help in finding and developing the energy resources in Alberta's portion of the Western Canadian Sedimentary Basin. He would not make Alberta's energy development a nationalistic issue. He knew the Canadian industry needed help, and he opened the province to investment and exploration from our neighbor to the south. It paid off in spades.

> "After Aberhart died in May, 1943, his successor, Ernest Manning, finally turned to American oil companies, "which were not only willing to invest in Alberta but also promised to bring along their expertise...something the central Canadian and British investors could not do. That sensible solution paid off. On February 13, 1947, after 133 dry holes, Imperial Oil hit black gold at Leduc, 20 miles south of Edmonton. In 1967, Alberta Premier Manning would proudly note that oil and gas revenues had put $2.25 billion into the provincial treasury over the previous twenty years." (Mary Janigan, Let the Eastern Bastards Freeze in the Dark, 2012)

CHAPTER 2: MANNING: CHAMPION OF THE PEOPLE

These resource revenues greatly helped Alberta recover from years of financial hardship. Although the provincial income was for all, Manning considered the individual as the most important unit in society, not the masses. He strongly believed that if his government looked after the individual, the masses would take care of themselves. It worked.

> "Our government's approach was meeting social needs through the private enterprise system, not through compulsory federal collectivism – statism."

To Manning, stimulating the economy and using proper fiscal management would do more to help the individual than increasing taxes to fund a mandatory, collective welfare program for every citizen.

Pierre Trudeau believed the exact opposite and applied it federally to Canada during his 15 ½ years as Prime Minister. He focused on the masses at the expense of the individual, and as a result, both the masses and the individual citizens suffered. His programs were mandatory, in line with a socialist spending platform. With large annual deficits, the welfare money was borrowed by the government, augmenting the national debt and damaging the Canadian economy.

> "Pre-Trudeau (1968) social programs were linked to increases in incomes and productivity in the 1950s and 60s. Trudeau lamented market-oriented mechanisms and criticized Mulroney (his successor) for weakening the power of the state, limiting social security and forcing the burden of economic adjustments on individuals (private enterprise) rather than society (i.e., the state). In 1968, the federal government spent more on OAS, national defense and transfers to other governments than it did on public debt. By 1984, interest costs on Trudeau's public debt were greater than OAS, UI benefits and family allowances combined. Under his

leadership Canada experienced a record number of bankruptcies." (Bob Plamondon, The Truth About Trudeau, 2013).

In 2020, Canada is on the collectivist/statist socialist course with another Trudeau at the helm, piloting Canada into very deep debt waters from which she may never recover.

Manning's government established a Censorship Board in 1947 to protect Albertans from "subversive material" being put out by communists and other groups. Many films were coming out of the U.S. with two messages; the more subtle one sowing doubts in the system of democratic freedom. The years since have vindicated his administration's concern for our free democratic society.

Note: "Fake news" is the modern version of this left-wing public subversion (i.e. CBC, Global, CNN, ABC, NBC, and most major newspapers like the Toronto Star, Calgary Herald, Winnipeg Free Press, etc.). As the American election looms in a few weeks all Global News radio broadcasts are pro-Biden, anti-Trump subtle invectives.

While Manning was trying to protect Albertan's from Communist subversion Pierre Trudeau was supporting the Soviets, admiring Mao Zedong and praising Fidel Castro.

> "Trudeau expressed overt fascination with communism and socialism during his academic training and in his early writings. As a private citizen he toured behind the Iron Curtain, China and post-revolutionary Cuba in the 1950s and 1960s. He visited the grave of Lenin's mother. In 1964 in Cuba, he said, "There were no elections in Cuba, but when you see mass rallies with Fidel Castro speaking for 90 minutes in 100° heat, you wonder what is the need for elections? Upon becoming prime minister,

CHAPTER 2: MANNING: CHAMPION OF THE PEOPLE

> Trudeau rekindled whatever feelings of affection he had for these three communist regimes he had visited." (Bob Plamondon, The Truth About Trudeau, 2013).

Ernest Manning's 7 election victories as premier were a "necessary evil" to be tolerated if he was able to advance the programs he envisioned to better the future of the citizens of the Province of Alberta. He loved administration; not politics. Organizing against Manning after the 1955 election was like "chiseling through granite" according to the Opposition.

After the landmark Imperial Oil Leduc oil discovery in 1947, the Premier said:

> "We may be confident that the future of this province will be the unfolding story of steady progress toward a place of eminence in our national economy."

The prosperity was not to last long however. Pierre Trudeau harbored a long-standing discomfort with the Canadian petroleum industry. He did his best to rob it with socialist policies designed to bring the industry to its knees and destroy Alberta in the process. He worked against everything that William Aberhart and Ernest Manning tried to do to help the Province of Alberta rise up out of poverty and deprivation.

> Trudeau's (1980) National Energy Policy was unprecedented interference in the functioning of the free enterprise system. It designed to seize Alberta's wealth by dramatic increases in Ottawa's share of production royalties and taxes. Stephen Harper said, "Beginning with the NEP, Mr. Trudeau showed me that economics and finance did matter." Gywn Morgan of AEC called Trudeau "world class" for the damage he caused. Jim Gray of Canadian Hunter said, "the NEP destroyed the oil patch. The NEP stands as one of the worst public policy decisions of any prime minister since

> Confederation." (Bob Plamondon, The Truth About Trudeau, 2013).

Ted Byfield described the NEP from a purely Albertan point of view revealing the heart and soul of Trudeau and the Liberal Party, and radical socialism working at its best...undoing the work of a quarter century of one of Canada's most respected and competent politicians, Ernest C. Manning. Justin Trudeau's government is an exact replica of the 1980 Liberals under Pierre Elliot Trudeau, and it is pursuing the same policies toward Alberta and the West.

> "History will one day record that it was on Tuesday, October 28, 1980, that a government of Canada by an act of deliberate policy tried to destroy the prosperity of the one section of the country that had escaped the recession and offered the best hope for the whole nation's future.
>
> **Why** have they done this to us? There are, I believe, two reasons. First, they must at all costs stay in power. Power comes from Ontario and Quebec. The purpose of the budget was to pay them off at the expense of the Western provinces. Second, Pierre Trudeau hates us, and passionately. **It is hatred** that runs to the roots of the man's being. It is the hatred of the <u>socialist for the individualist</u>, the cold fear of <u>the high-born for the self-made</u>, the aversion of <u>the theorist for the pragmatist</u>, the derision of <u>the urbanist for the peasant</u>, the disdain of <u>the intellectual for the uncouth</u>, the contempt of <u>the Gaul for the Slav</u>. All these hatreds have helped dictate the posture of the Trudeau government towards the west." (The Book of Ted, 1998, "The budget: a political payoff venting an unbridled hatred," November 7, 1980 column).

Beyond economics, and far more important to Manning was his life's mission; that of Christian evangelism – leading people to a personal relationship with Jesus

CHAPTER 2: MANNING: CHAMPION OF THE PEOPLE

Christ. He called on people first to make a public commitment to Jesus Christ and then take a stand for what they believed in as Christians.

> "Put your Christianity into action. Give God His rightful place in your life, home and the councils of your land. We need laymen behind desks, on farms and in factories who can get people away from the idea that Christianity is something to be ashamed of."

When criticized of political opportunism for going on an evangelical mission to Ontario and Quebec in November, 1952, he responded as follows:

> "I was teaching the Lord's Word long before going into politics, and I hope to be teaching it long after I leave politics."

Note: He kept this promise also.

He said that religion and politics were indivisible IF the politician was a "genuine Christian." Capitalization below by the writer.

> "If Christianity is giving you a new outlook on life, you can't divorce it from anything. When Christianity is genuine, it affects a person's outlook and attitude, and therefore affects his decisions. It isn't a matter of 'should they be mixed?' YOU CAN'T SEPARATE THEM."

The Premier said in 1949-1950 regarding the immense oil sands deposits in northern Alberta,

> "You don't just leave the largest oil deposit in the world sitting there and say, 'We don't need to be interested in it because we've got lots of conventional oil.'"

Ernest Manning and Howard Pew, President of Sun Oil, stood together on the bank of Athabasca River in 1953. Premier Manning said to him,

> "If you'll build the first commercial oil sand plant here, we'll carve out a market share for the oil of the future."

The result of this meeting was the "biggest gamble in oil patch history" and the birth of what would become Suncor, and the Ft. McMurray Oil Sands Project that has enriched Alberta and fueled the Canadian economy for many years.

Twenty-first century Marxism, masquerading as global warming – 'phony environmentalism' – is seeking to destroy the West's remaining prosperity in the oil sands and bring down the Alberta economy. Left-wing politicians and bureaucrats are fueling this nefarious agenda, with Justin Trudeau's Liberals leading the way. (See Appendix 4) They are in a very real sense, 'at war with Alberta,' seeking to destroy its economy and peoples' well-being.

Manning correctly had little patience with the environmentalists of his day (early 1980s), saying,

> "Today, you can't even open up a little coal mine without a parade of protestors screaming, 'It's going to chase the birds away or knock down a tree.'"

Ernest Manning's government felt that nothing should be able to interfere with resource development. The oil companies should be able to start drilling whenever they wanted. The "Crown Reserve" system prevented monopolies in Alberta.

CHAPTER 2: MANNING: CHAMPION OF THE PEOPLE

Premier Manning was a patriotic Canadian in the traditional sense. He was favorable to the English monarchy with sound reason.

> "I am a confirmed (but not fanatical) monarchist. There is a unifying influence that comes from affection for an individual who is above and removed from the political arena."

In stark contrast, Pierre Trudeau once observed that the British monarchy was less important to Canada than "skiing or snowboarding," but had no immediate plan to abolish it. When visiting Queen Elizabeth he did a tasteless pirouette behind her back as they were walking in Buckingham Palace. It was televised. (Bob Plamondon, "The Truth About Trudeau," 2013).

Premier Manning did not like the liquor trade because of his personal Christian convictions and the damage that it caused to so many lives. Yet, his government did not did not try to ban the sale of alcohol, recognizing the will of the majority as being in favor of it. In 1947 he said,

> "The liquor trade was controlled to the extent that you didn't at least encourage, aid, and abet the dire consequences that we saw so often."

The Alberta Government proposed a Cash Dividends Program in 1957 to give the citizens of the province a stake in the new found oil wealth. After polling a section of the populace Manning found that a majority of people opposed the program in favor of spending the surplus upon meeting the basic needs of Albertans. The Premier then cancelled the dividends plan in accord with the peoples' will. He said,

> "I like the attitude it indicated – a concern for others."

French thinker, Alexis de Tocqueville noted that public charity, like that shown above, combines the virtues of generosity and gratitude, which interact mutually, to improve society and exert a positive moral influence. Modern social welfare bureaucratizes the process of charity, the "donors" being the taxpayers who are forced to give up their wealth, rather than sharing it voluntarily, exacerbating conflicts between the rich and poor. De Tocqueville wrote,

> "One class still views the world with fear and loathing while the other regards its misfortune with despair and envy." (The Epoch Times, "How the Spectre of Communism is Ruling Our World," The Communist Economic Trap – Part 1, Chapter 9, 2020)

Mr. Manning rejected federally-imposed compulsory Medicare, saying it would put Canada on the road to a complete, central government-controlled socialist/collectivist welfare state.[4]

4. The path of progression of the left-wing progressive subversive agenda was intended to tear down and replace the Judeo-Christian institutions in the Western democracies. It was called, "The long march through the institutions," leading toward an authoritarian, and ultimately totalitarian, international socialist-communist government. It has largely succeeded. (see #s1 & 5)

Manning said,

> "We didn't believe in the welfare state approach. The state's responsibility was to care for people who were unable to care for themselves. Therefore, no one would be deprived of medical services for financial reasons. Moreover, a free citizen in a free society should be free to decide whether he wants to provide for his own medical needs from the many insurance programs

CHAPTER 2: MANNING: CHAMPION OF THE PEOPLE

available to him." (Brian Brennan, The Good Steward: The Ernest C. Manning Story, 2008).

<u>RE: Lester B. Pearson</u> (1897-1972): Canadian Prime Minister from 1963 to 1968. Ernest Manning described him as a great diplomat and administrator, but not a politician. He was easily influenced by socialist insiders in his administration.

> "Conrad Black writes in "Rise to Greatness," Lester B. Pearson was a congenial, urbane, and emollient (soothing) man – a model of restraint and fair-mindedness. He was no more a politician in manner and appearance than at heart and lacked the instincts of combat on the hustings and for legislative manoeuver for popular appeal." (The Epoch Times, p. B1, September 17-23, 2020)

Pearson, a classic Liberal who embraced Enlightenment values, was surrounded by social welfare advocates in the government who sold him on the socialist propaganda that only socialists are interested in people. They falsely labeled the people who believed in private enterprise and individual initiative as cold-blooded, hard-hearted parasites. (Brian Brennan, The Good Steward: The Ernest C. Manning Story, 2008) The Liberals followed Marx's error, not realizing the very prosperity of Canada and Alberta came from the free enterprise system, not from socialism. During Pearson's time in office most of the national socialistic programs – compulsory welfare, unemployment insurance and Medicare – were put in place. This was the great welfare gift to Canada, courtesy of the federal Liberals.

> "Frederick Hayek, the prominent Austrian economist and philosopher, cautioned against state-controlled planning and wealth redistribution, saying that it would inevitably lead to the rise of totalitarianism, regardless of whether the system was democratic or not. Hayek believed that

although the socialism practiced in Europe and North America was different from public ownership and planned economics, it would nevertheless come to the same result. People would lose their freedom and livelihood, just in a slower and more indirect fashion." (The Epoch Times, "How the Spectre of Communism is Ruling Our World," The Communist Economic Trap – Part 1, Chapter 9, 2020)

Brad Bird's recent Epoch Times article, "Pearson's Defense of Democratic Values 6 Decades Ago Rings True Today," admirably describes this 1957 Nobel Peace Prize winner. Pearson wrote that Western civilization's ideals came from Greece – quality/honor/principle before quantity/wealth/practice; Rome – order/organization, "one law for all citizens," responsibility of every citizen to do his duty by the state; and Israel – "spiritual heritage of one God and the worth and value and equal rights of every person under that God." Pearson was anti-totalitarian and anti-Soviet, abhorring his successor's support of the Soviets and opposition to Canada's allies in NATO (Bob Plamondon, The Truth About Trudeau, 2013)

> "Pearson talks about the threats to Western values from within: "quite as dangerous and in fact a part of that from without (communism)." He was wary of the welfare state. "There has been much of value of good in this concept, but only if we realize it is merely a means to an end, and not an end in itself. The end must be the better life, the freer life, the more expanding life of the individual. **The central value of our Western civilization is the stress that it rightly lays on the integrity and worth of the individual personality. Lose this and we lose everything. From this all our other freedoms flow.**" He opposed social engineering and collectivism – elements of Soviet totalitarianism were anathema to him. A citizen who believes "that government is not something to promote his dignity and worth, but merely something to increase his pension and free him from his own civic

CHAPTER 2: MANNING: CHAMPION OF THE PEOPLE

responsibilities, will give his support to those leaders which promise most to those ends." Then, **power will be gained by those who make the most alluring promises of immediate improvement, who appeal to selfish personal interests rather than to the sense of civic duty**." (Brad Bird, Pearson's Defense of Democratic Values 6 Decades Ago Rings True Today, The Epoch Times, p. B1, September 17-23, 2020)

Pierre Trudeau infiltrated Pearson's Liberal Party in 1965 to engineer it, and Canada, into radical socialism-communism, something that Pearson, himself, being an advocate of the essential values of Western civilization abhorred. Pierre and Justin Trudeau, along with Jean Chretien, and other key 'Liberal' insiders are today's proof-positive evidence that radical socialism-communism will destroy classical Liberalism.

Pierre Trudeau followed "collectivist" policies exactly opposite to what Pearson expounded. He reduced federal funding to Medicare and demanded increased federal control. He was upset some provinces charged extra fees because it violated his socialist ideology. In 1984 Trudeau established the Canada Health Act to deter doctors from charging user fees and penalizing provinces that did. Canadians who could pay for their own health care were denied freedom of choice. That's socialism; and that is what Ernest Manning strongly opposed. Pearson did not live to see the damage caused by Trudeau's radical socialist policies.

Note: This freedom applies to many areas of life, not just health care. We are losing these freedoms today (2020). Most of these losses can be traced back to Pierre Elliott Trudeau and his 1982 Charter of Rights and Freedoms.

Ernest Manning astutely observed very early on that –

"FORTRESS AMERICA" UNDER SIEGE

> "The pressure of social unrest (in the 1960s) was causing dissatisfied citizens to grope, often blindly, for a more meaningful and satisfying future."

Tragically for Canada, dissatisfied, blind citizens voted a flamboyant, unproven, rebellious dilettante into office for 15 ½ years.

Manning addressed this issue many times. Here is one example from his Back to the Bible Hour pamphlet, "The Face of the Sky," – Part 1, written in 1971, and concerning the future.

> "Herman Cann, who directs the Hudson Institute at Croiden, New York told 1550 top corporation executives and others, attending the first White House conference on the industrial world, the following: "Our biggest problem is religious – finding meaning and purpose. Why do we stay alive, and what are we here for?" "My Grandfather," he said, "walked with God and knew why, but we don't."

The election of Pierre Elliott Trudeau in 1968 was a socialist economic trap. He promised the voters much without increased spending, and they took the bait. He lied. Sound familiar? Justin did the same. Like father, like son. Canadians will look back some day and see their second greatest mistake.

> "It took 15 ½ years of incremental and radical change under Trudeau for Canadians to appreciate fully what he had in mind – and who would pay for it (i.e., his just society). He took office armed with a well-honed and coherent view of government as large, centralized, intrusive and indebted." (Bob Plamondon, The Truth About Trudeau, 2013).

The Epoch Times (March 5-11, 2020 ed.) stated,

CHAPTER 2: MANNING: CHAMPION OF THE PEOPLE

> "The majority of people working in major newspapers and TV stations are leftists, be they the owners of these organizations or the reporters and commentators. Their bias is obvious."

It is socialism/communism that they want, and it is nearly too late to save Canada and the U.S. from it.

Nearing retirement, Ernest C. Manning stated:

> "Times have changed; I haven't."

When the Alberta Legislature voted to allow professional sports to be played on Sundays, Premier Manning absented himself from the legislature on the day of the vote.

When the younger generation desired contemporary Christian music and new Bible translations on the Back to the Bible Hour programs he reaffirmed his commitment to the old paths. He said he had no intention of changing the program to make it more appealing to a younger audience. It would continue to feature readings from the Authorized 1611 King James Bible and the old hymns of the faith since,

> "any suggestion of modern beat music would give our audience a heart attack."

In his Farewell Address to the people of Alberta in December, 1968, Manning's leadership and subtle humor shone brightly.

> "Over the years, I have been portrayed by newsmen and commentators as an enigma; reserved, dour, cold and void of any emotions. But I am very happy to report to you tonight that none of these afflictions have caused me any pain."

He gave thanks for 33 years of –

> "innumerable memories and kindnesses; to the finest employer any man could have: you, the citizens of this great and dynamic province of Alberta."

Likened the Canadian Senate where he spent 13 years (1970 to 1983) after retiring as Alberta's premier to "a peaceful country graveyard," that should be reformed or abolished. It represented only Southern Ontario and Quebec.

When he asked Prime Minister Pierre Trudeau why he appointed him to the Senate, considering their conflicting political views, Trudeau answered that 'he would rather have Manning in the Senate than out on the street talking to people,' according to an archived newspaper article. Manning's strong Christian faith obviously represented a threat to Trudeau's ideology and plans for Canada.

In 1980, RE: Trudeau's National Energy Policy and Western separation, Ernest Manning wisely stated,

> "I know the feeling of frustration in the West. But it is not as simple as it sounds to set up a new nation or to tear an old one apart."

Westerners should keep this sage advice in mind when considering separation under Pierre Trudeau's younger son's divisive leadership. If Canadians exercise their democratic rights and vote wisely these problems can be solved with Justin out of the way.

RE: The establishment of the Manning Innovation Awards by Calgary businessmen for Canadian inventors, Ernest Manning gratefully said,

CHAPTER 2: MANNING: CHAMPION OF THE PEOPLE

> "You couldn't do anything I appreciate more. It was worth 72 years of life to have an evening like this."

He loved mechanics and innovation from his youth working on his father's farm in Saskatchewan (T. Cashman, 1958), so this later recognition was close to his heart.

Concerning the death of Social Credit in Alberta in 1982: He said to the remaining Party members,

> "Whatever you do, just keep the dignity of the party. It has served Albertans well."

Compare Manning's view of his former political party with Trudeau's attitude toward the Liberal Party of Canada in which he had served as an MP for about 19 years (1965-1984).

> "Trudeau was indifferent to Liberal fortunes before and after they had served his purpose." (Stephen Clarkson) "Trudeau left his party in ruins. He didn't care." (Donald Brittain) When Trudeau's personal interests and views collided with those of his party, the personal triumphed the political every time." (Bob Plamondon, The Truth About Trudeau, 2013, p. 320).

<u>RE: Pierre Elliott Trudeau</u>: Canadian Prime Minister (1968-1979; 1980-1984).

Trudeau was a left-wing intellectual who abhorred entrepreneurial individualism in a free market economy, a defining characteristic of Alberta and Albertans.

Manning was on record as saying Trudeau was...

> "the worst political leader in years from the standpoint of the Western provinces."

"FORTRESS AMERICA" UNDER SIEGE

Manning and Trudeau were 100% opposites philosophically and politically, and in how they viewed the needs of the average, everyday working man or woman. Manning saw through the charismatic Trudeau early on.

> "If you go and talk to him about how you're going to get money into the hands of other people to pay the rent, that's boring. He doesn't know how the other half lives. **He and his people have destroyed the pride of so many Canadians in their country.** This is not working for your country." (Brian Brennan, The Good Steward – The Ernest C. Manning Story, 2008)

Trudeau's Unemployment Insurance policies hurt Canadians badly.

> "Trudeau damaged the country by removing incentives to work and by diminishing the sense of self-reliance in many regions of Canada. His 'reforms' produced personal and regional stagnation. Unemployed had a 48% greater risk of having a major depression than those employed." (Bob Plamondon, The Truth About Trudeau, 2013).

He was remote and disinterested in everyday peoples' lives. A few of many examples are shown below –

> "Why should I sell their wheat? When there is too much sun they complain. When there is too much rain they complain. A farmer is a complainer." (Ibid, p. 305).

> "Trudeau was notoriously cheap on matters big and small. He rarely left an appropriate tip and did not provide his ex-wife sufficient funds." (Ibid)

Justin Trudeau said in his controversial, Canada Day message on July 1, 2017, on the anniversary of Canada's 150th anniversary celebration:

CHAPTER 2: MANNING: CHAMPION OF THE PEOPLE

> "As we mark Canada 150, **we also recognize that for many, today is not an occasion for celebration.** As a society, we must acknowledge and apologize for past wrongs." (Anthony Furey, How sad that even our flag now comes with a disclaimer, The Calgary Sun, June 30, 2020).

> "A newspaper based out of Nova Scotia, The Chronicle Herald, put a trigger warning on their front page, "You'll find a Canadian flag to clip and post to help celebrate July 1st. **We understand the flag doesn't mean the same thing to everyone.**" (Ibid).

On Canada Day, 2020, we now have to apologize for being Canadian. It ought to be a time to celebrate the positive things that make this country one of the best in the world to live in, and where people from many lands want to come to find a better life.

More about the fruit of both Trudeaus' divisive policies. Candice Malcolm wrote, "July 1 – the day we celebrate our unique achievements and proud history," wrote as follows:

> "Canada Day – or as I prefer to call it, Dominion Day, the name used by Canadians for over a century until former Prime Minister Pierre Trudeau re-engineered our national symbols to bury our rich history and traditions – should be a day of unity and patriotism. Instead, for many Canadians, it was just another day to push division, show off their woke credentials and try to smash the foundation of our free society. On Twitter, the hashtag "Cancel Canada Day" was trending, filled with vile and ignorant messages insisting that Canada is a uniquely evil country, purveyors of atrocities equal to Nazi Germany, and that Canada simply ought not to exist. **It seems that many Canadians, sadly, have lost all context and cannot show appreciation of Canada for even one day.**

> Brian Lee Crowley of the Macdonald-Laurier Institute said, the Canadian ideal is – a society where rights, freedoms, dignity and justice are upheld and protected for each and every one of us...and noted how rare this is in human history. **Canada is a rare jewel in human experience. We have every reason to be proud of Canada**." (Candace Malcolm, The Calgary Sun, July 6, 2020).

Ernest Manning stated that Pierre Trudeau had divided Canadians at many levels, and done inestimable harm to the social fabric of the country.

> "We are saddled with the most incompetent federal government in Canadian history."

Bob Plamondon corroborated his concerns almost 40 years later in his 2013 literary revelation, "The Truth About Trudeau." In that book, David Frum is quoted:

> "Trudeau's greatest disaster was his impact on the unity of Canada. He ascertained what each of Canada's regions most dearly wanted – and then he offered them the exact opposite..."the finger approach to national unity and – he nearly blew apart the country, and his own party."

Maybe Pierre Trudeau was not "incompetent," but was a fully committed, radical Marxist socialist-communist who was manufacturing his own **"class struggle**," and through it guiding Canada into his vision for its radical socialist-communist future. Justin is now trying to finish his father's work. His will succeed, if we let him. No doubt, the father coached his son concerning this agenda while Justin was still young.

Manning, while in the Senate, fought strongly against Trudeau unilaterally repatriating the Canadian Constitution from Britain in 1982, for this very reason. It

CHAPTER 2: MANNING: CHAMPION OF THE PEOPLE

alienated Quebec and nearly destroyed the nation. In 2020, Canada is reaping the fruits of this left-wing strategy causing strife and division through non-elected judges (i.e., judicial activism) making public policy and enshrining minority rights above the rights of the majority across the nation.

> "Trudeau repudiated the long-held British principle that Parliament, and not the courts, should reign supreme. His unilateral patriation of the Constitution in 1982, with an embedded Charter of Rights and Freedoms had the power to strike down federal and provincial legislation inconsistent with its interpretation of the Charter. The courts would soon rule on the great social and legal questions of the day, issuing a raft of new precedents that would define Canada for generations to come." (Bob Plamondon, The Truth About Trudeau, 2013, p. 117).

Manning's warnings were for the most part kept from the public eyes. He stated that Canadian newspapers are part of a –

> "universal brainwashing scheme...to make people aggressive in that which will destroy them...**state collectivism**." (Albertan, Dec. 2, 1955)

He saw far ahead the dangers free democracies would face. But he stood almost alone in trying to warn Canadians. Almost nobody listened.

> Marx stated, "the theory of the Communists could be summed up in a single sentence. Abolition of private property." (i.e., state collectivism). (The Epoch Times, "How the Spectre of Communism is Ruling Our World," The Communist Economic Trap – Part 2, Chapter 9, 2020)

> "Collective ownership inevitably leads to totalitarian outcomes; starvation wherever it goes. Collectivism is a yoke affixed on the necks of man by a totalitarian state.

> Freedom is stolen – including the freedom to be kind – and everyone is forced to follow the moral commands of the communist regime. Venezuela recently met its economic fate, believing Hugo Chavez's promise of "21st century socialism," where the government nationalized many, many private companies." (Ibid)

Pierre Trudeau fulfilled Manning's worst fears for the country he loved. Trudeau was a known admirer, friend and mentor of Cuba's Fidel Castro; and was enamored with Mao Zedong's China, both brutal socialist-communist regimes. His son, Prime Minister Justin Trudeau, is knowingly carrying his father's work to fruition – a totalitarian socialist, and ultimately communist, Canada; unless he is voted out of office. Now in 2020, Canada is in crisis and at a crossroads.

> "The divisions in (Justin) Trudeau's Canada run even deeper than traditional regional tensions, as the Liberals have introduced a toxic brew of identity politics into every aspect of federal politics. Federal budgets now consist of more rhetoric on feminism and intersectionality (see pp. 137-138) than they do cold, hard facts on spending, taxation, deficits and debt.
>
> Trudeau takes his own rigid ideology – dogmatically "progressive" on social issues and big spending – and attempts to exclude and silence those with dissenting views. Trudeau has allowed unprecedented illegal immigration; believes in unlimited access to abortion; believes in catastrophic predictions of man-made global warming; Trudeau treats all Conservative voters as members of a fringe movement who are unwelcome in polite society." (Candice Malcolm, Calgary Sun, May 25, 2020),

Please refer to Appendix 4 and read Zuzana Janosova Den Boer's warning to her adopted homeland, Canada, **"I Survived Communism – Are You Ready For Your Turn?"** written in Calgary in 2019.

CHAPTER 2: MANNING: CHAMPION OF THE PEOPLE

Conservative newspapers such as the Calgary Sun and The Epoch Times are full of articles on social engineering of society, the climate change 'crisis,' high government spending, social restrictions, cozy relations with Communist China, punitive gun laws on law-abiding citizens, restrictions on free speech, etc, etc. It is difficult to keep up with the flood of information on the war going on inside our country right now. The Liberal government is on a frenzied rush to impose a statist dictatorship in Ottawa.

Joe Oliver, Canada's former federal Minister of Finance under Stephen Harper's conservative government wrote:

> "Justin Trudeau leans farther left than any Prime Minister since his father. So he might not need a huge push to double down on his current tax and spending spree, costly and ineffective climate initiatives and treating Canada's energy industry as road kill." (Joe Oliver, Worst election outcome? Far-left social democratic coalition, The Calgary Sun, September 6, 2019)

The Trudeau Liberals accuse the Conservatives of what they themselves are – power hungry statists. Their leftist agenda is now out in the open. They are not hiding their intentions any longer. Mrs. Janosova (Appendix 4) thinks Canada's free democracy could end very soon, possibly in ten to fifteen years.

If freedom-loving Canadians do not open their eyes and resist the leftist take over by peaceful democratic means we will very soon end up in the totalitarian slave state predicted by William Aberhart and Ernest Manning so many years ago. It is coming! We are almost out of time to preserve our free democracy in Canada, and the United States is not far behind us.

"FORTRESS AMERICA" UNDER SIEGE

In 1979/1980, Manning repeated his warning and gave his advice for the only hope remaining for Canada. May God have mercy on us as it is now 40 years later, and later than we think concerning their fulfilment.

> "Beneath and behind so many of our social and political problems today is our abandonment of spiritual verities and our failure to give God and His truth their rightful place in our lives and the affairs of our nation. For this, many religious leaders who have rejected the Deity and Lordship of Christ and the infallibility of the Word of God must bear a heavy responsibility. The abuse of secular and political power for dishonest gain will ultimately lead to the destruction of any society. (E. C. Manning, "It is Written – No. 3: Wanted a Man," Vintage Radio Message on Back to the Bible Hour, July 5, 2020).
>
> Never has there been a more obvious need for people to develop a spiritual dimension and perspective, without which no (free democratic) society can survive." (Ibid)

Our choice is either traditional Judeo-Christianity – Jesus Christ and the Holy Bible – or socialism-communism – Karl Marx and the Communist Manifesto. We either return to free democracy with Judeo-Christian faith principles, or grope our way blindly into bondage under a dictatorial federal government. There is no other alternative.

Ernest C. Manning is our example to follow to get out of the mess we are currently in today in Canada. Chapters 1, 2 and 3 make this point unmistakably clear for all whose eyes are willing to see.

Pierre Elliot Trudeau is the example not to follow, because he, more than any other, brought us into the crisis of leadership we are now in today.

CHAPTER 2: MANNING: CHAMPION OF THE PEOPLE

> "Trudeau fils (the son) comes by his China naivete honestly; Trudeau pere (the father) fawned, serially, over Soviet Russia, China and Cuba." (Barbara Kay, Human Wreckage: Pondering Lenin's Legacy on 150th Anniversary of His Birth, p. B1, The Epoch Times, April 23-29, 2020)

Canadian voters have no choice but to remove his son, Justin Trudeau, from office as soon as possible.

What would Mr. Manning say if his grandchildren wanted to enter public life? He would consent – with one reservation:

> "Your number one concern in life should be your personal relationship to Jesus Christ. He's the Sovereign Lord of everyone. Settle that matter to start with. It'll do more to change your life and stabilize your life than any single thing you can do. Ambition is a wonderful thing. But in the process, don't barge off on your own. Just keep that other factor in mind: is this what God wants me to do?" (Brennan, 2008)

Mr. Manning's advice is confidently recommended for anyone desiring to enter public office in Canada today.

> "This land has been endowed with everything necessary to enable it to be a great nation under God, strong and prosperous, and free. Our great and urgent need at the present time is for strong, godly leadership, not only to resolve social and economic and financial troubles, but above all, to guide the feet of the nation into the paths of righteousness and principles of conduct based on the eternal verities which God has spelled out for our guidance in the pages of Holy Writ." (E. C. Manning, "It is Written – No. 3: Wanted a Man," Vintage Radio Message on Back to the Bible Hour, July 5, 2020).

The motivation should be the same as that held by Mr. Manning and Mr. Aberhart, back in 1933, as they entered

"FORTRESS AMERICA" UNDER SIEGE

politics to try and help lift Albertans out of despair and ruin caused in part by a UFA scandal-ridden government and mismanagement of the economy before and during the Great Depression (see Appendix 5).

CHAPTER 3

THE HON. ERNEST C. MANNING: THE PREACHER

*"For the transgression of a land many are the princes thereof:
but by a man of understanding and knowledge
the state thereof shall be prolonged."*
Proverbs 28:2

"FORTRESS AMERICA" UNDER SIEGE

E. C. Manning was a man of understanding and knowledge. He was a brilliant man and humble in all his ways. He won seven consecutive elections as Premier of Alberta, and was never defeated. His political life spanned 33 years (1935-1968). He also preached as a fundamental Baptist for over 60 years, beginning in 1930 with William Aberhart. He preached the gospel of Jesus Christ and gave warning to his generation of the deadly perils facing our nation. We ignore his wisdom and teachings at great danger to ourselves and to our nation.

This following sub-sections have been compiled from several of E. C. Manning's vintage printed messages provided by Mr. Dennis Snyder of Redlands, Alberta. Wider margins are used for the quotes, with some exceptions, because most of the material is copied directly from various parts of the hard copy pamphlets provided to me.

MANNING'S PERSONAL CONVERSION TO JESUS CHRIST

Alberta's eighth premier says he was saved as a teenage farm boy listening to William Aberhart over CFCN Calgary radio. He became convinced it was not enough to know ABOUT Christ – but that he wanted to know Christ personally. He found that personal relationship with Christ in 1925 (from *Ernest C. Manning-A Biographical Sketch* by Tony Cashman, 1958).

In a radio address in Chicago in 1948, Mr. Manning gave a more complete personal testimony of salvation. It is in Appendix 3.

MANNING ON TWO IRREFUTABLE CARDINAL TRUTHS

CHAPTER 3: MANNING: THE PREACHER

1. He stated, "Our first and foremost goal through these weekly broadcasts is to affirm clearly and unequivocally, and with all the conviction and emphasis possible, that the Bible is in very truth the verbally inspired (God-breathed), divinely preserved, infallible, inerrant, immutable and eternal Word of God.(3, #1144) I am not talking about original manuscripts which have long since passed out of existence; I'm not talking about the multiplicity of modern revisions and re-translations, so many of which mutilate and pervert the inspired text. I am talking about the old King James Bible that came down to us from the *Textus Receptus* or "received text," and which bears so many hallmarks of both verbal inspiration and divine preservation that we may say without doubt or reservation it is in very truth the infallible and inerrant Word of God."(4, #1175)

E. C. Manning preached only from the KJV Bible. His advice,

> "I commend it to you. Read it, believe it, and it will prove a lamp to your feet and a light to your path. It will change your life and point you to Jesus Christ, the only one who can forgive your sins and save your soul."(4, #1175)

His messages can still be heard on Canada's National Bible Hour/Global Outreach Mission on the first Sunday morning of every month.

2. Jesus Christ is the Son of God, the Creator and sovereign Lord of everything that exists. He died for our sins according to the Scriptures; He was buried and He rose again the third day according to the Scriptures; and by the miracle of His resurrection the Scriptures say He was "declared to be the Son of God with power" (Romans 1:4). After His literal, bodily resurrection, and after showing himself alive by many infallible proofs, He ascended back to heaven, where He is today seated at

God's right hand, from whence He will return someday to take over the management of this earth and reign as King of kings and Lord of lords. Today, through His message to mankind in the infallible Scriptures and the supernatural ministry of the Holy Spirit (His personal representative on the earth until He returns) He is calling to Himself out of the masses of humanity a people for His name.[3, #1144]

MANNING ON GENUINE BIBLE CHRISTIANITY

Genuine Bible Christianity is all about God reconciling men and women to Himself through Jesus Christ. It is a supernatural work of the Holy Spirit on those who are spiritually dead and alienated from God. Conversion to be genuine must be far more than a mental assent to the teachings of Scripture. Being saved is not a matter of creeds or dogmas, or subscribing mentally to this or that religious doctrine or ordinance, or sacrament. It means acknowledging your sinfulness in the sight of a Holy God and a whole-hearted turning from that sin (*repentance toward God*), and faith toward the Lord Jesus Christ. That faith is in Jesus' blood which was shed for the remission (forgiveness) of his sins, His death, burial and resurrection (Acts 20:20-21). Conversion brings new spiritual life in the form of a new spiritual nature.

> *"But as many as received him, to them gave he power to become the sons of God, even to them that believe on his name: Which were born, not of blood, nor of the will of the flesh, nor of the will of man, but of God." (John 1:12-13)*[3, #1144]

Biblical salvation is wholly dependent on the grace (*unmerited favor*) and mercy of God, as the Scriptures say,

CHAPTER 3: MANNING: THE PREACHER

> "For by grace are ye saved through faith; and that not of yourselves: it is the gift of God: Not of works, lest any man should boast" (Ephesians 2:8-9).

There is no salvation in good works or following the Golden Rule. Jesus warned,

> "Many will say unto me in that day, Lord, Lord, have we not prophesied in thy name: and in thy name have cast out devils? and in thy name done many wonderful works? And then will I profess unto them, I never knew you: depart from me, ye that work iniquity." (Matthew 7:22-23)[3, #1144]

When you enter into a personal relationship with the living, divine Person of Jesus Christ and turn your life over to Him, that new relationship will impact on every facet of your life.[3, #1144] It will change your thinking and give you a new outlook on life. Your priorities will change. Material things which once seemed so important will no longer seem important. You will begin to assess life's problems in the light of eternal considerations and in the light of the eternal truths affirmed in the Scriptures. You will live differently, talk differently and act differently. And your new-found living relationship with Christ will be reflected in your business ethics, in your political judgments, and in your family and social relationships.

> "Therefore if any man be in Christ, he is a new creature: old things are passed away; behold, all things are become new." (2 Corinthians 5:17)

God intends that each of His spiritually reborn children should be a consistent follower of Jesus Christ, yielding their lives in obedience to His will, doing what He would have them to do and being what He would have them to be.[1, #1140] Manning made no secret of his belief that the rapture of heavenly salvation was reserved for those who accepted Jesus Christ as their personal Savior. (Brennan, 2008)

MANNING ON SIN

Adam and Eve acquired a sin-infected, sin-prone nature when their willful disobedience to the express will of God alienated them from Him and brought about their spiritual death, as God had forewarned.(5, #1135)

> "Wherefore, as by one man (Adam) sin entered into the world, and death by sin; and so death passed upon all men, for that all have sinned" (Romans 5:12).

Consequently, their children were born dead spiritually, with sin-infected and sin-prone natures. The proof of inherent evil in human nature is our inclination to do what God tells us we shouldn't do. Sin lies dormant in our natures until the law of God says, "Don't do that." Then sin impels us to disobey and so brings us under the law's condemnation and sentence of death. Man fails to recognize the "exceeding sinfulness" of every thought and action that is contrary to the holy and perfect will of God. There is little sensitivity to sin today.(5, #1135)

In Romans 1:29-31, God goes on to describe human nature as follows:

> "Being filled with all unrighteousness, fornication, wickedness, covetousness, maliciousness, full of envy, murder, debate, deceit, malignity; whisperers, Backbiters, haters of God, despiteful, proud, boasters, inventors of evil things, disobedient to parents, etc,."(5, #1136)

All human beings, by reason of the sin-infected nature with which they are born, have hearts that are prone to evil and corruption and violence. In Psalm 14:2-3 we read,

CHAPTER 3: MANNING: THE PREACHER

> "The LORD looked down from heaven upon the children of men, to see if there were any that did understand, and seek God. They are all gone aside, they are all together become filthy: there is none that doeth good, no, not one."

In Psalm 51:5, King David records this explanation of his own inherent inclinations to evil,

> "Behold, I was shapen in iniquity; and in sin did my mother conceive me."

Jeremiah 17:9 affirms,

> "The heart is deceitful above all things, and desperately wicked: who can know it?" [5, #1136]

That is why there is no human solution for the problem of evil and corruption and violence in society. Man cannot change his own nature. He needs a new heart, and that is why genuine Bible Christianity is the greatest force in this world to bring about a transformation of attitude and lifestyle on the part of those who appropriate the salvation of God available to them only in the Person of Jesus Christ.[5, #1136] Reborn of God – that is the divine miracle that imparts to men and women new natures that delight in God and righteousness just as our old, natural human nature delights in things evil and destructive and violent. Jesus said in John 3:3,

> "Verily, verily, I say unto thee, Except a man be born again, he cannot see the kingdom of God."

The supernatural birth by God's Spirit is a divine imperative for sinful man.

"FORTRESS AMERICA" UNDER SIEGE

By Noah's day over 4000 years ago, sin had reached the crisis stage,

> "The earth also was corrupt before God, and the earth was filled with violence...for all flesh had corrupted his way upon the earth." (Genesis 6:11-12)[5, #1136].

The violence of a morally corrupt society was the main reason why God destroyed that world with a universal flood, sparing only just Noah and his family, eight persons in all.

Following the flood, the earth was re-populated by Noah's descendants, and soon the same social and moral trends reappeared. Once again the Genesis description of that ancient society is equally true of society today.[5, 1136] Again the earth has become corrupt before God, and again it is filled with violence. The plague of violence is fast becoming a normal characteristic of human behavior. With each passing year it increases in extent and intensity.

People don't like to be told that man is a morally corrupt, depraved sinner. They believe that the solution is to be found in more time, education and social reforms including a constant secular over-emphasis on so-called human rights, with little or no emphasis on the personal responsibility every right imposes.[5, #1136] They emphasize building tolerance, self-worth and self-esteem, and say society is collectively getting better and better. But all the while the levels of evil and corruption and violence continue to increase. Modern technology and the efforts of secular humanists have resulted in more sophisticated forms of evil and violence, and in better-educated criminals and terrorists.[5, 1136] But the basic problem remains unresolved. That problem is SIN.

CHAPTER 3: MANNING: THE PREACHER

MANNING ON THE SUBSTITUTIONAL ATONEMENT OF JESUS CHRIST

God's intervention in humanity involved providing an atonement for sin which alienates us all from God.

> "For all have sinned, and come short of the glory of God" (Romans 3:23).

The enormity of our sins was such that only by God'S Son shedding His own divine blood in <u>atonement</u> was our redemption possible.[5, #1135] Putting Himself in our place as our substitute, He bore the wrath of God the Father on the guilty sinner. Paul says of Christians in Romans 5:11,

> "We also joy in God through our Lord Jesus Christ, by whom we have now received the atonement."

God's Word remains true when it says,

> "Without shedding of blood is no remission (of sin)." (Hebrews 9:22).

The best of human efforts cannot atone for sin. Only the shedding of Christ's blood on the Cross could provide the redemptive payment for the sin of the whole world. God's forgiveness follows our acceptance of Christ and His atonement. We can't earn forgiveness, we don't deserve forgiveness; but when we repent of our sin and by faith receive Christ into our heart God extends it to us freely by grace, because of Christ's work of atonement and redemption on our behalf.[3, #1144]

> "Being justified (declared not guilty) freely by his grace through the redemption that is in Christ Jesus: Whom God hath set forth to be a propitiation (atonement) through faith in his blood," (Romans 3:24, 25a).

Having been redeemed by the blood of Christ, we are loved by God with an everlasting, measureless love, and are kept by the power of God through faith unto salvation.

MANNING ON THE CONCERNS OF MODERN SOCIETY

It is symptomatic of our times that sin does not appear sin to people today.[5, #1135] Even among professing Christians, there is no great concern or remorse over sin, few agonizing cries of repentance from hearts burdened because sin has broken their fellowship and communion with God. It is a rare thing to hear a sermon on sin today. This unwillingness to recognize sin for what it is is largely responsible for the corrupt social and moral conditions in society today. We don't have sinful people anymore; people who do evil are described by modern sociology and psychiatry as "sick", or "maladjusted," or "frustrated," or "emotionally unstable." Describe their conduct any way you like, as long as you don't call it "sin." Each and every human being is responsible for his or her own conduct and cannot pass that responsibility to others.[5, #1135] SIN is SIN.

The lack of concern and recognition of sin has led to society's abandoning the Biblical doctrine of the sanctity of life. God's breathing into Adam the very breath of life, made Adam a living soul related to God himself. There is a unique value and sanctity to human life, distinctly different from all plant and animal life, that should and must be respected.[5, #1135] No one can destroy a human life with impunity, and to do so by the evil of abortion and murder, including euthanasia, is "exceeding sinful" in the sight of God.

CHAPTER 3: MANNING: THE PREACHER

> "The total number of abortions in China between 1971 and 2012 were approximately 270 million, based upon the China Health Yearbook." (The Epoch Times, "How the Spectre of Communism is Ruling Our World," Destruction of the Family – Part 2, Chapter 7, 2020)

> The governments of the U.S. and Canada have killed approximately 40 million and 4 million unborn souls respectively in about the same period.

God will not pardon man from taking the lives, that is, the blood of innocents as recorded in the Scriptures (2 Kings 24:3-4). Both of these acts are a grievous sin in the sight of God and a violation of His perfect, divine law. God gave Noah and his descendants a divine decree,

> "Whoso sheddeth man's blood, by man shall his blood be shed: for in the image of God made he man" (Genesis 9:6).

Capital punishment for murder has nothing to do with revenge; it is solely a matter of justice, both human and divine. The severity of the penalty simply parallels the value and sanctity of human life as a living soul created in the image and likeness of God, though fallen in sin. God would not pardon the sin of killing innocents in the Bible.

> "In the 1990s, three professors, including Paul Rubin at Emory University, examined 20 years of crime statistics from 3,000 cities and towns across the United States and concluded that "each execution results, on average, in eighteen fewer murders." Even scholars who are against capital punishment must concede that **it has a deterrent effect**." (The Epoch Times, "How the Spectre of Communism is Ruling Our World," Using the Law for Evil, Chapter 10, 2020)

In June, 2016, Justin Trudeau's Liberal Government legalized 'doctor-assisted suicide,' the beginning of public acceptance of euthanasia or state-sanctioned murder. To date (March 2020), doctors have 'helped' some 7000 Canadians die since MAID (Medical Assistance in Dying) was enacted by Bill C-14. Dr. Harvey Shipper, a professor of medicine, and an adjunct professor of law at the University of Toronto warned,

> "Canada is moving too fast on changes to legislation that would expand eligibility for medically assisted death – down a pathway of immense societal consequence. A 'slippery slope' effect could lead to continuous expanding of the criteria. Faith-based and religious values are systematically excluded from the legislation,"

He called on the federal government –

> "to reject such changes, noting that there are serious ethical considerations that remain unanswered." (The Epoch Times, February 20, 2020).

The writer's only brother was euthanized on October 1, 2019 at the age of 78 years. He was not terminally ill. In October, 2020, Bill C-7 is about to be passed making it much easier to be euthanized by Canada's socialist government-controlled heath system.

Increasingly, society has discarded the moral and spiritual values and self-discipline which God intended as constraints against self-destructive human behavior.(5, #1139) Many have rejected pre-marital chastity and the monogamous marriage relationship God ordained for their protection. They flaunt and practice perverted homosexual relationships and defend them as an acceptable lifestyle and a right, but it is a sinful lifestyle that God condemns as evil and an abomination (Leviticus 18:22; Romans 1:26-27).

> "Homosexuality and other degenerate sexual behaviors were originally referred to as "sodomy" in English. Sodomy is a Biblical reference to the city of Sodom, which was wiped out under God's wrath for people's

CHAPTER 3: MANNING: THE PREACHER

> practice of sexual degeneracy. The word "gay" originally had a positive meaning, and was appropriated by the homosexual movement to lead people to sin further. In 2009, the CCP approved the first Chinese LGBT event – Shanghai Pride Week." (The Epoch Times, "How the Spectre of Communism is Ruling Our World," Destruction of the Family – Part 2, Chapter 7, 2020)

Sexual degeneracy has now become a worldwide phenomenon, setting the stage for God's coming judgment on mankind.

> "According to the adjustment standard of today's psychology, various perverted sexual freedoms advocated by the utopian socialist Charles Fourier, including incest, group marriage, bestiality, can also be considered normal psychological states. The devil is reducing man to a beast, without standards or morals, so that eventually he will be destroyed." (The Epoch Times, "How the Spectre of Communism is Ruling Our World," Destruction of the Family – Part 2, Chapter 7, 2020)

People inflict on themselves terrible damage through drugs and alcohol.(5, #1137) Today, the extent of the problem is staggering; afflicting adolescents of younger and younger ages. In numerous high schools drugs are readily available. Damage from alcohol is even more extensive, and is considered normal social conduct advertised on the media as a most blatant form of hypocrisy. There is no way to measure the incalculable price paid in impaired minds, wrecked bodies, emotional damage and wasted lives (see pp. 132-134).

Many young minds have been hardened against Biblical truth by educators in secular schools who ridicule or treat as fictional Biblical truth concerning the origin of man, the fact of sin, the deity of Jesus Christ, His literal resurrection from the dead and His promise to one day return to the earth.(8, #606) Newspapers, magazines, four

"FORTRESS AMERICA" UNDER SIEGE

letter word books, plays, motion pictures, TV programs (and the internet) daily spew into the minds of children and young people moral pollutants of every kind corrupting their characters. It is pathetic to hear parents say they don't want to teach their children anything definite about the Bible, God, Christ or man's need to be spiritually reborn – leaving them to decide later in life.[8, #606]

The materialistic society of our times is increasingly hostile to our historic Christian Judaic traditions. There are entrenched trends in that society that contain the seeds of self-destruction spiritually, morally, socially, economically and politically. Both the Christian minority and the secular majority that dominate society are being swept along by relentless tides towards the ultimate destruction of society itself. Man's best efforts to recover himself from these trends are proving futile, and we are rapidly reaching the point of no return. The key to national survival and recovery will be only through the divine intervention of God in our society.[2, #1141]

Note: Federal Bill S-202 was ratified by the Senate on 10/03/20, making it illegal to preach the gospel to the LGBTQ2S+, with the intention of converting them to Christ and back to natural affections and a normal sexual life.

If society persists in doing those things God has told them not to do, and goes deeper and deeper into sin, the time comes when God removes, if only slightly, His divine protection, without which none could survive. The consequence can be devastating.[5, #1139] God's judgment typically falls suddenly leaving no opportunity for repentance. "Fortress America," in 2020, is in danger of that happening to it in the near future.

CHAPTER 3: MANNING: THE PREACHER

MANNING ON END TIMES GEO-POLITICS

Premier Manning's knowledge of Biblical prophecy gave him an accurate understanding of end-times political developments. He wrote in the mid-to-late 1950s, the following concerning Communist China:

> "We hear (totalitarian) Communist China express constantly, vehement antagonism towards the nations of the western hemisphere. Aggressive tendencies on the part of this rising giant of the Far East are being made manifest, leading to a danger of international conflict.
>
> To offset this threat Western nations will form under *one head, the antichrist world leader of the future." (7, #44)
>
> **an international socialist confederacy: INAZI)*. Italics and acronym by the writer

The same warning proceeded from another source sixty years ago, and it is being born out, graphically and frighteningly, in our day:

> "China has now become the Communist country which arouses most indignation in Western non-Communist countries and especially in the United States. Today there is more hope of being able to live with Russia than with China. China today seems more doctrinaire, more fanatical, more ruthless, more likely to use military force directly to extend its power...and because of the hold it has on the overseas Chinese who are now living in many of the vulnerable countries." (John Bennett, Christianity and Communism Today, 1960)

China became Africa's largest trading partner in 2016. A scholar with the People's Republic of China boasted about his country's exporting its ideological approach and using poorer countries' natural resources as collateral against Chinese loan agreements.

> "China's progress over the past 40 years has proven that it doesn't need to do what the West did to achieve success. The impact of this on Africa is beyond what you can imagine."
>
> "Today, Ethiopia is called Africa's "New China." It's internet monitoring and censorship, the totalitarian nature of its government, its media control are all cast from the same communist mold as China's. The PRC has also held training sessions targeted at Ethiopian leaders and government officials from other African nations." (The Epoch Times, "How the Spectre of Communism is Ruling Our World," The Chinese Communist Party's Global Ambitions – Part 1, Chapter 18, 2020)

Chinese influence can be seen everywhere in Africa. The Zambian leader lamented in 2007, but was later as Zambia's leader forced to accept the CCP's control:

> "We want the Chinese to leave and the old colonial rulers to return. At least Western capitalism has a human face; the Chinese are only out to exploit us."

The recent COVID-19 pandemic has exposed the true nature of the Chinese regime for its lies and cover-up of the spread of the CCP – Chinese Communist Party virus.

> "Beijing is following in its global campaign to become the new leader of the world. There's just too much toxicity – aggressive, ultra-nationalistic, crude and dismissive diplomacy – coming out of the regime. The regime derogatorily referred to Australia as 'gum stuck to the bottom of China's shoe,' for wanting an investigation into the origin of the CCP virus.
>
> China seeks to reorder the world on its own terms. This plan threatens the well-being of the rest of the world and it's now a plain fact. Most of Europe is beginning to agree. European countries, especially the rich northern European countries, are breaking with China.

CHAPTER 3: MANNING: THE PREACHER

> Zi Zhongyun, of the Chinese Academy of Social Sciences said, Beijing's 'new' aggression toward the West has its roots in the anti-Western Boxer Rebellion of the early 20th century…making it impossible for China to take its place among modern civilized nations of the world." (James Gorrie, The Epoch Times, p. B1, May 14-20, 2020)

The same article went on to say,

> "That will make the immediate future more dangerous, not less. Is the world ready to reap that whirlwind?"

Another example of China's belligerent behavior toward the West follows:

> "Lu Shaye, China's past ambassador to Canada, in Toronto…called Canada and its Western allies white supremacists for asking for the release of Michael Kovrig and Michael Spavor, (innocent) Canadian citizens who have been incarcerated in China for almost a year following Canada's arrest of Huawei executive Meng Wanzhou. (Omid Ghoreishi, The Epoch Times, p. A10, Nov. 28, 2019)

Canada's current subservient behavior toward Communist China, as demonstrated by Justin Trudeau is shameful and worrisome. His father, Pierre Trudeau, became Canadian Prime Minister in 1968. He spoke repeatedly of the need to include Communist China in the United Nations. His support helped the totalitarian dictatorship's acceptance into the world body in 1971. As a result, democratic and free Taiwan was excluded and marginalized. And so it is today with the younger Trudeau in power.

> "Between the two adversaries (U.S. and PRC) that Pierre Trudeau set out to establish relations as he saw fit, one a rule-of-law based democracy and the other a communist totalitarian regime, which one is currently

holding Canadian citizens hostage?" (Omid Ghoreishi, The Epoch Times, p. A10, Nov. 28, 2019)

China's confrontation with the West, particularly the United States, seems to be playing out as Manning predicted in his early writings. Here is an example:

> "Thanks to Chinese censorship and state-controlled media, the Chinese people will only get the message the Chinese government wants them to get. And that message is that the blame for their problems doesn't belong with their own corrupt government, but with the West. I worry that things could deteriorate in such a way that the worst consequences of the COVID-19 epidemic won't be matters of public health or economics, but an escalating cold war that could turn hot." (Jonah Goldberg, The Calgary Sun, March 21, 2020)

We are living in very perilous times geo-politically as predicted by Manning. In "War of words heats up," in the June 1, 2020, Calgary Sun,

> "China rails against U.S., threatens new measures against Hong Kong. Cui Tianki, China's U.S. ambassador, wrote on Saturday that Hong Kong was 'a romantic fusion of the East and the West. To our regret, such romance is evaporating.'"

A future conflict between the East and the West is entirely possible as Manning wrote based upon his knowledge of the Bible, and the political developments of his day. He indicated that the West would move toward an alliance with Russia to counter China. President Trump has made some informal overtures toward Russia on that account according to the Epoch Times. A future U.S. Democratic government could follow through with such a policy. That would be a deadly mistake that could lead to a future Soviet U.S.A. The Epoch Times reports:

CHAPTER 3: MANNING: THE PREACHER

> "In Moscow alone there are almost 80 monuments to Lenin, whose body entombed in Red Square continues to attract to attract tourists and followers. **Red Square is still red**. The KGB has never been thoroughly exposed and condemned by the world. **Communism is still present in Russia, and believers of communism still abound**." (The Epoch Times, "How the Spectre of Communism is Ruling Our World," Exporting Revolution, Chapter 4, 2020).

With the genuine Christians raptured to heaven, the Anti-Semitic leftist, international socialist world dictator (antichrist) will deceive Israel into a false peace covenant (Daniel 9:27), and then turn on Israel and unsuccessfully try to destroy the Jewish people. Manning went on to write:

> "Poor Israel! Down through the ages she has repeatedly put confidence in those who in the end have betrayed her. When her Messiah came to win her back to God, and God's blessing, she rejected Him and had Him crucified. There will be no permanent recovery for Israel until she acknowledges her mistake (sin) and turns to Him in repentance and belief (faith) and then she will have the most glorious future of any nation on earth. (Middle East Conflict, Address by E. C. Manning, Dec. 1973, Back to the Bible Hour pamphlet)
>
> Today, Israel is still set aside (as the spiritual witness to the world) while God is calling out from all nations through Jesus Christ a people for His name. Through Israel's (temporary) fall, salvation is come to the Gentiles."

Manning's tract explains the origin of the intractable Arab – Jewish conflict from the Scriptures, and shows that the world's leaders will work in vain to solve it. Only God can, and will, solve it – in His time.

A sign that the end is nearing is the recent willingness of Arabic nations to accept Israel and establish diplomatic relations with her, over Palestinian objections. This has never happened before.

> "Last week's diplomatic breakthrough between Israel and the UAE (United Arab Emirates), establishing formal ties was met with only muted response in the Arab press. Today, the UAE, and a growing number of Arab states, recognize Israel as a force for good and normalization as a meaningful step in the quest to bring about lasting peace." (Shimon Fogel, The final unraveling of the 'Three Noes,' The Calgary Sun, August 24, 2020).

After the prophetic rapture of the genuine Christians, comprising the true Church, Israel will once again occupy the center of the world stage. Acceptance by the Arab nations is a big step in that direction, and to an agreement to build the Third Temple in Jerusalem. These developments also signal the nearing of the totalitarian one world government and the appearing of its leader, the Antichrist.

> "Israel will make a covenant with the Antichrist who at that time be working subtly to become the supreme head of a world government. When he gains his goal, he will break his covenant with Israel and once more she will face bitter persecution ending with the Battle of Armageddon." (Ibid)

Leftist socialism-communism is anti-Jewish, anti-Israel. What we are seeing today is the precursor to another holocaust implemented by future international socialism against Israel. It is Satan's last desperate attempt to try and thwart God's plan of bringing a repentant Israel back to her Messiah, Jesus Christ. Manning understood these truths.

CHAPTER 3: MANNING: THE PREACHER

"One of the most troubling developments in recent years is the resurgence of deeply entrenched Anti-Semitism on university campuses where Jewish students can feel unsafe. The Cultural Marxist ideology of 'intersectionality,' a victimhood hierarchy being taught by professors, makes everything a battle between the oppressor and the oppressed; Marx's "bourgeoisie and proletariat." I've had professors rant about Israel in classes about sexuality, and it never had anything to do with anything we were learning," said Lauren Isaacs, a student a York University in Ontario." (Shane Miller, The Epoch Times, p. A3, Nov. 28, 2019.)

Dennis Prager, founder of Prager University in California, warns:

"The left is racist. Leftists support racial segregation. That's why institutions such as Harvard and Columbia have black graduation ceremonies and why many universities have an all-black dorm. An all-black dorm is supported by the Ku Klux clan and the left. Universities are morally sick. What the college is doing is infantilizing its students, by censoring (by 'safe spaces') against conservative values and speakers that would damage the emotions of its indoctrinated leftist youth.

The left has never believed in freedom. Never. Of speech or anything else. (Classical) Liberalism and conservatism believe in freedom, but leftists oppose it. And "leftists will destroy liberalism." Yearning for freedom is a learned value. "People yearn to be taken care of, not to be free." In the ideal world of the leftist, "the government takes care of you. The government takes care of your family, the government takes care of your community." That's a nightmare. I want to take care of my family, my community. That was the American ideal.

The left is totalitarian. All leftism everywhere has a totalitarian temptation. The only thing that stops the left in America from being totalitarian is that they don't have full power. But wherever they have full power they are totalitarian. The college campus is the most obvious example." (I. Luo & J. Jekielik, The Epoch Times, p. B1, 5, Nov. 28, 2019)

The warning that "leftists will destroy liberalism" is documented in a book entitled, "Confessions of Stalin's Agent," by Kenneth Goff, a former communist in the mid-to-late 1930s.

> "The speaker was a young man from New York. He gave a report on the Seventh World Congress of the Communist Party. He called us Liberals, and said we were like armies without generals, or plans to carry out our campaign. Only by developing trained leadership could we attain to goal of a new world order, or international Communism. Cohen declared that the Communist Party was the vanguard of the masses and its membership comprised the generals for the coming revolution." (from "The Red Devil of Communism," by E. J, Daniels, D.D., 1954)

Maybe we're in the quiet revolution the leftists have been planning for a long time. Canada's Liberal Prime Minister says daily to Canadians..."we're (the government) here for you"...'taking care' of families, communities and businesses." That is, after he left the country open to the pandemic in the first place by allowing airlines to come into the country from viral 'hot spots' until the COVID-19 virus spread from coast to coast, creating the present lockdown, economic damage and government dependency the leftists like.

Ernest Manning wrote in his booklet, "The Future Complete Universal Dictatorship," Back to the Bible Hour Booklet No. 45, mid-to-late 1950s) as follows:

> "In recent times the progressive transfer, often the voluntary transfer, of responsibilities from the individual to the state, the surrender of individual freedom in return

CHAPTER 3: MANNING: THE PREACHER

> for some promised social or economic gain are conditioning the human race for universalism in every sphere to a degree unequalled in any previous period in human history.
>
> We can recognize in this, surely, the systematic destruction of the fiber of individualism and individual independence. These trends progressively destroy love of individual freedom and bring about the loss of man's capacity to successfully assume individual responsibility. All this is conditioning mankind to turn over to a world organization, a world government, a world tyranny (despotic), the autonomy of nations and the freedom of individuals in return for some promise of world peace or greater world social security for individuals and nations." (The Battle of Armageddon, E. Manning, Back to the Bible Hour booklet No. 48, mid-to-late 1950s.)

Manning's foresight can be fast-forwarded to 2020 with remarkable accuracy. It leaves one wondering if the CCP virus was unleashed upon the world for this very purpose. Of all the Western democracies, Canada seems the most passive and easily influenced by Communist China's propaganda and threats.

Prime Minister Justin Trudeau's incredibly naïve, even criminally negligent response and dealings with the totalitarian CCP has created for Canadians an enormous amount of emotional and financial pain across the country, grief and loss among business owners, our elderly and their families and finally, an unnatural dependence upon a debt-laden, 'benevolent' leftist federal government that is intent on increasing its power over the people.

And, incredibly, the same 'leader' is working with the communists to produce a vaccine to 'protect' Canadian citizens! Dr. Kulvinder Gill, a MD in the Toronto area and president of Concerned Ontario Doctors said,

> "Canada is literally the only country in the entire world offering up its own citizens as guinea pigs in this unethical, rapid, human clinical trial of the Chinese SARS-CoV-2 vaccine – in partnership with the communist Chinese military that is already under a cloud of global suspicion. This human clinical trial between the NRC and CanSino on the China's Communist Party vaccine is proceeding at an alarming rate," says Dr. Kulvinder Gill. She added, "It's fundamental for our government to abandon this dangerous endeavor and instead…fund vaccine trials with our allied nations who understand the importance of trust and ethics and transparency." (The Epoch Times, p. A3, May 21-27, 2020).

Justin Trudeau is a leftist. That may even be an understatement. In an article, **"Leftists remain too soft on communism,"** in the Calgary Sun on Dec. 19, 2017, Walter Williams wrote,

> "What about the greatest murderers in mankind's history – the USSR (Union of Soviet **Socialist** Republics) with Joseph Stalin and others, with 62 million lives lost (1917-1987): and the CCP in China (currently "**socialism** with Chinese characteristics") under Mao Tse Tung and others, with 76 million lives lost (1949-1987?" (statistics from Rudolf Rummel, Death by Government: Genocide and Mass Murder Since 1900, 1987)
>
> "Why (then) are leftists soft on communism? (Because) they sympathize with the chief goal of communist: restricting personal liberty."

There is a temptation for Trudeau's Liberal government to become totalitarian, if the people allow it to happen. Both Pierre and Justin Trudeau have shown a remarkable acceptance of, and favor toward Communist China, the most murderous regime in human history. That speaks volumes of their heart attitude toward their fellow man and their political agenda.

CHAPTER 3: MANNING: THE PREACHER

Manning put it this way:

> "Will godless totalitarianism establish itself permanently over the human race? Will atheistic communism triumph and achieve its goal of absolute world dictatorship?" (The Battle of Armageddon, E. Manning, Back to the Bible Hour No. 48, mid-to-late 1950s.

Jean-Louis Gagnon, a man who had abandoned the Communist Party to support the Liberals in Quebec said of Trudeau,

> "He was quite a radical. He was fresh out of the London School of Economics and a **Fabian socialist**." (The Truth About Trudeau, Bob Plamondon, 2013).

Pierre Trudeau left wide open the door for a possible totalitarian government to emerge at some future day in Canada. Perhaps he was thinking forward to the day when his son, Justin, might one day become Prime Minister. Justin was in his thirteenth year when his dad retired. After retirement Trudeau took his sons on trips to Russia and China, two communist countries he greatly admired. No doubt his sons knew why he was taking them there.

> "In 1977 Trudeau said that in certain countries and at certain times, a one-party (totalitarian) state would be preferable. "I wouldn't be prepared to think I would be successful in arguing that for Canada at the present time, but such a time might come, who knows?"

If a **totalitarian** regime takes over our country Canadians will suffer greatly. Conservatives will be the first victims, and genuine Christians like Ernest Manning will be at the top of the hit list. Jewish people will be victims again. The Bible foresees a universal persecution against the Jews by a totalitarian dictator before Christ's return.

"Totalitarian" is defined in the Winston College dictionary as "a state, conceived of as having one political party, coextensive with the population, in which the individual is entirely submitted unto the state." The People's Republic of China's flag demonstrates this point.

It has five yellow stars on a red background. The large star over the four others represents the Communist Party of China (CCP). The smaller stars represent the country's 1. Armed Forces; 2. Science and Technology; 3. Trade and Commerce; and 4. Agriculture. All of these parts of the society are under the Communist Party's pervasive and total control, as shown on the flag. That means every citizen in China. Furthermore, that is why no country can deal with China without dealing with the Chinese Communist Party (CCP), thoroughly integrated with the four smaller 'stars.'

Ernest Manning understood that you cannot negotiate in good will with communists. There is no basis for co-operation or agreement between a free democracy and a communist state. He said on his radio programs,

> "The rejection of God led to ignoring of moral and ethical standards. That stance meant it was impossible for atheistic (radical) socialists and communists to negotiate in good faith with people who had religiously- based moral constraints." (Brennan, 2008)

Modern democracies have been accommodating socialist-communist regimes today because they have largely departed from their own Judeo-Christian faith-based laws, morals and principles. This is incredibly

CHAPTER 3: MANNING: THE PREACHER

dangerous. The U.S. is trying to resist this trend under Donald Trump.

Manning wrote of sudden, unexpected crises that would come upon mankind toward the end of the present age.

> "The scriptures affirm that this present age will terminate in a world-wide state of crisis, of man's own making that will develop rapidly and take millions by surprise...the society of the period will be characterized by unprecedented material progress, with great emphasis on human self-sufficiency but an abandonment of faith in, and respect for, God's holiness and divine authority."
> (The Face of the Sky – Part 2, 1972)

COVID-19 may foreshadow a more catastrophic event ahead, or even the long anticipated international socialist 'revolution.' The suddenness of the pandemic, and the worldwide social and economic crisis it precipitated aren't isolated events, but a pattern that is further destabilizing and weakening the free democracies.

> "To "mitigate" this manufactured crisis, the world's governments have cancelled their economies and constitutions, and their citizens have blithely acquiesced to their own pauperization and self-imprisonment.
>
> It is just conceivable that there are certain ideological partisans in the United States and around the world who might be entirely sanguine (hopeful, optimistic) about the collapse of the Trump economic boom. These same people might be positively gratified by the unprecedented expansion of state power, its conscription (forced closure) of private enterprise, its massive new spending and redistribution of wealth, its new social programs and no-strings attached benefactions, and its abolition of such antiquated protections as the right to private property, free association, and religious assembly."

"FORTRESS AMERICA" UNDER SIEGE

(Harley Price, The Epoch Times, p. B 5, March 14-20, 2020)

The COVID-19 'crisis' has revealed just how far Manning's predictions of a descent into totalitarianism has come in Canada and the other Western democracies. In "Pandemic affording politicians great powers, Walter Williams writes concerning the U.S.,

> "There are other news tidbits about politicians drunk with power that we Americans have given them...The biggest casualty from the COVID-19 pandemic has nothing to do with the disease. It's the power we've given to politicians and bureaucrats. The question is how we recover our freedoms?" (The Calgary Sun, May 26, 2020)

COVID-19 (CCP virus) has essentially placed Canada in a *defacto* Liberal dictatorship.

There are worrisome signs that a future government in the United States could become dictatorial and totalitarian if the new breed of Democrats gain power over their own party, and if they take the presidency and gain control of the Congress and/or Senate. Put the Liberals in the Democrat's place, and you have Canada today.

> "For the enemies of Trump, a police state is more or less the price Americans are expected to pay for the restoration of the Democrats to power (the only natural right they recognize).
>
> The mark of the modern progressive state is the nauseating affection of superior wisdom and righteousness (virtue signaling) by its ruling class (elites), in telling the rest of us what to do, say, and think; and the advice they always give is backed up by violence.
>
> It takes little for democracies to revert to the norm; tyranny, despotism and totalitarianism. Indeed, Western

CHAPTER 3: MANNING: THE PREACHER

democracies have been regressing steadily in that direction since the early 20th century." (Harley Price, Civil Liberties, RIP: Big Brother's Lethal 'Cure,' The Epoch Times, p. B6, May 14-20, 2020)

In Canada, the Liberals and their affiliated socialist friends in the other non-Conservative parties are moving lockstep in the same direction. Canada has been essentially 'conquered' for Marxist socialism by the two Trudeaus. Communism, or so-called 'socialism with Canadian characteristics,' can't be far away (Appendix 4).

The primary remaining target for totalitarian conquest in 2020 is the United States of America, the leader of the Free World, as outlined by Ernest C. Manning in his 1973 pamphlet entitled, Middle East Conflict, printed by Canada's National Back to the Bible Hour.

> "The Soviet Union has a vested interest in weakening the economy of the United States which stands as the major obstacle in the way of communism's long range objective of world domination.
>
> The Arab oil boycott and Russia have vested interests aimed at weakening the economy of the United States and the economy of Europe, causing divisions among the member nations of the European Common Market group and between the NATO allies. This is one of the vested interests that world communism has because the more they can weaken the economy of these nations, the more they can sow discord and disrupt the normal pattern of life throughout the world, the more they can capitalize on that unrest to their own advantage."

The 2020 COVID-19 pandemic, coming out of Communist China seems to have accomplished what the Arab oil embargo could not do:

> "Economists believe the pandemic has created the worst downturn since the Great Depression (1929-1939). Many in Canada and the United States have started to worry that economic devastation caused by the lockdown will cause more damage than the virus itself...the U.S. jobless rate could soar to 25% this year." (Emel Akan, The Epoch Times, History Holds Lessons for Today's Economic Reopening and Recovery, p. A6, May 14-20, 2020)

> "They (leftist socialists-communists) talk about 'the oppressed of the Western world,' 'western capitalists,' and 'imperialists,' as the Soviets call them. And they're the greatest bunch of imperialists on the face of the earth themselves." (1947 Manning quote in Brennan, 2008).

The writer worked in Venezuela for 2 years and left when Hugo Chavez was elected in 1998. Since then communism has taken over the country, and ruined it completely. Notably; Cuban help has been used to keep the Marxist-Leninist dictatorship under Maduro intact and in power. China and Russia are complicit in this nefarious assistance. Russian bombers have landed in the South American country recently. This imperialistic, socialist-communist confederacy speaks volumes of where Russia's sympathies and strategic agenda lie today.

> "We look at China, then Russia, as our long term strategic competitors. Trump administration is fueling a Department of Defense modernization and readiness push to face great power competition with Russia and China. We see the trajectory China is on, and we know where Russia may be going in the coming years." (Simon Veazey, Looming Pandemic Debt Could Accelerate Tough Choices on US Military Strategy, The Epoch Times, p. A7, May 14-20, 2020)

MANNING ON MAN'S FINAL DESTINY[6, #51]

CHAPTER 3: MANNING: THE PREACHER

Mankind is divided into two great groups as far as man's relationship to God is concerned. In the one group are those who have been redeemed by the blood of Christ and reconciled to God through the death of His Son. They shall spend eternity in eternal bliss in the New Jerusalem – the great future city of God described in the Book of Revelation, Chapter 21. Those not reconciled to God remain throughout the endless ages of eternity without hope to face the inevitable consequences that sin and separation from God bring to men and nations.

> "The wicked shall be turned into hell, and all the nations that forget God." (Psalm 9:17).

Their destiny is described in the 20th Chapter of Revelation, verses 11 to 15, a part of which is quoted below:

> "And death and hell were cast into the lake of fire. This is the second death. And whosoever was not found written in the book of life was cast into the lake of fire." (Revelation 20:14-15).

Those whose sins have not been forgiven will be eternally separated from God and condemned to 'the second death' in the lake of fire, which was originally prepared for the devil and his angels, and not for man (Matthew 25:41). Those who perish are cast into the lake of fire to continue in conscious living torment throughout the endless ages of eternity. It isn't God's will that man should end up in a devil's hell.

> "God is longsuffering to us-ward, not willing that any should perish, but that all should come to repentance" (2 Peter 3:9).

Those who perish, perish because of they refuse to accept the redemption God has provided for them.

MANNING'S APPEAL

Christian people of this nation must respond to the divine promise before it is too late. The promise is,

> "If my people, which are called by my name, shall humble themselves, and pray, and seek my face, and turn from their wicked ways; then will I hear from heaven, and will forgive their sin, and will heal their land." (2 Chronicles 7:14) (2, #1141)

To the unsaved, E. C. Manning states the following:

So many are set out to defend the Christian way of life, but without any personal allegiance to Jesus Christ. They like to say they are a Christian nation; they want the social conditions that go with Christianity – but they don't want to enthrone the Person of Jesus Christ in their hearts and in their homes, and in the councils of their land.

My friend, you cannot successfully defend the things of righteousness without Jesus Christ being within you. He must be the One who does the work on your behalf as your intervenor.

> "Except the LORD build the house, they labor in vain that build it: except the LORD keep the city, the watchman waketh but in vain." (Psalm 127:1)

Where do you stand in this matter? You know about Christ; you stand for the things He stands for, but have you ever personally received Him into your heart and life as your Divine Redeemer and Living Lord? Have you acknowledged that you are alienated from God by sin? Are you willing to turn from your sin in repentance toward God? Have you confessed your sin before God

CHAPTER 3: MANNING: THE PREACHER

and asked Him for forgiveness on the grounds of Christ's death in your place? Do you believe that Christ died for your sins on the cross, and that after He had paid the price of your redemption in full with His divine blood, He was literally resurrected from the dead and is alive forever? Have you ever really opened your heart to Him, and invited Him to come in and be your Savior and the Lord of your life? If you haven't will you bow your head now and look up into His face and say,

> *"God be merciful to me a sinner and save me for Christ's sake."* (1, #1067; 9, #48)

> *"This poor man cried, and the LORD heard him, and saved him out of all his troubles." (Psalm 34:6)*

To read the Gospel of Jesus Christ, as preached by Ernest Manning, please refer to Appendix 1.

Messages by E. C. Manning used in compiling and writing this Chapter:

1. *Effective Discipleship*: #1067, Apr. 10, 1994
2. *The Lure of the Corn in Egypt*: #1141, Aug. 18, 1993
3. *A Call to Arms*: #1144, Jan. 7, 1990
4. *Let the Trumpet Sound*: #1175, 1980s
5. *The Concerns of our Times*: #s 1135/36/37/39, late 1980s
6. *Man's Final Destiny*: #51, mid-to-late 1950s
7. *The Time of the End*: #44, mid-to-late 1950s
8. *Good Seed in Poor Soil*: #606, mid-to-late 1970s
9. *The Battle of Armageddon: What! Where! When?*: #48, mid-to-late 1950s

CHAPTER 4

THE HON. ERNEST C. MANNING'S WARNINGS ON SOCIALISM – COMMUNISM

"The easiest way to take a fortress is from within."

Vladimir Lenin

Manning consistently warned for many years that Western free democracies were under attack from subversive elements within the state. An Alberta newspaper article quoted Manning:

CHAPTER 4: WARNINGS ON SOCIALISM & COMMUNISM

> "Two diametrically opposed ideologies which are irreconcilable and impossible to isolate are fighting in the political fields. One is Godless materialism in the face of Socialism, Communism and Collectivism; and the other is Christian (Free) Democracy." (Ken Kelly, Nov. 27, 1948)

Benjamin Franklin elucidated 13 virtues that should characterize individual behavior in a healthy society; namely "temperance, silence, order, resolution, frugality, industry, sincerity, justice, moderation, cleanliness, tranquility, chastity, and humility." (The Epoch Times, "How the Spectre of Communism is Ruling Our World," Popular Culture, a Decadent Indulgence, Chapter 14, 2020)

During the Great Awakening in America, Christian churches underwent genuine spiritual revival. It affected the whole nation bringing the virtues mentioned above into many homes and families, even affecting many outside the churches. Alexis de Tocqueville, the 19th century French thinker saw firsthand the effects of revival in America. He concluded that America was great because America was righteous, and when America ceased to be righteous America would cease to be great. Marxism's ultimate goal has been to seduce and destroy America's soul as a nation under God. It has largely succeeded by capturing the youth and destroying their character.

English scholar, Roger Scruton wrote:

> "The methods of the new literary theorist are really weapons of subversion: an attempt to destroy humane education from within, to rupture the chain of sympathy that binds us to our culture."

"FORTRESS AMERICA" UNDER SIEGE

Young students in the liberal arts programs are brainwashed by their professors and once inculcated with deconstructionist, postmodern Marxist ideology, it is difficult to get them to think in any other way.

> "Scholars have stigmatized tradition and morality by relativizing everything…with axioms like 'all interpretation is misinterpretation," "there is no truth, only interpretations," or "there are no facts, only interpretations." (The Epoch Times, "How the Spectre of Communism is Ruling Our World," Sabotaging Education – Part 1, Chapter 12, 2020)

> **"Ideology"** is a core concept in the Marxist-influenced humanities. Althusser's all-inclusive concept of **"all-inclusive state apparatuses**, (religion, education, family, law, politics, trade unions, communication, culture, etc.)" reflects communism's extreme contempt for human society – nothing is acceptable, short of complete rejection and destruction." (Ibid)

Yuri Bezmenov, a defecting KGB spy in the early 1980s, warned that communist infiltration and subversion targets thought, power and social life in four stages, all intended to produce unrest – Marx's "Class Struggle:"

1. Foster cultural decadence and demoralization of the enemy country (15-20 yr.);
2. Create social chaos (2-5 yr.);
3. Instigate a crisis leading to civil war, revolution or invasion by another country (3-6 mo.);
4. Normalization – bringing the country under the control of the Communist Party.

These methods have succeeded beyond the Soviet's wildest dreams. No. 1 has been going on for decades; no. 2 is going on right now with gender and identity politics and laws. Society is beginning to enter the third stage, no. 3, as a result of COVID-19 and the Black Lives Matter demonstrations and riots. We have not yet

CHAPTER 4: WARNINGS ON SOCIALISM & COMMUNISM

reached no. 4. Russian communism is not dead but alive and well. It just changed tactics; from the Cold War to the Covert War to defeat the Western democracies. Manning knew that!

Another warning was recorded in Manning's biography:

> "Socialists and communists, he maintained, had infiltrated Canadian society, namely the trade unions, universities and newspapers; their goal being to destroy freedom and democracy. The rejection of God led to ignoring of moral and ethical standards." (Brennan, 2008).

David Horowitz and Jacob Laksin identified about 150 leftist courses at 12 universities, noting that their political aims were hidden by scholarly language, and sometimes not, with all resembling closely mandatory political courses in communist countries. (The Epoch Times, "How the Spectre of Communism is Ruling Our World," Sabotaging Education – Part 1, Chapter 12, 2020)

Other prominent Christians gave warning of the dangers of socialism-communism to our personal freedom based upon the Judeo-Christian culture in the West.

> "Billy Graham warned us about this cultural shift in 1954 when he stated that communism "is here to stay. It is a battle to the death: either communism must die, or Christianity must die. Politically a communist is one who believes the state is supreme and the individual exists only for the welfare of the state, thus destroying the God-given status of the dignity of the individual." (Dr. Charles McVety, How Socialism is Ravaging Our Society, p. B6, The Epoch Times, June 19-25, 2020).

Pierre Trudeau, Canada's 15th Prime Minister, and the 'father' of Canadian socialism stated –

"FORTRESS AMERICA" UNDER SIEGE

"Some economists say all you've got to do is get back to the free market system and make it work. It won't. The government is going to take a larger role in running institutions. **And this means you're going to have big governments. The state is important.** It means there's going to be not less authority in our lives but perhaps more.

It was the best of times for public sector workers with Trudeau in power. He formed CUPE and 114 agencies and commissions, and 7 new government departments, doubling the number of ministries. In 1979 there were 464 crown corporations, 213 subsidiaries and 126 associated corporations. Public sector employees enjoyed a 20% pay advantage over the private sector." (Bob Plamondon, The Truth About Trudeau, 2013).

Ernest Manning continued to give the Canadian people warnings for many years afterward.

"People who regard communism as just another political movement are woefully misled. Communism is a godless philosophy, wholly incompatible with respect to God and truth, and that aggressively works to destroy all recognition of God just as its avowed goal is to destroy free and democratic society, and impose its tyranny of state regimentation and control on all people in all nations. May God help the people of this country and the government of this country to wake up to these facts before it is too late." (E. C. Manning, The Face of the Sky, Part 1, 1971, Canada's National Back to the Bible Hour Pamphlet)

In his 1972 Pamphlet, "The Face of the Sky" – Part 2, Ernest Manning gave 9 Communist Rules for fermenting revolution and destroying democratic societies. They are the following:

1. "Corrupt the young, get them away from religion, make them interested in sex; make them superficial. Destroy their ruggedness.

CHAPTER 4: WARNINGS ON SOCIALISM & COMMUNISM

2. Get control of all means of publicity, thereby getting peoples' minds off their government by focusing their attention on athletics, sexy books and other trivia.
3. Divide the people into hostile groups by constantly harping on controversial matters of no importance.
4. Secure the registration of all fire-arms on some pretext with the view of confiscating them and leaving the population helpless.
5. Destroy the people's faith in their national leaders by holding them up to contempt and ridicule.
6. Ferment strikes in general industries. Encourage civil disorders and foster a lenient and soft attitude on the part of the government towards disorders.
7. Always preach true democracy but seize power as fast and as ruthlessly as possible.
8. By encouraging government extravagance, destroy its credit. Produce fear of inflation with rising prices and general discontent.
9. By specious (fair-seeming or plausible, but not really so) argument, cause the breakdown in the old moral virtues, honesty, sobriety and faith in the pledged word."

Pierre Elliot Trudeau, Canada's leftist Prime Minister from 1968 to 1984, with one brief interlude in 1979, was fully aware of these same Communist rules. He knew that Manning knew them as well. Mr. Manning asked the Prime Minister why he appointed him to the Senate knowing their great ideological differences. Trudeau told Ernest Manning personally that he would rather have him in the Liberal-dominated Canadian Senate than out on the street talking with people.

Trudeau knew what he was talking about. Those who studied with Trudeau at the London School of Economics, a hotbed of socialist thinking, said that he went much further with his "flirtations with Marxism," with which he was fascinated. His main teacher, Harold Laski, was a proponent of Marxism and an executive member of the socialist Fabian Society from 1922 to 1936. Trudeau said, "we were witness almost on a daily basis to the spread of communism in Europe. Young people were truly fascinated by the Soviet Model." (Bob Plamondon, The Truth About Trudeau, Chapter 18, 2013).

> "Everything I have learned of law, economics, political science and political philosophy came together for me under Laski. I want a classless society. The party of the people – socialism, communism – will eventually come out the winner." (Ibid)

His fascination with socialism-communism, made him unique among Western leaders. Trudeau believed federalism was the best system by which to launch radical socialism in Canada. He said, "We're going to build socialism here. For a country with such a small population there is no alternative." Trudeau was a Fabian socialist. (Ibid) Fabians seek to implant socialism in a free democracy by gradual development and education rather than by open aggression. It is 'war' by the 'inevitability of gradualism.' That is exactly what Trudeau did to Canada, and we're suffering today because of it.

In Pierre Trudeau's own words,

> "Indeed, that superb strategist, Mao Tse-tung, might lead us to conclude that in a vast and heterogeneous country, the possibility of establishing socialist strongholds in certain regions is the very best thing. Federalism must be welcomed as a valuable tool, which permits dynamic parties to plant socialist governments in certain provinces from which the seed of radicalism can slowly spread." (Ibid)

Pierre Trudeau was not a Liberal. He was an old school, international socialist. He **used** the Liberal Party as a vehicle through which he could implement his socialist

CHAPTER 4: WARNINGS ON SOCIALISM & COMMUNISM

vision for the nation. He actually despised the Liberals but it was his best chance to get what he wanted. Trudeau's view of the Liberals:

> "The philosophy of the Liberal Party is very simple – say anything, think anything, or better still, do not think at all, but put us in power because it is we who can govern you best." (Ibid)

To Trudeau, joining the Liberals was the sort of maneuver demanded of great leaders.

> "If our intellectuals had read a little Marx, Lenin and Mao Tse-tung, they would know that true revolutionaries are ready to accept **a tactical compromise necessary to allow a still-young left to come into the world.**" (Ibid)

Manning had antipathy toward Trudeau's ideology. He had considered running federally for the Conservative leadership after retiring from provincial politics. He co-wrote, "Political Realignment: A Challenge to Thoughtful Canadians," with his son, Preston Manning in 1967. It proposed a national social conservative party as a clear alternative to left-wing liberals, socialists and "Red Tories." Manning's ideas received little support and the federal conservatives chose left-leaning Robert Stanfield as their leader. E. C. Manning may have been the man who could have blocked Trudeau's socialist aspirations for Canada. But we will never know. Only 1 copy of Manning's book is available in downtown Calgary's Central Library, and it can't be lent through another library branch or taken out of the facility.

Mr. Manning followed the preceding list of Communist rules with this comment:

"FORTRESS AMERICA" UNDER SIEGE

"Can anyone deny that we are surrounded on every hand with undeniable evidence that these rules have been very successfully applied in all free societies, including our own? The forces fostering world revolution and chaos have been successful in accomplishing almost all of the objectives spelled out in these guide rules for destroying free society, formulated over 50 years ago. (see The Epoch Times article immediately following)

So successful has their program been, that while they have moved the free world to the brink of chaos, they have at the same time largely succeeded through the mass news media in convincing society that fears of world domination by communism and kindred (socialist) champions of collectivism are groundless and mere figments of the imaginations of religious fundamentalists and ultra-conservative politicians. Nothing could be further from the truth.

The vital question is – "will enough people realize this in time? Will our governments come to their senses before it is too late?" There is no sign of this happening to date. Already, I repeat; it is later than we think.

The remaining hope is that the people themselves will demand that these issues be recognized and faced. What are you going to do to this end? Before you give politicians your support you would do well to ask where they and their parties stand on these issues which concern the future of us all. How desperately we need someone among those seeking public positions to give leadership in facing up to these matters and taking effective counteraction."

In the decades since Mr. Manning wrote these words (1972), and up until the completion of this writing in October, 2020, his concerns have been validated in all of the Western democracies. The origins of this infiltration and systematic destruction of our Judeo-Christian institutions have recently been exposed in many articles in The Epoch Times and Sun newspapers.

CHAPTER 4: WARNINGS ON SOCIALISM & COMMUNISM

The compelling essay by Mrs. Zuzana Janosova Den Boer testifies to her experience living under communism (Appendix 4).

In a recent article in The Epoch Times, "How Socialism is Ravaging Our Society," Dr. Charles McVety, president of Canada Christian College and School of Graduate Theological Studies, Whitby, Ontario, wrote:

> "Vast sectors of society are now dominated almost exclusively by socialist philosophy, including academia, media, bureaucracy and the judiciary.
>
> War is not the chief mechanism of this century's socialism. It has shifted to a much deeper level and is on track to result in equally devastating consequences. Philosopher Max Horkheimer stated that "the Revolution won't happen with guns, rather it will happen incrementally, year by year, generation by generation. We (Marxist socialists) will gradually infiltrate their educational institutions and their political offices, transforming them slowly into Marxist entities as we move towards universal egalitarianism (equality).
>
> **There is a battle raging for the soul of our society. It is not a battle of flesh and blood but a struggle between freedom and socialism. Individualism has been replaced by statism. Religion is now ridiculed as the opiate of society. Make no mistake, the socialists now have the upper hand and are ready to move in for the kill: full scale socialism."** (The Epoch Times, p. B6, July 19-25, 2019).

It is difficult to keep up with the tsunami of information coming in daily in the news on the socialist-communist revolution now taking place in our country, and in our neighbor, the United States. Each of Mr. Manning's nine Rules for a Communist Takeover of a free democracy will be summarized from articles taken from our daily newspapers.

"FORTRESS AMERICA" UNDER SIEGE

1. Destroy a nation's youth; infiltrate and corrupt the education system

"Corrupt the young, and get them away from religion, and make them interested in sex; making them superficial and destroying their ruggedness."

Corrupting the youth will make a free democratic society weak and susceptible for a socialist-communist take-over.

In the last 50-60 years Western society has suffered a precipitous decline as "rock and rap music, drug abuse, pornography, sexual liberation and promiscuity, homosexuality, the hippie culture, and spiritual emptiness have taken hold, seriously damaging the foundation of Western tradition. With the help of television, computers, the internet, mobile phones and various mass media the nation's foundation of morality and faith has been largely destroyed.

> "If the foundations be destroyed, what can the righteous do?" (Psalm 11:3)

A 1983 report prepared by a group of experts for the U.S. Department of Education, titled, "A Nation at Risk," stated:

> Quoting Paul Copperman – "For the first time in the history of our country, the educational skills of one generation will not surpass, will not equal, will not even approach, those of their parents." (The Epoch Times, "How the Spectre of Communism is Ruling Our World," Sabotaging Education – Part 1, Chapter 12, 2020)

John Stormer analyzed in "None Dare Call It Treason," the textbook reform program of the 1930s and found, "So pronounced was the anti-religious bias; so open was

CHAPTER 4: WARNINGS ON SOCIALISM & COMMUNISM

the propaganda for the socialistic control of men's lives," that the courses put down both American heroes and the U.S. Constitution. After several generations of public school textbooks and students taught from them, the nation has been separated from its original values and traditions, and it is almost impossible to go back. (from "How the Spectre of Communism is Ruling Our World," Sabotaging Education – Part 2, Chapter 12, 2020)

> "Economist Paul Samuelson described the power of textbooks thus: "I don't care who writes a nation's laws – or crafts its advanced treaties – if I can write its economic textbooks." (The Epoch Times, "How the Spectre of Communism is Ruling Our World," Sabotaging Education – Part 1, Chapter 12, 2020)

> "In some academic fields, the textbooks and required reading chosen by the professors contain more works of Marxism than any other school of thought." (Ibid)

> "The Modern Language Association, the largest U.S. academic association (25,000 members), have humanities and social science journal titles dominated by ideological Marxism, the Frankfurt School, deconstruction and many, many other radical and deviant leftist theories." (Ibid)

John Dewey, a democratic socialist, and a tenured professor for over 50 years at Columbia University, greatly enhanced the leftist agenda in education in America. He was influenced by Jean-Jacques Rousseau, the 18th century French philosopher who taught "natural education," where children would be left to their own devices in an atmosphere absent of religion, morality or culture. Twenty percent of all primary and secondary school teachers in America received instruction or advanced degrees from Columbia. Dewey, who was influenced by Darwin's theory of evolution, believed:

> "children should be weaned from the traditional tutelage of parents, religion, and culture and allowed the freedom to adapt to their environments. He was a moral relativist and signed "The Humanist Manifesto" in 1933." (Ibid)

> Albert Pinkevich wrote, "Dewey comes infinitely closer to Marx and the Russian Communists." (Ibid)

Dewey is credited with establishing progressive education that is responsible for dumbing down the past several generations of American and Canadian students, in both primary and secondary institutions. He did incalculable harm.

Communist elements in the West set their sights on education as a primary target. "The Naked Communist," written in 1958 listed goals for education as follows:

> "Get control of the schools. Use them as transmission belts for socialism and current Communist propaganda. Soften the curriculum. Get control of teachers' associations. Put the party line in textbooks." (Ibid)

> "Because instruction has been progressively dumbed down, students of the new generation are becoming less literate and mathematically capable. They possess less knowledge, and their ability to think critically is stunted. It is harder for them to handle key questions concerning life and society, and even harder for them to see through communism's deceptions. Four years of intensive indoctrination in university leave graduates with a predisposition for liberalism and progressivism. They are likely to accept atheism, the theory of evolution, and materialism without a second thought...narrow-minded hedonistic "snowflakes," lacking common sense, having a narrow worldview and knowing very little or nothing about the history of America or the world." (Ibid, Sabotaging Education – Part 1)

In the minds of students cut off from tradition by such propaganda, the standards of right and wrong, and good

CHAPTER 4: WARNINGS ON SOCIALISM & COMMUNISM

and evil are all evaluated according to radical left, socialist-communist standards. Senator Ted Cruz (Texas) attended a prestigious law school and found –

> "There were more self-declared Communists (in the faculty) than there were Republicans. If you asked them to vote on whether this nation should become a socialist nation, 80% of the faculty would vote, yes, and 10% would think that too conservative." (Ibid, Sabotaging Education – Part 1)

> "As one radical professor wrote: "After the Vietnam War (1974), a lot of us didn't just crawl back into our literary cubicles; we stepped into academic positions. With the war over, our visibility was lost, and it seemed for a while – to the unobservant – that we had disappeared. Now we have tenure, and the work of reshaping the universities has begun in earnest; with the greatest influence in the social sciences and humanities." (Ibid, Sabotaging Education – Part 1).

The three most powerful influences on the Humanities in America were Antonio Gramsci, Paulo Friere and Frantz Fanon according to Alan Kors, a historian at the University of Pennsylvania. The cumulative effect of their writings were utopian socialism and the overthrow of colonial capitalist hegemony, and the creation of a classless society. The preface of Fanon's book, "The Wretched of the Earth," says:

> "For in the first days of the revolt you must kill: to shoot down a European is to kill two birds with one stone, to destroy an oppressor and the man he oppresses at the same time: there remains a dead man, and a free man; the survivor, for the first time, feels a national soil under his feet." (Ibid, Sabotaging Education – Part 1).

The same principle of Marxist oppressor/oppressed has been raging as a gender class struggle in Western society for the past forty to fifty years. Preston Manning, on the inside cover of "The Book of Ted," wrote, "Ted Byfield is one of Canada's most provocative thinkers. He embodies the west – independent, proud and hopeful." Byfield, in an article on Gay Pride, wrote,

> "What is being sought by the homosexual lobbies is not mere tolerance. Homosexuality has become a missionary cause. It is now advocated as a "lifestyle," something all children should be familiar with and encouraged to investigate. If this seems exaggerated, then consider what is going on right now in the Toronto public school system, and is being proposed for B.C. and Alberta.
>
> The Toronto Board of Education called for a new sex education course for 13-18 year olds that would foster tolerance, to be followed by something similar for elementary school children. No parents objected...the committee charged with drawing it up included homosexual representatives but no parents. Last year (1992) the first draft of the course emerged. It seemed unbelievable. For page after page, homosexual practice was openly urged upon students. Story followed story on how this or that youngster had "come out." Videos had been made illustrating and advocating the gay lifestyle. The names of some eighty were appended with which students could consult. At least seventy of these were gay groups, one of them sado-masochistic.
>
> A parent's group vigorously protested (and) were dismissed as "right-wing" and "bigoted," and denied use of school property because "gay-bashing" violated school board policy. Two Toronto Board of Education counsellors, one gay and one lesbian, made (hundreds of) class by class presentations with illustrations and advice on homosexual practices. Opposing the course is legally dangerous. Under the new B.C. Harcourt government legislation, public criticism of any sexual lifestyle whatever is prohibited by law." (Ted Byfield, Why this magazine ran that 'disgusting' story on Gay Pride (August 30, 1993), in The Book of Ted, 1998).

CHAPTER 4: WARNINGS ON SOCIALISM & COMMUNISM

The fruit of this tragic selling of our children's morals to a debauched secular education system was on display recently,

> "Each year, society is progressively growing darker as morality is being eroded. Seeing nationally funded CBC parade onstage little boys, 10 and 12 years old, dressed in drag and performing stripper-like acts, is an indication that something is drastically wrong. Recently, we have seen euthanasia, marijuana, and sex clubs legalized. Marriage has been redefined and the family unit is under attack, with the use of "mother" and "father" being discouraged." (Charles McVety, How Socialism is Ravaging Our Society, The Epoch Times, p. B6, June 19-25, 2019).

Moral corruption is an outcome of rap music, rock music, alcohol and drug use prevalent today among our youth. The music of today is a prime mover in instilling rebellious attitudes among the young, and this leads into drugs as a spiritual outcome fostered by the devil.

> "The nature of much of our communicating one with another today, impairs rather than improves our capacity to pay attention to what we see or read or hear. In modern society, we are constantly bombarded with a babble of blaring and conflicting sounds and voices. Much of what passes for popular music today, frequently is a discordant din set to a jungle beat that does violence to all the basic laws of music composition. It is often accompanied by meaningless words and phrases produced at ear shattering volume by electronic amplification. It is not something anybody would listen to attentively for the genuine inspiration that quality music can give or for a meaningful message voiced in meaningful words. **It is a debased form of music** that most people hearing, hear not, in other words they simply tune it out." (E. C. Manning, It is Written – He that hath ears to hear (#6): Canada's National Bible Hour, vintage message, October 3, 2010).

"FORTRESS AMERICA" UNDER SIEGE

Ernest Manning commented on a book by Dr. Andrew Malcolm, "The Pursuit of Intoxication." Dr. Malcolm found that:

> "The drug problem has to be understood in terms of the inner man. In our society today (he writes) there is much evidence of disintegration. A person finds it easy to feel insignificant, expendable and lonely. For someone who needs a new way of looking at the world and his place in it, what quicker route is there than the speedway which chemistry offers through drugs that can radically transform the mind even if only for a short time. It is the fast road out of his troubles for a person who is having a hard time. That is one reason why many take them. Religion is basic to the drug problem therefore, because drug use results from an inner need, the kind of need which religion has been concerned about since ancient times." (The Face of the Sky – Part 1, 1971, Back to the Bible Hour pamphlet).

Manning also mentioned the results of a study of by an addiction research foundation.

> "The research shows young people's needs for values in a study of drug use in schools. A research team found part of the cause was the normlessness many students suffer, the absence of values which give purpose and direction to life, and conclude that this was a form of alienation explaining why some young people drifted into drugs. All of which suggest man is not ready to be non-religious. People may have less to do with church than they did a few years ago, but they still have the needs they used to believe the church could meet. **People still need something to give them a sense of identity, purpose and value. They still need guidelines for behavior.**" (Ibid).

In the same article Mr. Manning made the following comment:

CHAPTER 4: WARNINGS ON SOCIALISM & COMMUNISM

> "Man's sense of an inner need is something all experience. Drugs and alcohol temporarily create an artificial sense of well-being but when the trip is over or the hangover has passed, the inward emptiness returns and the longing for something that will really satisfy and give depth and meaning and purpose to life is still there. **There is only one way in which man's inner need can be fully and permanently satisfied, not by drugs, not by alcohol, not by sex, not by affluence, not by power, but by a personal relationship with the divine Person of Jesus Christ.** I commend Him to you. Be wise, open your heart and life to Him and ask Him to come in and take charge." (Ibid).

Justin Trudeau's Liberals legalized marijuana in October, 2018. Using pot is now normal social conduct in Canada. Cannabis (Marijuana) will have a great negative impact on our young people, mental health and impaired driving. It is a dangerous and highly addictive gateway drug into harder narcotics like cocaine, heroin and crack. Pierre Trudeau began this trend by loosening the marijuana laws in the late 1960s and Justin has carried his father's program to fruition. What better way to contribute to destabilizing a free democracy for eventual socialist-communist take-over?

> "Marijuana was legalized in Colorado in January 2014, and the consequences across the state have been negative with "no upside," says Ernie Martinez, a command officer with the Denver Metro Police Department for 35 years and director-at-large for the National Narcotics Officers Associations Coalition. "We've had a bevy of different issues since legalization. It has not been a good thing." "Because of the acceptability, affordability, and availability paradigm, we've seen increases in burglaries of dispensaries, burglaries of houses, robberies, home invasion robberies, aggravated assaults, and also the possession of marijuana for people under 21. That's across the state." Cases of people driving while high have risen too, as have addiction rates. "Legalization hasn't taken away

"FORTRESS AMERICA" UNDER SIEGE

the black market; it has mushroomed, including massive illegal grow operations." Police don't have the resources to keep up with them all. As of June, 2017, there were 491 retail marijuana stores in Colorado compared to 392 Starbucks and 208 McDonald's. Medical studies show that marijuana use can damage brain development in those aged between 12 and 24 (children/adolescents)." (Joan Delaney, 'We are seeing the ill effects' of pot legalization: Colorado police officer, The Epoch Times, 2018).

The natural outcome of this policy has been felt already in Colorado, the first state in North America to legalize marijuana for recreation use in 2012. A grieving family shares the account of the tragic death of their 19 year-old son, due to his drug addiction related directly to the law legalizing cannabis. Here are excerpts from their story.

> "Jonny was 19 and addicted to high-potency marijuana. Laura (his mother) said, "I just can't believe that he had to grow up in Colorado – everyone was doing it." He started smoking marijuana in 2014 at the age of 14. In 2016, he started taking "dabs," a marijuana concentrate or extract, and by 18 was dabbing every day. By 18, he became very suicidal and delusional. On November 20, 2019, Johnny took his life. Three days earlier he told his parents, 'You were right. You told me that marijuana would hurt my brain. And its ruined my mind and my life, and I want you to know I'm really sorry.'"

> "Canada legalized cannabis extracts, or concentrates, in October 2019…a drug so potent it's triggering cannabis-induced psychosis, especially in teens. Regular cannabis use, even without extracts, can increase the risk of developing psychosis and schizophrenia. The 2018-2019 Canadian Drugs Survey showed nearly 20% of students from grades 7 through 12 used cannabis over the past year. Most started around 14 years old. A 2019 Kids Colorado survey found 2.8% of high school students used marijuana 20 to 39 times a month. The trend is

CHAPTER 4: WARNINGS ON SOCIALISM & COMMUNISM

> toward more frequency and higher doses." (Charlotte Cuthbertson, High-Potency Marijuana, Psychosis, and Suicide: Johnny Stack's Story, The Epoch Times, p. A6, October 15-21, 2020)

The costs in human life are appalling, and our socialist governments are fully responsible for the carnage. Justin Trudeau's government has much blood on its hands. He will give account to God for that blood.

An epidemic of opioids (Fentanyl) killed 14,000 Canadians of all ages between January 2016 and June, 2019. In Alberta alone 806 died of them in 2018, and 617 souls in 2019. Thirty thousand Americans die annually from opioid overdoses. China, in a 21st Century 'Opium War,' is deliberately shipping these dangerous hard drugs to Canada and the U.S. to contribute to the downfall of North American society. (The Epoch Times, p. A3 – January 30, 2020).

Materialistic Western society ignored the socialist infiltration into their educational system in their pursuit of the "good life," and in the process set the stage for the socialist revolution that we are currently witnessing in Canada and the United States.

> "Unimpeded by any meaningful oversight or public concern about what schools teach, the progressive movement has literally captured the academic culture in North America." (William Brooks, Why Millennials Favor Socialism, p. B1, The Epoch Times, April 16-22, 2020)

Dr. Ralph Robey, Assistant Professor of Banking at Columbia University, made a survey of high school textbooks in the early 1950s with the following results:

> "The success of the United States of America is played down in too many of our school books and its failures are played up. That the success of Soviet Russia is played

up and its failures played down. This is an important and much-used Communist device." (E. J. Daniels, The Red Devil of Communism, 1954).

Schools are teaching children the essential elements of Marx's 'dialectical materialism' –

> "Dialectical reasoning points to dynamic, adversarial relationships, originally between proletarians (wage workers) and capitalists (business owners) but presently extended to black vs white ("Black Lives Matter"), women vs men (feminism), secular vs religious (Darwinian evolution), gay vs straight (LGBTQ2S), energy consumers vs environmentalists, and so on down the line. The imperative to resolve contradictory attributes always vindicates the Marxist commitment to some form of social action." (Ibid).

The writer recently observed his twelfth grade grandniece bringing home a textbook titled, "Ideology," with Liberal captions on almost every chapter heading. When I asked if I could see the book a year later she told me that it was kept at the school. I saw the same text book at another home where the young lady was in Grade 12 in a different Calgary high school. The word, ideology, is almost exclusively used by Marxist socialists. Our Canadian young people are being systematically brainwashed in radical socialism-communism with textbooks such as these without their parent's consent.

From hence comes the younger generation's support for carbon taxation, pipeline blockades, racial riots and gay-straight alliances in public schools, and much more – Marx's "class struggle." Both Trudeau the 'elder' and Trudeau the 'younger' were, and are, committed to this Marxist dialectical. That is why Justin Trudeau let protests rage on in January-February, 2020, over the pipeline blockades without intervening to stop them.

CHAPTER 4: WARNINGS ON SOCIALISM & COMMUNISM

The writer remembers the day when the Lord's Prayer was recited at the beginning of every school day. He remembers getting the strap and teachers enforcing their authority over rebellious students, sometimes physically. And it worked. There was order and learning in the classroom. Teachers were respected and students learned with discipline. Things today are different, very different. Why?

A key historical event causing the Marxist socialist movement to infiltrate and corrupt the Western democracies was presented recently in The Epoch Times.

> "In 1923, at the leftist Marx-Engels Institute in Moscow, socialist and communist subversives agreed to use the education system (schools and universities) to de-Christianize the "bourgeois" Western democracies, destroying traditional religion and the Christian culture it produced, collapsing sexual morality to deliberately undermine marriage and the family – a wrecking ball to infiltrate and demolish the existing institutions.
>
> From that early beginning, Marxist law professor, Carl Grunberg established the Institute for Social Research at Goethe University in Frankfurt, Germany with a group of international socialist and communist operatives; known as the Frankfurt School. After Hitler came to power in Germany in 1933, the ISR became unwelcome, and these professors moved to Columbia University in New York City, and other prestigious U. S. institutions, establishing themselves in Columbia's Teacher's College in 1934. They went on to collaborate with John Dewey, a humanist education reformer, to use 'education' as a key means of advancing their totalitarian, civilization – destroying philosophies through the medium of "Cultural Marxism.
>
> By 1950, about a third of principals and superintendents of large (U.S.) school districts had been trained by these

leftist professors. Their graduates left college with radical ideas about reality, government, society, family and the economy. Cultural Marxist ideology has since been passed on to successive generations of young, impressionable students and now infects the entire planet like a deadly cancer – mostly inherited through the education system."

In **"The Marxists are Winning the Education War,"** (Epoch Times, April 23-29, 2020) Rodney Clifton, Professor Emeritus of sociology of education at the U. of Manitoba wrote in substance that –

Progressive educators divide people in capitalist societies like Canada and the United States into one of two classes: Marx's Bourgeoisie (oppressor)/ and Proletariat (oppressed). Using Marxist "critical theory," "critical race theory" and "constructivism" they take out traditional teacher-led, knowledge-based course content and replace it with subversive and watered down progressive, student-led and experience-based 'learning.' Teachers are marginalized and children are in control of their learning. Clifton cited three examples from secondary schools in the Province of Manitoba.

He stated that children are taught that they are in a hierarchy **(neo-Marxist "intersectionality")** of oppressor/oppressed groups (e.g. male or female, white or colored, heterosexual or LGBTQ, white European or indigenous, etc. in which the oppressed are more deserving of elevation – attention, privileges and rights than the oppressor group. The oppressed group's 'truth' (experiences and beliefs) trumps the oppressor's truth, and is enforced by the legal system. Course content follows this pattern, removing proven, classical knowledge and course material from the classroom. The result is a loss of substance and real learning in the education of our children, making them less skilled, less

CHAPTER 4: WARNINGS ON SOCIALISM & COMMUNISM

disciplined, less resilient and less able to take their place in society as responsible, productive adults, and more willing to be submissive followers of an autocratic or totalitarian socialist state in the future.

If rural and urban education in Manitoba are so permeated by this neo-Marxist philosophy then it must be systemic through most of the schools across all regions of Canada. In fact, it is worldwide. Parents, "This is frightening!"

As Manning warned above, Clifton confirms:

> "Teacher education programs have been training teacher candidates in radical progressive methods, and teacher unions have been bargaining – and even striking – to get benefits enshrined in the progressive ideology." (Ibid)

American anti-communist pioneer and author of "You Can Trust the Communists...to Be Communists," Dr. Frederick Schwartz, observed that we already have an essentially communistic education system in our public schools.

> "The three basic tenets of Communism are atheism, evolution, and economic determinism. The three basic tenets of the American (and Canadian) Public School system are atheism, evolution, and economic determinism." (The Epic Times, "How the Spectre of Communism is Ruling Our World," Sabotaging Education – Part 2, Chapter 12, 2020)

English-speaking teachers were asked to evaluate a new 1979 history course curricula developed by a new Quebec government. What they found shocked them.

> "Little or no attention was given to the contribution of European culture, religion, customs, laws, or ideas on the development of Quebec and Canada. The social

democratic Parti-Quebecois (1968-1979) garnered more attention than the 350 year history of the Roman Catholic Church in North America. The course, we concluded, focused on dark relationships between "oppressors" and "oppressed." Canada's French-English discord was linked to class conflict. An inspiring story of "Colony to Nation" had been dismantled in favor of a smokescreen for the development of a Marxist, liberationist political agenda." (William Brooks, Why Millennials Favor Socialism, p. B1, The Epoch Times, April 16-22, 2020)

Opposing this leftist indoctrination was not easy. Their report was not allowed to circulate and considered too "provocative" to be taken seriously. They felt obliged to resign from the English-speaking organization.

Clifton gives the following advice in trying to effect change to these kinds of subversion:

> "Traditional educators that want to re-establish substance in the curriculum need the support of taxpayers, employers, post-secondary institutions and the general public to reverse these trends. Hopefully, citizens will become aware of the education war and join in. The future of both our students and our country is at stake." (Epoch Times, p. B6, April 23-29, 2020)

The left has acted with revolutionary zeal in the realm of education where the Christians have been complacent. These revolutionaries have succeeded in capturing the minds of generations of our children and have already transformed the morality-based Judeo-Christian world we older adults once knew in the 1940s and 1950s into their progressive and evolving Marxist utopia of...

> "isms", namely; feminism, communism, atheism, mass migration, globalism, humanism, multiculturalism, nihilism (*doctrine of nothingness; leading to violent revolution and anarchy to destroy all existing social*

CHAPTER 4: WARNINGS ON SOCIALISM & COMMUNISM

> *institutions*), hedonism (*doctrine of self-indulgence and pleasure as chief goal in life*), environmentalism, etc., etc.; all of which are presently undermining our individual liberty, traditional culture and morality." (Alex Newman, How the Frankfurt School Weaponized Education Against Civilization, p. B2, *The Epoch Times,* December 27, 2019).

Many students growing up under mass political indoctrination in our universities lose their resiliency and robust character traits that earlier generations possessed.

> "Many students growing up under this kind of academic atmosphere have easily hurt egos and try their utmost to avoid feeling offended. The group identity (communism's "class consciousness") that is preached on campuses leaves students ignorant of independent thought and personal responsibility…and against tradition – indulging in confused sexual promiscuity, alcohol addiction, and drug abuse…yet underneath are fragile hearts and souls unable to bear the slightest blow or setback, let alone take on real responsibility." (The Epoch Times, "How the Spectre of Communism is Ruling Our World," Sabotaging Education – Part 1, Chapter 12, 2020)

As Lenin predicted, "Fortress America," is being taken from within. The American people have forgotten that "eternal vigilance is the price of liberty," and Canadians have done no better. The great leader, Thomas Jefferson, said long ago:

> "I know no safe depository of the ultimate powers of the society but the people themselves; and if we think them not enlightened enough to exercise their control with a wholesome discretion, the remedy is not to take it from them but to inform their discretion." (Ibid)

> "Individuals with little knowledge and poor critical thinking abilities are unable to recognize lies and deceptions." (Ibid)

May God help us!!!

A recent example of this moral subversion comes from Columbia University, the 'womb' of American Marxism. There, Andrei Serban, a Romanian-born professor of theatre, who escaped communism in his home country, recently abandoned his tenured post claiming in a television interview that **the U. S. System of higher education is barreling toward communism**. As head of Colombia's hiring committee, he was pressured to hire a male-to-female transgender student for "Romeo and Juliet," because it would be better to choose a candidate from a minority group (applied "intersectionality"), or a woman, or a gay man (Marx's 'oppressed') to replace the departing teacher (Marx's 'bourgeois'). Hiring a more qualified, white, married, heterosexual male with children wasn't possible according to the university authorities. Professor Serban said,

> "I felt like I was living under communism again." (M. Vadum, Epoch Times, p. A8, Nov. 14, 2019)

An identical accusation is taken for Canada in an article entitled, "I Survived Communism – Are You Ready For Your Turn?" by Zuzina Janosova Ben Boer, a Slovakian (formerly Czechoslovakian) immigrant, now a Canadian citizen. She works as a Piping Engineer in a large oil company in Calgary, Alberta, Canada. Her story is reprinted in full in Appendix 4 with her permission. She said,

> "Having recognized all-too familiar signs of the same propaganda in my adopted country of Canada, I felt obligated to write the article below – because I do not want my adopted country to suffer the same fate as the country from which I emigrated."

CHAPTER 4: WARNINGS ON SOCIALISM & COMMUNISM

In North America, the generation of 1960s radicals gradually took over the elite universities...indoctrinating our youth in the socialist dream, and damning those that opposed their agenda.

The 1960s guru of this socialist intolerance was Herbert Marcuse, a far-left Frankfurt School radical socialist-communist whose famous essay, "Repressive Tolerance" is responsible for today's silencing of conservative voices of opposition and dissent against socialist indoctrination and legislation in schools, colleges, universities and greater society. He wrote that:

> "Tolerance is not a norm or right that should be extended to all people. Yes, tolerance is good, but not when it comes to people who are intolerant. It is perfectly fine to be intolerant against them, to the point of disrupting them, shutting down their events, preventing them from speaking, even destroying their careers and property. **He invented the argument that it is legitimate to be hateful against the haters.** For Marcuse, there were no limits to what could be done to discredit and ruin such people; **he wanted the left to defeat them "by any means necessary."** (Dinesh D'Souza, Herbert Marcuse: The Philosopher of Antifa, The Epoch Times, p. B4, June 18-24, 2020).

To Marcuse and his modern apostles, freedom of speech is OK as long as the socialist cause is espoused. Any conservative or Christian criticism or dissent is hateful and, therefore, illegal and must be silenced by whatever means, in universities or society in general.

In Canada, it is illegal today to oppose Bill C-16, which enshrined a fake "right" to gender identity and gender expression that has resulted in massive restrictions on free speech, religious freedom; and the privacy and security rights of women concerning sex-selective, coerced and partial-birth abortions. Trudeau's "conversion therapy ban," will put parents in jail for up to 5 years if they dare to encourage their gender-confused child to be at peace with their biological sex and stop their child under 18 to undertake a sex-change operation (Campaign Life Coalition letter, June, 2020). In Canada, free speech is being taken away. The Scriptures say,

> "Woe unto them that seek deep to hide their counsel from the LORD, and their works are in the dark, and they say, Who seeth us? And who knoweth us? **That make a man an offender for a word,** and lay a snare for him that reproveth in the gate, and turn aside the just for a thing of nought." (Isaiah 29:15, 21).

Dennis Prager (founder of Prager University in California) wrote,

> "For the first time in American history, free speech is threatened."

At Columbia University he was taught that Truman was a moral equivalent to Stalin and that America was as responsible for the Cold War as the Soviet Union. Thinking about this he suddenly realized that very bright people were teaching him foolish, silly things. The reason – they had no wisdom, because wisdom begins with the fear of God. He remembered Psalm 111:10a.

> *"The fear of the LORD is the beginning of wisdom:"*

and concluded the following:

> "That's why there's no wisdom at Columbia: there's no God at Columbia. The secular world produces knowledge and no wisdom. (In many cases) the secular intellectual is a moral idiot. The only people to support Stalin in the West were intellectuals. There's no such thing today as higher education –there's higher

CHAPTER 4: WARNINGS ON SOCIALISM & COMMUNISM

> indoctrination. When you send your kid to college, you are playing Russian roulette with their values. Christian seminaries are honest about their goals-namely to produce committed Christians – the university does not admit its goal to produce committed leftists." (I. Luo and J. Jekielek, The Epoch Times, p. B1, Nov. 28, 2019)

Corrupting of the educational system (schools and colleges) has had a profound impact on trade unions, the bureaucracy, political parties, the judiciary and journalism – particularly in the legacy media...moving these institutions further and further to the left, like Colombia University, as succeeding generations of adults emerge onto the scene as politicians, lawyers, judges and journalists in Canada and the United States.

Corrupting the education system has also fed down into all areas of everyday public life. Discipline in the form of corporal punishment has been wrested away from the family and from the school. Consequently, we have raised a bunch of rebels. Here is an example of a left-wing university-educated journalist:

> "There are zero upsides to spanking children. Here's what the science says about the kind of violence against children we call spanking... 1 – It permanently warps their worldview...2 – Spanked kids are measurably stupider...3 – Hitting kids retards development of parts of the brain associated with self-control...4 – Spanked children's DNA shows 1 to 3...5 – Spanking aged a child's cells prematurely...6 – The Canadian Medical Association wants spanking banned. Period...7 – Spanking increases aggression in children: American Academy of Pediatrics." (Ian Robinson, No more violence against kids. Ever. (The Calgary Sun, December 27, 2015)

The same kind of socialist-communist propaganda is found on pages 599-605 and 610, in Appendix 4.

"FORTRESS AMERICA" UNDER SIEGE

Concerning Ted Byfield, co-founder of the St. John's Boys School, author, and called in 1998, "the finest columnist in Canada today," Alan Fotherngham wrote:

> "Ted Byfield's entire philosophy – economic, political and social – could be summed up in one phrase, 'Bring back the strap!" (in Ted Byfield, The Book of Ted, 1998)

The Final Authority, God's Word, states:

> "Foolishness is bound in the heart of a child; but the rod of correction shall drive it far from him." (Proverbs 22:15)

Educating generations of entitled rebels who answer to no one and have no knowledge of God or moral convictions we now face the results of our actions at the highest levels of leadership in our country.

Roles in Canada's Judiciary, Parliament is Eroding Democracy," Two of the traditional pillars of free democracy, Parliament and the judiciary, have been undermined and changed by left wing ruling elites in the last generation. Centralization of power and privilege are in the Prime Minister's Office (PMO) and Privy Council Office (PCO), resulting in the Prime Minister enjoying almost absolute political power in the country. Members of Parliament (MPs) are completely subservient to their Party leader's policies and not to their constituents' needs or desires.

Canada's Judiciary has also been corrupted. Appointed judges, by activism, are no longer interpreting the law, but making the law; usurping the democratically-elected legislative body, Parliament. The nine Supreme Court Judges hold to the erroneous idea that they are superior to the public and therefore entitled to change Canada's social, political and cultural values to fit their cultural

CHAPTER 4: WARNINGS ON SOCIALISM & COMMUNISM

Marxist "isms" (see earlier). They are determining public policy, making Canada one of the most left-wing nations in the world. (G. Landolt, The Epoch Times, p. B1, Dec. 12, 2019)

In the USA, the same thing has happened. **"The Democratic Party has been infiltrated by socialists, Marxists, and outright communists at every level."** (T. Loudon, The Epoch Times, May 31, 2018).

Today in 2020, Canadian courts, mainstream media, universities and public education have become mainly anti-God, leftist institutions, and little free speech remains to be found.

> "Dewey's moral relativism, the Frankfurt School's rejection of inhibitions and Chisholm's "freedom from right and wrong," worked together to attack and undermine traditional values. They destroyed the moral fortifications of public schools in the United States." (see Chapter 5, pp. 326-328; Appendix 3, p.593)

The shocking results of this subversion has broken the moral foundations of America, of which few Americans are aware. The decay is so evident in the mass demonstrations and riots taking place across the country in 2020. "Fortress America" is indeed under siege, from within.

Phyllis Schlafly, scholar and U.S. constitutional lawyer provided statistics showing that from 1966 to 1970 the Supreme Court overrode lower court decisions in 34 instances, ruling against the prohibition of obscene content. She listed 9 methods activist judges use to undermine social morality.

> "They rewrite the Constitution, censor acknowledgment of God, redefine marriage, undermine U.S. sovereignty,

promote pornography, support feminism, handicap law enforcement, interfere with elections, and impose taxes. (The Epoch Times, "How the Spectre of Communism is Ruling Our World," Using the Law for Evil, Chapter 10, 2020)

To legalize behavior that deviates from traditional moral values is the same as having the government and laws train the people to betray morality and disobey God's commandments. The law has been twisted into a means of strangling people's ability to make moral judgments. It is essentially promoting homosexuality and encouraging people to give themselves to endless desire and degeneracy." (Ibid)

The product of modern secondary and university education has been on public display around the world. It is anything but commendable or honoring to the institutions that taught and nurtured them. Something has to change, the author of a recent article wrote –

"When mobs tore down a statue of Ulysses S. Grant and defaced a monument to African American veterans of the Civil War, many people wondered whether the protesters had ever learned anything in high school or college. These last several weeks of protests, riots and looting also revealed a generation that is poorly educated and yet petulant and self-assured without justification. Most of the young people in their 20s in protests appear juvenile, at least in comparison to their grandparents – survivors of the Great Depression and World War II.

Taxpayers who are hectored about their supposed racism, homophobia and sexism don't enjoy such finger-wagging from loud, sheltered, 20-something moralists. If being "woke" means the broke and unemployed are graduating to ignorantly smashing statues, denying free speech to others and institutionalizing cancel culture, then the public would rather pass on what spawned all of that in the first place. Taxpayers do not yet know what to replace the university with – wholly online courses and lectures, apolitical new campuses or broad-based vocational education – only that a once hallowed institution is becoming McCarthyite, malignant and, in the end, just a bad deal." (Victor Davis Hanson, Universities sowing the seeds of their own obsolescence, The Calgary Sun, July 4, 2020).

The COVID-19 'crisis' has revealed just how far Manning's predictions of a descent into totalitarianism has come in Canada and the other Western democracies. In "Pandemic affording politicians great powers, Walter Williams writes concerning the U.S.,

> "There are other news tidbits about politicians drunk with power that we Americans have given them...The biggest casualty from the COVID-19 pandemic has nothing to do with the disease. It's the power we've given to politicians and bureaucrats. The question is how we recover our freedoms?" (Calgary Sun, May 26, 2020)

The November, 2020, American election will determine which side wins this ideological war from within the United States – Marxists or freedom loving Americans. Canada faces the same choice in its next federal election soon to come.

2. Gain Control of the Media, thereby taking away Freedom of Speech

"Get control of all means of publicity, thereby getting peoples' minds off their government by focusing their attention on athletics, sexy books and other trivia."

The media is the 'voice of society,' guarding the nation's morals. Or it can be an instrument of evil. In communist countries it is the latter, and is fast becoming the same – with a few exceptions – in the Western democracies. Famous American leaders made these comments concerning the media:

> "Were it left for me to decide whether we should have a government without newspapers or newspapers without government, I should not hesitate a moment to prefer the latter." (**Thomas Jefferson**)

> "Our Republic and its press will rise or fall together. The power to mold the future of the Republic will be in the hands of the journalists of future generations." (**Joseph Pulitzer**, U.S. newspaper publisher)

Communist leaders have consistently viewed the media as a tool to promote, incite, and organize revolution; and a primary means to brainwash its citizenry. Therefore, socialists do their utmost to infiltrate and control the media – their ultimate goal being to deceive and poison the people with propaganda, misinformation and disinformation. The CCP employed as of 2010 it had about 1.3 million people employed in its propaganda apparatus. (The Epoch Times, "How the Spectre of Communism is Ruling Our World," Hijacking the Media, Chapter 13, 2020)

> "Have revolutionary energy and zeal in propaganda." (Ibid – Marx and Engels to The Communist League in 1847)

Candice Malcolm wrote an excellent article, **"Conflicts of interest threaten Canadian journalism."** In it, she stated the current condition of the mainstream Canadian media and its journalism:

> "A rigorous and independent media is vital to a free society. The only problem is that Canada's media is far from "free-thinking, independent, rigorous, robust and respected. Most members of the mainstream media are part of an exclusive club of left-leaning, urban elites who live in downtown Toronto, Ottawa or Montreal. They have a narrow world view, and frankly, they don't understand the values or concerns of most everyday Canadians.

CHAPTER 4: WARNINGS ON SOCIALISM & COMMUNISM

> Worse, Unifor, Canada's largest media union with 13,000 members, is waging an anti-Conservative campaign. It is an obvious conflict of interest. The Conservative government cut CBC's budget; the Liberals promised to increase it. Therefore, the Trudeau Liberals received glowing CBC coverage which helped them win the 2018 federal election.
>
> The media problem consists of left-leaning journalists but even worse, media outlets are corrupted by meddling political actors. The Liberals are offering a taxpayer-funded slush fund to dole out to more media outlets. Will journalists remain unbiased if other politicians threaten to end their funding? Unfortunately for Canadians, our media institutions are being corrupted and journalists are failing to provide the full story." (C. Malcolm, The Calgary Sun, November 17, 2018)

The government – media union partnership is a conflict of interest subsidized by taxpayer's dollars. That's immoral.

> Unifor President Jerry Dias said the Union will run an aggressive campaign to defeat Andrew Scheer in the Oct. 21 election. Dubbed "the resistance: and "Andrew Scheer's worst nightmare," to "stop Scheer stupidity." Obviously, the practice of media unions campaigning against Conservatives isn't going away." (Lorrie Goldstein, Media union won't stop attacking Scheer," The Calgary Sun, August 22, 2019)

The federal conservatives were defeated in the 2015 and 2019 federal elections where strong anti-Harper and anti-Scheer publicity was featured on most of Canada's public media. The reports could not be trusted due to bias. They swayed public opinion away from Harper and Scheer.

> "For every sin of commission...we believe that there are hundreds, and maybe thousands, of sins of omission (information left out) – cases where a journalist chose

facts or stories that only one side of the political spectrum is likely to mention." (Groseclose and Jeffery Milyo, 2005, "A Measure of Media Bias," in The Epoch Times, "How the Spectre of Communism is Ruling Our World," Chapter 13, 2020)

Omar Khadr, a repatriated, former teenage Islamic terrorist was compensated $10.5 million in 2017 by the Canadian government. He was interviewed by CBC's Radio Canada.

> "The Khadr appearance was a sophomoric effort to turn public opinion in his favor, to encourage him that he has plenty of elite support and tweak the noses of those who object to his current treatment by the federal government and courts. Yet the CBC never represents those opponent's views with the same amount of time or respect. It is once again taking sides on a contentious issue using taxpayer's dollars...an annual subsidy of $1.2 billion, roughly 4X what the P.E.I. government receives in equalization. The only way to stop that is to end Ottawa's massive annual subsidy to CBC." (Lorne Gunter, Khadr segment highlights problems with CBC's funding, The Calgary Sun, April 24, 2019)

A third applied to the American media:

> "A NPR/PBS 2018 Poll concluded 68% of Americans have very little or no confidence in our press. Fake news is harming our democracy and tearing us apart. Responsible media is at the core of a functional democracy. Media erosion starts small and then escalates quickly. When people stop trusting the press, a democracy struggles to succeed." (Gus Portela, Canadians should be wary of fake news, The Calgary Sun, November 17, 2018)

On August 18, 2018, 100 publications across the U.S. denounced President Trump's claim that the media "is the enemy of the American people." How did the Western media manage to accomplish this unpatriotic

CHAPTER 4: WARNINGS ON SOCIALISM & COMMUNISM

task? Communism expert, Trevor Loudon's commentary in the August 17-28, 2018, Epoch Times explains, in an article, **"How did the 'mainstream media' become the 'enemy of the people'?"**

"After WW II, hundreds of thousands of returning servicemen flooded into colleges and universities through the GI Bill. As young men they had read communist-infiltrated newspapers during the war – they were very open to "liberal" and leftist ideas, looking to build a world without want or war.

Into that perfect storm walked a man named Curtis MacDougall. His game-changing 1938 book, "Interpretive Journalism," said the goal of journalism was not to accurately report the news but to shape history – "advocacy journalism," Young idealistic journalism students lapped it up...and now it is the accepted "norm" in every major journalism school in the U.S.

MacDougall was Illinois state supervisor of the heavily Communist Party-infiltrated Federal Writer's Project (1939-42). He went on to teach journalism at Northwestern University till retirement in 1971. He was a leader of the communist-dominated Progressive Party, a sponsor of the Cultural and Scientific Conference for World Peace in 1949 – organized by the Communist Party USA front known as National Council of the Arts, Sciences, and Professions.

In the early 1960s MacDougall supported the Communist Party-controlled National Committee to Abolish the House Un-American Activities Committee. As late as 1970, he was vice-chairman of the communist-led Chicago Committee to Defend the Bill of Rights. **Modern American journalism was founded by a man who was at the very least a committed Communist Party "fellow traveler."**

Another U.S. icon of journalism was I.F. (Izzy) Stone, of the prestigious I.F. Stone's Weekly (1953-71). Stone was

"FORTRESS AMERICA" UNDER SIEGE

an early Socialist Party member who moved into Communist Party circles in the 1930s and 40s. He was an early supporter of the Democratic Socialists of America. In 1988, he endorsed Bernie Sanders for Congress.

Stone was a major enemy of Senator Joseph McCarthy, the anti-communist crusader from Wisconsin. Only later de-coded WWII messages reveal that for some time in the 1930s and 40s, Stone had been a paid Soviet agent.

Curtis MacDougall, I.F. Stone, and their leftist comrades in the journalism schools have created a leftist culture in American journalism. Journalists are typically liberal, and far more liberal than the public at large. Most journalists offer reflexively liberal answers to practically every question a pollster can imagine. 400 "progressive" and socialist journalists, academics, and "news media" activists supported Obama in the 2008 presidential election. Journalists were apparently willing to privately collude to attempt to steer public opinion in their desired political direction. More than 96% of media donations went to Hilary Clinton. **Trump is right. The mainstream media are the enemy of the people.** The President knows it, and the people know it. Only the "mainstream media" itself seems oblivious of its own contemptible status."

Television entered the mainstream of American society in the 1950s. It, as well as the movie industry, adhered to the Hays Code that restricted immoral content in their programming. But, by 1968 the Hays Code was abandoned and Hollywood and the television industry turned to violence and immorality – and more and more as the years went on. The writer can still remember the influence that the movie, "The Graduate," had on him as a young adult in the late 1960s, as well as the violence and sexual content in the movie, "Bonny and Clyde." They left a lasting imprint on a generation as well as many other productions. The movie industry and

CHAPTER 4: WARNINGS ON SOCIALISM & COMMUNISM

television took down public morality with startling speed.

> "Hollywood began to mass produce movies that cast a positive glow on degenerate behaviors such as sexual promiscuity, violence, illicit drugs, and organized crime...presenting dishonesty in a heroic light, criminal activity as something that pays off, heroes killing one or more people and heroines that were promiscuous to some degree." (The Epoch Times, "How the Spectre of Communism is Ruling Our World," Hijacking the Media, Chapter 13, 2020)

> "People tend to be subliminally persuaded by the themes and views represented on TV programs because they are in a relaxed mode where alpha "brainwaves" dominate, serious thinking and analytical ability decrease, and they become more impressionable. Violence and misleading sexual content is all over television. Ben Shapiro studied nearly 100 influential American TV series. He found as time progressed, these programs increasingly promoted liberalism and leftist viewpoints, atheism and belittling faith, sex and violence, feminism, homosexuality and transsexuality, the rejection of morality, ruthless antiheroes devoid of sympathy, and the rejection of the traditional relationships between husband and wife or parent and child....**a process of continual moral decay**." (Ibid)

We older folk see the fruit of progressive education; minorities given more rights and privileges taken from the majority. Free speech has been the casualty. We see non-elected, progressive judges making the law and forming public policy, usurping the authority of the democratically-elected legislative bodies, the Canadian Parliament and the provincial legislatures. These new laws are directly opposed to our historic Judeo-Christian culture and laws, and opposing them can mean prosecution in a court of law.

"FORTRESS AMERICA" UNDER SIEGE

The "new journalism" tactics used by legacy news outlets since the 1960s utilized psychological warfare methods to condition the public to react emotionally and irrationally to political stimuli, and not to facts (Joshua Philip, Emotion Over Logic: The Legacy Media Tool for Narrative Control, The Epoch Times, April 26-May 2, 2019). In that way people can be controlled by the media – much like Lenin's declaration that in place of individualism, "I want the masses of Russia to follow a communistic pattern of thinking and reacting." Below are comments on the "new journalism:'

> "Too often we wear liberalism on our sleeves. We do not tolerate other lifestyles and viewpoints. We are not hesitant to say that if you want to work here, you must be the same as us, and you must be liberal and progressive." (liberal editor of a major newspaper)
>
> The openness with which the Hollywood crowd admits its anti-conservative discrimination inside the industry is shocking." (author Ben Shapiro)
>
> "The academic left and its news media and Hollywood acolytes refuse to confront the horrifying record of Marxism's endless inhumanity." (Newt Gingrich, former Speaker of the House)

Using disinformation (stage events, evidence, conclusions, etc), misinformation (outright false information) and propaganda (true or falsely eliciting emotional response) they get people to react emotionally to surface issues along set partisan lines. The reporters start with their "issue," then engineer the interview to frame a story to fit their manufactured narrative. The sad victims of such reporting are politically conditioned and brainwashed. Here are a few of many recent examples of predetermined media narratives, one from the U.S. and two from Canada's CBC:

CHAPTER 4: WARNINGS ON SOCIALISM & COMMUNISM

"Contrary to a globally reported blunder by the media Friday, President Donald Trump did not say a positive report on U.S. job numbers was "good news for George Floyd." Trump's reference to Floyd was in the context of Americans agreeing everyone must be treated equally by police, not optimistic job numbers. Despite their obvious blunder about what Trump said, which quickly went global and erupted on social media, few media organizations have corrected it." (Lorrie Goldstein, Media got it all wrong, June 7, 2020).

"CBC Had 'Predetermined Narrative' for Reporting on Epoch Times, Says Scholar Interviewed by Broadcaster"

"'An expert interviewed by CBC as part of its recent coverage of The Epoch Times says he thinks the CBC reporters were trying to get a "predetermined narrative" (MacDougall's 'advocacy journalism') from him and that this has diminished his trust in the national broadcaster. Stephen Noakes, a senior lecturer at the University of Auckland said, "It seems to me that they were trying to reverse engineer information that would allow them to support a predetermined narrative – narrative-driven news reporting. There was a selective interpretation of facts that went on here." He says they ignored his answers in his area of expertise and he felt they were trying to get him to frame The Epoch Times negatively.'" (Omid Ghoreishi, The Epoch Times, pp A1, A3, June 4-10, 2020)

"The CBC, the CCP and COVID-19"

"The CBC remains as awful with reporting on COVID-19 as it has been with organ harvesting – the mass killing in China of prisoners of conscience for their organs. Falun Gong has been the primary victim of organ transplant abuse in China. The CBC announced the showing of Peter Rowe's documentary on Falun Gong in China, in November, 2007, and then pulled it after protests from the Chinese embassy. The documentary was shown later with criticisms of the CCP/Government of China deleted or softened.

A predetermined CBC narrative smearing The Epoch Times Special Edition for factual reporting on China and COVID-19 raised such a storm of protest that the CBC story and its headline were changed, more than once. Yet, the initial CBC report in its amended form and a subsequent report still report the concerns of those who misread the publication as if there were still some reality behind their concerns, but not the responses of any of the authors of the disputed pieces." (David Matas and David Kilgour, The CBC, the CCP and COVID-19, The Calgary Sun, May 11, 2020)

Ernest Manning described the newspapers of the mid-1950s as –

> "part of a universal brainwashing scheme to make people aggressive in that which will destroy them...state collectivism." (Albertan, Dec. 2, 1955)

In 1972 Mr. Manning quoted a news report from Quebec City, "Control Separatism on French Network in Ottawa is Urged." The issue again was the infiltration of national media by those who would report the news with predetermined narratives (MacDougall's advocacy journalism). In 2020, the separatism movement has receded for now, but the agenda and the news bias in the mainstream news outlets has not.

> "Acting Premier Mrs. Marie Claire Kirkland-Casgrain wants the federal government to impose some sort of control over the news on Radio Canada, the CBC's French language radio and television network. She said in an interview that the separatist radicals have infiltrated Radio Canada and slant news and documentaries to divide the country and sow revolution. Mrs. Kirkland-Casgrain added that when an autonomous corporation is not responsible to the elector, it can give birth to many

CHAPTER 4: WARNINGS ON SOCIALISM & COMMUNISM

abuses. She said Quebec is going through many of the experiences of pre-war Germany when the National Socialists infiltrated the news media. She said not only socialists but communists and extremists of all kinds are in Radio Canada. She said if she was in Mr. Pelletier's place she would cut off the funds of programs which divide the country and sow revolution. She said, "The infiltration of separatists occurs at all levels of the CBC management and staff. There is always time and publicity for protestors, but we never had a chance to state our case."

Mr. Manning's comments about the article are just as relevant today in 2020 as they were in 1972:

"Mrs. Kirkland-Casgrain Is only stating what many concerned Canadians have long known. How much longer will this insidious undermining of our free and democratic society be tolerated by an apathetic public and a government that lacks either the will or the fortitude to prevent a government-owned and publicly financed radio and television network, serving as a forum for anarchists and revolutionists who want to destroy our national unity and strength. We desperately need at least one political party and leader in this country with the backbone to call a halt to such subversive tactics." (E. Manning, The Face of the Sky – Part 2, 1972, Canada's National Back to the Bible Hour pamphlet)

Sadly, the left-wing 'revolutionary,' Pierre Trudeau was Prime Minister of Canada in 1972. Though he opposed Quebec separatism, he did not abandon his long term plan of making Canada a socialist country, with Quebec a net beneficiary of the country's wealth.

During the overblown COVID-19 'scamdemic,' the media has been fixated on the world caving in, keeping the people in a state of continual anxiety. And then, when and how will professional sports get going again? And back to stoking fear of a possible 'second wave' of the virus. The players' and owners' squabbles make news. People are being continually prepped to anxiously await the return of the virus and their millionaire sports idols playing again, while many of their own jobs, businesses and lives have been savaged first by government inaction and then by government overreaction. Of course, the mainstream news outlets follow the government line. They dare not do otherwise, and so become the government's propaganda machine.

> "Herein lies the problem with much of the mainstream media in Canada. National media reporters are mostly from downtown Toronto or Ottawa – or they moved there as soon as they could. These journalists are often progressive, secular, cosmopolitan urban elitists who always cheer on the latest leftist causes. They universally support unrestricted access to abortion, open immigration and the radical political organization Black Lives Matter. They likely don't know many Conservative voters, let alone people with traditional or religious values." (Candice Malcolm, Fair coverage of the Conservative leadership is badly needed, The Calgary Sun, July 27, 2020).

> "The response of Canada's federal and provincial governments to COVID-19 appears to have been driven by Dr. Neil Ferguson of Imperial College London, who predicted in March that as many as 510,000 people in the UK would die, along with 2.2 million Americans. Once unleashed, this wildly inaccurate "Ferguson Factor" infected the minds of politicians around the globe, as well as the media and the public at large. We now know that deaths from COVID-19 is within the range of deaths resulting from the annual flu." (John Carpay, Canada's Religious Leaders Should Stop Tolerating Unjustified Lockdown, The Epoch Times, p. B2, June 11-17, 2020)

> "The COVID-19 numbers were never as bad as the province's sunniest forecast. But still the fear machine cranked out the tales of woe." (Rick Bell, Ignore Nervous Nellies, The Calgary Sun, June 10, 2020)

CHAPTER 4: WARNINGS ON SOCIALISM & COMMUNISM

Though the churches were locked down, the adult movie and big box stores remained open. Apparently, sex entertainment is an 'essential service' in our hedonistic culture. Our spiritual well-being is apparently not that important. More sex material was sold during the COVID-19 lockdown than at any other time prior to the enforcement of the emergency regulations. But most churches still remained closed into mid-June due to meeting size restrictions, creating a subtle repression of free speech in public places of worship. Only The Epoch Times printed this important issue.

> "Freedom of conscience and religion is the most fundamental human right, and one which repressive regimes invariably seek to destroy. Why are most of Canada's religious leaders cooperating actively with the unjustified suppression of worship by chief medical officers and other government officials? When the government shuts down temples, churches, mosques, and synagogues on a pretext that ceased to hold water many weeks ago, there is no wisdom in blithely going along with government violations of a fundamental Charter Freedom. For Canada's religious leaders to embrace these continued, unjustified violations of religious freedom is not just foolish, but suicidal." (John Carpay, Canada's Religious Leaders Should Stop Tolerating Unjustified Lockdown, The Epoch Times, p. B2, June 11-17, 2020)

Concerning "the supreme value of our freedom to speak," journalist Max Maudie wrote in the December 27, 2015, Calgary Sun:

> "If you get to decide willy-nilly what can and can't be said (for whatever reason) – then be prepared for those in power to use their own matrix of fuzzy wuzzy to muzzle you. History proves it.

> Fighting to get people sacked because you disagree with them is a 21st century firing squad, and it's not at all uncommon for those offended to scurry to their rifles."

One week before the U.S. 2020 election, an article "Twitter and Facebook's Assault on Freedom of the Press," The Epoch Times Editorial Board writes on p. B1 in the October 23-28, 2020 edition:

> "Facebook and Twitter have taken extraordinary steps against the New York Post over an article about the son of former vice-president Joe Biden – the first action against a news article by a major U.S. Publisher. Their rules are so dangerously vague that the platforms can choose to censor content as they see fit."

Very perilous indeed are the days in which we are living. Truth has fallen in the streets under the heels of the mainstream media almost everywhere. The quenching of free speech accompanies the transformation of Canada into an international socialist-communist state. Ernest Manning said only the citizens of this country can stop this from happening, by demanding it stop and electing politicians who oppose it. That is, before it goes too far to stop which is where we are almost at today in 2020. Free speech is in jeopardy in Canada, as the Liberal government attacks through proxies like the CBC the few remaining conservative voices such as the Rebel Media and the Epoch Times. Who rules does matter.

> "Political parties are grossly imperfect and mirror all the imperfections of humanity. Still the political process remains the major means through which Christians can have an influence and bear witness. If Christians default they will get something far worse, so let's get on with it."
> (E. Manning, The Face of the Sky, Part 2, 1972)

Governments are involved in suppressing free speech among their elected members. Representing the people

CHAPTER 4: WARNINGS ON SOCIALISM & COMMUNISM

comes second to following party policy and protocol. The socialist parties are most repressive, but sadly so do the conservatives. For example:

> "Jason Stephan points to Justin Trudeau, the NDP and the Bloc and a socialism he says Albertans don't like. I wanted to ask Stephan about his statement. Sadly, Stephan is muzzled. The crew around Kenny don't want me hooking up with Stephan. "Our government was partly elected on the basis of giving a voice back to the people," says Nate Horner. Yes, they were. And they could start by giving the voice back to a member of the legislature with the guts to speak the truth to power." (Rick Bell, UCP Muzzles own MLA, The Calgary Sun, June 11, 2020)

3. Deliberately sow strife and division – Marx's "Class Struggle" in society

"Divide the people into hostile groups by constantly harping on controversial matters of no importance." Note: Also includes important matters as recent times have shown.

The basic tenet of Karl Marx, the 'father' of atheistic communism/socialism, was that of "<u>class struggle</u>," the concept of "oppressor" (bourgeois) vs "oppressed" (proletariat). Division and strife would be sown between these 2 groups in a society with the result that the so-called "oppressed" would tear down and destroy the existing social order and institutions through revolutionary subversion &/or violence, eliminating the so-called oppressors and all private property in the process. The so-called proletariat-ruled government would then build a socialist-communist 'utopian' (perfect) society that would reign supreme as the peoples' god.

"FORTRESS AMERICA" UNDER SIEGE

Much of the strife and division in Canada today in one way or another can be traced back to Pierre Trudeau's social policies established during his last term in office (1980-1984). Trudeau was a self-avowed Marxist. Columnist Andrew Coyne wrote –

> "Pierre Trudeau proclaimed himself a champion of individual liberties, yet his policies worked against free speech through an expensive human rights bureaucracy that operated like a separate police force and legal system, lacking any procedural restraints, rules of evidence or professional expertise." (Bob Plamondon, "The Truth About Trudeau," 2013)

Pierre Trudeau was a brilliant intellectual, and he was also a committed leftist, visiting communist countries as a young man and befriending socialist-communist dictatorships such as China and Cuba as Canada's 15th Prime Minister (1968-1984). He believed that these countries were 'just' societies, and that Christianity produced 'unjust' societies. Let's look at some of Pierre Trudeau's 'just' societies:

> "Stalin promised a great socialist-Marxist society with better food and working conditions," – the result: 62 millions murdered; Mao Zedong promised democratic constitutionalism and the dream that "farmers have land to till," – the result: 76 millions murdered, including 40 million farmers starved to death; Mao's CCP trained Pol Pot who murdered 2 million Cambodians; Venezuela's Chavez and Maduro took Cuba as their model and promised, "Have faith, we, in economic matters will be harvesting victories," – the result: critics jailed, hospitals lack basic medication, water and power supplies unreliable, rampant violent crime, child malnutrition at all-time high, millions have fled deadly food shortages and spiraling hyperinflation demonstrating the resounding failure of two successive socialist governments,"

CHAPTER 4: WARNINGS ON SOCIALISM & COMMUNISM

> Vietnam, - the result: 2 millions murdered, more than a million "boat people" refugees, re-education camp where inmates asked Red Cross for cyanide tablets with which to kill themselves;" etc., etc. (Sources: Walter Williams, Socialist Promises, The Calgary Sun, May 24, 2019; Brian Lilley, Why give Reds a pass?, The Calgary Sun, May 6, 2019; Gerry Bowler, The abysmal scorecard of socialist revolutions, The Epoch Times, November 2-8, 2018; Walter Williams, Leftists remain too soft on communism, The Calgary Sun, December 19, 2017)

Pierre Trudeau did not reject violence as a means to an end. Therefore, he justified the above socialist tyrants 'political ends' in creating their 'just' societies.

> "Terrorism does not constitute political violence if it is absolutely needed to attain the accepted political end of a given nation." (Bob Plamondon, The Truth About Trudeau, 2013).

So, Stalin, Mao, Ho Chi Minh, Fidel Castro et al were murdering millions because it was needed to consolidate totalitarian socialism, the 'accepted end,' in each of their countries. Their actions did not bother Trudeau.

Trudeau implemented the War Measures Act in the October Crisis of 1970 to counter FLQ separatists in Quebec. But he wildly overestimated and purposely exaggerated the threat posed by the FLQ. Forty years later his actions were analyzed in a collection of essays, the most comprehensive review on the event, concluding:

> "The October Crisis revealed Trudeau to be authoritarian, totalitarian, dictatorial and fascist." (The Truth about Trudeau, Bob Plamondon, 2013).

Pierre Trudeau was labelled a communist in his home province by Father Leopold Braun, once a priest in

Moscow. Another priest called Trudeau "the Canadian Karl Marx," in the Trois Rivers newspaper. When threatened with a lawsuit the priest replied, "I hesitate to call this libel," given Trudeau's writings. (Ibid)

Justin Trudeau, like his father, is very amicable and friendly toward China. His counterpart in that Communist country is President Xi Jinping,

> "Secretary of State Mike Pompeo almost daily articulates and advances Trump's understanding of the new Cold War with China we find ourselves in. If there is any doubt about that, consider a recent speech by Robert O'Brien, in which the president's national security adviser declared, "The Chinese Communist Party is a Marxist-Leninist organization. The Party General Secretary Xi Jinping sees himself as Joseph Stalin's successor." (Hugh Hewitt, Which do you prefer: Trump's agenda or Biden's?, The Calgary Sun, July 6, 2020).

> "China has never been stronger in its authoritarian and Communist ways than under the leadership of Xi Jinping." (Calgary Sun editorial, July 7, 2020).

All of these deaths and the suffering that accompanied the revolutions were supposedly for the "oppressed" in retaliation against the "oppressors" – a "class struggle" delusion in which all were the victims. Mao Zedong believed a class struggle should be repeated about every 8 years against some minority so that communism would remain pure. Every such cleansing in Mao's mind should punish about 5% of the country's population to terrorize the remaining 95% into submission. (The Epoch Times, "Nine Commentaries on the Communist Party," Special Edition, 2004).

CHAPTER 4: WARNINGS ON SOCIALISM & COMMUNISM

Ernest Manning commented on Pierre Trudeau's socialist legacy in Canada:

> "I think the outcome of all this is sown divisiveness – East against West, French against English, so many divisions. When people are split up into disagreeing factions like that, they become critical of everything. And that's what you primarily hear in Canada today. Everybody is finding fault with everything. They're mad at the government; they're mad at each other. You can't get 10 people together without them disagreeing on something. That is, I think, one of the most terrible effects of what Trudeau and his people have done to this country – not just this constitutional thing, but in the whole economic thing, the attitude and the philosophy." (Brian Brennan, The Good Steward: The Ernest C. Manning Story, 2008).

Bob Plamondon, in his 2013 book, The Truth About Trudeau, details the many ways this man sought to remake Canada in his socialist image, and deliberately sowed short-and-long term strife and division in the country, endangering its very survival.

> "He antagonized the West with his National Energy Program, subsidizing the East at the expense of the West."

> "He misled and betrayed Quebecers in the 1980 Referendum, by patriating the Constitution without their approval. **Senator Ernest Manning** in December, 1981, predicted, "Where does Quebec stand on the matter today? She stands more isolated than ever from the rest of Canada, more polarized, angrier and more resentful because she feels she was betrayed. There is no real profit in gaining a new constitution if in the process you lose a nation.""

> "He caused the failure of the Meech Lake and Charlottetown Accords meant to heal the wounds to

> Quebec. He weakened federalist leaders working on the ground to win the hearts and the minds of Quebecers, causing the near disastrous 1995 Quebec Referendum and the break-up of the country.
>
> Formed a Charter of Rights and Freedoms without consulting Canadians – with Human Rights Commissions and Tribunals – a huge state apparatus. Thirty years later, the Charter remains **a divisive document.** It replaced parliamentary supremacy with constitutional supremacy. The courts, and not the voters, now tell our democratically-elected politicians what they can and cannot do. It was a step backward as Canada already had the entire British legal tradition given at Confederation (ex. Magna Carta, Habeas Corpus Act, Petition of Right, Bill of Rights, plus court judgments, parliamentary conventions/royal prerogatives and international conventions."

The Charter imposed a new tyranny: that of interest groups twisting the legal system, to change laws in their favor. The pre-Charter legalities concerned, "guilt or innocence;" while the post-Charter issue was "police conduct," with guilt or innocence taking the back seat. This is one of many ways Trudeau engineered Marxist "class struggle" into his policies leading to strife and division, and social transformation of Canada from its historic Judeo-Christian roots. In speaking of Canada's Judeo-Christian cultural tradition that had shaped the political history of Canada Trudeau said,

> "All such politics are <u>reactionary</u>. **For the past 150 years nationalism has been an anachronistic notion.**" (Bob Plamondon, The Truth About Trudeau, 2013)

By definition, reactionary means: "one who favors a return to former conditions or state of affairs – a reverse action; or, one who seeks to undo or hinder (Marxist

CHAPTER 4: WARNINGS ON SOCIALISM & COMMUNISM

socialist) political advancement ... an **ultra-conservative**." A Bible believing Christian would be considered ultraconservative, and a reactionary – 'Public Enemy No. 1' – to radical socialists-communists.

Pierre Trudeau's use of the word **"reactionary"** exposed his communistic ideology. Persecution and liquidation of "reactionaries" was one of the first objectives of radical socialists-communists when they gained full power. It followed the Marxist agenda to destroy completely the pre-existing traditions and culture of the society they planned to transform into their communist utopia. The reactionaries were the primary holders of those traditions. In traditional Western culture conservatives, and particularly fundamental Bible believing Christians would be the socialist's reactionaries.

Justin Trudeau is far from an intellectual, but "leans farther left than any Prime Minister since his father." (Joe Oliver, The Calgary Sun, September 6, 2019). Justin Trudeau has continued his father's work and carried his divisive strategy to new heights.

> "And speaking of (Justin) Trudeau, let's not forget he once admitted the efficiency of the Chinese communist dictatorship and he also heaped effusive praise on the late Fidel Castro, a notorious communist thug who turned Cuba into a giant prison. He got a pass for such comments since for many on the left, communism is not that bad despite its record of gulags, mass murders and general overall crushing of human rights." (Gerry Nicholls, Who are the real hate-mongers?, The Calgary Sun, April 26, 2019).

Justin Trudeau may be even worse, and more dangerous, than his father. Right now, in 2020, Canada is more divided by far than it ever was under Pierre Trudeau. But

Pierre set the tone and laid the foundation for today's divided Canada with his Charter of Rights and Freedoms and the judicial activists that impose it.

Trudeau appointed Dr. Theresa Tam as Canada's chief public health officer, 'top doctor' and Liberal mouthpiece, a director in Beijing-controlled WHO, sympathetic to the Marxist cause. She mismanaged and continues to mismanage Canada's response to the COVID-19 pandemic.

> "the latest installment of her 86 page annual report, released Wednesday,... is a dead giveaway about seeing the pandemic through the lens of academic progressivism...(with) sections on ableism, ageism, **(neo-Marxist)** intersectionality and, of course, a fixation on race and how the "structural determinants of health...drive health inequalities....in society...**(Marxist class struggle)**." (Anthony Furey, It's time to start questioning agenda of Canada's public health officer, The Calgary Sun, October 29, 2020) brackets in text added by writer.

The Liberal left has used climate change to create "A Climate of Fear." (Mark Bonokoski, The Calgary Sun, April 28, 2019). They have used this fanatical fear to **exacerbate strife and division** throughout Canada, blocking pipelines, closing coal mines and coal-fired power plants, cancelling $2 billion in gas-fired power plants and spending multi-billions on green energy projects. The results:

> "Lots of former backroom types got rich...on green energy projects...but it wasn't the beleaguered taxpayer, because it was he who found himself having to choose between feeding his family or heating his home...outraged citizens living through trying times in home without heat or light."

CHAPTER 4: WARNINGS ON SOCIALISM & COMMUNISM

The list could go on endlessly. Suffice to say, strife and division, "class struggle," the Marxist strategy for undermining a free society, is running on eight cylinders in Canada in 2020. Pierre Trudeau, the Fabian socialist, made sure that would happen with his far-reaching policies and financial mismanagement.

> "After five years of Liberal rule, Canada is a weak and divided country. The Bloc Qubecois, which surged in the 2019 election and won enough seats to form the balance of power in the House of Commons, and a new Wexit movement in Western Canada no longer demanding a fairer deal within confederation, but now simply demanding a way out of the Canadian experiment." (Candice Malcolm, Divisive Grit tactics make Tory leadership race so important," The Calgary Sun, May 25, 2020).

And the Liberals are now taking aim directly upon law-abiding gun owners as the government moves toward civil disarmament for Canadians.

4. Carry out a program of civil disarmament

"Secure the registration of all fire-arms on some pretext with the view of confiscating them and leaving the population helpless."

The Liberal government of Justin Trudeau is making a determined push to civil disarmament in Canada. This move coincides with their socialist agenda to rule Canada as a Marxist dictatorship in the near future. COVID-19 is a major ingredient in this toxic mix to take away our freedom and render Canadian citizens vulnerable and helpless to Big Government.

"FORTRESS AMERICA" UNDER SIEGE

Western governments, under left-wing influence are seeking to disarm law-abiding citizens at just the time when crime and violence is increasing. Mr. Manning recognized that disarming such people rendered them helpless in the face of life-threatening criminals or a criminal government. The Epoch Times, "How the Spectre of Communism is Ruling Our World," Popular Culture, a Decadent Indulgence, Chapter 14, 2020) describes this trend.

> "In America, from 1960 to 2016, the total population increased by 1.8 times, while the total number of violent crimes grew 4.5 times. In the 50 years before the U. of Texas shooting in 1966 there were only 25 public mass shootings in which 4 or more people were killed. Since then, mass shootings have become more deadly and much more common over time...reflecting the culture of violence in society. In 2008, the Pew Research Center found that 97% of youths between 12 and 17 played video games, and that two-thirds of them played games that contained violent content. In addition, terrorist incidents worldwide increased from 650/yr. in 1970 to 13,488 in 2017, a twentyfold increase."

In an **"Open Letter to Canadians,"** in The Calgary Sun on July 4, 2020, the Canadian Coalition for Firearm Rights for commercial purposes wrote:

> "A determined group of Canadians are taking the federal government to court. This landmark case will affect the rights of all Canadians. The question is this: can the government take your property with no justification? Based on some past cases, it's looking like the answer is yes. Another question is what kind of property can they take? Apparently, anything: your land, bank account, personal possessions, whatever it is that they determine you don't need, or they want for their own reasons. In this case, a group of licensed gun owners is suing the government over the latest gun ban. The only justification offered by the government has been political sloganeering and a campaign of untrue rhetoric. This

CHAPTER 4: WARNINGS ON SOCIALISM & COMMUNISM

may appeal to Canadians who don't own guns, as they aren't losing any of their property, but the abuse of power and lack of accountability on behalf of the government should concern us all. **As it stands, it's looking like the government can simply use any motive to justify its improper exercise of its authority: pandemic, climate emergency, economic crisis, or any other reason could be used to take anything you own.** <u>Today it's RCMP-vetted, licensed gun owners, but tomorrow it could be you.</u> Take an interest in this case because it will affect your future, and the future of generations to come."

"FORTRESS AMERICA" UNDER SIEGE

ANNOUNCEMENT OF A FIREARMS PROHIBITION

On May 1, 2020, the Government of Canada reclassified the following firearms and devices as prohibited:

- Nine (9) types of firearms by make and model, and their variants;
- Firearms with a bore of 20 mm or greater, and those capable of discharging a projectile with a muzzle energy greater than 10,000 Joules;
- Upper receivers of M16, AR-10, AR-15 and M4 pattern firearms.

As the holder of a valid firearms licence, you are being contacted by the Canadian Firearms Program as you may be in possession of one of these firearms.

WHAT THIS MEANS FOR YOU:

1. An amnesty has been introduced which protects owners who were in legal possession of one or more of these newly prohibited firearms or devices on the day the amendments to the Classification Regulations came into force, May 1, 2020.

2. The Government intends to implement a buy-back program and is looking at a range of options. More information on the buy-back program will be available at a later date.

WHAT YOU SHOULD KNOW ABOUT THESE FIREARMS/DEVICES:

1. Owners of newly prohibited firearms are to keep them securely stored in accordance with their previous classification.
2. They cannot be sold or imported.
3. They may only be transported under limited circumstances.
4. They cannot be legally used for hunting unless allowed through the Amnesty Order.*
5. They cannot be used for sport shooting, either at a range or elsewhere.

*Exceptions are included under the Amnesty Order to allow for the continued use of the newly prohibited firearms and/or devices if previously non-restricted by individuals who hunt or trap to sustain themselves or their families, and by Indigenous persons exercising Aboriginal or treaty rights to hunt. At the end of the amnesty period, all firearm owners must comply with the new law.

WHAT ARE YOUR OPTIONS?

1. **Wait** for further instructions to participate in the buy-back program.
2. Have your firearm deactivated by an approved business.
3. Legally export your firearm, in which case individuals can engage businesses with the proper firearms privileges.

MORE INFORMATION:

For a list of newly prohibited firearms and information about the announcement or amnesty, go to the Canadian Firearms Program website:

www.rcmp-grc.gc.ca/en/firearms

 Royal Canadian Mounted Police   Gendarmerie royale du Canada

Canada

The July/August, 2020, NFA Journal had the following statements concerning the Liberal "gun grab" of May 1, 2020:

CHAPTER 4: WARNINGS ON SOCIALISM & COMMUNISM

"The Liberals have employed the most insidious and slimy tools at their disposal to ban and confiscate your property, the OIC (Order in Council). This is nothing more or less than Liberal economic and social warfare. Drive Canadian businesses to bankruptcy, cause job loss and government dependence for employees, manufacture criminal offences. They are warring against the hard-fought freedoms of previous generations...undermining the very foundations of English common law which have been enjoyed by Canadians for centuries. This is a very personal attack on the rights, freedoms and property of Canadians. The only solution to this mess will be the defeat of the Liberals in the next federal election. The Liberals must be defeated in the next federal election." (Blaire Hagen, The Only Solution).

"Langmann showed that none of Canada's gun laws worked to reduce homicide or suicide and Mauser demonstrated that moose kill more people than PAL holders. Not only does licensing stigmatize law-abiding citizens, but licensing exposes them to onerous police scrutiny and makes them vulnerable to false accusations." (Garry Mauser, The License Question – Should firearms owners be licensed?).

"OIC...a decision of the (Liberal) federal cabinet that is rubber stamped by the governor general...without need for reverting to an act of parliament. There is no bill filed in the House of Commons, no consultation of stakeholders, no debate and no vote. **If this sounds like totalitarianism, you are not entirely wrong.**

One need not be a Rhodes Scholar to figure out that these laws have no effect on criminal behavior. You are your own first responder. The police exist to investigate crimes after they've already occurred. You can choose to be a helpless victim, or you can fight back." (Chris McGarry, You Will Always Be Your Own First Responder).

The underlying, and often unspoken, consequence of 'gun control' is the issue of personal safety and freedom.

"FORTRESS AMERICA" UNDER SIEGE

The famous Western writer, Louis L'Amour, put it quite simply in two of his popular books, read by millions:

> "Men in this land could own guns, not to threaten their neighbor, but to ensure themselves of liberty. The men who shaped this land were men who had lately fought a war for their freedom and they did not wish it to be lost, and they must keep close to their hands the weapons with which they had won that freedom." (The Man from Skibbereen, 1973)

> "Understand one thing, Mr. Chantry. You can make laws against weapons but they will be observed only by those who don't intend to use them anyway. The lawless can always smuggle or steal, or even make a gun. By refusing to wear one you allow the criminal to operate with impunity." *Response:* "But we have the law." *Answer:* "But even the law cannot be in your bedroom at night." (North to the Rails, 1971)

It is no coincidence that former law professor and left-wing "progressive", Pierre Trudeau, upon entering Canadian politics in 1965 and becoming Minister of Justice, almost immediately initiated stricter gun control legislation. (Wikipedia).

His son, Justin, is focusing on the same issues today, as Canada is being pushed further away from the English-based, Judeo-Christian Common Law and culture that he and his father so despise(d).

> "The English (England) experience with the right to arms and the associated right to self-defence is deeply tied to civil liberties. The English, for most of their history, were an armed people, a fact which restrained arbitrary state power." (Bruce Gold, Canadian Gun Culture – English Roots; NFA Journal, July/August, 2018)

The CCP virus pandemic has made Canadians vulnerable to Liberal power opportunism. Trudeau's May 1, run

CHAPTER 4: WARNINGS ON SOCIALISM & COMMUNISM

around the COVID-19 end zone 'gun control' grab, is a prime example.

Veteran journalist Lorne Gunter wrote in the May 27, 2020, edition of The Calgary Sun newspaper, "Liberals shoot themselves in the foot,"

> "The federal gun ban, announced May 1, just gets worse and worse. Some 250,000 guns – maybe more – would be taken from 100,000 legal owners. The ban was authorized by an order-in-council (a Liberal Cabinet decree), not by an act of Parliament. And it was introduced when Parliament was not sitting due to the pandemic. Now the Liberals are plotting legislation that would permit municipal governments to outlaw the possession of handguns in homes. Almost all firearms crimes in Canada are committed by drug dealers and gang members, not law-abiding Canadians.
>
> In response to a constituents complaint Liberal MP Marwan Tabbara explained, "We can't get the necessary unanimous consent for introduction of a Bill on this subject and this has waiting too long for action."
>
> Since when is there a deadline for how long you have to try democracy before you can give up and shove whatever you want into law? If you're a Liberal, it's okay to bypass the democratic process. This is similar to them deciding early in the pandemic that they would like the power to tax and spend at will until the end of 2021, without Parliament having any say over it.
>
> Since mid-March, government in Canada has largely consisted of Prime Minister Justin Trudeau descending the steps at Rideau Cottage and decreeing what will and will not be done. This then is followed by a few questions from friendly journalists based largely in Quebec.
>
> **The longer the pandemic lasts, the more dictatorial the Liberals become."**

And now the minority Liberal government is moving rapidly forward to disarm law-abiding Canadian gun owners by stealth. They are not hiding their intentions.

> "Since May 1, the Liberals and RCMP have indeed been adding lots of shotguns to the ban. Worse yet, they have not been telling gun owners or the public...so they're sneaking around cramming as much in as they can under the cloak of the pandemic. It bans legal guns owned by law-abiding Canadians, and will be utterly useless as a crime-reduction strategy...it will increase the mistrust gun owners have for the police, especially the Mounties...and will undermine the rule of law." (Lorne Gunter, Liberals and RCMP have been quietly adding to the gun ban list, The Calgary Sun, June 7, 2020)

In their "long march through the institutions," the socialist left is now making its critical move toward UN-mandated, civil disarmament in Canada; and doing it while the country is distracted and preoccupied with the CCP virus pandemic.

> "In the fevered, sick minds of Statist Progressives, hell bent on the social re-engineering of Canadian society, government, culture and law...(who) hold the rights, freedoms and property of Canadians in contempt." (Blair Hagen, Our Future is Controlled at the Ballot Box, NFA Journal, September/October, 2019)

Socialists fear the law abiding gun owner because their form of Big Government necessarily means more and more restrictions on freedom. Those who prize individual freedom within a democratic society would be the first to oppose a complete, radical left-wing take over. Therefore, they must be disarmed before this happens. That is what the Trudeau Liberals are about, and the other socialist parties approve of their actions. There is also a broad faction within the Conservatives that supports gun control.

CHAPTER 4: WARNINGS ON SOCIALISM & COMMUNISM

"Compliance is not the goal. Confiscation of property and firearms prohibitions are the goal. Firearms confiscation and buybacks are popular programs for the *Utopian socialist civil disarmament lobby." (Blair Hagen, Non-compliance? NFA Journal, September/October, 2019)

* "Utopia – an ideal state where perfection exists in social life, politics and government (but) impossible of realization." (Winston College Dictionary)

RE: Public Health Board – "One could even say that their uncritical acceptance of this Marxist analysis, dividing society into oppressor (bourgeois) and victim (proletariat) groups, exposed their leftist politics. Understanding this way of thinking is important to the gun debate, because it is the same sort of thinking underlying a great deal of their anti-gun arguments." (Bruce Gold, The Public Health Approach to Violence, NFA Journal, March/April, 2020)

"The problems we face in Canada are, first, that bad gun control is deeply seated and ideological for the Liberals, and second, that the existing Liberal and Red Tory gun-control laws are broadly accepted by the Conservatives." (Sheldon Clare, History's Lessons, NFA Journal, March/April, 2020)

"For a government to arbitrarily demand the surrender of property based on ideological agenda, with no statistical evidence or mandate to back it up, defies explanation." (Blair Hagen, Predicting the Future, NFA Journal, January/February, 2020)

"Nowhere in the Canadian *Charter of Rights and Freedoms* is there a section that protects lawful gun ownership, as is the case in the United States with their renowned *Second Amendment*.

Even though Canadian (or American) society has not reached the point of chaos where citizens are forced to form militias, increasing instability is proof that people need the right to protect themselves." (Christ Mc. Garry,

> A Canadian Version of the Right to Keep & Bear Arms, NFA Journal, January/February, 2020)

> "The United Nations Human Rights Council has declared that only (national) states have the right to self-defence and there is no human right to personal self-defence." (Bruce Gold, Blaming Guns to Hide Failure, NFA Journal, January/February, 2019)

The UN is working through member states for universal civilian disarmament. Their main target is the Western democracies. The socialist parties in Canada, and the Liberal government in particular are in strong agreement with the UN disarmament agenda, whose basic premise is this, "there is no human right to personal self-defence."

The leftist mainstream media continue to demonize gun ownership and promote gun bans and buybacks, supporting the UN, Democrat and Liberal civil disarmament agendas.

> "The UN Small Arms Programme of Action is aimed squarely at destroying firearms cultures in first-world nations like Canada and the United States...civil disarmament through economic, political, legal and bureaucratic warfare. I can assure you this new kind of warfare has just as many ramifications on your future, your family's future, your culture, your beliefs and your values as the violent conflicts of the past. We either stand and fight this now or fade into the misty oblivion of UN globalist civil disarmament." (Blair Hagen, Consultations to Confiscate, NFA Journal, January/February, 2019)

John Lott, an economics professor at the U. of Chicago, statistically examined over 54,000 observations taken across 3,000 counties in the U.S. for 18 years, and in his landmark 1998 book, "More Guns, Less Crime," concluded the following:

CHAPTER 4: WARNINGS ON SOCIALISM & COMMUNISM

> "Allowing citizens without criminal records or histories of significant mental illness to carry concealed handguns deters violent crimes and appears to produce an extremely small and statistically insignificant change in accidental deaths; deters all types of murders; all areas benefit (but) urban areas benefit the most; women and minorities obtain the largest benefits; there is a drop in the murders of children; causes criminals to leave an area; is the most cost-effective means of reducing crime; and is an equalizer for physically weaker victims (women and elderly) and states with the most guns have the lowest crime rates.
>
> The fundamental issue (for non-discretional conceal-carry) is personal protection. Preventing law-abiding citizens from carrying handguns does not end violence; it merely makes victims more vulnerable to attack.
>
> Will allowing law-abiding citizens to carry concealed handguns save lives? The answer is yes, it will."

Lott's research, taken in a professional and unbiased manner, has never been refuted or proven wrong. Yet, the leftist legacy media continue to demonize gun ownership and promote gun bans and buybacks, supporting the leftist UN, Democrat and Liberal disarmament agenda.

Massad F. Ayoob, "recognized internationally as one of the world's leading authorities on police weaponry," wrote in his book, "In the Gravest Extreme: The Role of the Firearm in Personal Protection," 1980, as follows:

> In his book Dedication – *"To my mother, Mary Elizabeth Ayoob, who approved when my father taught me defensive weaponry at an early age...and thus probably preserved me to write this book."*
>
> "The author believes personally that the citizen has the right to kill in defense of innocent life; the dead attacker

> waived his own right to live when he threatened to wrongly deprive a victim of his." (p. 2)
>
> "The license to carry concealed, deadly weapons in public is not a right, but a privilege. To be worthy of this privilege, one must be both discrete and competent with the weapon. The gun-carrying man (or woman) who lacks either attribute is a walking time bomb. The responsible man who carries a gun does not respond to emotional provocation as he might if unarmed." (pp. 81-82)
>
> The lethal force of a handgun is only warranted when the citizen is in the *gravest extreme of immediate, unavoidable, deadly danger* – of death or grave bodily harm to oneself or another innocent person." (pp. 90 & 93)

Alberta's current UCP government is defending the gun owners under its jurisdiction. Unless other provincial governments act the federal government will disarm law-abiding Canadian citizens.

> "An expert panel will craft firearms policy upholding "Alberta values alongside a push to do all forensic testing in the province. Those moves accompany an earlier vow to establish a provincial chief firearms officer and an Alberta parole board. "Those law-abiding Albertans should not be used as scapegoats for criminals by politicians in Ottawa," said Premier Jason Kenny."

Law-abiding is the key word. Disarming law-abiding citizens works against safety and crime reduction simply because, as Manning wrote; it "leaves the population helpless." A helpless society or individual is easily subjugated by malignant force.

The Second Amendment in the U.S. Constitution (notwithstanding an individual state's intervention) was put there by the founding fathers who believed –

CHAPTER 4: WARNINGS ON SOCIALISM & COMMUNISM

> "that an armed citizenry is the ultimate bulwark against tyrannical (despotic, cruel, overbearing) government. Possibly our trust in government has risen so much that we no longer fear what future governments might do." (Lott, More Guns, Less Crime, 1998)
>
> "Totalitarianism remains a constant temptation for our rulers." (Harley Price, Civil Liberties, RIP: Big Brother's Lethal 'Cure,' The Epoch Times, p. B6, May 14-20, 2020)

It is much easier for a leftist government seeking uncontested rule and authority to do it over a population that has no recourse to resist. This is the real reason behind the restrictive gun legislation from the start. Leftist politicians fear the people. It does not target criminals but law-abiding citizens who would most object to authoritarian rule. In the last issue of the NFA Journal (September-October, 2020) the seriousness of Canada's erosion of civil liberties is made plain. If this travesty can happen to law-abiding gun owners, it can happen to any citizen under any future pretense.

> "As we have seen, this whole process of RCMP-driven, OIC (Order in Council)-promulgated law is offensive to justice and contrary to our most basic legal traditions. The process is secretive. This is, in its effect, **a bill of attainder** nullifying that person's civil rights and their right to property. As Canadian citizens, the law is our property just as much as it is any bureaucrat, politicians or judge's. Neither Trudeau nor his Liberal party have the right or privilege of abusing our laws or us in this manner."

The basic tenet of Marxism is the abolition of private property. Guns are property, so the root of this socialist gun-control project is civil-disarmament prior to more draconian laws taking away further citizens' rights and properties in the future. It is a tried and proven method of establishing dictatorships all around the world.

Rudolf Rummel, a professor at the University of Hawaii wrote, "Death by Government" in 1987. He concluded that the more centralized power a government has, the more lethal its use of that power becomes. That is why the greatest murderers of all time have been totalitarian governments of their own unarmed, innocent civilians. That is why Mr. Manning, as a law-abiding lover of democratic freedoms, opposed civil disarmament.

5. Undermine faith and confidence in the country's leaders

"Destroy the people's faith in their national leaders by holding them up to contempt and ridicule."

There is an old saying that if you get the head, you get the body too. If you can discredit the leader you can beat their party and win the election. It is all about power, and truth is not the issue. That is why the left-wing media concentrate on casting doubt and fear on political leaders, especially conservatives. They do it everywhere, all the time.

> "CBC and Antifa have a common enemy – Donald Trump and conservatives more broadly – and thus, apparently, the CBC feels comfortable promoting Antifa tactics. CBC once did a friendly interview with the author of an Antifa political handbook, where the author repeatedly justified violence while the host nodded along." (Candice Malcolm, Antifa, encouraged by the media, grows by spreading fear and paranoia, The Calgary Sun, August 18, 2018)

Increasingly, the purpose of a mainstream media interview or in-depth study isn't to inform or explain the views of a public figure, but to ruin their reputation. The interview is designed to trap the person into saying

CHAPTER 4: WARNINGS ON SOCIALISM & COMMUNISM

something that will expose or cause loss of confidence in him or her in the public arena.

> "We see this most obviously in the obsessive preoccupation of the mainstream media with Trump-bashing – the so-called Trump Derangement Syndrome (TDS). Concerning Trump's triumphant welcome by a huge crowd of well-wishers in India NPR reported – about the damage resulting from Trump's mispronunciation of Indian names...nothing to do with the size or importance of the mass welcome or its political significance to U.S. – India relations. I don't recall any discussion on NPR of any of the president's many achievements, economic, social, or in foreign policy, where the emphasis wasn't on belittling those achievements or denying them outright.
>
> Those who should be professionally committed to truth and objectivity renounce such concerns in practice, and often deny their possibility in theory. Habits of mind so evident in the media become vehicles for propaganda and indoctrination rather than information and education." (Paul Adams, Gotcha! The High Cost of Hit-Piece Journalism, p. B1, The Epoch Times, March 12-18, 2020)

Justin Trudeau's agenda, with the mainstream media's help, is to delegitimize, exclude and marginalize whoever he disagrees with, especially all Conservative voters. He considers them a fringe group not welcome in his polite society. In the 2019 federal election Trudeau and his Liberal henchmen –

> "used every dirty trick in the book to paint their conservative opponents as white nationalists, white supremacists and members of the alt-right. The media happily played along, grasping at straws to vindicate the invented Liberal narrative." (Candice Malcolm, Divisive Grit tactics make Tory leadership race so important, The Calgary Sun, May 25, 2020)

"FORTRESS AMERICA" UNDER SIEGE

The Liberals under Trudeau are mean, very mean. That is the character of the leader. He will pull no stops in destroying anyone who gets in his way, including his own people. That is a far-left characteristic. It is Marxist hate.

> "Last week, Canadian witnessed Trudeau's new, disgusting, ultra-personal smears against Conservative Leader Andrew Scheer, calling his main rival soft on neo-Nazism and white supremacy. The PM's character assassination is one of the lowest, most-despicable attacks we can recall in Canadian politics." (Editorial, The Calgary Sun, April 28, 2019)

Nearly identical methods were used by Rachel Notley's socialist NDP against the United Conservative Party and its leader, Jason Kenny, in the 2019 provincial election. Here are some examples:

> "Most Alberta voters ignored spurious allegations Kenny's secret agenda was to install an anti-immigrant, anti-woman, pro-white supremacist government. The highest volume from the NDP didn't come from saying Kenny had the wrong ideas. He was not a political opponent. He was a bad man. It naturally followed for the NDP faithful to ask who could vote for such a bad man...In short, sewer rats. (Rick Bell, Campaign and suffering – Notley NDP, this historic defeat is your fault, The Calgary Sun, April 17, 2019)

The NDP also attacked a Nigerian-born black man, Kaycee Madu who was running for the UCP in Edmonton:

> "Madu was defamed as a white supremacist sympathizer by his opponent after Madu posted a photo of himself with a campaign sign on a lawn that said, "StopNotley.com," which had a small logo from The Rebel media organization in the right top corner. Madu, who has a law degree, responded, "Our focus remains ensuring that we rebuild our economy. We have zero

CHAPTER 4: WARNINGS ON SOCIALISM & COMMUNISM

> interest in divisive and identity politics and politics of personal attacks and destruction, which are the focus of the NDP because they cannot afford to campaign on their record of economic failures." (Licia Corbella, How not to run a campaign, The Calgary Sun, April 18, 2019)

Premier Jason Kenny has since appointed Mr. Madu to the position of Alberta's Minister of Justice.

Exactly the same thing is going on in the United States with the incessant, vitriolic attacks on Donald Trump by the Democratic Party and their media friends. Donald Trump currently stands in the way of this totalitarian leftist movement in the United States and his influence is effecting the whole world. On Independence Day, 2020, President Trump visited Mt. Rushmore, South Dakota, and said:

> "Make no mistake, this left-wing Cultural Revolution is designed to overthrow the American Revolution. Our children are taught in school to hate their own country." (Jeff Mason, 'Left-wing revolution' ripped, Reuters, in The Calgary Sun, July 5, 2020).
>
> He accused "angry mobs" of trying to erase history with efforts to remove or rethink monuments to U.S. historical figures and used a speech at Mount Rushmore to paint himself as a bulwark against left-wing extremism." (Ibid).

That is why there is so much hatred toward him from the left. He is blocking their agenda. The leftist Democratic Party wants to see him defeated in the November, 2020, U.S. election, **no matter what**!

> Re: the 3 main U.S. media networks: "In 2017, 90% of media coverage on Trump was negative; in 2018 it was 91%..."Without question, no president has ever been on the receiving end of such hostile coverage, for such a sustained period of time, as has Trump. His outspokenness threw liberals into a panic. Armed with

the mainstream media, they lashed out with an all-out assault against Trump." (Media Research Center, in The Epoch Times, "How the Spectre of Communism is Ruling Our World," Hijacking the Media, Chapter 13, 2020)

Trump is attacked and demonized because he strongly advocates the restoration of tradition, and his ideals cannot coexist with the anti-traditional ideology of the left.

It is not the slightest exaggeration to say that the communists and socialists drive Democratic Party policy formation. The Congressional Progressive Caucus is effectively part of the world communist movement and it's about to become the dominant faction in the Democratic Party."

The mainstream media is treasonous. They suppressed and ignored reporting on bombshell allegations against Joe Biden and his son Hunter just before the U.S. election.

"Now Joe could be on the verge of winning the presidency and there is little or no reporting on the Hunter Biden laptop story, a Biden family business transaction involving agents of the Chinese government, and how all the Biden family business relates back to Joe's political connections. The American media's treatment of negative stories about Joe..Ignore anything that might hurt the guy we like. **The American people deserve to know the whole truth on both candidates before voting. Too bad they won't get it on one of them.**"
(Brian Lilley, Biden their time, The Calgary Sun, October 29, 2020)

The virulent attacks on President Trump and his administration are coming from a country infiltrated at most key levels by committed socialists and communists. For example, a New York Times columnist wrote:

CHAPTER 4: WARNINGS ON SOCIALISM & COMMUNISM

> "Mitch McConnell, Barr and almost everyone else in the GOP, have made themselves numb to abhorrent (loathsome, detestable) actions because of self-interest." To support Trump is to be morally flawed. Let's face it, most of the media thinks most of Trump supporters are stupid or evil. Incredibly, secular elites have appointed themselves judges of moral character. This contempt of the left for ordinary Americans is not new." (Hugh Hewitt, The searing, self-destructive disdain of the left, The Calgary Sun, May 31, 2019)

These attacks are meant to undermine and destroy the peoples' confidence and faith in their leaders, past and present, particularly the conservative ones like Mr. Trump. The same situation prevails in Canada.

> "Dinesh D'Souza in his book, "The Big Lie: Exposing the Nazi Roots of the American Left," 2017, attributes the current narrative that socialism is somehow separate from Nazism and fascism and, even more so, the belief that these are somehow divorced from their communist origins is a 'narrative shift' to what Sigmund Freud called "transference," based on his idea that people who commit terrible acts often transfer blame onto others, including their victims, of being what they themselves are."

The attacks documented above on conservative politicians are eerily similar everywhere because of worldwide infiltration by international socialism-communism. Mr. D'Souza shows that what the communists accuse their victims (mainly conservatives) of being is exactly what the socialists-communists are themselves, a case of "transference," or the 'pot calling the kettle black.' If they think of conservatives as the Democrat Hillary Clinton's "basket of deplorables" or the "sewer rats" of Rachel Notley's NDP now, then what would they do to them if they had control in a totalitarian environment? Here are some indications.

"FORTRESS AMERICA" UNDER SIEGE

> "Hollywood is one leg of the Axis of Indoctrination, with media and academia completing the trifecta. "This place hates Republicans, and hates Donald Trump to a degree I've never seen. You're the enemy, and they're blatantly against you and proud of it." (Larry Elder, Hollywood in the Trump era: Conservatives not welcome, The Calgary Sun, March 9, 2020)

> "Peter Fonda called for Trump's youngest son to be taken away and placed alongside pedophiles. A sometimes CBC comedy writer wrote to Donald Trump, Jr., "We're coming for Chloe, too." Chloe Trump is the president's 4-year-old granddaughter." (Anthony Furey, Trump hatred has become a drug, an addictive and dangerous drug, The Calgary Sun, June 26, 2018)

What we are witnessing is a communist revolution right in our midst without guns being fired, with the people unaware of what is happening. That is, until it is too late to stop. Nikita Khrushchev said in 1959/60 that the communists would defeat us without firing a shot. He was right. It doesn't stop at Trump.

> "The left has gone positively berserk in their almost maniacally hateful persecution of Supreme Court Associate Justice Brett Kavanaugh. Throwing out due process and abandoning any pretense of caring about the truth, hate-filled leftists have adopted a scorched-earth campaign against Kavanaugh that spills over onto his family." (Mark Hendrickson, Ominous Signs of Hated in Politics, The Epoch Times, p. B1, October 17-23, 2019)

Fortunately, there is still some coherent, sane reporting in the media. Here is an unusual example:

> "There can be good fun to be had in watching peoples' heads explode when you make the case for the re-election of Donald Trump, which I am about to do. Trump has not only been right on many of the key big issues, but the gut impulses of this real estate developer turned

CHAPTER 4: WARNINGS ON SOCIALISM & COMMUNISM

> reality TV star have been further ahead of the curve than those schooled at the finest public policy institutes." (Anthony Furey, Looks like it's time for a pro-Trump column, The Calgary Sun, June 28, 2020).

The media wields extraordinary power in the communications age; for good or for bad. It can sway public opinion 10 or 15 points and mean the difference in elections. It probably determined Stephen Harper's defeat in the 2015 election, and Andrew Scheer's loss to Justin Trudeau in the 2019 election. The people end up believing the lies.

> "The liberal media have been killing entire forests telling us about how badly Andrew Scheer and the Conservatives did in the Oct. 21 election." (Lorrie Goldstein, Panicking Conservatives only help Trudeau, The Calgary Sun, November 7, 2019)

The Conservative defeat was far from lopsided, as Mr. Goldstein showed.

The Bible explains it this way:

> "Be not deceived: evil communications corrupt good manners." (1 Corinthians 15:33)

Those who watch and listen to the leftist-controlled legacy media are persuaded of the leftist agenda through misinformation, disinformation and propaganda (p. 155). This is a form of psychological warfare that the leftist socialists-communists are masters of. The TV viewers are unaware of it.

Erasing history and tradition is a communist strategy. The CCP has done that in China. Now it is being done in America because "Black Lives Matter." Nancy Pelosi, Democratic House Speaker, and closely allied with the influential socialist-communist faction in her party wants to do away with 11 statues of historical American figures, including Jefferson Davis and Alexander Stephens, the president and vice-president of the former Confederate States of America. Socialists would like to erase or deconstruct vital parts of American and Canadian history, thereby destroying the people's connection to their past. That is part of leftist (communism's) strategy of discrediting Western democracies' historical leaders, past or present.

A statue of Sir John A. Macdonald, Canada's first prime minister and an architect of Confederation was defaced in Charlottetown, P.E.I. on June 19, 2020.

> "A statue of Sir John A. Macdonald was doused in red paint...the latest in a series of defaced sculptures and monuments depicting historical figures across Canada...(and) across the world are being vandalized and torn down in the wake of protests against anti-black and anti-indigenous racism, and similar incidents in Canada are mounting." (Teresa Wright, The Canadian Press, in The Calgary Sun, June 20, 2020)

Brad Bird, an award-winning reporter of English and Cree background wrote concerning Macdonald:

> "Liberal opponent Wilfred Laurier called him, "the foremost Canadian of his time." Another contemporary said, "his work – a nation – stands as his monument." John Thompson, his successor, said he was a man of "great amiability" and "gentleness of nature;" his devotion to Canada, unmatched. Macdonald, in the 1880s, was the first leader in the world to try to give women the vote. In 1885, he tried to give Indigenous men the vote, but the Liberals opposed it." (The Epoch Times, Macdonald's Record Refutes the Campaign Against Him, p. B5, June 25-July 1, 2020)

This attack against the founders of our great nation is a planned, concerted attack our traditional culture. What

CHAPTER 4: WARNINGS ON SOCIALISM & COMMUNISM

are they going to replace these statues with? Marx, Stalin, Jinping, Castro?

Communism expert and author Trevor Loudon called the statue defacing and toppling a "Maoist tactic of erasing the form of culture." (Bowen Xiao, Amid US Unrest, Some Now Call for Toppling of Jesus Statues, The Epoch Times, June 25-July 1, 2020). The article continued:

> "'As statues of historical American figures, including those of former presidents, are being forcibly torn down across the U.S., Black Lives Matter activists are now beginning to target Christianity, calling for statues of Jesus to be torn down...labelling them as "racist propaganda." "They are following the line of the Chinese Cultural Revolution that wiped out the previous Chinese culture. They toppled statues and desecrated monuments," said Loudon.'"

> "Senate Majority Leader, Mitch McConnell noted on June 23, "This far-left anger is sparing some heroes of their own. I understand that in Seattle, a large statue of Vladimir Lenin stands quite untouched."

Sir Winston Churchill, Britain's great wartime leader helped his country overcome National Socialist (Nazi) Germany. He opposed socialism-communism, and rallied the British people in their darkest hour in 1940-41. In 2020, his memory is held in contempt by young radicals, as statues of historical figures, including Churchill's, are being vandalized, boarded up or covered to protect them from further damage because of anti-racism "Black Lives Matter" protests over the death of George Floyd in Minneapolis. Britain's Prime Minister Boris Johnson tweeted,

> "It is absurd and shameful that this national monument should today be at risk of attack by violent protesters."

"FORTRESS AMERICA" UNDER SIEGE

(Michael Holden and Elizabeth Piper, Reuters, in Calgary Sun, June 13, 2020)

"Destroying national heritage is a fundamental communist tactic used to indoctrinate societies with Marxist ideology as a prelude to revolution." (Ryan Moffatt, Erasing Historical Statues a Monumental Mistake, The Epoch Times, June 25-July 1, 2020). The article continued:

> "One of Marxism's primary aims is to sever a population's link to the past. The longer and richer the history, the more resistant a nation is to the influence of foreign ideologies. In China, communists realized early on that political, cultural, and philosophical traditions gave people a measuring stick to assess the Marxist ideology they were promoting. To mitigate this problem, Mao Zedong, a man responsible for the death of 80 million Chinese citizens, launched the 10 year Cultural Revolution to purge society of its traditions and impose (Marxist) Maoism as the dominant ideology. Violent class struggle, purges, exile and persecution of anyone or anything with ties to China's past rendered China wholly disconnected from its 5000 year history...the fear-ridden populace was readily assimilated to Marxist ideology.
>
> Destroying statues is symbolic; burning down and trashing cities is a premeditated assault on American civilization, not hot-headed and aggrieved impetuosity. BLM is not principally an organization that mourns the fate of victims of mistreatment like George Floyd; it is more notably an anti-white racist and urban guerilla movement that is going to have to be dealt with as a threat to the elemental rights of all citizens of every pigmentation and to public security." (Conrad Black, Ignorance, Malice, and Racism Assault the Reminders of Past Generations, The Epoch Times, p. B1, September 3-9, 2020).

The left has taught an entire generation of the most privileged Americans to view the world through "race-

CHAPTER 4: WARNINGS ON SOCIALISM & COMMUNISM

tinted glasses." Larry Elder, a colored conservative journalist wrote as follows:

> "There were 13 Baltimore high schools where, in 2017, 0% of students could do math at grade level, and another half-dozen high schools where only 1% were math proficient. Do you really think these students even know enough about Gen. Thomas "Stonewall" Jackson to be mad at him? Shouldn't monuments and schools dedicated to Barak Obama come down? After all, Obama's ancestors on his white mother's side were slave owners. Can we skip to the part where the "protesters" who burned and looted stores denounce business owners as racist for refusing to rebuild?
>
> A 2013 Rasmussen poll of Whites, Blacks and Hispanics ranked Blacks as the group with most racists. Blacks are more than twice as likely to be anti-Semitic than whites. If the USA is "institutionally racist," why stop at defunding the police? Why not defund public school education? There are far more, bad public school teachers than there are bad cops. And it practically takes an act of Congress to get a bad public school teacher fired." (Larry Elder, Random thoughts while not out protesting, The Calgary Sun, July 6, 2020).

In "Welcome to Maoist America," Roger Simon writes, "This cultural revolution began decades ago on our campuses and in our media. Now, it's taking over our streets." (The Epoch Times, p. B6, June 18-24, 2020).

> "But it's our schools, primarily, that have been the instigators of this...from kindergarten through Ph.D. Viewpoint diversity is a thing of the past, with faculty meetings morphing into our own versions of Maoist "struggle sessions," teachers and professors first shutting their mouths if they disagree, then exercising what amounts to "self-criticism" to save their jobs or just gain some peace. Our media, of course, are the products of the same educational system and have long been prepared to ratify and amplify these same behaviors and

views. The communications and journalism departments of our universities are literal fonts of groupthink, training students to be propagandists for the glorious new future. **While for Mao, social class was the lever of control, in our society today, it's almost always race."**

In Calgary, a few years back the Langevin Bridge across the Bow River had its name changed by City Council to Reconciliation Bridge without any input from the citizens. Another case of 'groupthink,' apologizing for past injustices against indigenous peoples, taking away another small part of our local history. There are better ways to do this.

Anyone can be disgraced and destroyed today, not only political leaders but any person with views diverging from the new-leftist normal, no matter how distinguished or credible. For example, the destruction of free speech for a renowned Canadian professor:

> "Tomas Hudlicky, a 70 year old distinguished Tier 1 Canada research chair in organic chemistry at Brock University in Ontario, disapproved of "preferential" hiring from among selective identity groups, "is counter-productive if it results in discrimination against the most-meritorious candidate." (And his) remarks on "masters and apprentices" for skills transference. His opinion, "many students are unwilling to submit any level of hard work demanded by professors...the university views students as assets and protects them from any undue hardships demanded by the "masters."
>
> Ominously, Brock's VP and provost (chief official) wrote, "further steps are being considered and developed," (against Hudlicky). Kay spoke with Hudlicky...the show trial he was subjected to reminds him of the totalitarian environment he thought he had left behind, The Twitter mob – all chemists – "managed to destroy my career in chemistry." Hudlicky's family had "escaped communist Czechoslovakia...and built their home in the free West.

CHAPTER 4: WARNINGS ON SOCIALISM & COMMUNISM

> It would be ironical if "the very same forces of censorship and intolerance that forced Tomas Hudlicky from his homeland would silence him in Canada." (Barbara Kay, Show Trial of Distinguished Professor Over Essay a Disgrace, The Epoch Times, p. A5, June 18-24, 2020).

"Why do we see the campus in such an intolerant condition today? People are afraid to speak out. The work they completed from high school on, that secured a favorable nod from superiors, has been internalized into a general state of mind: "I want your approval." They pass through their professional spheres to tenured professor in a more or less binding chill. Only a firm counterforce will reopen the campus to a wider spectrum of opinion. We need more professors to stand tall. The more of them who do, the easier it will be for others to do so." (Mark Bauerlein, The Reasons Behind Conformity in Academia, The Epoch Times, p. B6, August 7-12, 2020).

Those who are part of the mainstream media should recognize that objectivity and impartiality are the basic ethical requirements of their profession, and are key to the trust people place in it. If they wish to remain the propaganda arms of the left wing political movement, one day they, too, and their children and grandchildren will suffer the wrath of totalitarianism. It's not worth it. They need to return to the basics of truth and tradition.

The reader is invited to refer to Appendix 4 to read first-hand the kind of life the Czechoslovakian people lived under communism.

We have very little time left to try and preserve our free speech and free democracy.

6. Create civil strife and disorder, and allow it to continue

"FORTRESS AMERICA" UNDER SIEGE

"Foment strikes in general industries. Encourage civil disorders and foster a lenient and soft attitude on the part of the government towards disorders."

As the U.S. convulses with violence in the summer of 2020 the American Attorney General, William Barr, stated:

> "Democrats grilled William Barr over the Justice Department's crackdowns on racial justice protests. Barr said liberals are intent on "tearing down the system. They are a revolutionary group that is interested in some form of socialism, communism," he said of Black Lives Matter. "They're essentially Bolsheviks." (The Calgary Sun, August 11, 2020).

Bolsheviks were the followers of the party of revolutionary socialism which established the Soviet form of government in Russia in 1917.

Two recent articles show that the violence is still continuing in some areas.

> "Protests in several major cities across the country turned violent this weekend, as weeks of civil unrest and clashes between activists and authorities boiled over, sending thousands of people teeming into public squares, demanding racial justice." (Protests explode across U.S., The Calgary Sun, July 27, 2020)

> "Crowds swarmed Chicago's luxury commercial district early Monday, looting stores, smashing windows and clashing with officers for hours, police said. Police sent 400 officers into the area, where they were met by caravans of people arriving in cars." (Looters run riot in Chicago, The Calgary Sun, August 11, 2020).

To obtain their objective of winning power, a pattern of violence is coming from Leftist activists, particularly

CHAPTER 4: WARNINGS ON SOCIALISM & COMMUNISM

those affiliated with the group that calls itself Antifa, a group of...

> "Young adults, brainwashed by Marxist university professors about the supposed evils of Western liberal democracy, believe in communism, anarchy, open borders, street-fighting and constantly organize protests. They hate the police, the media and conservatives. Despite their open hostility, CBC, CNN and many other biased news outlets have provided glowing coverage of Antifa. In May, 2020, the group released a terrorist how-to guide, including instructions on how to build bombs, sabotage infrastructure and evade the police." (ibid)

Black Lives Matter's website says, "Together, we can – and will – transform. This is the revolution. Change is coming." The organization's founders refer to themselves as "trained Marxists." (Kevin Richard, Revolution is Dangerously Overrated, The Epoch Times, p. B3, August 6-12, 2020).

> "BLM states that it wants to abolish the nuclear family, police, prisons and capitalism aiming to transform the U.S. – and the entire world – into a communist dystopia. Their mentors include former members of a radical, 'left-wing' terrorist group that sought a communist revolution in the U.S. in the 1960s and 1970s. They are training militias. Their immediate goal is to remove President Donald Trump from office. Donations are linked to the Democratic Party. If there is systemic racism today it is racism against white people, in the sense that white people are told they are responsible for all the evils in the world." (Soeren Kern, The Gatestone Institute, from ACT for America, July, 2020).

Canada also experienced anarchical protests in 2020. Illegal blockades set up by deceitful, radical environmentalists claiming to speak for Indigenous people, shut down much of Canada's railway system early in 2020.

"FORTRESS AMERICA" UNDER SIEGE

> "The illegal blockades were not only inconveniencing the public but damaging the economy, endangering jobs and risking public safety by, for example, choking off vital supplies to hospitals and chlorine to water treatment plants." (Lorrie Goldstein, The 'Un-Prime Minister,' The Calgary Sun, February 16, 2020)

Journalists covering this event shied away from the real source of the damaging protests, except for Candice Malcolm. In "Country in Turmoil – Trudeau Missing in Action," she wrote, "The far-left in Canada is out of control":

> "The Coastal GasLink pipeline has already been approved by the courts as well as every level of government, and was given the green light from 20 band councils, including the elected band leaders of the Wet'suwet'en First Nation.
>
> Deceitful environmentalist protesters claiming to speak for Indigenous people have set up illegal barricades across the country. They've blocked railways and highways – closing major thoroughfares, shutting down commercial and passenger rail and grinding our economy to a halt.
>
> Mainstream media have distorted the issue with euphemisms (pleasing words) to downplay the actions of the radical environmentalist left, calling their illegal actions "civil disobedience" and "peaceful protests." While an overwhelming number of First Nations voices are in support of the project and the pipeline, too many in the media have described these as "First Nations protestors: and the Indigenous cause." Even CBC's John Tasker pointed out the media's biased and erroneous coverage.
>
> We are on the brink of a national crisis. The rule of law is breaking down, the economy is in disarray and any remaining confidence in our system is quickly vanishing. And Trudeau is off on a vanity tour of Africa vying for a

CHAPTER 4: WARNINGS ON SOCIALISM & COMMUNISM

seat on the UN Security Council." (Candace Malcolm, The Calgary Sun, February 16, 2020).

Trudeau was out of the country when the blockade chaos was boiling, and when he returned he would not intervene with determination to end it, deferring the matter to the police, who did little to nothing, thus allowing the civil strife and disorder to continue and grow.

> "First Nations leaders gave a press conference (and) distanced themselves from these blockades and encouraged them to wind down. Instead, Trudeau continued to pretend that the radical activists who are appropriating the First Nations agenda to serve their own goals somehow represent the voices of all First Nations. Non-First Nations activists who are focused on climate change activism are the driving forces behind the blocking of major intersections and rail lines we're seeing across the country. **Trudeau would not acknowledge that.** Conservative Andrew Scheer did. Trudeau then said Scheer had "disqualified himself" from the conversation, and banned Scheer from a meeting of party leaders to discuss how to deal with this unfolding situation. Meanwhile, lawlessness continues." (Editorial, The Calgary Sun, February 20, 2020)

Only the conservatives were banned from the discussion for telling the truth, while four radical socialist parties would plan the way 'forward,' which went nowhere. They don't want it to go anywhere, for its suits their agenda. This is how a country loses its democratic freedom.

The Prime Minister thought that discussion and talk could resolve the blockades. They could not resolve the problem because the radical activists would settle for nothing less than a full-on "settler" (non-Indigenous whites) submission to revolution.

> "It should go without saying that reliance on "dialogue" or hesitation to enforce the law will only embolden those behind the blockades." (Shane Miller, Rail Blockades: The Destructive Spirit of the 1968 Paris Revolt Lives On," p. B1, The Epoch Times, (February 27-March 4, 2020)

The Liberal government and the mainstream leftist media qualify as Malcolm's "far-left" by virtue of their cooperation in creating and exacerbating this crisis. Trudeau's unjust environmental policies caused the turmoil over pipelines in the first place, and his reluctance to act to quell the unrest fits communism's sixth rule for destabilizing a free democratic society.

> "Yuri Bezmenov, a former Soviet spy who defected to Canada, called Marxist ideological subversion in universities' humanities departments "demoralization," which is delegitimizing the state by taking legitimate issues (institutionalized racism, sexism, etc.) and teaching they are endemic to the capitalist system and building a narrative that these issues can only be reversed by destroying the capitalist system and rebuilding a pure communist system.
>
> The fact that millions of former students were influenced by this ideology has, over the decades, led to fundamental changes coming about in society, so that today, radicals feel empowered to engage in unlawful acts like the rail blockades." (Ibid)

Trudeau allowed the radical environmental left to create the crisis, control the course of events and silence the overwhelming number of First Nations voices who were in support of the project and the pipeline, using a minority of hereditary chief's opposition as an excuse for the illegal blockades.

> "Members of the Mohawk nation block the line in support of the hereditary chiefs of the Wet'suwet'en in their opposition to a natural gas pipeline across their

CHAPTER 4: WARNINGS ON SOCIALISM & COMMUNISM

> traditional territory in northern British Columbia." (The Canadian Press, 'Situation very tense,' The Calgary Sun, February 16, 2020)

Three other Calgary Sun columns from February 20 give a sense of what Trudeau's handling of these blockades accomplished for Canada:

"'Rule of law' gets the finger" (Bonokoski)
"PM talking to no one" (Lilley)
"Express train to anarchy" (Bell)

An editorial in the Calgary Sun (June 28, 2020), "Cities must stand up to protestors," stated what needs to be done concerning protests that cross the line and become illegal.

> "The lesson is that municipal governments cannot indefinitely allow protestors to take over public or private property...it will be time for the occupiers to leave, first by asking politely, but then, if necessary, doing what needs to be done."

Shortly after the Canadian blockades the COVID-19 pandemic occurred.

> "The nationwide mass quarantine, social distancing and mandated lockdowns for months have been the source of endless fighting between the people and their governments. Red (Republican) and Blue (Democrat) states often adopted diametrically opposed policies." (Victor Davis Hanson, Bitter irony of revolution, The Calgary Sun, June 11, 2020)

COVID-19 lockdowns in the U.S. led to abuses of power by local politicians in many states. People responded angrily in demonstrations as they saw their Constitutional freedoms challenged:

> "In a growing number of states across the US, 10 so far, crowds of Americans are taking to the streets to protest against lockdown measures that have up-ended nearly every aspect of their day-to-day lives. They declared this crisis and we lost our rights overnight. Their life savings are being dwindled away. They're shuttering their businesses and are not allowed to work.
>
> Based on what we now know today, the lockdown measures, let alone the arrests and fines, are both unlawful and inappropriate," Matt Pinsker, an attorney and constitutional law professor at Virginia Commonwealth University, told the Epoch Times." (Bowen Xiao, Anti-Lockdown Protests Surge in US Amid Ongoing Fight Against Virus, The Epoch Times, p. A1, A5, April 23-29, 2020).

While it was peaking in some areas a cruel police action in Minneapolis led to the death of unarmed George Floyd, a colored man. His unfortunate death sparked violent "Black Lives Matter" protests across the U.S. and around the world.

The pattern of the protests were almost identical to the Canadian blockades. Radical far-left elements, not part of the black community, took control of peaceful protests, stirred up the people and initiated violence and destruction on a revolutionary scale. The mainstream media did not call out the radicals but tried to deflect the blame on President Trump, much like Trudeau and the mainstream media did toward Andrew Scheer in the Canadian blockades.

> "The (Minneapolis) police chief said the vast majority of protestors had been peaceful but there was a core group of demonstrators who had been focused on causing destruction." (Brendan O'Brien, Reuters, in The Calgary Sun, May 29, 2020)

CHAPTER 4: WARNINGS ON SOCIALISM & COMMUNISM

> "The violence is planned, organized and driven by anarchic and left extremist groups – far-left extremist groups...many of whom travel from outside the state to promote violence," U.S. Attorney General William Barr said in a statement." (Brendan O'Brien & Carlos Barria, Reuters, in The Calgary Sun, May 31, 2010)

The response to the riots in the U.S. was a paradox. The Democratic municipal and state governments of the worst hit areas, responded poorly. President Trump took a strong stand, and was bashed by the left-wing media for doing so. Conrad Black wrote in The Epoch Times (June 11-17, 2020), "Mayors, Generals and Journalists Vie For Most Dishonorable Response to US Crisis," the following:

> "In the chaos of the last two weeks, most of the corrupt, interminably incumbent Democratic municipal regimes were exposed as useless and cowardly. Minneapolis mayor Jacob Frey panicked, abandoning a police precinct encouraging the immediate destruction by fire of almost 200 businesses. New York's and Los Angeles' mayors announced cuts to police budgets in the week that saw the worst riots in the history of either city (in quantum damage).
>
> Trump made the right speech and the right gesture: churches and people's right to use them, peaceful protest, public and private property, and the public spaces of the country will be protected, and riot, arson, looting and general assault will be discouraged with whatever means are required."

The week before Trump displayed strong leadership and decisive statements concerning the crisis affecting America's cities:

> "President Donald Trump spoke for 99% of Americans in denouncing the tragic and criminal death of George Floyd, and for approximately 90% of Americans in denouncing in about equal voice the widespread looting

and arson in more than a score of the country's greatest cities."

The Democrats, and their mainstream media responded to the riots like Canada's Liberal Party and mainstream media responded to the illegal blockades. The only redemption for the U.S. was that the country had a conservative Republican government with a strong leader.

> "Instead of allowing him to speak for the country...the wall-to-wall Democratic national media downgraded the very extensive violence, prattled on about the right to peaceful protest – which the president specifically upheld – and accused Trump of tear-gassing peaceful demonstrators (untrue) in order to enjoy a photo-opportunity at St. John's Church, beside the White House. The Democrats, led by Joe Biden, effectively sided with the rioters, uttered the usual bunk about sources of discontent and comprehension of the frustration that causes righteous people to "lash out," and railed at the president...imputing nasty motives and twisting Trump's words." (Conrad Black, With Riots Threatening U.S., Trump Navigates Multiple Crises, p. B2, The Epoch Times, June 4-10, 2020)

Matthew Vadum wrote concerning Black Lives Matter, founded in 2013:

> "BLM grew out of the death of Black teen Trayvon Martin at the hands of George Zimmerman in 2013, (but) Zimmerman was later acquitted when evidence showed Martin was the aggressor. BLM is a radical left-wing movement that calls for defunding the police and providing Blacks with "reparations," for their slavery before the U. S. Civil War (1860-65). Alicia Garza, one of its founders, admires the Marxist revolutionary and convicted cop-killer, Assata Shakur, and reveres Angela Davis, who ran for vice-president in 1980 and 1984 on the Communist Party USA ticket with Gus Hall." (Matthew Vadum, Black Lives Matter Began With Claim

CHAPTER 4: WARNINGS ON SOCIALISM & COMMUNISM

of Systemic Racism, The Epoch Times, June 11-17, 2020)

Notably, the head of the Board of Directors of the University of British Columbia was censured for saying Black Lives Matter is a leftist organization. He resigned his position after being accused of white racism and being a supporter of white colonialism. (Global News, Calgary, June 21, 2020)

Heather Mac Donald, a fellow at the Manhattan Institute, and author of "The War on Cops," said –

> "Blacks commit about 60% of all homicides and robberies in the largest counties in the U.S., and they commit gun homicides at about 10 times the rate of whites and Hispanics combined. She said in 2016, 4,300 people were shot in Chicago – one person every two hours, and virtually all were Black. (Yet) BLM has never turned its focus to Black to Black crime, which is astronomically higher than any other grouping. "They (BLM) don't give a damn about Black Lives," said Mac Donald." (Charlotte Cuthbertson, Radical Call to Defund Police Emerges From Protests, The Epoch Times, p. A1, A5, June 11-17, 2020)

BLM isn't interested in Black Lives except if a life is lost that may help it fulfill its left-wing political agenda. People who peacefully protest in good will in BLM demonstrations do not know what the organization's real agenda is. They are among the "useful idiots" being used to accomplish the totalitarian socialist-communist takeover of North America.

> "As to the narrative that blacks hate and fear the police, polls say otherwise. A Monmouth University poll found that both blacks and whites gave "very-to-somewhat" satisfied responses to the police of 72%. As rapper Tupac Shakur said in a 1994 interview, blacks living in the ghetto fear and oppose the same criminal "villain"

element that police fear and oppose. The racial "diversity" achieved by city police departments, as in New York City and Los Angeles, has not and will not stop charges of "institutional racism" as long as many of the "reformers" true intent is for black criminals to go unpunished." (Larry Elder, Protesters seek diverse police forces, but will that matter? The Calgary Sun, June 15, 2020).

Lorrie Goldstein writes, "Use police race-crime data properly, or don't use it at all," in the August 13, 2020, Calgary Sun.

> "Thirty-one years ago (1989), Julian Fantino released statistics suggesting Black people in a trouble Toronto community were disproportionately involved in crime to counter allegations Toronto police were racist. He later became Toronto police chief and a cabinet minister in the Harper government."

Fantino later commented regarding Pierre Trudeau's Charter of Rights and Freedoms.

> "I never believed the Charter was designed to invent unreasonable and truly mind boggling schemes to protect criminals, but to a large degree that is exactly what has happened."

> Pre-Charter police focus was "guilt or innocence; post-Charter police focus was "conduct of police officers," and guilt or innocence took the back seat. (Vern White – assistant commissioner of RCMP). (Bob Plamondon, The Truth About Trudeau, 2013).

Goldstein (above) added, "If race-crime data are to be released, release all of it, not just arrest and charging data based on race, but data on those convicted of crimes based on race."

CHAPTER 4: WARNINGS ON SOCIALISM & COMMUNISM

All of this divisiveness and confusion makes policing more difficult and frustrating. It undermines law and order. What better way for a *Fabian socialist to cause Marxist class struggle and weaken a free democratic society from within.

> Fabian Society: a group of English socialists who seek to bring about change or reform by gradual development and education rather than by open aggression. Like the tactics of Fabius, a Roman general who overcame Hannibal by delays and harassments rather than by open battle. (Winston College Dictionary).

Trudeau said that everything he learned he learned from the Fabian socialist professor Harold Laski at the London School of Economics in the 1940s. To Laski, Marxism and individual equality aligned as fundamental principles of justice. Hence, Trudeau's Charter of Rights and Freedoms. Through this Charter with its apparent good intents came the undermining of the Judeo- Christian laws that governed our land from its inception. The writer believes that this was deliberately done for this exact purpose.

BLM seeks to weaken the police and render them ineffective bystanders to anarchy and coming revolution. That is the "true intent" behind their goal "for black criminals to go unpunished." The left-wing Democratic and Liberal political, academic and social justice ideologues applaud this objective in Canada and the United States, and elsewhere:

> "Black Lives Matter across Canada, in conjunction with Greenpeace, is calling for total elimination of both police and prisons. They are self-appointed activists who were not elected to solve anything. It is beyond doubtful that the majority of the public, regardless of race, gender or any other group has such a radical view.

> The problem is that many politicians at the moment are paralyzed with fear and the activists know it. Activist voices are amplified by the vacuum left through the inability of cowardly politician to fight back." (Jerry Agar, Time for push-back against this 'defund the police' narrative, The Calgary Sun, June 30, 2020).

Radical socialism seeks to intimidate their victims, demoralize and discredit them, and then destroy them. Strong public leadership is necessary to defend free democratic society from such radicals taking control. A weakened police force cannot properly defend the law-abiding citizens of a free democracy from far-left radical violence and intimidation.

> "Politicians across Canada are turning their back on the men and women who risk their lives to keep our communities safe. Desperate to keep up with trendy protesters and the radical demands of the far-left, hapless officials from all levels of government have been scoring cheap political points by needlessly and baselessly denouncing Canadian police officers. During a Black Lives Matter rally on Parliament Hill on June 5, Trudeau took a knee as part of the political theatre. Singh's words and Trudeau's actions are telling Canadians, particularly Indigenous and Black Canadians, that the police are racist and out to get them. Rather than supporting the heroes that keep us safe, politicians on the woke left are making their job even more difficult." (Candice Malcolm, Politicians are turning their back on Canada's police, The Calgary Sun, July 11, 2020).

Jonah Goldberg, in the August 8, 2020, Calgary Sun wrote:

> "Black people don't view police the same way the activists and journalists who dominate the debate do. Eighty-five percent of Black people reported that traffic stops they were involved in were conducted properly. The vast majority of Americans, of all races and

CHAPTER 4: WARNINGS ON SOCIALISM & COMMUNISM

ethnicities, don't want the police to leave their communities because a police-free modern society is simply unworkable – Just ask the former denizens of that "autonomous zone" in Seattle."

Of course the radical socialists and anarchists would like a police-free environment in which to conduct their Bolshevik revolution. Removing authority would make tearing down free democratic society much easier and taking power much simpler. And the story goes on here in Canada –

> "Calgarians can take part in a nationwide protest in support of Defund YYC, Black Lives Matter, Idle No More and Land Back movements. "We must keep putting pressure on those in power to make swift change...to alleviate all oppressions." (Alanna Smith, Calgary among cities hosting nationwide protest to urge police defunding, The Calgary Sun, August 29, 2020).

> "The annual Pride festival began Friday...with workshops on topics like Black queer leadership, LGBTQ 101 and 2S (2 spirit) identities." (Alanna Smith, COVID-19 can't stop Pride, The Calgary Sun, August 29, 2020).

Politicians who prostrate themselves by "bending the knee," like Trudeau did publicly, become useful idiots for the revolution. The same goes for those 'bending the permissive knee' toward the LGBTQ2S$^+$ movement. In the future they will be challenged further...to 'bow the permissive knee' to incest, pedophilia and bestiality. It's coming! The floodgates are open!

The communist government of China used such debasing and degrading tactics to gain and consolidate their power, forcing submission upon their citizens. The Epoch Times details some of their more recent torture methods, many of which resort to terrifying sexual means.

"FORTRESS AMERICA" UNDER SIEGE

> "Mao was particularly adept at forcing his victims to abase themselves, publicly confessing to assorted failures and "crimes" against the state.
>
> Police officers across the country kneel in homage to Black Lives Matter hooligans. We haven't quite got to the Struggle Sessions of Mao's Cultural Revolution...epitomized by the Tennessee police officer who declared that he knelt only before God as the mob screamed at him.
>
> What is wanted is the "decolonization" of one's personal library and private reading. From a woke writer for NPR, "If you are white, take a moment to examine your bookshelf."

Where is all of this headed?

> "The destructive, race-based histrionics we are seeing unfold before us on the nightly news are secretly orchestrated by the Democrats as one more assault on the administration of Donald Trump...as the laughable "Russia Collusion" narrative, as the bogus "abuse of power" and "contempt of Congress" charges, as blaming Trump for COVID-19 fallout, as the weaponized racial unrest from Black Lives Matter riots – the deep state's desperate attempt to defeat Trump in the 2020 election.
>
> A great contest – a stark choice – seems to have opened up. Partisans of Lincoln who think the U.S. was "conceived in liberty and [is] dedicated to the proposition that all men are created equal." The other side repudiates Lincoln and believes that the country was founded as a "slavocracy" and that the despicable behavior of a handful of white policemen and police brutality in general renders the whole American experiment a failure.
>
> **It's a choice between those who believe that the United States, whatever its imperfections, is a land of economic opportunity and political liberty and**

CHAPTER 4: WARNINGS ON SOCIALISM & COMMUNISM

> **those who think it is a transnational socialist regime in the making. I know what side I'm on."** (Roger Kimball, Adventures in Self-Abasement and Ideological Conformity, The Epoch Times, p. B5, B6, June 11-17, 2020)

What is happening today in the U.S. cities is approaching the kind of anarchy that the radical left desires to foment revolution for an eventual take-over of the country. The timing is critical and the stakes are high.

> "Mobs are taking over some U.S. cities, acting Department of Homeland Security Secretary Chad Wolf said on July 6 (2020). "It's very disturbing. It's lack of political leadership in that city. I think any city that is having increases in violence, is burning, is having the rioting, the looting, it's by choice at this point. But the president's been doing everything on our part from the federal side and saying that this is unacceptable and it's time for these Democrat governors and mayors to step up." Wolf believes the movement to defund the police is a contributing factor to violence in the cities. Nearly every top 20 U.S. city in terms of population is run by Democrat mayors." (Zachary Steiber, 'Criminal Mobs" Taking Over Cities Amid Spike in Violence: US Official, The Epoch Times, July 9-15, 2020).

The U.S. republic is in real peril, for the first time since its founding in 1776 as the greatest repository of freedom and democracy in the world.

> "White America is temporarily so shaken by the horrible and sadistic killing of George Floyd that it is ignoring or misreading movements that do not seek reform, fraternity, or leadership to "bring us together," but rather are trying to strike a mortal blow at the entire American project. President Trump has stumbled seriously, and the pandemic and coordinated media hostility have put his reelection in some doubt, though he has condemned racism, lawlessness, and attacks on rights and property

of individuals and on public monuments. He will have to raise his game or jeopardize the cause he is leading.

Americans should see Black Lives Matter clearly, and the threat of its New York leader, Hawk Newsome, to "burn society down." Unless what Mr. Lincoln called, "the better angels of our nature" prevail, the United States will enter a possibly irreversible decline on November 3, 2020." (Conrad Black, A Movement of Vindictive Hatred is Tearing Down Historic Statues, The Epoch Times, p. B2, July 2-8, 2020).

The continuity and violence of the current disorder when mixed with COVID-19 and damaged economies is a perfect storm for social change and revolution. Both Canada and the U.S. are in dangerous territory, and at a cross roads. It is time for the silent majority to take a stand.

> "A half century after the 60s revolution, today's cultural revolution is vastly different – and far more dangerous. America is far less resilient, and a far more divided, indebted and vulnerable target that it was in 1965...a welfare state, soaring divorce rates, waning nuclear family and skyrocketing immigration. Today, radicals are protesting against old liberals – radicals of the 60s – who now hold power, and sympathize with them. Their college debt impedes maturity, marriage, child-raising, home ownership and saving money. They are far more desperate and angry. The two blue (Democrats) coasts despise the red (Republican) interior, and vice versa. Now there are no conservatives in Hollywood, on campuses or in government bureaucracies. The war now pits socialists and anarchists against both liberals and conservatives. **In the 60s, a huge "silent majority" elected Richard Nixon and slowed down the revolution. Today, if there is a silent mass of traditionalists and conservatives they remain in hiding. If they remain quiet, the revolution will**

CHAPTER 4: WARNINGS ON SOCIALISM & COMMUNISM

> **steamroll on**." (Victor Davis Hanson, Why this revolution isn't like the 60s, The Calgary Sun, July 24, 2020).

It does not take a large number of committed revolutionaries to take over a country if people remain silent and do nothing to stop it. J. Edgar Hoover, head of the F.B.I., said that there were more Communists in America in the 1950s (1/1,814 persons) than there were in Russia when they overthrew that government in 1917 (1/2,227 persons). Their genius is not to have too many "known Communists," or members of their party, but to have the right people placed in the right places for the right and "ripe" time for the revolution (E. J. Daniels, The Red Devil of Communism, 1954). That may be what we are seeing today in the U.S. as the violence rages on. Certainly, there are many more socialist-communist subversives and their "fellow-travelers" in that country in 2020 than in the mid-1950s. The same can be said for Canada. That is why North America is in such peril today.

It is in China's strategic interests that turmoil continue in the U.S. especially as the election nears. Their primary objective is to remove President Donald Trump from office and see a Democratic candidate elected in his place. Using Canadian connections to fuel riots in the U.S. is alluded to by John Mills, in an October 15-21, 2020, Epoch Times article entitled, "Coincidences in Vancouver Suggest China Money Laundering Could Be Funding Disruption in US."

> "A Vancouver-based group nondescriptly called "Adbusters" is also the group that was, and perhaps still is, planning the "Siege of Washington D.C." to disrupt the U.S. election. The Chinese Progressive Association also has a large footprint in Vancouver (and) has been tied directly to the CCP as well as to Black Lives Matter. Canada and the United States should exercise their

historic relationship and friendship to more diligently address the curious, high-cash operations enabled by CCP-associated groups in Vancouver."

It is questionable whether the Liberal government would be willing to address CCP activities in Vancouver. The current Prime Minister has not shown a strong hand to date in confronting the Beijing regime. It appears to be distancing itself from the U.S. waiting for the election results, and hoping for a Trump defeat at the polls.

What is going on in the U.S. is becoming more apparent by the day. This is the **real** push for a communist takeover of the American republic. The news reports are coming in like a tsunami. Conservative-minded people are being overwhelmed by the elite control of nearly all of the institutions. The media is public-enemy number one. The election is only two weeks away as of this entry in the book. What the future holds is uncertain.

> "The Democratic Party is ruled by the revolutionary left. If they win, Antifa and BLM will be used to attack and intimidate opponents of the regime – morphing from storm troopers to S.S. Like France in 1789, Russia in 1917 and Germany in 1932, **we stand at the brink**. Thank God Trump is no Louis XVI. Don't think civil war. Think firing squads, gulags and death camps. Think the Black Lives Matter flag flying over the White House and Capitol." (Don Felder, The Elements of Revolution are all in Place, Front Page Magazine; in ACTS for America, October 9, 2020)

In Canada, the Liberal government is doing everything possible with the help of the NDP to stonewall and block the opposition Conservatives from holding it to account over transparency concerning the WE scandal, out of control spending and its going forward concerning COVID-19. Trudeau's agenda speaks loudly by its silence.

CHAPTER 4: WARNINGS ON SOCIALISM & COMMUNISM

As an example of radical socialists hiding their true intentions, Pierre Trudeau, as Prime Minister, hesitated to admit his socialist beliefs. The day after he became Prime Minister in 1968, he said at a press conference that he was not a radical or a socialist, but a pragmatist. (Bob Plamondon, The Truth About Trudeau, 2013). **He lied – with a bald face.** Yet, *"you shall know them by their fruits,"* held true by his policies.

In Canada today, Justin Trudeau and the Liberals are in power and represent the same threat as the Democratic Party and the activists in the U.S. Whether Trudeau resigns, or the returning Mark Carney takes over leadership, Canada will remain in peril under a corrupt Liberal government. Therefore, the great fight for Canada is here, too. What side are you on? What stark choice do you need to make?

7. Take power by any means possible through violence, craft and deceit

"Always preach true democracy but seize power as fast and as ruthlessly as possible."
"In the 1968 federal election Trudeau reassured the Canadian people he was not 'Santa Claus,' and would not open the 'fiscal floodgates.' He promised a Liberal government would not increase taxes or increase spending. He eagerly abandoned his pretense at the first opportunity. Eventually, he imposed socialist economic policies that were experimental, extravagant, and ultimately destructive. **Canadians entrusted their robust, strong economy to a wealthy intellectual with little practical experience.**" (Bob Plamondon, The Truth About Trudeau, 2013).

And they paid the price. The only thing we learn from history is that we – the people – never learn from history.

Canadians repeated their mistake in 2015, with equally damning consequences. When Justin Trudeau was elected Prime Minister of Canada on October 19, 2015, he promised the citizens of Canada –

> "I know that I am on stage tonight for one reason and one reason only: because you put me here. And you gave me clear marching orders," *he said*. "You want a prime minister who knows if Canadians are to trust their government, their government needs to trust Canadians, a PM who understands that openness and transparency means better, smarter decisions." (Ezra Levant, The Libranos, 2019).

Here are some additional charges and promises made by Justin Trudeau as he sought to win power over the Harper Conservatives.

> "Harper has turned Ottawa into a partisan swamp promoting partisan interests at the expense of public trust. We will clean up his mess." (Ibid)

Yet, when the rubber meets the road,
> "Literally 20% of Trudeau's cabinet-by- gender would end up caught up in some scandal or other in their very first term. "Some people who got in were borderline idiots," according to one Liberal insider. Maybe counting genitals isn't such a great way to pick a cabinet after all." (Ezra Levant, The Libranos, 2019)

Once achieving power in 2015 Justin Trudeau's Liberals did exactly the opposite of what he had promised. Ezra Levant's expose of the Trudeau government in "The Libranos" is somber and alarming. It was written before the 2019 federal election, and before COVID-19. The

CHAPTER 4: WARNINGS ON SOCIALISM & COMMUNISM

concerns raised in it are magnified 10X today. Read it! "The Libranos" summary statements are as follows:

> "Few could have imagined that he (Justin Trudeau) would end up leading what is arguably the most unethical, corrupt, even criminal government in modern Canadian history. He lied, cheated, deceived and plundered. He has used his fake compassion, feminism and progressivism to mask a dark, angry, vengeful side. This is the very real story of one man who has resorted to breaking the law and undermining our economy, our democracy, our values and even our justice system to get everything he wants."

In "We'll never know the truth,"

> "We now have two legal cases where individuals who were trying to do the right thing – then attorney general Jody Wilson-Raybould and Vice-Admiral Norman – were treated unjustly by their own government. By a government that ignored some of the most fundamental precepts of the rule of law, including prosecutorial independence and the obligation to disclose in a timely fashion, relevant information sought by the accused in a criminal trial. Marie Henein, Norman's lawyer said senior officials within Trudeau's government withheld relevant information to the defence and the prosecution regarding her client. Which leads to the question of what this government will do next, if it wins on Oct. 21, 2019?

Concerning Trudeau's promise of "openness and transparency," here is the 'fruit,' only three of many, many examples to date:

> "The Liberal MPs who dominated the Commons' justice committee probing the SNC-Lavalin scandal shut down their meeting before opposition MPs could get Jody Wilson-Raybould to testify, something she was keen to do....and the Liberal MPs on the ethics committee immediately voted to shut things down...After Ethics Commissioner Mario Dion's scathing report about how Prime Minister Justin Trudeau violated a Conflict of

> Interest Act law, Liberal MPs used their majority to reject the opposition bid to allow Dion to testify." (Calgary Sun editorial, Yes, yet another Lavscam coverup, August 22, 2019)

The Liberals did win the October 21st, 2019, election, albeit with a minority government; and here is where we are at today in Canada in mid-2020. Due to the CCP virus 'scamdemic' and Liberal opportunistic corruption, Canada is in a political crisis and soon-to-come fiscal calamity. They are ruthlessly fast-tracking an unprecedented "grab for power" over a democratically elected Parliament.

> "The (socialist) Liberals – who only have a minority – have largely governed without opposition for the past three months and intend to continue doing so for at least three more…because the NDP and Bloc Quebecois let them get away with it…unprecedented spending (and) no budget. The pretend Parliament consisted of Justin Trudeau descending the steps of Rideau Cottage in Ottawa to give a daily news briefing, followed by a handful of softball questions from reporters hand-picked by the PM's communication staff and disproportionately selected from Quebec." (Lorne Gunter, Where's outrage at Liberals crushing Parliamentary procedure? The Calgary Sun, June 20, 2020)

In "Democracy in Danger," Licia Corbella of the Calgary Sun wrote on June 16, 2020 –

> "'Christian Leuprecht a Macdonald-Laurier Senior Fellow, in a report called *COVID's Collateral Contagion: Why Faking Parliament is No Way to Govern in a Crisis*, makes an impassioned case for why Parliament should immediately resume…says the extraordinary measures employed by the minority Liberal government demonstrate "unprecedented disregard for parliamentary convention."…has capitalized on the virus to limit democratic debate on measures it has implemented (and) effectively put the very ability of Parliament to carry

CHAPTER 4: WARNINGS ON SOCIALISM & COMMUNISM

> out its functions up for debate wholesale. Never has a Canadian Parliament sat less: only 40 sitting days between July, 2019, and June, 2020. "In unprecedented disregard for parliamentary convention, the government cancelled the budget it had planned to table and refuses to provide a fiscal update." On June 17 only 4 hours were allocated for Parliament to debate total spending of $150 billion. Sharpest criticism for NDP leader Jagmeet Singh, who shamefully negotiated away our democracy to have Trudeau announce additional employee sick days, something under provincial jurisdiction. Other Westminster parliaments (U.K., NZ, AU) have remained sitting through the pandemic."'

And on and on it goes, with Liberal Marwan Tabbara facing charges for assault, break and enter and criminal harassment. Trudeau's response –

> **"MP's charges kept secret,** Grits keep litany of alleged bad behavior out of the public eye...Instead Tabarra continues to sit in Parliament." (Brian Lilley, The Calgary Sun, June 21, 2020)

Remember that one of communism's nine rules for destroying a free democracy is to "preach democracy but seize power as fast and as ruthlessly as possible."

> "Trudeau's complete betrayal of those who naively expected he would actually be accountable and transparent is important to highlight because it's the background for his entire modus operandi." (Ezra Levant, The Libranos, 2019)

Here is the real Justin Trudeau in his 44th year, as shown in 2016 on the floor of the House of Commons:

> "He thought they were taking too long to get to their seats. So the prime minister stormed onto the floor to grab the Conservative party whip, Gordon Brown, and physically drag him to his seat. "He looked very, very angry and he pushed some people, grabbed the arm of

the whip and pulled him saying stuff like, you know, **'get the fuck out of my way,'** and when he turned back he hit Ruth Ellen Brosseau and she was shocked and hurt. So he pulled [Brown] to the end of the room," Another MP added: "He said, 'Get the bleep out of the way.' There was some resistance by the whip [Brown] and on the final pull he elbowed Ruth Ellen Brosseau and knocked her over. Ruth Ellen was clutching her breast and her chest and she had a big red mark on her chest." (Ezra Levant, The Libranos, 2019)

The only other Prime Minister to ever use such vile speech publicly in Parliament was Pierre Trudeau. Both father and son showed no moral compass or character in speaking this way. Yet, the country kept electing them to the highest office in the land. No wonder we're in such a mess!

> "When an opposition MP was getting under his skin, he mouthed **"fuck off"** on the floor of the House of Commons. Trudeau was not one to apologize or seek forgiveness." (Bob Plamondon, The Truth About Trudeau, 2013).

At the colored woman, MP Celina Caesar-Chavannes' resignation Justin Trudeau's –
> "reaction was another one of those burst of rages like he showed to Ruth Ellen Brosseau. 'He was yelling. He was yelling that I didn't appreciate him, that he'd given me so much,' said Caesar Chavannes." (Ibid)

Ezra Levant, in "The Libranos" writes, "This was the same Justin Trudeau who, having defeated Indigenous Senator Patrick Brazeau in a charity boxing match in 2012, took as his prize the senator's scalp – literally chopping off the long black hair of a proud Indigenous man. Live on television."

> "He that hath no rule over his own spirit is like a city that is broken down, and without walls." (Proverbs 25:28)

CHAPTER 4: WARNINGS ON SOCIALISM & COMMUNISM

A leader like this leaves Canada wide open to bad actors, both from without and from within the country. Candice Malcolm nailed it in the Prime Minister's resume in his bid for a UN Security Council temporary seat, and his loss:

> "While the media are busy covering for him, fair-minded observers know why Canada lost: the countless examples of Trudeau's juvenile superficial stunts on the world stage:
> - He danced in ethnic costumes for photo ops in India and was snubbed by the Indian government.
> - He invited a convicted terrorist to a state dinner.
> - He was directly involved in the SNC-Lavalin scandal.
> - He dressed in blackface, a despicable and racist trope (turn), and he did it multiple times.
> - He missed important trade meetings, and according to Australia's former PM, he was "flaky" and "humiliated" other world leaders.
> - He was caught on a hot mic bashing Donald Trump, acting like a mean girl not a leader.
> - He pandered to the murderous Iranian regime, insulting Canadians, Iranian dissidents and our closest allies.
> - And he shamelessly uses every opportunity to virtue signal." (C. Malcolm, Canada's back? More like increasingly irrelevant, The Calgary Sun, June 20, 2020)

Here is yet another breaking story of Justin Trudeau's abuse of power, lack of integrity and reckless disregard of parliamentary Conflict of Interest rules. It is happening as I write:

> "Prime Minister Justin Trudeau's mother and brother were paid more than $350,000 to appear at WE Day events run by the same charity that his government attempted to give a sole-sourced $912 million contract to just weeks ago. The issue before us now is the conflict of interest the Prime Minister faces for awarding this lucrative contract to his friends and donors. This deal Trudeau struck with WE stunk from the beginning.

> **Remarkably, Trudeau continues to see no conflict of interest in this contract or in his involvement in awarding it.** Did you know that Craig Kielburger (ME to WE co-owner) was part of the Leaders' Debate Commission to set out rules for the televised election debates?" (Brian Lilley, WE pay well – Trudeaus paid big to appear at WE Day events, The Calgary Sun, July 10, 2020).

Concerning this blatant misuse of Trudeau's authority, the PM "suddenly has a big problem with the Conflict of Interest Act." Ethics Commissioner Mario Dion said,

> "he would investigate Trudeau under subsections 6(1), 7 and 21 of the Conflict of Interest Act." (Lorrie Goldstein, Trudeau didn't learn his lesson about conflict of interest, The Calgary Sun, July 9, 2020).

It appears that the man Canadians elected as Prime Minister is unqualified for the position. How many times do the eastern voters need to be told that before they open their eyes?

> "When he says one day that the civil service along arranged WE to be given a sole-source contract to distribute nearly $1 billion in pandemic emergency grants to students who volunteer their time and then admits days later he pushed for and voted for the deal at cabinet, **I'm convinced he hasn't the intellectual perception to see those as contradictory.** To Liberals, particularly in Toronto, Montreal and Ottawa, the WE scandal no more proves that Trudeau is corrupt than the Kokanee grope proves he is sexist or his multiple blackface antics prove he is a bigot. They're sure he's none of those things and there are enough of them to keep re-electing him." (Lorne Gunter, Here's why PM keeps making ethics blunders, The Calgary Sun, July 12, 2020).

Canadian's moral compass is being dulled by the actions of our leaders, and Trudeau is a prime example. Ernest Manning wrote:

CHAPTER 4: WARNINGS ON SOCIALISM & COMMUNISM

"How many there are who will ride roughshod over others to gain their own ends. How many there are who will stoop to deception and the exploitation of public dissatisfaction and grievances to further their own interests. **We are constantly being made aware of the appalling lack of integrity in the conduct of individuals, businesses, labour unions and governments. Many people often wonder who there is left that they can really trust.**" (E. C. Manning, The Spirit of Anti-Christ, vintage message on Canada's National Bible Hour, September 6, 2009).

Manning added his insight to the deceit and deception that we have come to regard as normal in society today.

"The constant exaggerated use or misuse of adjectives in modern advertising robs the words of their literal depth and meaning. When everything from laundry soap to automobiles is described as stupendous, fantastic, unprecedented, unparalleled; in time, those words lose their true meaning and become words which hearing, we hear not. Most of us read our newspapers with considerable skepticism as to the accuracy and the reliability of what we read. Our experience has taught us that there is probably very little similarity between what we read and what is true. For the same reason, many people pay very little attention to the statements and promises of politicians. All too frequently, their performance has been so at variance with what they say, that the public no longer regards their statements as dependable. Their words therefore fall into the category of words which hearing, we hear not, and effective communication between the people and their governments becomes almost non-existent." (E. C. Manning, It is Written – He that hath ears to hear (#6), Canada's National Bible Hour, vintage message, October 3, 2010).

Perhaps the Laurentian elite Justin Trudeau betrayed his true nature and philosophy of government prior to becoming Prime Minister in 2015. For once he spoke the truth. When asked in 2013 what country he most admired, the then leader of the Liberal Party of Canada answered,

> **"There's a level of admiration I actually have for China. Their basic dictatorship is actually allowing them to turn their economy around on a dime."** (Yao Liang & Tanya Du, Pandemic Perspective: The Ties Between Beijing and Canada's Powerful and Elite, The Epoch Times, p. A6, June 18-24, 2020)

> "The sinister phenomenon known as "elite capture" through offering lucrative financial deals in exchange for the elite's spine, as they're required to essentially toe the regime's propaganda line on matters of diplomacy and governance. Canada (is) a favorable place for subversion because of the ease with which it can be achieved. Politicians often think of themselves as "global citizens" (in this case under Beijing's spell) rather than representatives of a particular nation (in this case Canada) and citizenry that they're obligated to." (Shane Miller, The Chinese Regime's 'Elite Capture' in Canada, The Epoch Times, p. B2, October 8-14, 2020)

As China makes its end run to try and conquer the world, it has ramped up its espionage globally to "off the scale" proportions. Using elites gives the communist government an open door to government, business and academia. A former senior American intelligence expert with thirty years of experience warned:

> "There's almost no way of knowing the true scale of the regime's global espionage program. It could range from "easily" in the tens of thousands of cases to even hundreds of thousands. The regime has adopted a "whole of society" approach to acquiring foreign intellectual property (IP), as it "energizes all of society to support national, economic, and military development goals." It has innovated to combine human and cyber espionage, "in many cases, masterfully executed.

CHAPTER 4: WARNINGS ON SOCIALISM & COMMUNISM

> Western industries as a whole remain quite ignorant of what's happening," he added." (Cathy He, Chinese Global Spy Operations Are 'Off the Scale,' Analyst Says, The Epoch Times, p. A1, 10, October 8-14, 2020)

The Scriptures speak to Trudeau's and the other elites' attitudes, when they praise or support China's corrupt communist government:

> "O generation of vipers, how can ye, being evil, speak good things? for out of the abundance of the heart the mouth speaketh." (Matthew 12:34)

Trudeau has used the WE Charity to promote his progressive leftist agenda to impressionable youth. Far more than a charitable mission it is a mission of indoctrination in the international socialist "new world order" that his father so fondly embraced and promoted.

> "WE Day rallies (many which are available for viewing online) are a combination of Korean boyband concerts and revivalist religious shows. **Leaders preach "progressive" ideology and social justice campaigns during which WE executives and celebrities – such as the prime minister and his family – whip up attendees (mostly junior-high students) into a virtue-signaling frenzy.**" (Lorne Gunter, Province is right to ditch scandal-plagued charity, The Calgary Sun, July 25, 2020).

"Since his failed bid for a seat on the United Nations Security Council, Trudeau has been mildly more critical of Beijing," for imprisoning two innocent Canadians in retaliation for Canada's arrest of Meng Wangzhou of behalf of the US. (Lorne Gunter, "Trudeau right not to engage in hostage diplomacy, The Calgary Sun, June 28, 2020).

> "Trudeau responded, "If the Chinese government concludes that is an effective way to gain leverage over

"FORTRESS AMERICA" UNDER SIEGE

Canadians and over the government of Canada...then no Canadian will be safe." (Yet) he is still weak on China."

Despite Trudeau's proven corruption he is still a significant threat, and far from finished in his plan move Canada past the point of no-return in a radical leftist direction, following his father's example. When the WE Charity scandal looked like it might bring the Liberals down Trudeau made an unexpected move.

> "The PM has proven one thing over the past little while: He's a shrewd political operator. A month ago several polls showed that the WE scandal was damaging the Liberal brand with voters. So, Prime Minister Justin Trudeau did what he had to do to knock the WE scandal off the front pages. **He prorogued Parliament.** Now polls show that Liberal support is bouncing back. The numbers, if translated into votes, would likely deliver Trudeau a stronger majority than he got in 2015." (Brian Lilley, PM's play worked: Poll, The Calgary Sun, September 16, 2020)

If the Canadian people don't open their eyes and stop Justin Trudeau and the Liberals in the next election, then that vengeful, virtue-signaling "fake and egocentric man" (Tarek Fatah, The Calgary Sun, September 24, 2019) and his corrupt Liberal government will overcome and destroy Canada's democratic freedoms. They are on course to do that with a coming fiscal nightmare for the country.

8. Destroy the fiscal structure through excessive spending and government debt

"By encouraging government extravagance, destroy its credit, Produce fear of inflation with rising prices and general discontent."

CHAPTER 4: WARNINGS ON SOCIALISM & COMMUNISM

Pierre Trudeau, the patriarch of Canadian socialism, did not believe in capitalism despite inheriting a fortune from his father who profited from a capitalist system. He won 4 out of 5 elections, losing every contest outside the Province of Quebec, and decimated the Liberal Party in the process. Excerpts from Bob Plamondon's book, "The Truth About Trudeau," are given below. He said that everything he learned about economics came from Harold Laski, a Marxist. Obviously, they both knew about **point #8** (above).

> "Trudeau had a disdain for capitalism and the free enterprise system. At the 1981 G-7 meeting in Canada, Trudeau pitched socialism – rich nations sharing their wealth equitably to developing ones. Margaret Thatcher and Ronald Reagan proposed free enterprise (capitalism), rather than socialism, as the preferred solution, and Trudeau's pitch went nowhere. In 1983 in the House of Commons Thatcher again observed that her remarks more powerfully defended values and principles of freedom and free enterprise than did those of Canada's own government." (Bob Plamondon, The Truth About Trudeau, 2013).

Ernest Manning adopted the same economic policy of free enterprise and individualism that so benefitted Thatcher's and Reagan's countries during their times in office. Alberta under Manning grew in prosperity during his 25 years as premier, benefitting its citizens. But Trudeau would not listen to any of their advice though he knew Manning personally having appointed him to the Canadian Senate in 1970. In Trudeau's own words, "I was thus able to institute policies that I had been dreaming about for a long time." Dreams don't balance budgets any more than budgets balance themselves.

> "The prime ministers who served before him endowed Trudeau with a healthy, balanced Canadian economy. He inherited a strong hand and squandered it, passing

on to those who followed him a nation deeply indebted, pushing up the spending (15%/yr. for 15.5 years) and borrowing curve so irresponsibly that later governments of both parties took more than a generation to pull Canada back from what we know today as the "Greek brink." The national debt increased 10X; from $19.4 billion in 1968 to $194.4 billion in 1984. His policies caused investment to flee Canada, businesses to close and the real estate market to crash. His response to Canada's economic problems was to stimulate the government on borrowed money – DEBT. His record of operational deficits – 10 out of 15.5 years – stands mercifully unmatched by any other prime minister.

Trudeau had a federal spending addiction: 72-74 increased 27.8% and 20% in consecutive years; 82-84 increases of 16.8%, 22.5% and 22.5%. After the 1980 election government officials complained that spending controls were virtually non-existent. Officials warned Trudeau that most new spending had ongoing costs that would lead to annual deficits of at least $40 billion per year. In 1968 federal spending was $12.3 billion/yr. When Trudeau left office in 1984 it was $106 billion.

Over 18 budgets and 15 ½ years in office Trudeau's economic legacy constitutes a succession of failures. His government spent $55 billion more on socialist programs than he collected in revenue, which with $131 billion in interest costs formed a $186.5 billion compounding debt hole by 1984. The interest costs on Trudeau's debt handcuffed his successors and the country. It took 2 successive administrations and 20 years of hard work and sacrifice by the Canadian people to get a handle on Trudeau's legacy of debt. From the year Trudeau resigned up to the fiscal year-end of 2012, the Canadian government recorded operational surpluses of $634 billion. But they also paid over $1 trillion in interest costs, all of which can be traced to Trudeau's debt. In 2012 the country was still more indebted than under Lester Pearson in 1968, thanks to Trudeau." (Ibid)

CHAPTER 4: WARNINGS ON SOCIALISM & COMMUNISM

Former Prime Minister (2005-2015) Stephen Harper's verdict on Pierre Trudeau follows:

> "Flailing from one pet policy objective to another, he expanded the welfare state, created scores of bureaucratic agencies, offices and ministries, and encouraged the regulation and control of major industrial sectors. Under his stewardship the country created huge deficits, bloated bureaucracy, rising unemployment, record inflation, curtailed trade and declining competitiveness. From these consequences <u>we have still not fully recovered</u>, and they <u>continue to have an impact</u> on my pay cheque, and my family's opportunities, every single month."

Therese Cosgrain said that Trudeau was something of a ***dilettante**, and although a prodigious intellectual, he lacked perseverance. He liked launching ideas and movements, and then lost interest and turned to something else. He did not complete his PhD thesis on the Interplay between Christianity and Marxism. No wonder he had trouble; Marx was an atheist, and Marxism is atheistic. He was a radical socialist in his own words but could not even complete his thesis on Marxism. Even his friends described him as a **dilettante**, a spoiled brat and an intellectual snob. Nearly everything he did as Prime Minister he left in a mess as Bob Plamondon so carefully describes in his masterfully researched and carefully documented book, The Truth About Trudeau, 2013.

> *dilettante – One who pursues the fine arts, literature, or science, for amusement; therefore an amateur, a dabbler, a trifler.

The April, 1944, issue of The Prophetic Voice stated succinctly the nature of the dilettante. At this time Trudeau and a friend were travelling through northern Quebec dressed in German uniforms in opposition to WW

II, while our own men were dying in defense of our freedoms. Pastor William John Laing of Bible Institute Baptist Church in Calgary wrote concerning such a man, in a column titled, "Concentration;"

> "Words of philosophy may appeal but lack the conviction of one word from the Bible. The man who scatters himself on many objects soon loses his energy, and with his energy his enthusiasm. Often we speculate in life-study by speculation – an aimless learning of things because they may be useful someday."

Canadians should have been wary of electing and re-electing a man with a radical past whose "dreams" and ideas had never been tested. We should also have been wary of electing and re-electing his son, a part time actor and drama teacher who had no political qualifications beyond having the last name, Trudeau. And as we have seen the name Trudeau is anything but special among former prime ministers. We know this from our current Prime Minister and the news surrounding him.

The Calgary Sun Headline for July 9, 2020 read, **"343 B! Oh, Canada! Morneau reveals projected federal deficit – as debt soars past $1 trillion**. The Sun editorial read, in part, as follows:

> "We knew the deficit would be bad. But no one expected it would be this bad...a shocking, staggering $343 billion for this fiscal year. That record-breaking figure has also pushed the debt to over $1 trillion. Finance Minister Morneau's speech to Canadians had zero mentions of the actual deficit or debt totals. Instead, he offered a rosy sales pitch..."This support is helping Canadians back on their feet, and has prevented long term damage."
>
> The Liberal's "snapshot" offered no plan about how to move from economic support to economic recovery. We should have received more than just a "snapshot," one

CHAPTER 4: WARNINGS ON SOCIALISM & COMMUNISM

that offers no numbers beyond the current year. **Other countries have managed to table a full budget during the pandemic. Canada could have done likewise.** Meanwhile, Canadians are left wondering what these massive deficit figures mean for the country and for future generations."

In the July 11, 2020, Calgary Sun newspaper, an article, "Trudeau spent rainy day fund back when sun was shining," Aaron Wudrick, federal director of the Canadian Taxpayers Federation writes –

> "When the economy was growing and times were good, the Trudeau Liberals ran deficits and racked up nearly $100 billion in new debt. Even more troubling than their track record is the Liberals complete lack of a plan for the future. There was no indication of how they would wind down expensive temporary spending; no sign they've begun to look at ways to reduce the cost of government; no hint of a plan to revive the economy, even as every day brings news of more businesses going bankrupt."

Trudeau and his father are almost identical in their financial management. It is almost as if they had agreed together how to mismanage our economy to fulfill socialism's agenda in our fiscal demise.

Trudeau 'managed' the COVID-19 (CCP virus) "scamdemic' to engineer this fiscal crisis to its present intolerable levels, in hope of eventually destroying Canada's fiscal structure (Point #8). He has no plans to change anything.

> "If the totals aren't troubling enough, there was little indication offered of what comes next. "Trudeau has no plan to help you get back to work or to restart our economy," said Conservative Leader Andrew Scheer, pointing out we now have the highest unemployment in the G7. Why are the Liberals seemingly reluctant to retool their responses and get people working again? Here's a theory: Trudeau has been faring well in the polls

because his main job is now throwing cash to anyone with their hands out, which plays well with some voters. Maybe Trudeau likes things just the way they are. **So for now, we're left with the news that <u>Canada's finances are a total mess and there's no plan to get us out of it.</u>"** (Anthony Furey, We're in a trillion-dollar hole – and no plan to dig us out, The Calgary Sun, July 9, 2020).

Ernest C. Manning understood the socialist-communist fiscal agenda for destroying a free enterprise based democratic society. He spent a lifetime in provincial politics (1935-1968) working to advance the economic well-being of the citizens of Alberta through an individualistic free enterprise system of government. William Aberhart and Ernest Manning led Alberta out of near bankruptcy during the 1930s to ultimately become the country's economic powerhouse, in later years generating far more to the financial well-being of the country than any other province. Following are some excerpts from "The Good Steward – The Ernest C. Manning Story," by Brian Brennan, 2008, that reveal some of Mr. Manning's beliefs on fiscal management –

> "It seemed to Manning that Canada's federal and provincial governments should adopt the same "pay-as-you-go" policy that Social Credit used in Alberta. "Only spend what you collect," he told the business leaders. If the governments kept their spending under control, they should be able to weather any future economic storms."

Concerning the driver of the Alberta economy after the Leduc Oil Discovery in 1947, Premier Manning said,

> "Let Americans keep taking the risks – "How any government could have remained in office while gambling $20 million of the people's money in dry holes is something the socialists have never explained."

CHAPTER 4: WARNINGS ON SOCIALISM & COMMUNISM

"Prevent the continent from becoming increasingly dependent on crude oil imported from Venezuela and the Persian Gulf."

Concerning labor relations and the free market economy –

"We did discover after we got into government that it was extremely difficult to provide as much as organized labor felt we should have without, in our view, being unfair to the other side – the management end – thereby impairing the economy as a whole and costing people jobs."

"Don't replace the free market economy (by socialism) but fix it (by free enterprise); "stimulate the economy through encouraging the 'money barons' to invest in Alberta."

Ernest Manning sat in the Canadian Senate for 13 years (1970-83) as "a self-described advocate of reduced federal spending and debt." He left the Senate at the mandatory retirement age of 75.

"Pierre Trudeau would not scale back rapidly growing government spending. He blamed society when he should have blamed himself. When Trudeau came to power in 1968, he found the fundamentals of the Canadian economy in solid shape. During his second term in office (1972-76) every economic indicator ($, jobs, economic growth, interest rates, unemployment) veered strongly in the opposite direction and stayed there until he resigned from office." (Bob Plamondon, The Truth About Trudeau, 2013)

President Ronald Reagan followed the same kind of fiscal restraint advocated by Ernest Manning. America's economy rebounded sharply during his presidency.

"Trudeau called Reagan an imbecile, and a reckless and dangerous simpleton. At a 1982 summit, a self-indulgent Trudeau constantly contradicted, refuted and needled Reagan.

"FORTRESS AMERICA" UNDER SIEGE

> To Reagan, the key to taming inflation was a balanced budget. Therefore, defending the public treasury demanded the same action as protecting one's virtue. Just say, NO!" (Ibid)

After Ernest Manning left office the Progressive Conservatives ruled Alberta for 44 years. Successive administrations led Alberta into deeper and deeper debt until finally, Premier Ralph Klein brought the province out of an approximate $30 billion provincial debt. After Klein, Alberta again slid back into the red. The NDP took government in 2015 and ruled until their defeat in early 2019 by Jason Kenny's United Conservatives. An article near the end of Rachel Notley's NDP term describes Alberta's fiscal condition up to the end of 2018. It contrasts starkly with Manning's fiscal example and advice.

> "It pays well to be a government employee in Alberta. According to the Fraser Institute, government employment in Alberta surged upwards between 2014 and 2018, while jobs outside of government declined. The Alberta government has continued the spending spree increasing its purchases from $48.4 billion in 2014 to $56.6 billion this year. Government employees in Alberta earn a 10% wage premium compared to their counterparts in business. It's the same story at the municipal level. Calgary is still suffering from the highest unemployment rate of Canada's major cities, total workers' pay in Alberta remains below pre-recession highs and the job situation facing young men is nothing short of alarming." (Franco Terrazzano, Booming government is out of touch with Alberta's realities, The Calgary Sun, December 7, 2018).

Canada's fiscal well-being at the federal level has deteriorated massively since the Harper Conservatives left power in 2015. People remember with scorn Justin Trudeau's infamous comment that "budgets balance themselves." By 2019, and before COVID-19, the lying

CHAPTER 4: WARNINGS ON SOCIALISM & COMMUNISM

Liberals had already plunged the country deeper and deeper into debt as documented by Lorrie Goldstein:

> "In April, 2015, he (Trudeau) said: "Our platform will be fully costed, fiscally responsible and a balanced budget." In July, 2015, he said, "I've committed to continuing to run balanced budgets...Liberals balance budgets. That's what history has shown." During the leader's debate (August 5) Trudeau hammered Harper for turning the Chretien/Martin surpluses into deficits. Then-flip-flop...on August 27, Trudeau now said a Liberal government would run three years of "modest deficits" to pay for a "middle class tax cut" followed by a balanced budget in Year 4. On September 17 leader's debate Trudeau assured voters deficits would only be for a short time..."I am looking straight at Canadians and being honest the way I always have. We will balance that budget in 2019. He promised "not to break our promises like politicians of all parties have done in the past – including my own. I'm being honest with Canadians." After the December, 2015, election his promise to balance the budget in 2019 was "very" cast in stone. **For the next 4 years Trudeau broke every promise he had ever made on running modest deficits and returning to a balanced budget.**
>
> **This year (2019), where he promised a $1 billion surplus, there will now be a $26.6 billion deficit, with no plan to ever return to balanced budgets."**

The COVID-19 **'scamdemic'** has since exacerbated the country's finances at the federal level to beyond alarming, setting the stage for a future financial crisis that fits well with communism's eighth rule for taking down a free democratic society; "By encouraging government extravagance, destroy its credit; produce fear of inflation with rising prices and general discontent."

How absolutely insanely tragic that our leaders have followed medical advisors and academic modelers' advice causing exponentially more harm to our economies than the CCP virus ever should have. President Trump was fiercely attacked for suggesting that the pandemic overreaction was more damaging than the virus itself. Yet, he was showing the kind of leadership needed to carry the nation safely through this crisis.

> "Prior to the virus afflicting him Trump was already emphasizing that 99.997% of Americans under the age of 60 who contracted the coronavirus survived it, and that of all those above the age of 60, 95.04% survived it. He was already emphasizing that of those who died from COVID-19, the great majority suffered from other illnesses that compromised their immunity. (He said) "I have experienced this problem and quickly overcame it and I am in the category of higher risk, **and I say the nation must face the coronavirus with prudence and boldness**." (Conrad Black, Having Been Infected, Trump Beset by Perceptions of His Attitude Toward COVID," The Epoch Times, p. B2, October 8-14, 2020)

In "Democracy in Danger," Licia Corbella documented the unprecedented erosion of Parliamentary powers and radical spending prerogatives usurped by the Trudeau government in response to the COVID-19 pandemic. She wrote the following:

> "Christian Leuprecht, a MLI Munk Senior Fellow, likens Canada's Parliament to Britain under King Charles I, an unrepentant absolutist (despot) famous for quarreling with Parliament over royal prerogative and – the large fiscal deficit that had built up – during the tyranny of his 11 year-long personal reign. Charles I was beheaded.
>
> On June 17, 2020, only 4 hours were allocated for Parliament to debate total Liberal spending of $150 billion. In unprecedented disregard for parliamentary convention, the government cancelled the budget it had

CHAPTER 4: WARNINGS ON SOCIALISM & COMMUNISM

planned to table and refuses to provide a fiscal update. **An un-democratic Liberal government** is exposing Canadians to unprecedented levels of spending and restrictions on personal freedom – with an unprecedented lack of parliamentary debate and scrutiny.

By May 2020, direct federal spending announcements related to the pandemic had amounted to $152.8 billion...while the federal deficit is expected to exceed $250 billion this year. The Government of Canada's total balance sheet is expected to be $1 trillion in red, while total public debt in Canada is anticipated to amount to $3.2 trillion, or 166% of GDP." (The Calgary Sun, June 16, 2020).

Radio news reports on July 8, 2020, are saying that Canada's federal deficit this year, according to the parliamentary budget officer, will likely exceed $343 billion. The Canadian economy will shrink by over 6.8%, the greatest contraction since the Great Depression. Unemployment will remain high while the media continue to hype the possibility of a "second wave" of COVID-19.

Since the Liberals have avoided transparent fiscal accountability no final, fixed number is currently available. It will be huge, however; a product of the "scamdemic," and a perfect storm leading to the erosion and eventual destruction of our freedom and democracy in the years ahead. We're in deep trouble.

"The size of the deficit alarmed Conservative Leader Andrew Scheer who said, "Over the past five years, the Trudeau Liberals have completely abandoned their fiscal anchors. The debt-to-GDP ratio is rising, the deficit has exploded to $343.2 billion, and they have completely lost control over the federal debt, which for the first time will reach over $1 trillion this year." Canada will have to live with a higher level of debt and risk having to refinance it at higher rates in the future." (Rahul Vaidyanath, Morneau Forcused on Spending to Restart Economy Despite Jobless Spike, Surging Deficit, The Epoch Times, p. A4, July 9-15, 2020).

It appears that this opportunistic Liberal grab for power and reckless spending has long been planned. Many people who lost their jobs due to COVID-19 are on federal $2,000/month income support and, sadly, some don't want to go back to work. By dragging Canadians down economically it will be easier to enslave them with debt and future financial dependence upon a despotic federal government...a socialist-communist strategy.

> "Parliament's budget watchdog said the federal deficit could be on track to hit $256 billion this fiscal year due to the COVID-19 pandemic...due to $169 billion in spending on emergency aid and a historic drop in economic output. Figures don't include an 8 week extension of Canada emergency response benefits." (Editorial, Federal deficit could hit $256 billion, PBO says, The Calgary Sun, June 19, 2020).

Trudeau seems to want to drag out the pandemic fiscal crisis, spending more and creating more uncertainty among the population about the way forward out of this mess. The mainstream media feeds this frenzy. They are non-stop COVID-19 mouthpieces.

> "Trying to kick-start the Canadian economy into recovery from the COVID-19 recession through federal and provincial stimulus spending will fail warned a new report by the Fraser Institute. The result will be weak economic growth along with substantial increases in already soaring government deficits and debt. The best way to speed up Canada's economic recovery is through deficit-financed, broad-based tax cuts, paid for by reducing government spending over the long term." (Lorrie Goldstein, Can't buy our way out of this problem, The Calgary Sun, June 25, 2020).

CHAPTER 4: WARNINGS ON SOCIALISM & COMMUNISM

Sadly, for Canada and Canadians the present federal government will likely have little interest in following the Fraser Institute's advice. It is not concerned about crippling debt.

> "We're clearly talking about more than $20 billion for the eight-week extension of the Canada Emergency Response Benefit (CERB)...the costs could be dire depending on how policies are implemented going forward. "The federal government hasn't provided a fiscal update or a budget," Jason Clemens of The Fraser Institute tells The Epoch Times. Economist Jack Mintz last month in the Financial Post noted that "Canada's debt burden is $3.2 billion." In a memo for the C.D. Howe Institute, Saskatchewan's former minister of finance and social services Janice MacKinnon writes that there's no real incentive for people to return to work." (Shane Miller, National Debt Skyrockets Even Higher With CERB Extension, The Epoch Times, p. A4, June 25-July 1, 2020).

A next to last excerpt from this sordid saga to be recorded in this book is in the August 18, 2020, Calgary Sun. Brian Lilley, in "Sold Bill of Goods," wrote as follows:

> "Justin Trudeau got back to work Monday after more than two weeks spent between two different cottages and just in time to fire his finance minister. So Morneau is out because he didn't pay $41,000 for a family vacation with WE Charity, while Trudeau keeps his job despite his mother getting $479,000 in speaking fees, travel and other expenses. This is a government that even Liberal standards now show should not be in office. Trudeau simply hasn't read the memo yet."

Morneau, Trudeau's finance minister since 2015, is out for more than $41,000. A Bay Street business man could not continue Trudeau's 'drunken sailor' spending. In "Trouble in Paradise," (Calgary Sun, August 17, 2020), two Reuters correspondents wrote:

> "Confidants say Morneau is alarmed by ballooning budget deficits, the amount of money Ottawa is spending to combat the coronavirus. **Total coronavirus support is nearly 14% of GDP (Gross Domestic Product).** His resistance to expensive environmental initiatives reflects his roots in Bay Street, and a view held among <u>right-leaning Liberals</u> that deficits are out of control. Morneau has been saying, "We need to get a grip." He was not very keen on a huge deficit; that's not what he wanted as his legacy," said another source.

Former Liberal attorney general Jody Wilson-Raybould, a central figure in LavScam, weighed in on Bill Morneau's resignation on Twitter;

> "Whether voluntary or not, resignation day for a Minister and their family is a tumultuous one by any measure and for many reasons. **I have to think there is <u>more</u> to this story."**

That "more" may be Pierre Trudeau/John Turner (1980s); Jean Chretien/Paul Martin (1990s) repeated in 2020 by Justin Trudeau/Bill Morneau. Three radical socialist prime ministers destroying three financially "right-leaning" Liberals who were in line for succession, possibly to reverse the far left agenda to bring totalitarianism to Canada. Each finance minister was destroyed in almost an identical way. These examples support the statements by Dennis Prager and E. J. Daniels that radical socialism and communism will destroy Liberalism.

> "He called us Liberals, and said we were like armies without generals, or plans to carry out our campaign. Only be developing trained leadership could we attain the goal of a new world order, or international Communism." (E. J. Daniels, The Red Devil of Communism, 1954, p. 74).

CHAPTER 4: WARNINGS ON SOCIALISM & COMMUNISM

This may explain Mrs. Raybould's "more," as well as Pierre Trudeau's "new world order," and "citizen of the world," philosophy that he applied to himself and to his future plans for Canadians. (Bob Plamondon, The Truth About Trudeau, 2013). It is hard to believe that Jean Chretien, Trudeau's understudy, who travelled to Communist China 17 times in 10 years as Prime Minister, isn't somehow 'in the know' about what is going on here.

The Liberal's modus operandi is increasing and consolidating its power in a single person, the Prime Minister. That control, started in earnest during Pierre Trudeau's administration, is beginning to extend over all aspects of Canadian life. Unaccountable and unrestrained spending, a characteristic of Pierre Trudeau's administration, and now his son's, is a recipe for disaster and a way forward to creating a full blown "collectivist welfare state," as William Aberhart and Ernest C. Manning warned so many years ago. (Brian Brennan, 2008). Manning's government relied on democratic Cabinet decisions with strong, but not dictatorial leadership, from the Premier, according to Ray Speaker, a MLA in the Manning Cabinet. (Brian Brennan, The Good Steward: The Ernest C. Manning Story, 2008).

Both Trudeau's exhibited and exhibit a disregard for the well-being of those under their authority. That is a typical mindset for socialist leaders in general and radical socialist leaders in particular. Justin Trudeau's second carbon tax is an issue at point –

> "Hitting families and businesses struggling to get by with even more costs is exactly the approach Trudeau is taking with his second carbon tax. Only a few weeks ago Trudeau promised Canadians that the feds "are not going to be saddling Canadians with extra costs…the last thing Canadians need now is to see a rise in taxes right now." Economist Jack Mintz, of the U. of Calgary said, "It

makes no sense for Trudeau to promise Canadians that he will not saddle us with extra costs, then hammer us with a second carbon tax that will increase fuel bills (gasoline by 10-20% & natural gas by 3-4%), and destroy jobs (up to 30,000 nationally) at the same time." (Aaron Wudrick and Franco Terrazzano, Trudeau's second carbon tax coming at the worst possible time, The Calgary Sun, October 3, 2020)

Perhaps it hasn't occurred to those trying to make sense of this government's moves that their policies have little to do with the environment, social equality or any other of their pet issues, but are entirely designed to bring Canada under a radical socialist dictatorship, a precursor to their vision of an international socialist utopia – as envisioned by Marx and others of his kind. All of the petty issues are really a smokescreen for their greater agenda. As Lenin said long ago, "Only a few at the top really know what is going on."

Out of control government spending is occurring at all levels, from Ottawa to the provincial legislatures and down to the municipalities. It is as Ernest Manning warned, "Debt leads to more debt," if hard decisions are not made. The principal culprits are socialist governments; the 2 greatest federal spenders, the 2 Trudeaus, and the greatest Alberta spender, the NDP's Rachel Notley. The future does not look good for our free democracy, as socialism's goal of destroying public finances is achieving its end. The last entry in this sorry saga for this book is in the August 29, 2020, Calgary Sun, by Licia Corbella, "Screwed up: Everyone from taxpayers' advocates to rating agency worried about future as governments keep spending."

> "They call themselves Generation Screwed. It's hard to argue with them. Alberta's debt is forecast to hit $99.6 billion next March, an increase of $25.4 billion from 2020. A person born in 1990 will pay a tax bill of $706,099.

CHAPTER 4: WARNINGS ON SOCIALISM & COMMUNISM

> Someone born in 2000 will pay $1,661,504, a 235% increase (Generation Screwed website). That does not included the projected federal deficit of $334 billion this fiscal year, wracked up as result of necessary COVID-19 measures, but also reckless spending as well.
>
> According to the Canadian Taxpayers Federation website, every hour of every day our federal debt grows by $39 million or $940 million/day. Every man, woman and child owes $22,629 towards that growing debt. We're seeing politicians plugging holes with money and **we're in a sinking ship**. It's clear Alberta's provincial government intends to take action, **but the spending spree appears to be just ramping up on the federal side, which means in the long run, <u>we're all going to be screwed</u>.**"

Sooner or later, massive government debt will lead to higher taxes. Socialist leaders will target the businesses and wealthy segment of society – the wealth generators – which already bear a heavy tax burden.

> "High taxation is the forcible nationalization of private assets for redistribution on a massive scale." (The Epoch Times, "How the Spectre of Communism is Ruling Our Society," The Communist Economic Trap – Part 1, Chapter 9, 2020)

As Prime Minister Margaret Thatcher sagely noted, **"Socialism works until you run out of other people's money."** (also see Appendix 4)

Joshua Philipp noted in The 'Nordic Model' Narrative is a Lie, that socialists like Bernie Sanders used the so-called 'Nordic Model' to justify socialism. They use Sweden for their example, but their narrative is a lie.

> "Sweden's economy is a market economy. It's a private market economy with a lot of taxes. On the Economic Freedom of the World Index, which rates countries on a zero to 10, with 10 being the most capitalist...the United States ranks high, so does Sweden – which sits in the

top 25% of all the countries rated." (The Epoch Times, August 22-28, 2019)

Socialism, in lieu of the free market economy, is unsustainable. This is precisely what the leftist Marxists want; to bankrupt the country. It is one of their key rules in overthrowing a free democracy. After ruining the economy they can take full control. Pierre Trudeau groomed his son, Justin, to do that very thing. Jean Chretien, and other Liberal insiders, have coached Justin Trudeau through the years, and now he is succeeding in making Canada another Greece, courtesy of COVID-19 – the Chinese Communist Party virus.

COVID-19 IS CHINA'S WAR ON THE FREE WORLD!
It is a carefully planned attack on the Free World intended to gradually demoralize the targeted free democratic societies – a form of 'death by a thousand cuts' – to weaken the resolve of our citizens from resisting the erosion of our individual and collective freedoms, to prepare the target country for a pre-planned socialist-communist future take-over. The leftist mainstream media fuel the fear and perplexity of the people with non-stop reporting of statistics, a "second-wave" and outbreaks of the virus daily. People are kept primed to a high degree of anxiety by this psychological conditioning. Considerable strife and division has been sown throughout Canadian society as a result. Gradually it wears individual citizens down. Len Webber's 2020 Annual Community Survey for the Calgary Confederation Constituency showed 53% of respondents favoring mandatory masks in public places where physical distancing is not always possible, and even more worrying, as well as 84% concerned that unvaccinated people could be putting their health at risk. These kinds of concerns could easily translate into more punitive legislation and erosion of personal freedom in

CHAPTER 4: WARNINGS ON SOCIALISM & COMMUNISM

the future, if conditions worsen. We are in a very real war today in October, 2020.

9. Destroy the moral fabric and character of society

"By specious (fair-seeming or plausible, but not really so) argument, cause the breakdown in the old moral virtues, honesty, sobriety and faith in the pledged word."

"Before the 1950s, the moral standards of most people generally met a respectable, common standard." (The Epoch Times, "How the Spectre of Communism is Ruling Our World," Popular Culture, a Decadent Indulgence, Chapter 14, 2020). Since then, it has gradually deteriorated and now is in a freefall that is accelerating at frightening speed.

The Bible describes the last days as perilous times. We are living in the last days. It is a time of decadent indulgence.

> *"This know also, that in the last days perilous times shall come. For men shall be lovers of their own selves, covetous, boasters, proud, blasphemous, disobedient to parents, unthankful, unholy, Without natural affection, trucebreakers, false accusers, incontinent, fierce, despisers of those that are good, Traitors, heady, high-minded, lovers of pleasures more than lovers of God." (2 Timothy 3:1-4)*

In, How the Modern World Breeds Narcissism, Conan Milner writes of an epidemic of egocentric self-love in the world. This epidemic is prevalent among young people in the Western democracies, but in no way absent in other cultures either. Narcissism is defined as an abnormal tendency to derive sexual gratification from admiration of one's own body. It is self-love.

"FORTRESS AMERICA" UNDER SIEGE

"According to Campbell, we are now living amid a narcissism epidemic, as many features of modern society fuel it. It's easy to see how our culture promotes a sense of entitlement and selfishness. Influential entertainment and advertising industries have stimulated our desires for decades, whetted our appetite for status, and cultivated an aspiration for fame. **More than any generation that's come before, we yearn to feel special, and we've never had more opportunities to express it.** We can show off any moment of our lives with a carefully staged selfie, or post a scathing public review whenever any product or service doesn't meet our expectations. Narcissism fares best in big cities and online – places where you can maintain some degree of distance, and treat those around you as disposable. It is pushed out of small towns and close-knit communities because people don't want it around. It destroys relationships.

There's often a point where you have to sacrifice your own desires for the team or the family. But what you get is to be part of a group. It's about trading some of your own individual desires for the betterment of the group. In the long term, it benefits you, and the group. This is classic social theory, but you have to give up something you love to have something more. If you live for yourself, you don't get that much. You have a very limited life. If you're super-talented, you can get away with it for a while. But eventually, people won't want you in their lives." (The Epoch Times, pp C4-5, September 17-23, 2020)

As a member of the baby-boom generation the writer was exposed to these influences. He was a young university student in 1966-69 living in men's residence. He and others complained that the men's and women's residences were separate and that no co-ed visiting was allowed. We murmured against the Christian premier in Edmonton, blaming it all on him. But the issue was larger than that.

CHAPTER 4: WARNINGS ON SOCIALISM & COMMUNISM

In France, in May, 1968, a violent student revolt broke out that shook the world. Parts of Paris were destroyed. The reason – students protesting the separation of young men and women in college residences, exactly like that in Calgary. So, the restrictions were about more than one politician in Edmonton; it was about Western moral traditions. The young people wanted to destroy these traditions and, in Paris, marched holding up "huge portraits of Mao Zedong, and the three "M's" – Marx, Mao, and Marcuse – became their ideological mainstay." At the same time as the Paris riots, protests were occurring in other countries. Chinese Red Guard youth applauded these rebels as part of a universal uprising against traditional customs and authority. (The Epoch Times, "How the Spectre of Communism is Ruling Our World," Popular Culture, a Decadent Indulgence, Chapter 14, 2020)

Yesterday's students become today's leaders. The examples that the leaders in society set become the norm for the citizens of that society. Since Karl Marx sought the destruction of the nuclear family, basic human morality was rejected in place of unrestricted moral degradation. The current LGBTQ movement is an outgrowth of utopian socialism (the perfect society) promulgated by Karl Marx. Every example of past immoral utopian societies resulted in complete disintegration of that society, including Lenin's early U.S.S.R. and many closed communities started by Marxian socialists (The Epoch Times, "How the Spectre of Communism is Ruling Our World," Destruction of the Family – Part 1, Chapter 7, 2020)

> "The lesbian, gay, transgender (LGBT) movement has been closely associated with communism ever since the first utopians began touting the practice of homosexuality as a human right. Since the communist movement claims to emancipate people from the bondage of traditional morality, its ideology naturally calls for supposed LGBT

rights as a part of its program of "sexual liberation." David Thorstad, a Trotskyite founded the North American Man/Boy Love Association (NAMBLA) in 1978. Alan Ginsburg, an American communist and **admirer of Fidel Castro, and a promoter of LGBT and pedophilia**." (Ibid)

In "Nine Commentaries on the Communist Party", Part 9 – The Scoundrel Nature of the CCP, p. 23:

> "The inconsistency between Communist leaders' actions and words can be traced all the way back to their founding father, Karl Marx. Marx bore an illegitimate son; Lenin contracted syphilis from prostitutes; Stalin was sued for forcing a sexual relationship with a singer; Mao Zedong indulged himself in lust; Jiang Zemin is promiscuous; the late Fidel Castro hoarded hundreds of millions of dollars in overseas banks; North Korea's demonic killer, the late Kim Il Song and his children, led a decadent and wasteful life, etc., etc."

As Brian Brennan so aptly put in his 1996 tribute to Ernest C. Manning –

> "By and large, no provincial leader has ever earned and won more public respect, confidence and admiration than has been sustained over a remarkably long period (25 years) by Premier Manning." (B. Brennan, Ernest Manning left indelible mark on Alberta, The Calgary Sun, Calgary Herald, February 21, 1996).

Pierre Trudeau, another admirer of Fidel Castro, was completely different. He repudiated any reference to, or dependence on God, in his government and its policies. Asked what his "just society" was, he said,

> "It means freeing an individual so he will be free of his shackles to fulfill himself in society in the way which judges best without being bound up by standards of morality which have to do with prejudice and religious superstition."

CHAPTER 4: WARNINGS ON SOCIALISM & COMMUNISM

> Prime Minister Trudeau's government passed legislation in 1969 "initiating the decriminalization of homosexuality in Canada." (Shawn Jeffords, LGBTQ2 coin marks progress, The Calgary Sun, April 24, 2019).

In the United States, "as early as 1980, the Supreme Court had banned the Ten Commandments from being displayed in public schools. This decision was the catalyst for an overall movement across the country to have the Ten Commandments removed from public view. In Utah, the ACLU even offered a reward to anyone willing to report those plaques and slates that had not yet been taken down." (The Epoch Times, "How the Spectre of Communism is Ruling Our World, Using the Law for Evil, Chapter 10, 2020)

By removing Biblical standards from society moral corruption set in and we are rapidly approaching a complete breakdown in morality in government, education, the judiciary and business. Manning said that unless we return to the 'old paths' our society is doomed.

> "All God needs to do is let society go down the destructive path it so often chooses for itself and it will ultimately self-destruct. In other words, individuals and nations ultimately reap what they sow. If we permit the seeds of immorality and permissiveness to be sown in the lives and minds of our children, the ultimate harvest will be moral corruption. If we plant the seeds of hate and intolerance, the harvest will be brutality and violence. If we build our economy on debt and usury, we will reap the inevitable consequences. Immorality produces more immorality. Hate produces more hate. Violence produces more violence. Debt produces more debt. All these things feed on themselves and produce after their kind which is why society has within it the seeds of its own self-destruction." (E. C. Manning, "It is Written, #3: Wanted a Man," vintage message on Back to the Bible Hour, July 5, 2020).

"FORTRESS AMERICA" UNDER SIEGE

Dear Reader – please read Mr. Manning's warning again. Only a return to God will save our society from self-destructing.

"The current bastion of communism in the West is located in our universities. Moral corruption coming from these institutions has permeated society. Today, the typical citizen of modern Western democracies now lives in complete individual freedom with respect to all things private, personal, sexual, and moral that he or she can imagine and defend as compliant while not harming others." (William Gairdner, Libertarian socialism: How modern democracy overcame its own contradictions, The Epoch Times, October 9-25, 2018).

> "But with respect to all things public, a bureaucratic statism extends the tentacles of state control into a myriad of private lives, properties, social, artistic, and athletic activities, and commercial operations, while positioning the state as the generous benefactor, regulator and protector of all, equally. The unspoken trade offered as a lure was the understanding that the people wouldn't bemoan their diminished political, property and economic freedoms and the permeation of their lives by high taxation and minutely invasive regulation of they were allowed more sexual and bodily freedoms in exchange... In a nutshell: "Give me (the state) control over your broader citizen liberties and I (the state) will give you all the private rights and pleasures of the body.
>
> "These are states where one-third of the people work to create wealth, one-third are employed by government and one-third receive significant annual income or benefit from the state. In the voting booth the second and third group gangs up on the wealth-creators – and an eventual irreversible catastrophic decline of society occurs."

For the record, Pierre Trudeau ballooned the public sector by 42% in 15 years; Rachel Notley's NDP ballooned

CHAPTER 4: WARNINGS ON SOCIALISM & COMMUNISM

Alberta's public sector by 21.5% in just 4 years. Both were international socialists and fit the above category very well.

Canada is in social and economic decline today, and COVID-19 is fast hastening it along. Alberta is in decline also, courtesy of fossil fuel-hating federal and provincial governments bent on 'bowing the knee' to global warming activism, a smokescreen for international socialist revolution.

People need to remember that both Manning and Aberhart were genuine Bible believing Christians who walked with God. They set an example that has not been equaled since. Our deliverance as a nation depends upon following their example in our personal lives, families and institutions, including government. We need a leader like Manning in Canada today.

Moral virtue begins early in life with such principles instilled in early childhood. Those qualities will feed into all aspects of the adult life later on. If a nation's youth can be corrupted that nation cannot endure; it will disintegrate. The writer remembers being in a small town Canadian movie theatre as a young boy in the 1950s and listening to the girls screaming as Elvis Presley appeared singing on screen. That was only the beginning...the music of rebellion, rock and roll, was only just beginning.

> "After destroying tradition with modern music, the avant-garde used rock n' roll to supplant the role of classical music in people's lives. Sidney Finklestein, the leading music theorist of the Communist Party U.S.A., openly declared that the boundaries between classical and popular should be eliminated. At the same time, **strongly rhythmic rock music** was gaining an increasing foothold in the United States, as classical and traditional music was squeezed out and marginalized.

> The characteristics of rock n' roll include inharmonious sounds, unstructured melody, strong rhythmic beats, and emotional conflicts and contradictions – quite similar to the communist idea of struggle. China's foremost ancient historian, Sima Qian, said only when sound conforms to morality can it be called music. Typically, the lives of rock n' roll musicians are full of sex, violence and drugs.
>
> Rap music followed rock n' roll in the U.S. Rap lyrics are replete with swear words and obscenities, and make plain their rebellion against tradition and society through depictions of drug use, violence and promiscuity." (The Epoch Times, "How the Spectre of Communism is Ruling Our World, Desecrating the Arts, Chapter 11, 2020)

Elvis Presley died tragically of a drug overdose in his forties.

Ernest Manning reported on a Toronto news report in one of his pamphlets, The Face of the Sky – Part 1, 1971:

> "The mother of a teenage boy was absolutely seething because a Toronto homosexual group that had received more than $39,000 in federal grants, mailed her obscene literature for her son to read. The mother's strongest objection was against six panels of cartoons in the March-April edition of "The Body Politic," a bi-monthly newspaper produced by homosexuals in Toronto. Leaving nothing to the imagination, they graphically showed crude scenes of homosexual acts presented as humor. She commented: "In heaven's name what is the federal government doing with the taxpayers of Canada's money in handing out grants to spread such depraved and crude scenes. I am absolutely seething."

The Prime Minister at this time (1971) was Pierre Elliott Trudeau. Some of his first legislative policy changes as Minister of Justice after 1965 was to relax laws on homosexuality in the Canadian legal system. The grant mentioned above likely came from these new policies. Manning commented on this development as follows:

CHAPTER 4: WARNINGS ON SOCIALISM & COMMUNISM

> "Some time ago the criminal code of Canada was amended to remove from the category of offences against society, homosexual acts between consenting adults.
>
> The condoning of homosexual acts is a by-product of the twentieth century permissive society. This article says homosexual groups are now receiving government grants. Contrast this with what the Bible says on this subject."
>
> *"For this cause God gave them up unto vile affections: For even their women did change the natural use into that which is against nature: And likewise also the men, leaving the natural use of the woman, burned in their lust one toward another; men with men working that which is unseemly, and receiving in themselves that recompense of their error which was meet." (Romans 1:26-27).*
>
> "This is a far cry from the attitude of society today." (The Face of the Sky – Part 1, 1971, Back to the Bible Hour pamphlet).

Sexual morality came under siege with popular music enticing youth to rebel and indulge in their sexual instincts and desires. Shockingly corrupt musical productions like hip-hop, rock-and-roll, with drums and guitar behind the vocals, and the focus on promiscuity, murder, violence and drugs dragged the young listeners into the vortex of strife and rebellion against traditional culture.

> "With America as the de facto leader in the tone of global popular culture, the decadent corruption of American cultural productions has had a huge impact on the world...with many other countries, such as China and Japan, emulating them. The sexual revolution struck at traditional morality, promoting radical feminism, abortion, premarital sex and homosexuality. Society became flooded with pornography with the resultant destruction of the family and marriage. The porn industry has been

normalized as part of Japanese society bringing a serious and negative influence on all of Asia. China now exports a large number of prostitutes" (The Epoch Times, "How the Spectre of Communism is Ruling Our World," Popular Culture, a Decadent Indulgence, Chapter 14, 2020)

Nearly all countries are suffering moral decline and decadence as this decadent culture has spread around the world with the aid of the internet, modern smart phones and international travel. Western nations, once the standard for morality and righteous laws are now near the top regarding decadent indulgence. In the Bible, God severely judged Sodom and Gomorrah for their sexual perversion and decadence. The Bible details God's judgment in Genesis chapters 18 and 19.

> "Even as Sodom and Gomorrah, and the cities about them in like manner, giving themselves over to fornication, and going after strange flesh (homosexuality), are set forth for an example, suffering the vengeance of eternal fire." (Jude 7)

Consider the moral condition of our youth in 2020 with the inculcation of left-wing morals over the last 50 years. In a report this spring, Violence in Alberta's Urban Schools: The Perspectives of School Resource Officers," young peoples' exposure to immoral material was documented in six jurisdictions across the province:

> "Multiple officers brought up the prevalence of pornography and sexual relationships among students. "What surprised me when I went into the school? Sexual stuff," said one female officer. "I could not believe it started in Grade 7. What surprised me the most was the level of what they know, what they do, and what they have experienced already at that age." Another officer said the breakdown of sexual relationships was frequently a source of tension, fights and bullying."

CHAPTER 4: WARNINGS ON SOCIALISM & COMMUNISM

>(Jonny Wakefield, Time for training, The Calgary Sun, June 28, 2020).

"The modern concept of Pornographic sex education was first introduced by **Georg Lukacs**, founder of the (Marxist) Frankfurt School of social theory and philosophy. His purpose was to **completely overturn traditional Western values**. In 1919, Lukacs developed a radical sex-education program that taught students about free love and how "outdated" marriage was." (The Epoch Times, "How the Spectre of Communism is Ruling Our World," Sabotaging Education – Part 2, Chapter 12, 2020)

>"The purpose was to pollute children. Children are very curious, but have an immature moral foundation. New and strange content stimulates their curiosity and can lead them down a dark path. Moral relativism, death and drug prevention education, and sex-education courses became a tool for destroying youth – traditional values of family, individual responsibility, love, chastity, a sense of shame, self-control, loyalty, and more."

Canadian public schools have been implementing this perversion for decades, twisting the morality of our young children and youth away from innocence and chastity to pre-pubescent sex and later promiscuity ruining our country's morals and families. Even the provincial conservatives are guilty of continuing this leftist indoctrination.

>"In its absurdity, the (Liberal) Wynne-(Conservative) Ford sex-ed curriculum – as it must now be officially denominated, since Premier Doug Ford's campaign promise to repeal it has been revealed as a sham – is nothing new. If parents continue to sit by and submit blithely to the corruption of their children in state-run moral re-education camps, they should hardly be surprised when little Johnny comes home one day and, after hectoring them as usual on the size of their carbon footprint, demands a sex-change operation.

And now that Ford has eternized Wynne's progressive agenda, if they (the parents) don't withdraw their offspring from school *en masse* – with whatever legal consequences that entails – **they will have convicted themselves of complicity in the sexual abuse of their own children**." (Harley Price, The Absurdity of the Wynne-Ford Sex-Ed Curriculum, The Epoch Times, p. B2, August 29-September 4, 2019)

The effect of this 'dumbing down' and moral corruption is to produce a citizenry lacking adult maturity.

> "Studies have found that there is a tendency in American society for adults to remain in a kind of adolescence longer than in other populations. The National Academy of Science (2002) defined adolescence as 12 to 30 years of age; the MacArthur Foundation argued up to 34 years of age (in the U.S.). The educational system and the media bear the responsibility for this extended period of adolescence that many (American and Canadian) adults find themselves in." (Ibid)

Canada's current prime minister is a perfect case-in-point for this kind of childish behavior. He shows many of the characteristics of the self-serving, hedonistic younger generations that followed the counterculture revolution of the 1960s. His dad was exactly the same.

> "American and Canadian education exaggerate the ideas of freedom and self-centeredness in the name of sentimental self-esteem, from whence issues our current prime minister's habitual virtue-signaling. Generations of young people who don't value morality and don't assume responsibility are the result; young people and adults whose common mindset is: "I want to do what I want, how I want and when I want, and nothing and no one is going to stop me."

This is the perfect society into which to introduce COVID-19 as a communist destabilizing strategy to subvert,

CHAPTER 4: WARNINGS ON SOCIALISM & COMMUNISM

demoralize and ultimately destroy Canada and the United States.

Leaders in the Western democracies fail too often in regard to character and integrity. Political correctness, situation ethics, failure to answer questions honestly, and outright lies by some in high office are often put before the public. Our current Prime Minister's virtue signaling on irrelevant issues such as gender and diversity; as well as his blatant disregard for telling the truth on important issues – nay, lying time and time again – teaches Canadians to disregard the truth and accept lies from the highest office in the land. It weakens Canada's moral foundation from the top down.

One of the most destructive policies of Pierre Trudeau's government was his social welfare programs. They had a negative impact on the recipients.

> "He extended the welfare state damaging the country by removing incentives to work and by diminishing the sense of self-reliance in many regions of Canada. Atlantic Canadians became dependent on equalization rather than following market incentives. You need to pull people into work and out of dependence on government support. "Our economic development" system was deeply infected with politics. It became a prop that promoted Liberal Party fortunes," said visiting economist, Crowley." (Bob Plamondon, The Truth About Trudeau, 2013).

Perpetuated welfare state economics destroys the work ethic and character of the people.

Justin Trudeau is using the same approach today in his COVID-19 extended "emergency relief" programs. He seems unlikely to change this approach.

"FORTRESS AMERICA" UNDER SIEGE

Pierre Trudeau used the welfare state policy to morally undermine regions of Canada, making them dependent upon federal transfers and unemployment benefits rather than giving incentives to diversify their economies and develop self-determination and economic independence from Ottawa. The Maritimes suffered through perpetual dependence upon the federal government that translated into habitual voting in favor of the Liberal Party. Later Conservative administrations found it difficult to break this patronage.

> "Visiting economist Crowley said, "Trudeau presided over an income-redistribution machine that did nothing to equalize the productive capacity of Canadian regions. Atlantic Canadians became dependent on equalization rather than following market incentives with the result – the welfare state perpetuated poverty there. You need to pull people into work and out of dependence on government support. Our system with Trudeau's economic development programs was deeply infested with politics. **It became a prop that promoted Liberal Party fortunes**." (Bob Plamondon, The Truth About Trudeau, 2008)

> "Forbes business magazine summarizes the **Curley Effect**: "A politician or a political party can achieve long-term dominance by tipping the balance of votes in their direction through the implementation of policies that strangle and stifle economic growth. Counterintuitively, making a city (or region) poorer leads to political success for the engineers of that impoverishment." (The Epoch Times, "How the Spectre of Communism is Ruling Our World," Communism Sows Chaos in Politics – Part 2, Chapter 8, 2020)

The federal Liberal Party's attack on Alberta and its efforts to degrade its economy by blocking pipelines, using global warming as a counterfeit pretext, may be part of the same agenda to create poverty and dependence, and ultimately dictatorial control in the

CHAPTER 4: WARNINGS ON SOCIALISM & COMMUNISM

West – similar to what it has already done in Atlantic Canada.

> "In free societies, the government is moving toward authoritarianism, with 'big government' coming to control almost everything." (Ibid)

The Fraser Institute reported that the relative size of Canada's government share of 40.3% in the economy, prior to COVID-19, significantly exceeded that which is necessary among OECD countries for optimal growth of the economy, which is approximately 26%. The trend to bigger and bigger government continues unabated.

> "Government spending levels, along with associated deficits and debt, have reached historic highs across the country – including in 8 of the 10 provinces. Increased debt today means higher taxes tomorrow. If we continue the decade-long trend of growing the size of government in Canada, we will impede rather than foster economic growth and prosperity for Canadians and their families.
>
> Government spending in the optimal level of around 26-30% of the economy provides basic functions needed for society to function optimally such as independent courts, effective policing and basic universal education. Going further usually entails government becoming active in areas where its efforts are counterproductive to growth, such as redistributing income from certain groups to others, rather than incentivizing economic growth; favoring certain industries and sectors of the economy through corporate welfare and protectionism." (Alex Whalen and Steve Globerman, Government is just getting bigger, The Calgary Sun, September 16, 2020)

Nineteenth century French thinker, Alexis de Tocqueville, commented long before our day:

> "If despotism were to be established amongst democratic nations of our days, it might assume a different character; it would be more extensive and more-mild; it would

degrade men without tormenting them." **The welfare state is thus described.** (The Epoch Times, "How the Spectre of Communism is Ruling Our World," The Communist Economic Trap – Part 1, Chapter 9, 2020)

A degraded society is a demoralized society dependent upon the government, and ripe for the relinquishment of its freedoms and a full socialist-communist takeover. Appendix 4 offers a further explanation of this process.

"The Libranos" and "Stop Notley," teach how not to lead by example. With leaders like Trudeau and Notley, people begin to think, "What is truth?" as did Pilate who condemned Jesus Christ to be crucified. How do these kinds of examples effect the conduct of aspiring leaders and those already in responsible positions? It ruins them. After all, the democratic process should rely on truth and integrity at all levels.

The end result of a government that ignores truth is a regime like Communist China which has no truth at all, except the Party line. People are taught that the Party is truth, no matter how bold or how often the Party lies. And they accept those lies without question. God forbid if Canada should ever end up like that. Communism will win then.

CHAPTER 5

SOCIALISM – COMMUNISM

FULFILLING MANNING'S WARNINGS

"Dictatorship is the only means of government that can bring people together in a society devoid of faith."

Alexis de Tocqueville
Socialism-communism is a collectivist killing machine, a death cult that, given free rein knows no limits on brutality. Regard for the sanctity of human life is totally lacking when Marxism reaches its pinnacle of development, as it has in China,

where 'socialism with Chinese characteristics' is how the CCP describes its regime. Here is its fruit:

> "After the Chinese Communist Party seized the reins of power in 1949, it initiated "land reform," to eliminate (liquidate/kill) the landlord class, the "socialist reform" in industry and commerce to eliminate capitalists, the "movement of purging reactionaries" to eliminate folk religions and officials who held office before the communists took power, the "anti-rightist movement" to silence intellectuals, and the "Great Cultural Revolution" to eradicate traditional Chinese culture. It killed young pro-democracy demonstrators in 1989 and initiated persecution and killing of people of conscience, including Falun Gong practitioners, in 1999 until present, using many living prisoners for commercial organ harvesting." (The Epoch Times, "Nine Commentaries on the Communist Party," On How the Chinese Communist Party is an Evil Cult, Part 8, p. 19).

Communists love killing one another, showing it to be a 'Death Cult' at its very worst.

> "Internal fights of Communist Parties are well known. All members of the Politburo of the Russian Communist Party in the first two terms, except Lenin, who had died, and Stalin himself, were executed or committed suicide. Three of the five marshals were executed, three of the five Commanders-in-Chief were executed, all 10 of the secondary army Commanders-in-Chief were executed, 57 of 85 army corps commanders were executed, and 110 of the 195 division commanders were executed." (The Epoch Times, "Nine Commentaries on the Communist Party," On the Chinese Communist Party's History of Killing – Part 7, p. 17, 2004).

> "By the time of the Cultural Revolution in China (1966-1976), almost all the senior members within the Party had been eliminated. None of the former CCP's secretary-generals met with a good ending." (Ibid)

CHAPTER 5: SOCIALISM & COMMUNISM FULFILLED

Far away from the killing fields voices were warning of the dangers of socialism-communism. Ernest C. Manning's Alberta provincial government from 1943 to 1968, was –

> "a free individual enterprise movement opposed to socialism and all forms of statism." (B. Brennan, 2008)

Premier Manning recognized that Canada was headed in a collectivist direction during his day. He sounded the warning that "all forms of statism" were a growing threat to free democracy. That is what we are witnessing in Canada today in federal politics with four of our national parties; namely the Liberals, NDP, Bloc and Greens being socialist and collectivist in policy and character. Only the Conservatives offer an opportunity to preserve our free democracy though there are also within that Party "Red Tory" elements with statist affections.

"As violent communism lost its appeal in the latter part of the 20th century, 'non-violent' forms were devised. These variant strains of socialism infiltrated all of society to the extent that they are difficult to identify." (The Epoch Times, "How the Spectre of Communism is Ruling Our World," The Communist Economic Trap – Part 1, Chapter 9, 2020)

This change of behavior does not make socialism-communism any less dangerous in 2020, as recent social upheaval in the Western democracies and elsewhere demonstrates.

Brian Lilley, in a January 3, 2020, article, "Red scare returns," in the Calgary Sun wrote:

> "I've covered protests across the country during the last 20 years and seeing the old flags of the Soviet Union or banners from various communist groups is not unusual.

What is surprising to me is the mainstreaming of this deadly ideology. Famine, work camps, ethnic cleansing – all have been carried out in the name of supporting the communist state. Here at home we have Maclean's publishing a column calling for the left to stand against capitalism and embrace Karl Marx. A recent poll found just 7% of baby boomers in America hold a favorable view of "communism," and 36% of millennials and 28% of Generation Z. I doubt the numbers would be much different in Canada, quite possibly higher, to tell you the truth."

In "Marx Didn't Distinguish Between Communism and Socialism; Why Should We?" Diana West writes:

"Marx and Engels were emphatic in their insistence that the Communists do not form a separate Party and that they ally themselves with all the forces which work towards a socialist society. Anti-communists need to bear in mind the common aggression of socialists and communists – and "democratic socialists," Fabians, progressives, Alinskyites (not to mention most Democrats and an awful lot of Republicans) – believe in the same centrally planned, varyingly totalitarian vision for America that our Founding Fathers would have to declare independence from all over again. They all travel to the same soul-crushing destination of collectivism." (The Epoch Times, p. B6, February 13-19, 2020).

Alexander Solzhenitsyn's book, "One Day in the Life of Ivan Denisovich," is a 200 page book describing one 24-hour day in the life of an inmate of an inhuman Soviet concentration camp. Every occasion where the political system was mentioned by one of the inmates or guards, the word "socialism" was always used, not "communism." Socialism is, therefore, a dead end path to totalitarianism with the ever out-of-reach Communist "Utopia" as its ultimate end.

CHAPTER 5: SOCIALISM & COMMUNISM FULFILLED

The plight of the Western democracies today is part of a trend begun long ago. For example, Alberta Premier William Aberhart –

> "dismissed the post-war social security plan proposed for Canada by Ottawa social scientist Leonard Marsh as a work of a socialist colluding with international financiers to destroy Christianity and create a world slave state." (Brian Brennan, 2008)

> **"Europe is already in the grip of socialist ideology and policies."** (The Epoch Times, "How the Spectre of Communism is Ruling Our World," How Communism Sows Chaos in Politics, Chapter 8, 2020)

In "Young People's Embrace of Socialism is Partly Their Boomer Parents' Fault," Mark Hendrickson writes:

> "Collectively, our generation has set a poor example. Look at the public policies that have proliferated on our watch. Social security, Medicare, and numerous lesser government programs were established for the purpose of having the government provide for and take care of us. Every politician knows that a formidable majority of boomers and older Americans will fight tooth and nail to resist any reduction of promised benefits, even if the programs look like they'll go bankrupt without such concessions. Therefore, does it offend you that young voters are embracing socialism in the hope and expectation that the federal government will give them free college, free health care and other valuable benefits? They got the idea that the most important parts of our lives are public rather than private matters from their elders – both our generation and a couple of generations before us. **We have done nothing significant to dismantle Big Government or at least to get it to live within its means (i.e., balanced**

budgets, no unfunded liabilities)." (The Epoch Times, p. B6, March 12-18, 2020).

We're blazing a trail into the socialist-collectivist sunset of our free democracies all across the Western world. Totalitarian socialism-communism is at the bottom of this slippery slope; exactly what Manning warned us against.

"Few people know the full facts about what Communism is and what Communists are seeking to do in an effort to capture the world. Because of the ignorance of so many people about what Communists stand for, what their methods for capturing a nation are, and how strong they have become, these terrible termites have been able to all but destroy the very foundation of our nation. I firmly believe that 95% of all Americans would shun them like poison if they knew the real truth." (E. J. Daniels, The Red Devil of Communism, 1954)

Socialism and Communism are the same movement under different names working in a little different way to accomplish the same goal. International Secretary of the Socialist Party, Morris Hilquist, who headed the legal department of the Soviet Bureau in the United States in 1919, said with authority:

> "It is high time that the American public abandon the myth of 'diverse meanings of socialism' and the 'diverse kinds of socialism.' There is not, and probably never was a theory and movement of more striking uniformity than the theory and movement of Socialism. The International Socialist movement is all based on the Marxian (Karl Marx's) program and follows substantially the same methods of propaganda and action. There is no such thing as EUROPEAN socialism or AMERICAN socialism. There is only one kind of socialism the world over –

CHAPTER 5: SOCIALISM & COMMUNISM FULFILLED

> INTERNATIONAL SOCIALISM, which means everywhere the same." (Ibid)

Former Prime Minister, the late Pierre Trudeau had pinned on his dorm door at Harvard University in the 1940s, "Pierre Trudeau, citizen of the world." He said,

> "I want a classless society." To Trudeau the world was evolving to socialism, and more: "The party of the people – socialism, communism – will eventually come out the winner." Trudeau wrote that his personal and political choices had been made for life when he left the London School of Economics in the 1940s." (Bob Plamondon, The Truth About Trudeau, 2013).

Trudeau's statements are fully compatible with those of a diehard, radical socialist-communist.

> "Trudeau believed that massive state intervention can and should be accomplished on borrowed money." (Ibid)

Proof of their sameness is that the CCP (Chinese Communist Party) calls China politically, "socialism with Chinese characteristics," Vietnam, an atheistic communist country, is called the "socialist Republic of Vietnam." Both of their national emblems are the "hammer and sickle" of the original U.S.S.R., the Union of Soviet Socialist Republics, where communism first became established and from where it spread around the world. Those who say they are for Socialism but are opposed to Communism are ignorant of what Socialism is, for the two are the same in principle and purpose. Please refer to Appendix 4 (pp. 601 & 607) to see their deceptive nature in trapping people into totalitarianism.

In, "Nazism, fascism, and socialism are all rooted in Communism, Joshua Philipp writes:

"The concept of a "far left" that is opposed to a "far right" is false. The systems placed on the two ends of that spectrum, including socialism, fascism, and Nazism, are all rooted in communism. And all of them share beliefs in core communist concepts, including state collectivism, planned economies and class struggle." (The Epoch Times, p. A9, June 8-14, 2018).

"A 1926 Nazi pamphlet titled, "Thoughts About the Tasks of the Future," stated, "We are Socialists, enemies, mortal enemies of the present capitalist economic system." It would be easy to mistake this for a Marxist proclamation." (Cid Lazarou, Globalism: Hybrid ideology of the 21st century, The Epoch Times, October 19-25, 2018).

WHAT IS COMMUNISM?

Communism is a universal world philosophy that: in religion, means atheism; in the state, a democratic (totalitarian-1 Party) republic (e.g., The Republic of Vietnam); in industry, a popular collectivism; in ethics, a measureless optimism (utopia); in metaphysics (dealing with nature or being), a naturalistic materialism; in the home, an almost entire loosening of family ties and of marriage bonds." (E. J. Daniels, The Red Devil of Communism, 1954). It advocates the following radical ideas:

1. The abolition of all forms of religion;
2. The destruction of private property and the abolition of inheritance;
3. Revolution under the leadership of the Communist International (Comintern);
4. Engaging in activities in foreign countries in order to cause strikes, riots, sabotage, bloodshed and civil war;
5. Absolute social and racial equality;
6. Destruction of all forms of representative or democratic government, including civil liberties, such as freedom of speech, of the press, and of assemblage;

CHAPTER 5: SOCIALISM & COMMUNISM FULFILLED

7. The ultimate objective of world revolution to establish the dictatorship of the so-called 'proletariat' into a universal union of Soviet socialist republics with its capital in Moscow;
8. The achievement of these ends through extreme appeals to **hatred**."

J. Peters, Russian head of a Communist spy ring in the U.S.A., has said:

> "The Communist Party is like a submerged submarine; the part that you see above water is the periscope, but the part underneath is the real Communist organization; that is the conspiratorial apparatus."

Here are some other key points on how socialism-communism works...by infiltration and camouflage. All of these things are happening today in Canada and the U.S., and in other free democracies around the world.

> "The real power in Communism is within the professional classes (incl. the elites). Taken as a whole the Party depends for its strength on the support it gets from teachers, preachers, actors, writers, union officials, doctors, lawyers, editors, businessmen, and even from millionaires." (E. J. Daniels, The Red Devil of Communism, 1954).

> Communists carry on their work primarily through organizations not generally known as Communistic. They are called "Fronts." (100 Things You Should Know about Communism in the U.S.A.," Committee on Un-American Activities of the U.S. House of Representatives, in E. J. Daniels, The Red Devil of Communism, 1954)

Most of socialist-communist subversion in Western democracies is hidden from the general public. They don't know what is going on, except that society is changing. They generally don't like what is happening but feel powerless to stop it. They are deceived. **Deception** is the essence of socialism-communism, and people have no way to grasp it in its entirety.

The Epoch Times weekly newspaper has been running installments, since July 13, 2018, of a book entitled, "How the Spectre of Communism is Ruling our World." For a complete understanding of socialism-communism and its beginnings you can read the whole series online at **theepochtimes.com**. Many quotations from this excellent book are used by the writer. The Epoch Times published a three volume book set of the entire series in 2020. It can be obtained from their website for $25.

Karl Marx, a German philosopher, wrote "The Communist Manifesto," the 'Bible' of socialism-communism in 1848. It and his 3 volume work, *Das Kapital*, influenced Europe and spread around the entire world. By 1950, one-third of the world's population was enslaved by communist governments in the U.S.S.R., China and Eastern Europe. Today the movement is worldwide and is threatening the Western democracies by infiltration and internal subversion. It has its tentacles around the U.S.A.

> "Marx and Lenin are still the intellectual and the spiritual fathers of Communist societies and of Communist parties around the world."
>
> "Even Khrushchev, when he looks around the world, sees other nations through a Marxist lens." (John Bennett, Christianity and Communism Today, 1960)

When visiting the U.S.S.R., Pierre Trudeau visited the grave of Lenin's mother. He also playfully threw snowballs at Lenin's statue. He obviously liked Lenin who advocated violence to overthrow the existing order. (Bob Plamondon, The Truth About Trudeau, 2013).

CHAPTER 5: SOCIALISM & COMMUNISM FULFILLED

The writer can still remember seeing the communist Russian President, Nikita Khrushchev, banging his shoe on his desk at the UN General Assembly in New York in about 1959 shouting to the Western democracies, and particularly the U.S.,

> "We will bury you. Your grandchildren will be our subjects."

Mr. Khrushchev was right. Communism is not dead; it is alive and well and thriving around the world, including in Canada and the United States.

Though communism says it is atheistic, it is not; it is a religion unto itself. It has all the forms of a religion as shown in Table 1 [see next page]. Though it may seem for a while to co-operate with a religion, the Party will ultimately destroy that religion after it gains complete control, as evidenced by the CCP in China today.

	A	B
1	THE BASIC FORMS OF A RELIGION	CORRESPONDING FORMS OF THE CHINESE COMMUNIST PARTY (CCP)
2	Church or Platform (podium)	All levels of the Party committee; platform from Party meetings to all CCP-controlled media
3	Doctrines	Marxism-Leninism, Mao Zedong's ideology, Deng Xiaoping's Theory, Jiang Zemin's "Three Represents" & Party Constitution
4	Initiation Rites	Ceremony in which oaths are taken to be loyal to the CCP forever
5	Commitment to one religion	A member may only believe in the Communist Party
6	Priests	Party secretaries and staff in charge of Party affairs on all levels
7	Worshiping God	Slandering all gods, and then establishing itself as an unnamed "God"
8	Death is called "ascending to heaven or descending to hell"	Death is called "going to see Marx"
10	Scriptures	The theory and writings of the Communist Party leaders (see above)
11	Preaching	All sorts of meetings; leaders' speeches
12	Chanting scriptures; study or cross-examination of scriptures	Political studies; routine group meetings or activities for the Party members
14	Hymn (religious songs)	Songs to eulogize the Party
15	Donations	Compulsory membership fees; mandatory allocation of gov't budget - money from peoples' sweat & blood - for Party's use
16	Disciplinary punishment	Party discipline - from "house arrest & investigation" and "expulsion from the Party" to deadly tortures and even punishments of relatives and friends
18	TABLE 1. CCP'S SOCIALISM WITH CHINESE CHARACTERISTICS: A RELIGION (from "Nine Commentaries on the Communist Party," - Part 8, p. 19, 2004)	

CHAPTER 5: SOCIALISM & COMMUNISM FULFILLED

An excerpt from Chapter 15, **The Communist Roots of Terrorism,** in "How the Spectre of Communism is Ruling our World," in the June 4-10, 2020, instalment of The Epoch Times follows:

> "From the Paris Commune and Lenin's institutionalization of violence, to the CCP's state-sponsored persecutions, communism has always used terrorism to achieve its aims. Standing with terrorists against Western democratic states is part of the radical left's long march to destroy Western society from within."

In "The Face of the Sky – Part 2, 1972, Ernest Manning listed the 9 rules for a Communist takeover of a democratic society (pp. 119-120). At least 7 of them are in one way or another afflicting the United States in 2020, namely: the oil price collapse caused by Russia and Saudi Arabia, the COVID-19 pandemic caused by Communist China and the targeted "Black Lives Matter" violent riots and looting of US cities following the death George Floyd, accompanied by the incessant and self-denigrating focus on racism and vilifying the police. They are a combined mixture of toxic Marxist methods to deconstruct American free democracy and make the U.S. a socialist slave state. This kind of revolutionary effort is tried and proven.

Ernest C. Manning wrote about this covert war on our democratic freedom in another pamphlet entitled, Middle East Conflict, 1973, that:

> "The Soviet Union (and in 2020, Russia and China) has a vested interest in weakening the economy of the United States which stands as the major obstacle in the way of communism's long-range objective of world domination. It is completely consistent with communistic strategy to foster any action on the part of the Arab states that would weaken the U.S. economy especially at a time when the United States is beset by domestic instability at home

and is suffering the aftermath of her prolonged involvement in Viet Nam as a result of communist aggression there."

Communism is the greatest menace in the world today. The Union of Soviet Socialist Republics (U.S.S.R.) sided with the Middle East Muslim nations in supplying arms and logical support for their attacks on Israel, to destroy the Jewish state. Russian armaments spurred the Arab nations' to plans to attack Israel prior to the 6-Day War in 1967, and to attack it during the Yom Kippur War in October, 1973. It also supported Yasser Arafat and the terrorist Palestinian Liberation Organization (PLO) in the 1970s and onward.

> A 2004 study by American scholar David Horowitz titled, "Unholy Alliance: Radical Islam and the American Left" reveals the nefarious (very wicked) connection between Islamic extremists and the radical leftists. According to his analysis, the radical left around the world has served to cover for Islamic jihadis.

As Canada has moved further to the left in recent years we see government policy enshrine LGBTQ, etc. rights into law, adopt euthanasia, introduce sexual education and gender ideology, and legislate more and more against Christian churches.

Pierre Trudeau, Canada's Prime Minister from 1968 to 1984 had a history of close attachment to murderous communist regimes.

> "Trudeau travelled to China in 1949 as a young man, and again in 1960 on a trip sponsored by the regime (CCP). "We are convinced that we are witnessing the beginning of an industrial revolution." Their trip was during the famine caused by Mao's Great Leap Forward that led to the deaths of about 40 million Chinese farmers."

CHAPTER 5: SOCIALISM & COMMUNISM FULFILLED

As Ernest Manning noted, Pierre Trudeau through his 'Laurentian elite' intellectual bias, could not understand the lot of the common people, their needs and their suffering.

> "He doesn't know how the other half lives." (Brennan, 2008)

Pierre Trudeau put forth his political philosophy while on one of his trips as a younger man.

> "While on a visit to Moscow to attend a propaganda conference in the 1950s, Trudeau, then a young political activist from Quebec, had reportedly told the wife of the U.S. charge d'affaires that he was a communist and a Catholic and had come to Moscow to criticize the United States and praise the Soviet Union, according to the 2013 book, "The Truth about Trudeau" by Bob Plamondon."
>
> "Intellectuals tend to be fooled by radical ideologies. British historian analyzed the lives and radical political views of Rousseau and a dozen intellectuals who followed him. He found that they shared the fatal weaknesses of arrogance and egocentrism." (The Epoch Times, How the Spectre of Communism is Ruling Our World, Infiltrating the West – Part 2, Chapter 5, 2020).
>
> RE: Pierre Trudeau; "His lack of respect for others…Even his friends described him as a dilettante, a spoiled brat and an intellectual snob." (Bob Plamondon, The Truth About Trudeau, 2013).

Canada's hard turn to the left began in 1965 when Pierre Trudeau became Minister of Justice and shortly thereafter, Prime Minister of Canada from 1968 until 1984. He was the first Western leader whose main foreign policy objective was to establish diplomatic relations with Communist China in 1970 and help it join the UN shortly after. More than anyone else he set

Canada on the course to socialism. Trudeau's understudy and close friend, Former Prime Minister (1993-2003), Jean Chretien boasted,

> "For the 10 years as the prime minister, I met the president of China (Jiang Zemin) 17 times, so I was close to China." Jiang went on to launch a brutal campaign of persecution against the traditional meditation discipline Falun Gong in 1999." (The Epoch Times, "How the Spectre of Communism is Ruling Our World, Infiltrating the West – Part 2, Chapter 5, 2020)

One of the Chretien government's first actions on Parliamentary procedure after winning a huge majority in the 1993 election was to immediately change the opening prayer in the House of Commons. Three times, "in the name of our Lord and Savior Jesus Christ," was mentioned in the prayer. It was taken out, removing a link to Canada's Judeo-Christian heritage (Hansard). Trudeau mentored Chretien. Therefore, his understudy was also sympathetic toward socialism-communism where there was no room for God.

Hundreds of thousands, or more, of innocent people have died in Jiang Zemin's persecution of peaceful people of conscience, many of whom have been victims of China's organ 'harvesting' business. Xi Jinping has carried forward this bloody business to the present.

Prime Minister Pierre Trudeau visited China in 1973, during Mao's Cultural Revolution (1966-76), and met Mao and Premier Zhou Enlai,

> "Trudeau praised the regime for its governance...is striving to provide human dignity and equality of opportunity for the Chinese people." (Ibid)

CHAPTER 5: SOCIALISM & COMMUNISM FULFILLED

The writer remembers as a younger man Zhou Enlai's 'moderate' image, compared to Mao's, as presented in the mainstream media. Pierre Trudeau said Zhou Enlai was the most impressive leader that he had ever met. Looks are deceiving, even to a prodigious intellect like his.

> "Party (CCP) nature overwhelms human nature so completely that the Chinese people have lost their humanity. For instance, Zhou Enlai and Sun Bingwen were once comrades. After Sun Bingwen died, Zhou Enlai took his daughter, Sun Weishi, as his adopted daughter. During the Cultural Revolution, Sun Weishi was reprimanded. She later died in custody from a long nail driven into her head. Her arrest warrant had been signed by her step-father Zhou Enlai." (The Epoch Times, "Nine Commentaries on the Communist Party" – Part 2, 2004)

The Cultural Revolution was, according to writer Qui Mu:

> "an unprecedented calamity: [the CCP] imprisoned millions, ended the lives of millions more, shattered families, turned children into hoodlums and villains, burned books, tore down ancient buildings, and destroyed ancient intellectuals' gravesites, committing all kinds of crimes in the name of revolution." (The Epoch Times, "Nine Commentaries on the Communist Party" – Part 3, On the Tyranny of the Chinese Communist Party, 2004)

Other descriptions of this "class struggle" are described in the Nine Commentaries on the Communist Party. The very people Trudeau praised were behind this 10 year event that was still going on at the time of his visit in 1973.

> "students beating their teachers, fathers and sons turning against each other, Red guards wantonly killing the innocent...The CCP has covered up the direct instigation

of and involvement in the violence by party leaders and government officials...their logic that the enemies of the class struggle deserved any violence against them." (Ibid, Part 3, On the Tyranny of the Chinese Communist Party & Part 8, On How the Chinese Communist Party is an Evil Cult)

"Another one of Mao's claims is that the Cultural Revolution should be conducted "every seven or eight years." Every struggle and movement served as an exercise in terror, so that the Chinese people trembled in their hearts, submitted to the terror and gradually became enslaved under the CCP's control." (Ibid, Part 1, On What the Communist Party Is)

In 2020, China is still the same, and she is confident that she will soon rule the world.

"Central party officials run the government, military, media and universities collectively in a manner reminiscent of the science-fiction Borg organism of *Star Trek*, which was a horde of robot-like entities all under the control of a central mind." (Victor Davis Hanson, China's government is like something out of '1984,' The Calgary Sun, February 21, 2020)

Justin Trudeau is not ignorant of these well-known atrocities yet continues to hold China's dictatorship in "admiration."

China and Russia still have a mutual interest in overthrowing the West; it is socialism-communism. In their quest to be 'top dog' of the nations they will work together, then afterward will fight it out with each other. Germany and Japan had the same kind of agreement in the Second World War. Russia is still meddling in Venezuela's political crisis.

"China may be the more dynamic partner in the Communist alliance, but Russia may still at times run

CHAPTER 5: SOCIALISM & COMMUNISM FULFILLED

interference for China internationally and give many kinds of support to Communist expansion by the combination of outside pressure and internal revolt. **We shall have to live for a long time with the problem imposed by the imperialism of international Communism even if it should turn out that Russia is not the prime mover."** (John Bennett, Christianity and Communism Today, 1960).

The Bible speaks prophetically of a great invasion into the Middle East by the "Kings of the east" in Revelation 16:12.

> "And the sixth angel poured out his vial upon the great river Euphrates; and the water thereof was dried up, that **the way of the kings of the east** might be prepared." (Revelation 16:12)

The Scripture describes the size of this army as 200 million strong. This invasion indicates that China succeeds in pushing America out of eastern Asia and gains dominance over the lesser Asian powers such as Japan, Korea, Taiwan, Indochina and the Philippines who become her subjects. They are united to form the invasion force mentioned in Revelation. India is probably the first victim of this huge army. This event is quite near as China's current geo-political intentions become clearer in Asia.

> With the OBOR (One Belt One Road) strategy China has successfully integrated British geographer/historian Halford Mackinder's 1904, "Whoever rules Central Asia (the Heartland) commands Eurasia (the World-Island); whoever rules the World-Island commands the World," with American naval historian Alfred Mahan's strategy to "dominate sea power by controlling the sea lanes, choke points and canals by policing global trade," completed by Nicholas Spykman's contrasting view that, "Who controls the Rimland (coastal land encircling Asia) rules EuroAsia; who rules EuroAsia controls the destinies of

the world." The CCP assumes to extend its leadership across Asia, Africa and Latin America in its struggle against the free world, and ultimately become the world's number one power." (The Epoch Times, "How the Spectre of Communism is Ruling Our World," The Chinese Communist Party's Global Ambitions – Part 1, Chapter 18, 2020)

China has succeeded in sowing its divide and rule strategy to weaken unity in the European Union and every country where its fingerprints or footprints appear. Through the PRC's influence Europe is gradually becoming estranged from its traditional ally, the U.S.

> "Europe's gates are wide-open with political and professional elites starting to embrace Chinese rhetoric and interests, including where they contradict national and/or European interests. Beijing's political, economic, and cultural infiltration and espionage in Europe are purposed to plunder sensitive information regarding major states' economic assets."

Canada's democracy is under a severe threat from China's communist government. Beijing finds areas where its enemies are weak then works to target and use elites from the Chinese diaspora in those countries to advance and promote their interests. A weak, malleable and socialist Liberal government is a soft target for China to bully and destabilize. It wishes to use a weak pro-Beijing, elite-controlled Canada to encircle its enemy, the U.S., along its northern border. Former Liberal PMs Pierre Trudeau and Jean Chretien were close to tyrannical Mao Zedong and Jiang Zemin respectively, aiding and abetting this long term strategy. Here is the current situation as described by Omid Ghoreishi in The Epoch Times, pp. A1, A3, October 8-14, 2020:

> "Foreign governments (in this case China) go after (key) members of their diaspora, in some cases "somebody

CHAPTER 5: SOCIALISM & COMMUNISM FULFILLED

who's second, third generation," so that "there's the old country connection." A relationship is formed, the individual is offered trips back to the home country. When the individual later assumes a position of power, "all of a sudden decisions aren't taken on the basis of the public good but on the basis of another country's preoccupations." The CCP's United Front builds ethnic Chinese-based political organizations, makes political donations, supports ethnic Chinese politicians, and deploys votes to swing close-run elections. **The program is most advanced in Canada,** where the diaspora's flow of money bought political influence.

If the candidate is a prominent member of the United Front or avoid saying anything critical of the regime they are under CCP influence. **Canada is in deep trouble because of the elites**, where the business political elite have become entangled with the Chinese political and corporate elite resulting in Canada's diplomatic dealings with China becoming embarrassingly submissive. "**The kind of intimidation and bullying that Canada has been subject to from Beijing is shameful for any nation with a modicum of self-respect. <u>If Canada is going to reassert its independence, this is not something that will be done in a month or two. THIS IS A 10-YEAR STRUGGLE, because the influence of the CCP runs very deep in Canadian institutions.</u>" <u>Britain "has passed the point of no return</u>," said Australian author Clive Hamilton in his book, "Hidden Hand." ACT by 1. Exposing it; 2. Holding to account the political and business leaders involved; and 3. Enacting foreign interference laws as Australia has done making United Front activities illegal."

Canadians have put in the highest office in their land admirers of Communist China. Pierre Trudeau, Jean Chretien and Justin Trudeau doted over this regime. That speaks volumes for the value and respect they had, and have for Canada's free democracy patterned after the British Parliament? They have made Canada subject to China together with other highly-placed eastern elites primarily from Quebec and Ontario.

1. The abolition of all forms of religion;

Marx and Engels wrote in The Communist Manifesto, that under their system, "the bourgeois family will vanish as a matter of course." They stated clearly their goal that "communism abolishes eternal truths, it abolishes all religion, and all morality." (The Epoch Times, p. A10, May 4, 2019).

Communism is the greatest foe of Christianity. It is anti-God, anti-religion, anti-church, anti-society, anti-home, anti-America and anti-everything else that is dear to the hearts of true Christians and Americans. It is a more deadly "ism" than even Fascism or National Socialism (NAZISM), bad as these were. (E. J. Daniels, The Red Devil of Communism, 1954)

Communist leaders, knowing the teachings of the movement, try and hide their anti-Scriptural doctrines from those who love God, the Bible, and right, UNTIL THEY GET FULL CONTROL. But the truth is, Communism is at "war with God and religion." (Ibid)

The writer worked and lived in Venezuela in 1997-1998. Hugo Chavez was elected President in 1998. One of his first objectives after he took control of the country was to target the children's education. No Christian curriculum or Bible was allowed in any schools in Venezuela within a few years after Chavez took power. A socialist curriculum was imposed.

Socialism-communism is particularly malevolent and hateful toward genuine Bible Christianity because it is Marxism's greatest adversary.

CHAPTER 5: SOCIALISM & COMMUNISM FULFILLED

> "Genuine (Bible) Christianity is the most potent force in the world to change human nature through the miracle of a spiritual new birth." (Ernest Manning, The Face of the Sky, Part 1, 1971, Canada's National Back to the Bible Hour pamphlet)

The new birth produces something that socialism and communism cannot combat, and that is spiritual regeneration and the love of God.

> "But the fruit of the Spirit is love, joy, peace, longsuffering, gentleness, goodness, faith, meekness, temperance." (Galatians 5:22-23)

Socialism-communism may begin benignly, but soon shows its true nature. It is a death cult with more blood on its hands than any other system of belief ever devised by man. To demonstrate this point, Jim Jones began as a charismatic Indiana preacher and led his Peoples Temple flock of over 900 souls to death in the jungles of Guyana, S.A., on November 18, 1978. His radicalism wasn't revealed at first but later the truth came out.

> "By the mid-1970s Jones admitted he was, in fact, a communist. 'If you're born in capitalist America, racist America, fascist America, then you're born in sin. But if you're born in socialism, you're not born in sin.' Later that day the 909 residents of Jonestown gulped down cyanide mixed with purple Kool-Aid. Members sobbed as their leader spoke. 'Stop these hysterics. This is not the way for people who are socialists or communists to die,' adding that they were committing 'revolutionary suicide.'"
> (Brad Hunter, Followed Leader into Death, Calgary Sun, November 11, 2018)

> "The leader of the infamous Peoples Temple of the Disciples of Christ called himself the reincarnation of Lenin, was a Marxist believer and set the original teachings of Marxism-Leninism and Mao Zedong Thought as the doctrine of the Peoples Temple." (The

"FORTRESS AMERICA" UNDER SIEGE

> Epoch Times, "How the Spectre of Communism is Ruling Our World," The Revolt Against God, Chapter 6, 2020).

The people had been deceived. And that is the nature of communism...deception. One of the survivors wrote in her 1995 memoir:

> "I never wanted to go to Guyana and die...I didn't think Jim would do a thing like that." (ibid)

In, Remembering Solzhenitsyn and the brutality of the Gulag, Gary Greg in The Epoch Times (December 21-27, 2018) reminds us of that iconic Russian writer's depiction of the horrors of totalitarian socialism in Russia during Stalin's regime when 62 million civilians were murdered by their own government. The Gulag Archipelago (1973) describes this time of suffering and despair for the Russian people. That is the true face of socialism-communism, just as in Jonestown. It is the "works of the flesh," described in the Bible:

> "Now the works of the flesh are manifest, which are these; Adultery, fornication, uncleanness, lasciviousness, idolatry, witchcraft, hatred, variance, emulations, wrath, strife, seditions, heresies, envyings, murders, drunkenness, revellings, and such like: of the which I have also told you in time past, that they which do such things shall not inherit the kingdom of God." (Galatians 5:19-21)

Vladimir Lenin, a leftist icon, and follower of Karl Marx, who took power in Russia in 1917, forming the U.S.S.R., exhibited hatred for traditional society and advocated destroying it. Their modern followers have the same mindset.

> "It's important to realize that people recognize the extent to which hatred has found a home on the political left." (Mark Hendrickson, Ominous Signs of Hatred in Politics, The Epoch Times, p. B1, October 17-23, 2019)

CHAPTER 5: SOCIALISM & COMMUNISM FULFILLED

In Ernest Manning's The Face of the Sky – Part 2, a News Report from Moscow reads as follows:

> "I lined the pupils up and ordered all those who considered themselves Baptists to come forward two paces. About thirty came forward. I asked them if they intended to go on praying. They all replied that they would. Then I ordered the teachers to give them all low marks for conduct."

> "This is how the headmaster of a Soviet school described his favorite method of combatting religion among children. His method is criticized in an atheist manual for teachers and parents, published in Leningrad. It demands that all school children be so indoctrinated with scientific atheism that they will stop their grandmothers from praying. Schools are advised to organize their own museums of atheism to which pupils are asked to bring their parents." (Canada's National Back to the Bible Hour pamphlet)

Communism always aims to indoctrinate the children as soon as possible after taking power. In Russia, between 1920 and 1989, over 6 K-12 'generations' of school children were thus indoctrinated, making socialism-communism a part of the peoples' mindset even to the present day. Their present leader, Putin, was part of the KGB. Russia, today, is anything but a free democracy.

> "The Soviet Union crumpled, but Lenin's mindset has shaped our political world and endures everywhere, including the progressive dream palaces on western campuses. Lenin hated capitalism because it is generally a win-win for buyers and sellers." (Barbara Kay, The Epoch Times, Human Wreckage: Pondering Lenin's Legacy on 150th Anniversary of His Birth, p. B1, April 23-29, 2020)

Kay quotes Gary Morson, professor in Southern University as follows"

"FORTRESS AMERICA" UNDER SIEGE

> "I know of no other society, except those modeled on the one Lenin created, where schoolchildren were taught that mercy, kindness, and pity are vices." Empathy might lead to hesitation in denouncing one's parents, after all."
> (Ibid)

America faces Lenin's potential wreckage as a future threat – even a mortal peril – to its free democracy and Christian churches.

> "A recent Victims of Communism Memorial Foundation survey found that 51% of American millennials would rather live in a socialist or communist country than in a capitalist country, and 25% view Lenin favorably. Some of their beliefs represent their having been indoctrinated by their K-12 teachers and college professors." (Walter Williams, Young people and troubling views on socialism and communism, The Calgary Sun, December 7, 2018)

In 1951, at age 32, Trudeau visited the U.S.S.R. He reflected admiration for Soviet methods.

> "Contrasting the evils of capitalism with communism, Trudeau wrote of his Soviet hosts, "From a material point of view your system can be excellent for countries such as yours." (Bob Plamondon, The Truth About Trudeau, 2013).

He returned to the U.S.S.R. in 1971 as prime minister and addressed the regime saying that Canada's and the Soviet's regimes had similar constitutional frameworks. (Ibid) What a joke! Few Canadians would have agreed with him. Actually, he wanted a Soviet Canada.

Trudeau had little pity for Soviet dissidents. Incredibly, Trudeau shrugged off the Russian occupation of Eastern Europe. He did not seem to care about the brutality of Soviet suppression in Hungary, Czechoslovakia and Poland, despite the great suffering inflicted on people

CHAPTER 5: SOCIALISM & COMMUNISM FULFILLED

who desired only freedom from communist suppression. He felt the Yalta Conference in 1945 gave the Soviet Union the right to rule Eastern Europe as they wished. (Ibid)

> "The notion that Trudeau was a respected world statesman is utter bunk. He had nonsensical ideas about the legitimacy of the Soviet occupation of Eastern Europe...despite being a civil liberties advocate. He had a very weak record raising such point with left-wing dictatorships. Robert Ford, Canadian Ambassador in Moscow and Michael Gauvin. ICC in Viet Nam, both highly regarded men **"thought Trudeau was an unmitigated jackass."** (Conrad Black in Bob Plamondon, The Truth About Trudeau, 2013).

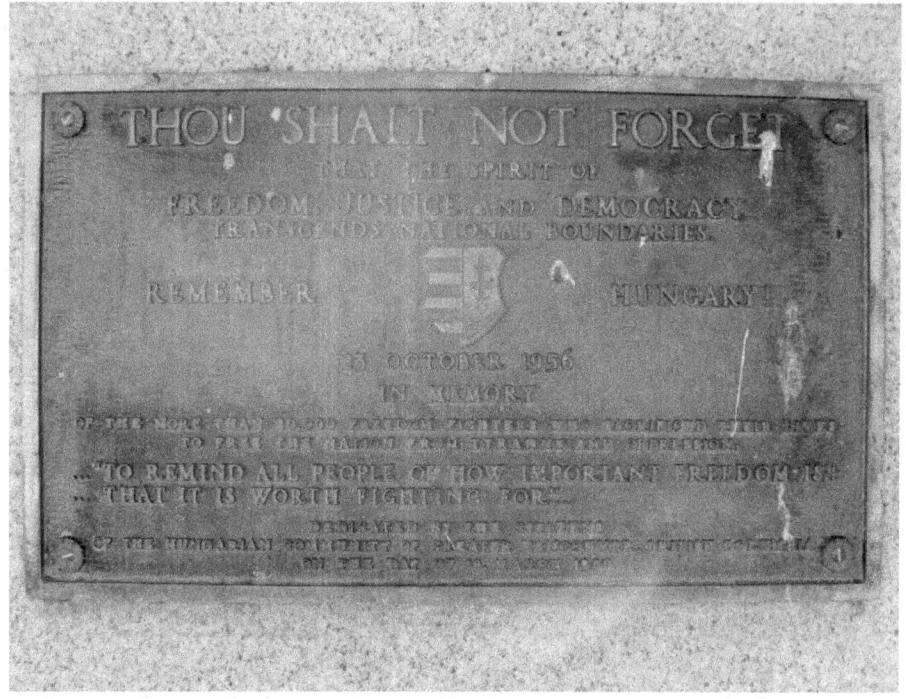

Please examine closely the plaque that the writer recently photographed in Queen Elizabeth II Park in Vancouver, B.C. commemorating the 1956 Hungarian Revolution against Soviet tyranny. The writer still remembers the fear felt as a nine-year old boy at the news of the Russian army invading Hungary and killing those desiring free democracy and an end to totalitarian communist rule. The fear of nuclear war accompanied the news reports.

In light of all of this Soviet tyranny, Trudeau was a "foe of NATO and fan of unilateral Canadian disarmament." (Ibid) He sided with the Russians.

Pierre Trudeau's 1983 "Peace Initiative," lacked credibility. After unilaterally disarming Canada and diminishing its military over 15 years, he naively thought he could bring peace to the world. He was called a comic figure who was playing a game without making the defense spending to be taken seriously. Newsweek correspondent, Eleanor Clift wrote,

> "Trudeau does not have enough country to support his ambitions." (Ibid)

Some day in the near future another leader like Trudeau will bring about a world peace treaty. He will be the international socialist world leader called the **antichrist** and **beast** of Revelation chapter 13. His peace will be a fake peace like all socialist treaties, and will end up causing worldwide suffering and destruction.

> "And through his policy also he shall cause craft to prosper in his hand; and he shall magnify himself in his heart, **and by peace shall destroy many**: he shall also stand up against the Prince of princes (Jesus Christ); but he shall be broken without hand." (Daniel 8:25).

Manning warned in his writings that free democracies should never make treaties in good faith with socialist-communist governments because they don't have the moral grounds of faith to keep them. "How the Spectre

CHAPTER 5: SOCIALISM & COMMUNISM FULFILLED

of Communism is Ruling Our World," Infiltrating the West – Part 1, Chapter 5, 2020, states:

> "A study conducted by the U.S. Senate Committee on the Judiciary in 1955 found that in the 38 years since the founding of the Soviet regime, it had signed nearly 1,000 bilateral or multilateral treaties with various countries around the world, but breached nearly all the promises it had made. **The authors noted that the Soviet Union (U.S.S.R.) was probably the least trustworthy of all major nations in history.**"

Russia is just as untrustworthy today though it has changed its outward appearance. Its heart is unchanged. The West cannot trust Russia, and especially NOT as an ally against China. That would be fatal. Putin proves that.

No free democracy can make a treaty with any socialist-communist dictatorship or oligarchy. They will be betrayed...sooner or later. The end times peace treaty between Israel and a totalitarian socialist leader will end in another Holocaust for the Jews, (Daniel 9:27, Ezekiel 38 & 39) and death for multitudes of Gentiles around the world. It will be a false peace.

> "For when they shall say, Peace and safety; then sudden destruction cometh upon them, as travail upon a woman with child; and they shall not escape." (1 Thessalonians 5:3).

Communists took power in China in 1949 after many years of infiltration, subversion and false peace pacts with the Chinese Nationalists. The communists soon began jailing religious leaders, driving out missionaries, and dismantling or destroying churches, typical of everywhere communism spreads. Killing was epidemic and continues to this day.

> "In February, 2019, Liberal MP Borys Wrzesnewskyj said that since the Second World War, the world hasn't seen such "human horrors on an industrial scale by a state, by a government" as the organ harvesting carried out by the Chinese communist regime.
>
> "After the live organ removal, some of their bodies were directly thrown into the crematory oven. No trace of their bodies was left," he said. Her ex-husband, a surgeon told Annie he had removed corneas from about 2000 Falun Gong adherents between 2001 and 2003." (The Epoch Times Special Edition, "How the Chinese Communist Party is Endangering Canada and the World," May/June, 2020)

Fifty years later, The Epoch Times reports, "Beijing Orders Churches to Promote the Chinese Communist Party – or Else." Stephen Mosher writes:

> "On February 1, 2020 new and onerous restrictions on churches, temples, shrines, and all forms of organized religious activity will come into force in China. The "Control Measures for Religious Groups," consist of 41 articles that deal with every facet of religious life. Also, each and every religious group, as a condition of being allowed to exist at all, must first register with the "Civil Affairs" office of the communist regime. The Falun Gong, and other groups such as the Early Rain Covenant Church were called "heretical," and banned from registering."

Consider Article 17 –

> "Religious groups must propagandize the principles and policies of the Chinese Communist Party, along with national laws, regulations and ordinances, to all of their religious staff and followers to embrace the Chinese Communist Party's leadership, to embrace the socialist system, to uphold the path of socialism with Chinese characteristics, to obey national laws, regulations, ordinances, and policies; correctly resolve the relationship between national laws and religious

CHAPTER 5: SOCIALISM & COMMUNISM FULFILLED

commandments; strengthen awareness of the nation, the rule of law, and the people.

Replacing the worship of God with the worship of the Party-State is precisely what the CCP is trying to do today in China. This is precisely what the Nazis attempted to do in the 1930s to German Catholic and Protestant Churches – turn them into supporters of National Socialism and promoters of its ideology.

Upon reading the new regulations, a Chinese Catholic priest commented to Asia News: "In practice, your religion no longer matters if you are Buddhist or Taoist or Muslim or Christian; the only religion allowed is faith in the Chinese Communist Party.

Or, as another believer put it to me even more succinctly, "The walls are closing in."' (Stephen Mosher, The Epoch Times, p. A9, January 23-29, 2020)

Exactly 200 years after his birth on May 5, 1818, **a statue of Karl Marx given by the Chinese Communist regime – itself responsible for the deaths of nearly 80 million** (innocent Chinese) **people – was erected** (as a gift) **in Trier, Germany, the city of Marx's birth.** (The Epoch Times, May 11, 2018).

In a keynote speech in November 2018, Xi Jinping, China's most Mao-like leader since the Chairman Mao's death in 1976, emphasized the need to "remain unmoved in upholding Marxism's guidance. We must persist in having the party lead all work."

> ""The Communist Party holds up Marxism as its religious doctrine and shows it off as 'the unbreakable truth.'" In China, where the Communist Party is the state religion, groups with different opinions are not allowed to exist." (The Epoch Times; "Nine Commentaries on the Communist Party," – Part 8, On How the CCP is an Evil Cult, p. 19, 2004)

"FORTRESS AMERICA" UNDER SIEGE

Even a small number of truly committed socialist-communist believers can take control of a country, and then transform it into their ideal of a Marxist utopia, annihilating all those whom they consider opposed to their agenda.

> "True communist believers have no life apart from the Party (Partinost). George Orwell understood that the essence of totalitarianism is a citizen who does not himself distinguish between right and wrong. **Right** is what the Party says; everything else must therefore be **wrong**. In the "Gulag Archipelago," Alexander Solzhenitsyn observed that Shakespeare's tragic protagonists are content to murder only a handful of people. They stop killing, he explained, because "they have no ideology." (Barbara Kay, The Epoch Times, Human Wreckage: Pondering Lenin's Legacy on 150th Anniversary of His Birth, p. B1, April 23-29, 2020)

Joshua Philipp, "In Socialist Theocracy, Getting 'Woke' Brings Absolution," writes:

> "Socialism is very much a theocratic system. In it destruction of God, it aimed to replace God; and in its destruction of morals it has looked to create a new morality. The statist theocracy now rules.
>
> To be forgiven for politicized sin, the socialists must proclaim their hatred of who they are. The white person must proclaim their hatred of "white privilege," the man must proclaim his hatred of "toxic masculinity," and the business owner must announce his opposition to "capitalism." (The Epoch Times, p. B5, December 27, 2019 - January 5, 2020)

Socialism-communism has no such restraints. There is a truly frightening prospect for conservatives and the Christian churches if a totalitarian government gains control of the United States.

CHAPTER 5: SOCIALISM & COMMUNISM FULFILLED

Consider China in 2020, forty-four years after the death of Mao Zedong. Beginning with the persecution of Falun Gong in 1999 until the present day (2020), hundreds of thousands of people of conscience have been imprisoned, tortured, killed and brainwashed by the CCP. Forced organ removal causing death has gone on unabated among these innocent civilians in China's booming organ transplant business. Falun Gong's core beliefs are "Truthfulness, Compassion and Tolerance." Why would such people be killed? Because the regime is the antithesis of what they believe.

The CCP is a slave to the atheistic **Marxist imperative**. The revolution has to move forward; the communist Utopia has to be realized historically, and to this day. *This required, in communist eyes, that actual and potential opponents be eliminated* (killed) *and that, like cogs in a machine, those that remain* <u>obey commands from the party, absolutely</u>. No competing power structure could remain; not religious leaders, not village and hamlet leaders, not alternative voices. Nor could land or productive machinery be allowed in private hands, to be possibly used contrary to the communist restructuring of society. <u>Anyway, capitalists were "evil."</u> This was after all a revolutionary war, a war against domestic capitalism, ultimately for Utopia, so murder by the state was implemented, no matter the number of civilians sacrificed. (Rudolf Rummel, Death by Government, 1987).

A column, **Freedom of religion disappearing in Canada** appearing in the June 22, 2018, Calgary Sun. Brian Giesbrecht, a retired judge, wrote:

> "Freedom of religion received two blows recently – one from the Trudeau government and a second from the Supreme Court.

> First: The federal government announced that any group wishing to apply for summer job grants had to sign an agreement pledging to follow the Liberal Party's official policy on a woman's "freedom of choice," with respect to abortion. There is no law about abortion at all in Canada, (only) an absolute and unrestricted freedom to abort right up to the moment of delivery of the baby. Many religious groups cannot, in good conscience, sign the form – and won't be eligible for grants of their own tax money.
>
> Second: In the Trinity Law School Case, the Supreme Court ruled they would allow provincial Law Societies to override religious choices made by candidates who freely chose to abide by the principles of certain Christian law schools, as a condition of entry.
>
> We are being required to bow down to some strange Gospel of the Secular, as interpreted by unelected judges, and a self-described feminist Prime Minister, who both insist on telling us all what we must think."

Calgary City Council passed a bylaw banning 'conversion therapy' on May 25, 2020, thus making it illegal to counsel anyone on gender identity. A city councilor said the bylaw represented a "societal shift." Businesses face a fine of $10,000 for advertising it. Christian counselling or witnessing to a member of the LGBT group is now made illegal by this law. Anyone in the LGBTQ group could accuse a Christian witnessing or passing gospel tracts of 'trying to convert me.' This bylaw is a serious attack on religious freedom.

In 2016, Rachel Notley's NDP socialist government set out Alberta provincial guidelines directing schools to fully accommodate LGBTQ students, particularly transgender ones. Roman Catholic Bishop Fred Henry, in a written statement called the move "dictatorial" and an assault on Catholics, forcing their schools to violate

CHAPTER 5: SOCIALISM & COMMUNISM FULFILLED

their own doctrines. An outcry arose against Mr. Henry calling his remarks:

> "fanatical," "dangerous bigotry", "out of touch with modern realities," "harmful and hateful rhetoric," "a distressing assault on LGBTQ youth," and "this is a scared man who is clearly anti-gay, anti-transgender, and anti-LGBTQ." (Bill Kaufmann, 'Harmful and hateful rhetoric' – Calgary bishop assailed for LGBTQ views, The Calgary Sun, January 15, 2016)

Welcome to religious persecution under socialist 'lite.' It can only get worse in the years to come wherever left-wing parties form government. Thankfully, the NDP was defeated in the 2019 provincial election and replaced by a conservative government.

No wonder the Christian churches are under assault by Justin Trudeau's government. His father, Jesuit-educated intellectual Pierre Trudeau, scorned Christianity, and hence, Christians. His true feelings came out in an appearance as Prime Minister among young people in Saskatchewan, in an incident documented by the Hon. Ernest C. Manning.

> **"News Report: Regina (1972)**
> John Diefenbaker commented today on Mr. Trudeau's reply when the Prime Minister was asked at a Regina High School what had happened to the Liberal's promise four years ago, of a just society. Mr. Trudeau replied: "The next time you see Jesus Christ, ask Him what happened to the just society He promised 2,000 years ago." Mr. Diefenbaker said: "Such a statement is sac-religious if not blasphemous. It is a statement no Prime Minister in history has made and is indicative of an attitude of mind, not in keeping with what one expects from a Prime Minister. It is more than shocking. It is revolting." The Prime Minister's statement was made during an open line broadcast from the high school. The students laughed at his reply.

"FORTRESS AMERICA" UNDER SIEGE

Ernest Manning's Comment
Mr. Diefenbaker is absolutely right! Sacrilege practiced by the Prime Minister of a nation should not be tolerated. It should be condemned by every responsible citizen. As sickening as the Prime Minister's offensive comment, is the fact that it elicited only laughter from the students who heard it. Children and young people reflect the spiritual and moral standards of society, and of the homes from which they come. This is a sobering thought. The Prime Minister's office should have been deluged with thousands of letters and wires of condemnation. Where are our churches, our Christian ministers, our community leaders, our Christian Activists? How long, O God, how long?

Through Canada's National Back to the Bible Hour, we are trying to bring home the seriousness of the spiritual and moral decline of our times. We want to see Canada prosper and be blessed of God. It cannot be, unless people recognize that we need spiritual as well as political leadership. It is righteousness that exalteth a nation, but sin is still a reproach to any people." (The Face of the Sky – Part 2, 1972)

Years ago, Baritz, the organizer of the Socialist party in Canada, said in the *Toronto Globe*:

> "The Socialist party is against the worship of Christ, Socialists do not believe in any God. The church will find us its mortal enemy." (E. J. Daniels, The Red Devil of Communism, 1954)

> "Our teachers directed their hardest blows against Fundamentalist Christianity. We hate Christians. Even the best of them must be regarded as our worst enemies. But I never heard one of them say, at any time, a single word against Modernism." (Kenneth Goff, Confessions of Stalin's Agent; Ch. 6, in The Red Devil of Communism)

> "'But Comrade Mironov,' one of the men present spoke up, 'isn't there a danger that the new generation, which will one day take our place, may be spoiled by religious

CHAPTER 5: SOCIALISM & COMMUNISM FULFILLED

superstition?' "'Don't worry on that score,' he replied, smiling. "There is neither soil nor sap on which religion can feed in the U.S.S.R. After all, the press, theatre, radio, schools, literature, all the forces of the mind are in the Party's sole control. It's clear that a young man with religious inclinations cannot possibly make a career. If he is not on our side spiritually and politically, there is no place for him. This is our supreme advantage." (Victor Kravchenko, I Chose Freedom; Ch. 3, in The Red Devil of Communism)

Prime Minister Justin Trudeau should seriously re-think his father's anti-Christian Marxist bias, not adopt it for himself. He has a wife and children to protect from future socialist tyranny, should it ever come to Canada. Justin Trudeau was born on December 25, 1971. Christmas Day is when Christians celebrate the birth of Jesus Christ. Providentially, God was speaking both to the elder Trudeau and to his son, not to treat lightly or despise the churches and God's Son. Justin Trudeau will have to walk over Christ to follow in his father's footsteps.

A few lines from the late American Communist Langston Hughes' song, "Good-Bye Christ," shows how much Communists hate Christ, and how sacrilegious their teachings are:

> "They ghosted you up a swell story, too.
> Called it the Bible –
> But it's dead now.
> The popes and the preachers've
> Made too much money from it.
> They've sold you too many
> Kings, generals, robbers and killers –"
> (Ibid)

America (and Canada), if ever taken over by radical Socialism – Communism, will take away forever the blessings of free democratic society, that we have known, as so vividly portrayed in writing by the late William Upshaw, a Georgia Congressman:

> "If Communists ever take over America, every loyal Christian who has opposed Communism and refuses to renounce his faith and adopt Communism, will be slain or made a slave. This is what has happened again, and again, according to reliable authorities.
>
> Gone every high incentive of the 'Little Schoolhouse on the Hill!' Gone the sacred music of the 'Little Church in the Wildwood!' Gone the chimes of the bells everywhere! Gone the holy call of the Lord's Day. Gone the blessed benediction of the old-fashioned family altar where mother and father read God's Word and pray with their children – that family altar which, if preserved in the majority of American homes, would have saved this suffering land from its present moral and economic debacle! Gone forever, the beauty and comfort of every religious funeral where 'Rock of Ages,' and 'Nearer My God to Thee,' let their heavenly comfort fall into broken hearts and shadowed homes! Gone, gone forever, that miracle of regeneration in triumphs of God's Gospel which have made countless millions of 'Twice-born Men' and women the wonder of the world – which has turned hovels in palaces, slums into paradises, and gutters into crystal streams of beauty and blessing amid the desert places of the earth! That is Communism!" (E. J. Daniels, The Red Devil of Communism, 1954). Read Appendix 4 also.

The writer's Baptist church sponsored building a home for orphans in Vietnam a few years ago. Putting the word "church" on the plaque was forbidden by the government of the Socialist Republic of Vietnam. Only "From Your Friends at 'Name' (word 'church' omitted)," was allowed by the Communist regime.

In Calgary recently, forty-four 'faith leaders' from religious organizations near and far sent a letter standing for the Calgary "Conversion therapy" bylaw

CHAPTER 5: SOCIALISM & COMMUNISM FULFILLED

(see above). These Modernist compromisers, and others of all stripes, will face the wrath of totalitarian socialism, should it ever gain political control here in Canada:

> "Dennis said, 'Dialectic materialism and religion don't mix. Anyone with religious tendencies would be a menace to the Communist State.' I asked him about the thousands of Modernist Ministers who have defended and furthered the Communist cause. He replied, 'These liberal chameleons are of great value at present, but once our goal is reached, they will either have to change their belief, or pay the price with their heads along with the rest.'" (Kenneth Goff, Confessions of Stalin's Agent, in The Red Devil of Communism, 1954).

There are many ideologues in the west from all walks of life, from academia to social justice warriors of all stripes (environmentalism, feminism, etc., etc.). Most of these people are not knowingly Leninists. But – they are following a movement which at its core has a Leninist mindset. That is why hate is so common in ideological differences, particularly from the left. And therein lies the danger to our democracy.

> "As Lenin pointed out in "What is to be Done," there's a spectrum. A few people at the top understand what is going on. Then there are those "who just practice the appropriate responses." Finally, there are the entirely innocent, but supremely gullible foot soldiers. "The real questions are," Morson said, "is there such a spectrum now, and how do we locate people on it? And if there is such a spectrum, what do we do about it?"
>
> **And if we do not find answers to those questions now, when we are faced with a communist regime whose ambitions are as boundless as Lenin's and their vision of life as ruthless, but their version of terror simply a little more nuanced** (shaded in tone or expression) **and sophisticated, then what?"** (Barbara Kay, The Epoch Times, Human Wreckage: Pondering

Lenin's Legacy on 150th Anniversary of His Birth, p. B1, April 23-29, 2020)

The writer would venture to say that Jean Chretien is one of the few who knows what is really going on in Canada today. He was mentored by Pierre Trudeau. He developed close ties and a friendship with Jiang Zemin, the tyrannical communist leader of China, visiting that country frequently during his term as prime minister. He worked behind the scenes to get Justin Trudeau elected, and he continue to guide his mentor's son in the backroom, concerning the political future of Canada. As Pierre Trudeau once speculated, "Who knows whether Canada will one day have a totalitarian government?" We may be on the verge of having one in the very near future...for the 'ghost' of Pierre Trudeau is living his life through his son.

No one can hide when, and if, totalitarian socialism – communism takes full control of Canada.

Dr. Joseph Paul Goebbels, a Jesuit-educated Liberal Arts intellectual, was an ardent National Socialist in NAZI Germany, and Propaganda Minister for Hitler's Third Reich. In the Goebbels Diaries (1942-1943) we see totalitarian Socialism's view of Russian Communism (Bolshevism) and of the Christian churches. In Goebbels' own words:

> "In the final analysis it would be better for us to end our existence under Bolshevism than to endure slavery under capitalism." (Oct. 23, 1925)

> "I think it is terrible that we and the Communists are bashing in each other's heads...Where can we get together sometime with the leading Communists?" (January 31, 1926)

CHAPTER 5: SOCIALISM & COMMUNISM FULFILLED

> "Goebbels (was) the unflagging motive force behind the vicious anti-Semitism of the Nazi regime. He makes it clear that while he wants to devote himself to the extermination of all Jews during the war, he plans to deal with the churches after the war and reduce them to impotence. He prepared the ground well for Hitler's war on civilization." (The Goebbels Diaries 1942-1943, Edited, Translated and with an Introduction by Louis P. Lochner, 1948).

When Goebbels speaks of Jews, he meant **all** Jews; when he spoke of Christian churches, he meant **all** Christian churches. Hitler failed; but the threat still remains from the growing influence of socialism-communism in the twenty-first century.

Lest anyone think that communism is benign regarding killing on an ethnic basis they need only look to Pol Pot of the Khmer Rouge of Cambodia, trained under Mao Zedong whom he "worshipped." "Beginning in 1965 he visited China four times to listen to Mao Zedong's teachings in person." His murderous rampage was ethnically-centered as the prejudiced, dark-skinned Khmer despised other 'races,' including the Vietnamese whom they slaughtered along with just about any other group that differed from Pol Pot's Khmer. That included 200,000 ethnic Chinese in Cambodia whom Mao allowed the Khmer to massacre (The Epoch Times, "Nine Commentaries on the Communist Party," On the Chinese Communist Party's History of Killing – Part 7, 2004).

Thus socialists, whether Bolsheviks, Maoists or Nazis (National Socialists), or any other far-left group for that matter, will murder ethnically if their totalitarian leader's ideology finds a reason to. The Soviet-engineered "Great Famine" of 1932-33 in the Ukraine is another example.

"FORTRESS AMERICA" UNDER SIEGE

In "The Big Lie – The Nazi Roots of the American Left," 2017, Dinesh D'Souza wrote:

> "Marxism split into 2 camps; Leninism and Bolshevism, and fascism and Nazism. Fascism and Nazism are two different things. There are deep and profound connections between the left and fascism but also between the left and Nazism. The progressive Democrats (in the U.S.) are closer to the German Nazis than to the Italian fascists."

The churches will face great danger in the years ahead, no matter what brand of totalitarian socialism takes control in our own nation, or over our own nation, or internationally, as the Bible predicts. Severe persecution will come, if the Lord Jesus Christ does not return to rapture his people first.

Canadian churches' assets are in peril, and have been for many years. The tax-exempt status of most churches opens them up to Revenue Canada's expropriation of, or order to, dispossess the charity (local church) up to 100% of their total assets should they be de-registered voluntarily or involuntarily.

I attended a church which asked to be de-registered in 1986. Revenue Canada's reply is shown on the attached letter. Fortunately, the government did not act on their legal option, and formally de-registered the church seven years later. After that time we were free from any penalty imposed by Revenue Canada.

CHAPTER 5: SOCIALISM & COMMUNISM FULFILLED

Revenue Canada   Revenu Canada
Taxation   Impôt
Head Office   Bureau principal

Western Baptist Church
4324 - 19th Avenue North West
Calgary, Alberta
T3B 0R7

45733
Tel. (613) 954-1174

Attention: Pastor Larry Jones

August 25, 1986

Dear Sirs:

Re: Western Baptist Church of Calgary

Thank you for your letter of March 17, 1986 requesting deregistration of the Church's charitable status. Reference is also made to our telephone conversation on May 7, 1986. We sincerely regret the delay in replying caused by our present workload.

We would advise that if the Church no longer requires its registered charitable status with this Department, voluntary revocation of its registration would be in order. Please note, however, that when a charity's registration is revoked it loses both its exemption from tax and its authority to issue donation receipts for income tax purposes. Moreover, a charity that does not distribute all of its assets to qualified donees described in paragraphs 110(1)(a) or (b) of the Income Tax Act within one year of the date its registered status is revoked is subject to a one hundred percent tax based on the value of the assets not so distributed.

If voluntary revocation is desired after taking the foregoing into consideration, please confirm so in writing and forward the following within 6 months of the end of the charity's fiscal year in which dissolution took place:

Not dissolving

... 2

Ottawa, Ont.   Ottawa (Ont.)
K1A 0L8   K1A 0L8

Canada

Revenue Canada may not be so gracious with such church properties in the future, especially with an entrenched radical socialist 'Liberal' government. Pastors and congregations need to decide which is more

303

important, my tax receipt or my church's assets, including the building where I worship?

The United States has enacted laws which can rule against churches that are designated registered charities creating threatening circumstances similar to what Western Baptist Church experienced in the 1980s.

> "In 1954, Sen. Lyndon B. Johnson of Texas, who later served as the 36th President of the United States, introduced the Johnson Amendment, which prohibits nonprofit organizations, including churches, from engaging in certain activities. Violators could have their tax exemptions revoked. Wary of this, some Christian churches have instructed their priests to avoid certain political topics when speaking at the pulpit, including controversial social issues such as abortion, homosexuality, euthanasia, stem cell research, and so on." (The Epoch Times, "How the Spectre of Communism is Ruling Our World," Using the Law for Evil, Chapter 10, 2020)

"In 1951, the Chinese Communist Party ordered all members of churches, temples, and religious societies to register with government agencies and to repent for their involvement. Failure to do so would mean severe punishment." (The Epoch Times, "Nine Commentaries on the Communist Party," On the Tyranny of the Chinese Communist Party – Part 3, p.6, 2004).

> "By persecuting large numbers of God-worshipping and law-abiding people, the CCP cleared the way for Communism to become the all-encompassing religion of China." (Ibid).

Nos. 2, 3 and 4 are discussed as a single subject below.

2. The destruction of private property and the abolition of inheritance;

CHAPTER 5: SOCIALISM & COMMUNISM FULFILLED

> "Karl Marx said that if a single sentence would summarize the goal of communism it would be the abolition of private property." (The Epoch Times, "How the Spectre of Communism is Ruling Our World," 2020)

The Trudeau government has very discretely floated the idea of taxing inheritance in Canada, but knowing how unpopular this would be has not made any moves in that direction. It is testing the waters.

3. Revolution under the leadership of the Communist International (Comintern);

> "Lenin said the goal of the Communist International was to establish a World Soviet Republic." (The Epoch Times, "How the Spectre of Communism is Ruling Our World," Globalization and Communism, Chapter 17, 2020)

4. Engaging in activities in foreign countries in order to cause strikes, riots, sabotage, bloodshed and civil war;

The Epoch Times July 5-11, 2019, issue published, A History of the Chinese Communist Party's Killing, going back to the communist take-over of China in 1949. Perhaps no country in human history has seen such a blood bath. This killing spree epitomizes the Marxist doctrine of "hatred and "class struggle," destroying lives until there is no opposition left. This behavior summarizes points 2, 3 and 4 (above).

> 1950-1953: Killing landlords during the 'Land Reform' Movement (nearly 100,000 killed)
> 1953-1956: Eliminating the capitalist class (at least 20,000 killed)
> 1957-1959: Re-educating intellectuals – the Anti-Rightist Campaign (at least 46,000 killed)

1959-1961: Starving the populace – the Great Famine (about 40 million died)

1959 and beyond: Suppressing Tibetans (more than 1 million deaths)

1966-1976: Destroying Tradition – the Great Cultural Revolution (at least 7.73 million deaths)

1979-2015: Enforcing the One-Child Policy (about 400 million unborn killed)

1989: Killing pro-democracy student in Tiananmen Square (thousands killed)

1999 to 2020[+]: Persecuting Falun Gong and other people of conscience (deaths in the many thousands, organ harvesting)

Now the same kind of socialists have set their sights on the United States of America. In 2020, Manning's prediction (pp. 196-198, 327, 530) is being played out on the world stage. The players and the circumstances are, in part different, but the same objective remains; to bring down the U.S.A. and transform her into a socialist-communist slave state. The attacks are coming from without and within that great nation today. God help those evil designs not to succeed!

> "According to Marxist logic, the 'oppressed' are morally correct in all circumstances, and many people do not dare to question the authenticity of their absurd, twisted moral claims. The "bourgeoisie" and "landlord" classes (akin to white males in 2020) must recognize their original sin as members of the colonial oppressive class."
> ("How the Spectre of Communism is Ruling Our World," Sabotaging Education – Part 2, Chapter 12, 2020)

The entire ethnic, gender, global warming, etc. narrative playing out in Canada and the United States today has this underlying Marxist doctrine as its agenda. And the strategy, if successful, will destroy our freedoms and usher in a **totalitarian dictatorship of the 'so-called oppressed proletariat'** (i.e. gender and diversity minorities, and pro-global warmers).

CHAPTER 5: SOCIALISM & COMMUNISM FULFILLED

"America Imploding," "Those Burning US Cities Aim to Destroy American Civilization," "American Uprising, With Riots Threatening US and Foreign Agitators" are just a few of the recent articles describing the mayhem following the unjustified death of the colored man, George Floyd, at the hands of Minneapolis police.

> "The United States is burning and it's horrifying to watch as our neighbor to the south tears itself apart. Legitimate protests in many cities have been hijacked and turned into riots and looting." (Michele Mandell, The Calgary Sun, June 3, 2020)

> "The first thing to understand about the destructive mob riots sweeping the United States is that they are not race riots. Many of the thugs looting and destroying property are white...young beneficiaries of the richest and most generous society the world has ever seen. At school, they were taught to despise their country as racist, sexist, colonialist and exploitive; attitudes that were reinforced in college and from the megaphones of the media, Hollywood and our elite universities...Waugh was right. The more elaborate the society, the more vulnerable it is to attack, and the more complete its collapse in case of defeat." (Roger Kimball, The Epoch Times, p. B1, June 4-10, 2020)

> "The rioting isn't about angry grieving over George Floyd or even mob rage, but skillfully coordinated precision looting and vandalism directed by cellphone and supported by pre-positioned weapons and Antifa medics. It is a paramilitary operation. Under Obama and his loyalists, the Democrats have shifted to the virulently anti-American far-left, while trilling the virtues of the brave new socialist and anti-Caucasian America they conjure." (Conrad Black, The Epoch Times, p. B2, June 4-10, 2020)

> "Barr said foreign groups are also using social media campaigns like those mounted by Russia during the 2016 presidential election to widen divisions in U.S.

society. Some of the foreign hackers and groups that are associated with foreign governments are focusing in on this particular situation we have here, and trying to exacerbate it in every way they can." (Lynch and Sullivan, The Calgary Sun, June 5, 2020)

We find that these radical groups have been implanted in strategic positions across the U.S. They have been incubating and waiting for the right moment to rise up and cause mayhem and carnage in America's great cities. The communists are emboldened because they have the support of one of America's political parties, the Democrats, and the mainstream media – both of which support left-wing causes, for the sole purpose of grabbing political power by any means.

In "Antifa, Other Far-Left Groups Exploit US Protests for 'Revolution,'" Bowen Xiao, assisted by Ivan Pentchoukov, of the June 4-10, 2020, Epoch Times write:

> "Communist groups – including the extremist organization Antifa – are hijacking what started out as peaceful protests over the death of an unarmed black man to usher in a revolution, according to officials, experts, videos and anarchists' own words...they're basically hijacking the black community as their army. Numerous social media posts and videos also depict African American protestors objecting to rioting perpetrated by groups of white men in full black outfits.
>
> It's in 40 different states and 60 cities...an unprecedented and coordinated effort behind the riots, the likes of which have never been seen before...up to 80% of the rioters came from outside Minnesota" (Gov. Walz). 'It's a radical, leftist, socialist attempt at revolution,' said Bernard Kerik, former police commissioner of the NYC Police Dept.

CHAPTER 5: SOCIALISM & COMMUNISM FULFILLED

> Communism expert, Trevor Loudon, told The Epoch Times that Antifa is only one part of the picture, noting that, 'every significant communist or socialist party in the United States has been involved in these protests and riots from the beginning.' According to Loudon, Communist Party USA, Liberation Road, Freedom Road Socialist Organization, Democratic Socialists of America, Revolutionary Communist Party, Worker's World Party and the Party for Socialism and Liberation, have been involved, among others.
>
> Loudon said, 'If the death of George Floyd in Minneapolis hadn't sparked these riots, the next one would have. People need to understand that there are hundreds of foreign-trained agitators and organizers operating in this country, and tens of thousands more disciplined communists.'" (The Epoch Times, pp A1-2, June 4-10, 2020)

The violence is continuing in an effort to destabilize the country and defeat Donald Trump in the November, 2020, U.S. election. Democratic governors and city councils are acting in a treasonous manner allowing it to continue.

> "Gordon (Uncle Fabe's owner) said city and state officials seem to be handling the situation by hamstringing the police and pointed to the new prosecutorial policy of presumptively dismissing charges that include riot, disorderly conduct, and interfering with officers." (Zachary Steiber, Businesses Flee Portland, Citing Local Government Failure to Protect Against Riots, The Epoch Times, p. A9, September 3-9, 2020)

Labor Unions are susceptible to socialist-communist infiltration and even take-over. Manning reported that radical socialists were infiltrating the trade unions, universities and newspapers in Alberta in the 1950s and onward. (Brian Brennan, 2008).

> "By capturing labor unions, the Communists can create discord between "capital" and labor. They can paralyze our industries by constant strikes and make people dissatisfied with the American industrial system." (E. J. Daniels, The Red Devil of Communism, 1954).

In spite of Mr. Manning's concerns about trade unions, his twenty-five years as Premier of Alberta brought no serious conflict with the unions. He was a leader who genuinely cared about the individual citizen and he conducted his government wisely with respect to labor relations. His words of wisdom given below are good for both sides of the negotiating table. It is balance and fairness where everyone profits.

> "We always felt that the working man was entitled to fairness and justice and equity, and it was the government's responsibility to fight to get it for him. But we did discover after we got into government that it was extremely difficult to provide as much as organized labor felt it should have without, in our view, being unfair to the other side – the management end – thereby impairing the economy as a whole, and costing people jobs." (Brian Brennan, The Good Steward – The Ernest C. Manning Story, 2008)

> In 1944 Alberta Labor recognized, 'Alberta was singularly fortunate in having a government that has done more to work for, and with, labor than any other government in Canada.'" (Ibid)

"Lenin believed that the formation and legalization of trade unions was an important means for the working class to seize the leadership of the democratic revolution from the capitalist class. The Soviet regime built during the October Revolution of 1917 originated from the trade union." (The Epoch Times, "How the Spectre of Communism is Ruling Our World," The Communist Economic Trap – Part 2, Chapter 9, 2020)

CHAPTER 5: SOCIALISM & COMMUNISM FULFILLED

> "Lenin proposed that trade unions become "a school of communism" and "a reservoir of the state power," between the Communist Party and the masses."

> "The Heritage Foundation said of unions: 'They function like an albatross around a company's neck – making it less flexible, less able to react wisely to the demands of a changing marketplace. Union contracts compress wages: They suppress the wages of more productive workers and raise the wages of the less competent.'"

Alberta's former radical socialist premier, Rachel Notley, was closely connected to the unions:

> "Notley isn't a moderate. She's not a liberal. She's not a left-wing Albertan. She's an **old-school international socialist**. She's a crusader from the international labor movement, (and) anti-oil/anti-business. Her husband, Lou Arab, is even the communications officer for the Canadian Union of Public Employees (CUPE), the same union that campaigned against Canada's fight against the Islamic State; that accuses Israel of "unjust and disproportionate violence" in its defence against rocket attacks from Gaza; and most recently has supported Venezuela's socialist tyrant Nicolas Maduro, despite the Canadian government refusing to recognize his rigged election and corrupt rule." (Sheila Gunn Reid, Stop Notley: The Case for Throwing out the NDP, 2019).

In democratic countries, and provinces like Alberta, labor unions, infiltrated by communists and progressives, have largely become a tool for leftists to fight against capitalism, as the example above shows, and the excerpt below explains:

> "They (labor unions) single-mindedly demand "social justice" and "fairness," creating a huge welfare burden on society and industry, and becoming an obstacle for reform and attempts to improve efficiency in the manufacturing, service, and educational industries, as well as in government administration. When the time is

not ripe, they hide, but when conditions are favorable, they come out and mobilize a social movement to promote their ends. **Labor unions have thus become a wedge communism uses to divide free societies.**" (The Epoch Times, "How the Spectre of Communism is Ruling Our World," The Communist Economic Trap – Part 2, Chapter 9, 2020)

Pierre Trudeau and Rachel Notley would have been soul mates politically, in the 'Socialist Political Union.' Both hugely enlarged the public sector unions and received their votes during elections. Notley's NDP was rewarded by their union friends by dominating the provincial capital, Edmonton, during the 2019 election, while losing out nearly completely across the rest of Alberta. The bureaucracy voted socialist, as it usually does.

When Albertans and Canadians put socialists in office they typically suffer thereafter. Rachel Notley is a case in point (see the next chapter). "The Libranos" by Ezra Levant (2019) makes the same case for Justin Trudeau and his corrupt federal Liberal government.

As Leader of the Opposition in the Alberta Legislature, Notley is currently working through the Alberta Union of Public Employees (AUPE), to take the United Conservative government of Jason Kenny to court for its legislation preventing blockage of key transportation lines, such as railways, by radical protestors. In February, 2020, Canada's economy ground to a halt through such illegal protests (pp. 198-201). Notley farcically calls such legal government action to protect the economy "undemocratic." Perhaps she should have said, unsocialistic.

Communism and radical Islam have much in common. Marx's teachings helped spawn radical Islam in the 1960s through Sayyid Qutb, and allied it with communism to attack and overthrow the Western democracies. The bombing of the World Trade Center in 1993 and the final destruction of the Twin Towers in 2001 can be traced back to this source.

> "The ideological source of Osama bin Laden's Islamic extremism can be traced back to Sayyid Qutb, the Egyptian pioneer of Islamic terrorism, a man who could be described as the Marx of Islamic jihad and who is often referred to as the "godfather of Islamic jihad." (The Epoch Times, How the Spectre of Communism is Ruling our World, Chapter 15, The Communist Roots of Terrorism, May 14-20, 2020)

5. Absolute social and racial equality; add to that gender in 2020;

The economist Milton Friedman said:

> "A society that puts equality before freedom will get neither. A society that puts freedom before equality will get a high degree of both." (The Epoch Times, "How the Spectre of Communism is Ruling Our World," How Communism Sows Chaos in Politics, Chapter 8, 2020)

Hatred and covetousness (**envy**) are the origin of communism's absolute egalitarianism (absolute equality). It is an attitude of "I want what you have; I deserve it more than you do; and I'm going to get it from you any way I can." Jesus Christ was delivered by the Jewish leaders to the Romans to be crucified because of "envy" in the hearts of the Jewish religious leaders. The Christian Scriptures teach,

> "Let your conversation (life) be without covetousness; and be content with such things as ye have: for he hath said, I will never leave thee, nor forsake thee. So that we may boldly say, The Lord is my helper, and I will not fear what man shall do unto me." (Hebrews 13:5-6)

"FORTRESS AMERICA" UNDER SIEGE

In the Marxian view, whether an individual is good or bad is not based on his morality or actions, but on his place in "the hierarchy of "capital. This makes the poor good; the rich bad. The poor have the moral high ground, so they can treat the rich any way they want and still hold their heads high." The same thinking can be carried to any human behavior, ethnic background, skin color, gender or sexual conduct – no matter how deviant or distasteful. This reversal of right and wrong, good and evil has encouraged evildoing. Socialism's "class struggle" comes out of this Marxist doctrine. It pours hatred and scorn on the existing economic and social order – to undermine and overthrow it. Yet, Marx himself acted superior to others around him, as shown in Chapter 7. (The Epoch Times, "How the Spectre of Communism is Ruling Our World," The Communist Economic Trap – Part 2, Chapter 9, 2020)

Pierre Trudeau boasted that he wanted a "classless society," yet acted superior to most people around him, treating many of them despicably. That is certainly not according justice or equality to your fellow man, but superiority. His son Justin's incessant virtue signaling at home and on the international stage is the same kind of condescending hypocrisy.

> "Trudeau made Canada a chain of ethnic enclaves. He wouldn't pronounce any culture superior to any other, despite certain cultures practicing barbarous rites.
>
> Concerning Trudeau's 1983 misplaced "Peace Initiative," Allan Gotlieb, Canada's Ambassador to the U.S. wrote, when a leader sought to perch himself on high moral ground through "a solemn international mission to save the world, then it was time for that leader to step aside." (Bob Plamondon, The Truth About Trudeau, 2013).

CHAPTER 5: SOCIALISM & COMMUNISM FULFILLED

Plamondon's book also describes Pierre Trudeau's shock at the collapse of the Soviet Union in 1991. He blamed the Western democracies for its demise, instead of accepting it as the victory of a free enterprise market system over a collectivist, government-controlled economic system. Pride and arrogance kept him from admitting the truth. He was wrong-headed.

Justin Trudeau is exactly like his father, a narcissistic, self-deluded virtue signaler who impresses no one but himself with his court jester antics. He 'took the knee' at a recent BLM demonstration in Ottawa.

Recent peaceful 'Black Lives Matter' demonstrations in the U.S. have been co-opted by the radical left to overthrow the Trump administration and bring in a Democrat-led radical socialist-communist government in the U.S. in November, 2020.

> "ANSWER (**Act Now to Stop War and End Racism**) is an anti-war organization with prominent exposure in the media. Its members are mostly socialists, communists, and leftists or progressives."

Black Lives Matter is not what it appears to be in the public and mainstream media eyes. Many well-intentioned people have demonstrated in its protests, not knowing that they were being used for nefarious purposes.

> "(BLM) is, in fact, the latest and most dangerous face of a web of well-funded socialist/communist organizations that have been agitating against America for decades, said Maryland-based researcher James Simpson, formerly a contributor to The Epoch Times and now a candidate for Congress." (Matthew Vadum, Black Lives Matter Began With Claim of Systemic Racism, The Epoch Times, June 11-17, 2020)

"FORTRESS AMERICA" UNDER SIEGE

> "In the name of attacking racism BLM promotes a more virulent, minority-based racism. The spectacles of U.S. senators and representatives kneeling in silence with multicolored scarves on their shoulders, replicating traditional West African ceremonial garb, etc., etc., are all indications of a widespread state of public madness. BLM is more of a sentiment than an organization and the program it espouses, beyond respect for human life and dignity, is nonsense – and in practice, dangerous and violent nonsense. People removing BLM graffiti from monuments and public buildings in Washington are accused of racism. People stating in gentle and diplomatic terms that all lives matter and that some of BLM's other nostrums (remedies) won't fly have been fired from their jobs." (Conrad Black, Revulsion at Floyd's Killing Triggers National Derangement, The Epoch Times, p. B2, June 18-24, 2020).

There is no such thing as 'absolute' equality of any kind. More Jews win Nobel prizes than any other group. More Blacks dominate basketball than any other group. More women are nurses than any other group...etc., etc.

> "In no worldly sense are we born equal. We are decidedly unequal in physical strength and co-ordination, in mental capability, in natural virtue, in mental stability and nerve, in mechanical aptitude and in a hundred other ways. Yet the lie of our supposed equality continues to deceive us with amazing tenacity. It has proved particularly alluring to the modern educator, in fact is the basis of much of the mischief he has wrought. And in this he could always count on the eloquent support of his equally befuddled devotees in the ivory towers of the media.
>
> For nature is not egalitarian. The numbers of genuinely talented born among us, will in natural occurrence be severely limited. Those able to become skillful engineers, violinists, physicists, writers, salesmen, will be statistically few. They are, as it were, rationed to us. And whether we progress, prosper or even survive as a society depends almost entirely on the performance of that few. However undemocratic it may sound, the reality

CHAPTER 5: SOCIALISM & COMMUNISM FULFILLED

> is that there is among us an elite (the best or choicest part of); there always has been; there always will be. And the rest of us are very much dependent upon it." (Ted Byfield, The Book of Ted, 1998).

Tragically, much of the elite in our society today have rejected the Judeo-Christian precepts upon which Western civilization has been built, and that very much involves the values and customs of our free democracies. In the realm of education this failure has had a huge impact on our institutions and value systems. Here is a recent example.

Two Canadians, Michael Kovrig and Michael Spavor, have been imprisoned illegally for about two years in China by a totalitarian communist government with no rule of law, except 'CCP law'. All in retaliation for Canada's legal arrest of Huawei chief, Meng Wanzhou, upon a legal U.S. extradition warrant. Her detention is supported by a vast majority of Canadians, and rightly so. So, what did a band of our Canadian elites do?

> "A former Supreme Court justice, two former ambassadors to Washington, a former NDP leader, three former foreign ministers, four former ambassadors to the UN and a former Liberal justice minister – a group of foreign policy **grandees** (any person of high rank-an elite) released a letter urging Prime Minister Trudeau to release Meng Wanzhou in the hope of convincing China to release the two Michaels." (Lorne Gunter, Trudeau right to not engage in hostage diplomacy, The Calgary Sun, June 28, 2020).

These **elites** urged the Prime Minister to jeopardize the rule of law by arbitrarily (imperiously or dictatorially) stepping in to bypass the Meng extradition case now moving forward in a Vancouver courtroom. Thankfully, he refused to take their advice. But he has left Meng in her million-dollar mansion in Vancouver while two innocent Canadians suffer intolerably in Chinese prisons.

> Peter Dahlin, co-founder of China Action, a NGO supporting human rights was detained for 23 days in a Chinese prison, and subjected to intense interrogation. He guesses "Kovrig's (and Spavor's) days (numbering 652 as of September 21, 2020) in custody are spent, being grilled for hours by a "good cop-bad cop" interrogation duo across from his suicide-padded cell, with the sessions often going late into the night to ensure he "doesn't get proper sleep." There have also been reports that lights are kept on in their cells day and night, which is a form of torture in sleep-deprivation, said Farida Deif, Canadian director at Human Rights Watch." (Omid Ghoreishi, Hell on earth: Horrors of Chinese torture methods, The Epoch Times, p. A 1, February 15-19, 2019)

The sad thing today in the Western democracies is that most of the elites have been hijacked in their younger years by a leftist education system that has produced thousands of 'brainwashed,' leftist intellectuals and skilled scientists, who have greatly influenced society, but not for its good. In past generations when the Bible was honored it was not this way.

> "The fear of the LORD is the beginning of knowledge: but fools despise wisdom and instruction." (Proverbs 1:7)

> "The fear of the LORD is the beginning of wisdom: and the knowledge of the holy is understanding." (Proverbs 9:10)

The grandees' letter to Prime Minister Trudeau was without wisdom or understanding. They have no fear of God. And so it is throughout most of our educational, legislative and judicial institutions in Canada today. Ernest Manning's wisdom came first and foremost from the Word of God, and he was not ashamed to say so.

CHAPTER 5: SOCIALISM & COMMUNISM FULFILLED

6. Destruction of all forms of representative or democratic government, including civil liberties, such as freedom of speech, of the press and of assemblage;

The incessant and virulent attacks on Donald Trump since his victory in the 2016 U.S. election were all planned by the left-wing Democratic Party and their media allies, assisted by Republican defectors, for the express purpose of removing him from office. The attacks have now shifted to try and defeat him in the 2020 U.S. Presidential election. Political power is the sole objective. Freedom of speech no longer exists in the mainstream media. Social media is following the same agenda. Everything is skewed against conservatives. The same situation exists in Canada only to a far worse degree with the Liberals in power in Ottawa. Conservatives seek to win elections; socialists seek to win POWER.

> "To see an opposition leader say, 'we don't need Parliament right now,' is really, really troublesome," adds Bratt. (NDP's) Singh shamefully negotiated away our democracy to have Trudeau make an announcement about additional sick days for employees, something that is under provincial jurisdiction. "That's all he held out for," points out Bratt." (Lisa Corbella, Democracy in danger, The Calgary Sun, June 16, 2020).

Justin Trudeau has just prorogued Parliament for a month after it has hardly met since March, 2020. That is because he is facing some hot-button issues related to his ethics violations in the WE Charity scandal, and who knows what else? He is not willing to take adult responsibility for his actions.

Though Pierre Trudeau devised a Charter of Rights and Freedoms he left the rights of the unborn untouched. He avoided taking responsibility.

"FORTRESS AMERICA" UNDER SIEGE

> "Canada remains one of the few countries in the world with no official policy on abortion." (Bob Plamondon, The Truth About Trudeau, 2013).

Ernest Manning pointed out many times the sanctity of life and the murder of the unborn.

> "Killing a child shortly before birth is as wrong as killing a child shortly after birth. When we get used to killing the not-yet-born because we do not want them, on the excuse that they are less than fully human, and we have very quickly grown used to it, it will be easier to decide to kill the already born, whom no one wants." (Ernest Manning, The Face of the Sky – Part 2, 1972, Back to the Bible Hour pamphlet).

Now, many years later Canada still has legalized abortion at all stages before birth. Our country has since carried out 4 million abortions, and the U.S. 40 million killings. Free speech again came under attack when the movie, "Unplanned," was offered for screening in theatres across Canada.

> "A film that tells the story of a Planned Parenthood clinic director turned vocal pro-life activist has been effectively banned from Canadian movie theatres, and was rejected by virtually every Canadian distributor. The movie follows the story of Abby Johnson... after seeing an ultrasound-guided abortion of a 13-week fetus, which shocked her. "Seeing that child fight and struggle for his life against the abortion instrument," made her realize "there was life in the womb, humanity in the womb," Johnson said." The movie was previously screened once in Edmonton, twice in Ottawa – once for members of Parliament and once after a press conference." (Margaret Wollensak, Pro-Life Movie 'Unplanned' Rejected by Canadian Theatres, The Epoch Times, May 24-30, 2019)

Cineplex's CEO later recanted and offered to show the movie explaining that free speech should be upheld for "Unplanned." He showed courage.

CHAPTER 5: SOCIALISM & COMMUNISM FULFILLED

It should be noted that any media going against the accepted government narrative is suppressed and attacked by the mainstream media, and censored by the government wherever possible. The Rebel News is currently taking the Liberal government to court over such censure, the freedom of the press. Rachel Notley's radical socialist NDP provincial government tried ardently to suppress the publication of Sheila Gunn Reid's excellent book, "Stop Notley" before the 2019 Alberta provincial election. Such governments will crush free speech, and the freedom of the press if given the opportunity...communist countries being the prime example.

The writer worked in Venezuela in 1997/98 when the country had a democratic government. With the election of Hugo Chavez in late 1998, the new leader moved quickly to shut down the democratic process and install himself as a totalitarian communist leader with close ties to Cuba. He changed the constitution, rigged elections, suppressed the middle class, indoctrinated the younger generation and destroyed what had once been a free democratic country. His protégé, Maduro, a former bus driver now runs a ruthless avowedly Marxist-Leninist socialist regime with Cuban, Russian and Chinese support. The Venezuela that we once knew is no more. Socialism has triumphed there.

The reader is encouraged to examine Chapter 4 and Appendix 4 for additional examples of the destruction of civil liberties and democratic government. Whether the process is slow (Canada) or quick (Venezuela) the end result is the same...freedom is gone.

7. The ultimate objective of world revolution is to establish the dictatorship of the so-called 'proletariat' into a universal Union of Soviet Socialist Republics with its capital in Moscow;

Khrushchev's warnings to the West in the late 1950s and early 1960s such as, "We will bury you," need to be remembered. That is because Russia has a unique position in relation to Europe and the Western democracies; it is neither fully European, nor fully Asian, though part of both continents. Yet, from this enigmatic nation communism spread to the world and, as The Epoch Times warns in its 2020, 3-volume series, "How the Spectre of Communism is Ruling Our World," is still a very present threat to free democracies everywhere in the world.

> "The messianic role of Russia has had a long history in Russian culture. This adds a quality to Russian Communism that is peculiarly difficult for Americans and western Europeans to understand. Berdyaev once said, "Something has happened which Marx and the western Marxists could not have foreseen, and that is a sort of an identification of two messianisms, the messianism of the Russian people and the messianism of the proletariat. (i.e., socialism-communism)." (John Bennett, Christianity and Communism Today, 1960)

Biblical prophecy has much to say about Gog, Magog, Meshech and Tubal that are identified by Bible scholars with modern day Russia. They are always in conflict with God, and God's chosen people, Israel; and lastly as a worldwide confederacy against Jesus Christ in Jerusalem at the end of the Millennial reign of Christ (Revelation 20:8). Russia and Germany will enter into a union near the end of this present church age and, together with Shiite Iran and Sunni Libya, etc., attack an unprepared Israel (Ezekiel 38:1-9). The foreshadowing of this socialist/Islamic confederacy is beginning to take shape with Russian influence and infiltration of Western European society, particularly Germany, its largest economy. The purpose, as always, is the formation of a one-world socialist government.

CHAPTER 5: SOCIALISM & COMMUNISM FULFILLED

"Germany is on the "front line" of the West's "new Cold War" against Chinese and Russian influences, a lead British think tank says. Royal United Services Institute (RUSI) states, "Russian and Chinese involvement in, and potential infiltration of, Germany's society, politics, and its economy is a threat not just to Europe's largest economy, but also to the continent itself and for wider Western democratic institutions." (Alexander Zhang, Germany on Front Line in 'New Cold War' Against Chinese, Russian Influence: Report, The Epoch Times, p. A12, August 6-12, 2020)

"The "Intelligence Digest" of April, 1946, said, "In Germany propaganda is being spread that the nation can only redeem itself and become a great world power again under the Communist regime. Will Germany swing to Russia? The menace to world peace lies in that mighty combination, and that is the declared path of Germany's future reconstruction in the political realm." (Cyril Hutchison, What Lies Ahead of Germany? June, 1947)

World revolution is still the primary, immediate objective of international socialism-communism. The main target at this time is "Fortress America," comprising the free democracy of the United States, and secondarily Canada. Israel is next on the list. Other countries are subsidiary, but still objectives. The left-wing institutions in academia, the media and judiciary are spearheading this attack. Wherever possible violence or a 'bio-warfare lite' attack like COVID-19, will be used to soften up society as in the recent riots and strife over the handling of the pandemic and events following the death of George Floyd. Riots are still going on as of October, 2020.

At some point in the not-too-distant future an alliance comprised of Russia, Germany and certain Muslim nations will attack Israel. This is almost certainly a Russian-led socialist-Islamic confederacy. It is described in some detail in the Bible (Ezekiel 38:1-9). These prophetic events were often preached in Aberhart's

"FORTRESS AMERICA" UNDER SIEGE

Prophetic Bible Institute in Calgary. Marxist socialism will most certainly drag Germany and many other nations into the Russian orbit, and a subsequent invasion of Israel. Russia is currently lying in wait, first for America's demise, then its next move.

> "First turn to the 38th chapter of Ezekiel. In verses 2-3 we read the root names Gog, Magog, Meshech and Tubal, which correspond to modern Russia, here shown as entirely anti-God. In verses 8 and 16, plus Ezekiel 39:2 and 4, the attempt of this nation to conquer the land of Palestine (now Israel) is clearly set forth. That is coming! Now turn back to Ezekiel 38:5-6. **And here is GOMER! And here she is WITH RUSSIA!** They are shown as marching together to war, perhaps <u>more as leader and satellite than as allies, and certainly with Russia as the leading power</u>. The Bible says that in the last days Germany and Russia will MARCH TOGETHER! (Ibid)

Revolutions do not usually turn out as the revolutionaries anticipate. As Lenin pointed out only a few people at the top really know what is happening and where the revolution is headed. The rest are followers, used by the few at the top. In Canada, Jean Chretien remains the central personage from the Trudeau years, when Canada was engineered to the left by economic and social legislation. Trudeau's affection for the Soviet and Chinese form of government is well known. We are again moving to the far left. At some point our society will become so unstable that a radical socialist revolution could well take place. The U.S. is in the same situation.

> "Throughout history, revolutions often do not end up as their initial architects planned. The idealists who ended the French monarchy in 1789 thought they could replace it with a constitutional republic. Instead, they sparked a reign of terror, the guillotine and mass frenzy. Yet the radicals who hijacked the original revolution and began beheading their enemies soon were themselves

CHAPTER 5: SOCIALISM & COMMUNISM FULFILLED

guillotined. It was not democracy but rather the dictator Napoleon who put an end to French domestic unrest.

Blue (Democratic) states pride themselves for their liberal governors, big-city mayors, But progressive urban bastions like Los Angeles, New York, Minneapolis and Philadelphia are also ground zero sites of arson, violence and looting, where racial relations are the worst. White Antifa arsonists occasionally helped torch black-owned small businesses – in the name of Black Lives Matter." (Victor Davis Hanson, Bitter irony of revolutions, The Calgary Sun, June 11, 2020).

During the counter-culture revolution of the 1960s that tore apart the traditional social fabric, university radicals and their professors would demonstrate and chant the "3 Ms"; Marx, Mao and Marcuse; the latter, Herbert Marcuse, being the German-born American Marxist philosopher and radical political theorist, who would later become known as the "Philosopher of Antifa." He was associated with the Frankfurt School of Critical Theory and fled to the U.S. before Hitler came to power in 1933. Dinesh D'Souza outlines this radical's poisonous influence on today's society. He summarizes it in the following words:

> **"Today, socialist indoctrination is the norm on the American campus, and Marcuse's dream has been realized."** (Dinesh D'Souza, Herbert Marcuse: The Philosopher of Antifa, The Epoch Times, June 18-24, 2020)

Marx's "class struggle" today does not currently involve the wage earners (proletariat) overthrowing the (bourgeois) middle class property owners. That was an unworkable proposition in American society.

> "The socialist left today is concerned less with worker exploitation by the bourgeoisie and more with the race, gender, and transgender grievances of identity politics. I

call it identity socialism. Today's socialists want an America (and Canada) that integrates the groups seen as previously excluded while excluding the group that was previously included.

> **"If you are white, male, heterosexual, and religiously and/or socially conservative, there's no place for you"** on the progressive left," writes Rod Dreher, senior editor at The American Conservative. On the contrary, it should now be expected that in society, "people like you are going to have to lose their jobs and influence." That is, blacks and Latinos are in; whites are out; women are in; men are out. Gays, bisexuals, transsexuals, together with other, more exotic types are in; heterosexuals are out. Illegals are in; native-born citizens are out. It's not only inclusion; but to exclude their opponents from their native land." (Ibid)

Herbert Marcuse brought us to this perilous place of current revolution in society through identity socialism. His 'Marxian' philosophy of "social struggle" is detailed in his book, "Eros and Civilization," 1966.

> "Marcuse influenced a whole generation of young radicals...after stints at Colombia, Harvard, Brandeis and U. of California-San Diego. He became the guru of the New Left in the 60s...egging on activists to seize buildings and overthrow the hierarchy of the university as a kind of a first step to fomenting socialist revolution in America. Angela Davis, who ran for V.P. for the Communist Party said (Marcuse) "taught me that it was possible to be an academic, an activist, a scholar, and a revolutionary." (Ibid)

Marcuse needed, like Lenin, to find a proletariat (outcast group) willing to advance socialism in America. He searched for such groups for his Marxist "class struggle," to take Bohemian (one indifferent to the conventions of social life-an outcast) culture mainstream. In doing so he would "normalize the outcasts, and turn the normal people into outcasts." Which is what we are seeing today. Just speak or take action publicly against the

CHAPTER 5: SOCIALISM & COMMUNISM FULFILLED

LGBTQ2S⁺ and see what happens. You WILL be persecuted!

> "Marcuse started with the young people of the 1960s, already somewhat alienated from the larger society – living in these socialist communes called universities. These slack, spoiled products of post-war prosperity, these parodies of humanity; these horny slothful loafers completely divorced from real-world problems and neurotically focused on themselves, their drugs, their sex lives, and their mind-numbing music. They sought "something more," a form of fulfillment that went beyond material fulfillment. Here was the raw material out of which socialism is made in a rich, successful society – they would serve as the shock troops of revolution." (Ibid)

Ernest Manning recognized the young peoples' problems in that generation, saw the need and recommended the solution. But the Christian churches were asleep in their materialism, and left the door wide open for men like Marcuse to capture the younger generation. He even alluded to discontented young adults in the then fledgling environmental movement (pp. 555-596).

In, The Face of the Sky – Part 1, 1971, Ernest Manning quoted a news statement made by the Director of University Health Services at Harvard University:

> "The so-called calmness and quietness now attributed to some of the colleges is a case of people turning inward and looking for peace and meaning in their lives. People who have given up on the outward values in society – success as measured by money, fame, prestige. The most desolate thing is when a person has turned inward after having abandoned those outward values as worthless and then can't find anything either."

Ernest Manning made the following comment on these young peoples' situation, and the tragic reason why so many of them were left to fall prey to men like Marcuse:

> "When young people can't find satisfaction in the superficial, external values of a materialistic society it is understandable. But it is tragic that when they seek something to give peace and fulfillment within, and they grope but cannot find. What an indictment on the Christian Church and individual Christians who should be on hand to tell those looking for inward peace of the One who waits to enter into their lives, the lives of all who will admit Him, and give them an inward fulfillment and peace that passeth all understanding. That One is Jesus Christ, the One who brings to a life committed to Him a satisfaction and sense of purpose beyond all expectations."

The Vietnam War helped Marcuse recruit young American youth to consciousness-raising (indoctrination) by portraying communist Ho Chi Minh and the Vietcong as Third World Vietnamese "freedom fighters" opposing the evil capitalists, the American soldiers. The students were –

> "the "freedom fighters" within the belly of the capitalist beast...collaborating with the communist Vietcong "freedom fighters" to end the war and redeem both Vietnam and America to, in Marcuse's own words: "Collective ownership, collective control, and planning of the means of production and distribution." In other words, classical socialism." (Dinesh D'Souza, Herbert Marcuse: The Philosopher of Antifa, The Epoch Times, June 18-24, 2020)

Marcuse captured the young people and then looked for more disgruntled proletarians, the so-called 'disenfranchised,' for his future socialist revolution. In each case, by Marxist transposition he made them the oppressed "working class" and the other side the oppressor "capitalist class." He found 3 groups ripe for the taking:

CHAPTER 5: SOCIALISM & COMMUNISM FULFILLED

> 1. "The Black Power Movement – Blacks had grievances that dated back centuries. Blacks became the "working class," whites the colonizing "capitalist class."
> 2. The feminists – Women became the "working class," men the patriarchal "capitalist class."
> 3. Gender – abolish the monogamous heterosexual family to hasten the advent of socialism – today's LGBTQ⁺ become the proletariat and heterosexuals, even Black and female heterosexuals, become their oppressors."
>
> "Marcuse advocated "polymorphous sexuality," and the "reactivation of all erotogenic zones," leading to the current bizarre preoccupations, from bisexuality to transsexuality and beyond." (Ibid)

Marcuse's oppressed groups went on to expand and co-mingle to produce multiple intersecting oppressed groups long after his death producing today's "intersectionality," a favorite term used by Canada's current prime minister and his chief health officer, Dr. Theresa Tam. For example:

> "a black or brown male transitioning to be a woman with a Third World background who is illegally trying to get into this country because his country has been wiped out by climate change." (Ibid)

Marcuse saw the university as the ideal breeding ground for students, environmentalists, Blacks, feminists, gays to produce a new culture in the Western democracies, a generation of socialist and left-wing radical activists. This new breed of 1960s activists would then infect the larger society by taking over the elite universities, and since infecting all of society – the media, the movies, the schools, the judiciary, political parties and even the lives of the capitalist class itself. He opened the door to hate and have no tolerance toward his capitalist "oppressor" groups because he called them intolerant.

Thus it was ok to persecute them. Hence, Marx's "class struggle" is everywhere today in the news and Western society today, and Marcuse's legacy lives on.

Marcuse also recognized the emerging environmental movement, and saw it as an –

> "opportunity to restrict and regulate capitalism, the goal, he emphasized, was **"to drive ecology to the point where it is no longer containable within the capitalist framework."**

In that way environmentalism could be used to cripple the economies of the Western democracies, fomenting strife and division as it did so. Alberta today is in the midst of such a crisis through the false premise of global warming, and the attendant carbon taxation that left-wing politicians are imposing upon unwilling citizens in Canada and elsewhere. So far the U.S. under Donald Trump have rejected this Marxist strategy. Ernest Manning would never have allowed this form of socialist agenda to drag down Alberta.

> "Manning didn't have much patience with environmentalists. He said, "Today (early 1980s) you can't even open up a little coal mine without a parade of protestors screaming: 'It's going to chase the birds away or knock down a tree.'" (Brian Brennan, 2008).

The impact of environmentalism, and its attendant, **anti-middle class** aberrations such as global warming, green power, anti-coal, anti-pipeline, anti-oil and carbon taxes have grown over the years to the point where it has nearly shut down Alberta's oil and gas industry and ravaged the main engine of the Canadian economy which Ernest Manning worked so hard to build. Socialism has, therefore, impacted that province both from without, and more recently from within, through electing a NDP government hostile to Alberta's very 'life blood,' the energy sector. Fortunately, a friendly conservative government is in power in 2020, trying to reverse the damage done by Notley's and Trudeau's socialist policies. The next chapter will deal with this subject; but before that, the reader is encouraged to read Appendix 4, written by a lady Engineer who currently works with a major oil and gas company in Calgary. She has kindly given permission for her essay to be reprinted in this book.

8. The achievement of these ends through extreme appeals to "hatred;"

We have already looked at the hatred-based Marxist-Leninist philosophy of socialism-communism throughout its history from the Paris Commune in 1871 to China and Venezuela in 2020. This system of government is the exact antithesis of "God's government," as exhibited by William Aberhart and Ernest Manning. For example:

> "Videos appeared of children screaming in cruel fashion that their own parents were racists." (Victor Hanson, Bitter irony of revolutions, The Calgary Sun, June 11, 2020).

> "They despised rather than cherished their parents for the sacrifices made on their behalf." (Dinesh D'Souza, Herbert Marcuse: The Philosopher of Antifa, The Epoch Times, June 18-24, 2020).

> "Russian school-teachers receive a special course in atheism, and are compelled to teach 'anti-Godism' in schools. Thus the children are being reared to hate even the idea of God." (E. J. Daniels, The Red Devil of Communism, 1954).

> "There are no human beings here, Eliena Petrovna, only humble guardians of the revolution. There's no room for

sentiment here. Our tools against enemies of the State are pain and death. The sooner you realize it the better." (Ibid).

To the extent that God is shut out of society and genuine Bible Christianity is denigrated, despised and marginalized that country's citizens' capacity to love and show compassion one toward another declines. Thus, China, today has probably the most hateful, cold and pitiless society in the world, not due to the Chinese people's capacity to love, but due entirely to the sinister, evil influence of the atheistic Chinese Communist Party.

> "**The Chinese Communist Party's (CCP) ideology runs on hatred.** The patriotism it promotes entails hating Japan, hating Taiwan, hating Tibetans, hating the ethnic minorities of Xinjiang, hating religious believers, hating dissidents, and, **most importantly, hating the United States.** The Party painted itself as China's savior by stoking hatred against the United States and other foreign nations. It has indoctrinated the younger generation intending to use them to infiltrate the United States and its allied democratic states in various fashions, participate in an all-out armed conflict, wage unrestricted warfare, and should the need arise, sacrifice themselves in a nuclear holocaust to establish a communist "new world order." Currently, on major Chinese political and military forums, one commonly sees sentiments like, **"China and the United States must have a war."** This is a long-term, gradual mobilization for war, deliberately planned and systematically carried out. The Party directs the global forces of anti-Americanism, as **the People's Republic of China now leads a formidable new axis of evil, <u>an adversary more threatening to the free world than the Axis alliance</u>** (Germany, Italy & Japan) **during the Second World War**." (The Epoch Times, "How the Spectre of Communism is Ruling Our World," The Chinese Communist Party's Global Ambitions – Part 1, Chapter 18, 2020)

CHAPTER 5: SOCIALISM & COMMUNISM FULFILLED

By destroying the morality of the Chinese youth over decades of propaganda and indoctrination the Party has produced a violent "wolf culture" that is now immoral, aggressive and self-centered. This is precisely what is happening in our own country as Marxist doctrines are being instilled in our younger generations since the 1960s.

With this kind of CCP-induced systemic anti-America hatred fueling the mainland Chinese people, there is nothing that that country's leadership would stop at to achieve its delusional quest for world supremacy. The writer firmly believes that China deliberately planned the COVID-19 pandemic, and was willing to take losses itself, to destroy Trump's presidency in favor of a Democratic victory at the polls, thus weakening the U.S.'s capacity to wage a future war.

The PRC, under top CCP directives, may have followed the pattern of Tom Clancy's fictional novel, "Rainbow Six," where a paramilitary elite organization sought to use doomed human guinea pigs to test a pathogenic virus prior to unleashing it on the world; a plan that ultimately failed. Nevertheless, the Chinese communist regime may have used the same template; and been responsible for the disappearance of Malaysia Airlines Flight 370, that was en route from Kuala Lumpur to Beijing on March 8, 2014. The plane vanished from off the face of the earth with 239 souls aboard. It could not be located, no matter how hard or far subsequent searches were conducted. Could the CCP, whose virologists had just engineered the SARS-pangolin or bat virus particle, capable of infecting humans – as published in international journals about the same time – have planned a human experiment with a large enough sample of humans to predict the eventual outcome of a future bio-warfare pandemic unleashed against the West? The plane's flight path would bring it over Chinese territory slightly to the west of Wuhan toward Beijing. This idea seems far-fetched, but is entirely within the realm of a communist government that has never placed a high value on human lives, and whose tentacles of malignant influence and control know almost no limits.

A war with China is a war which America could very easily lose. If the U.S. is pushed out of East Asia, the next battleground could very well be on our own soil here in North America. The enemy is already well-entrenched by infiltration and degradation in Canadian and American societies.

Published in 2020, a report entitled, "Violence in Alberta's Urban Schools: The Perspectives of School Resource Officers," found cell phones and social media to be a big problem contributing to bullying and violence in schools.

> "When asked what they would do with a magic wand, one officer replied: "No cell-phones...that's a start. Number 1 would be cellphones. Ban cellphones." According to officers, apps like Snapchat and Instagram are a constant source of conflict in schools.
>
> One officer who works at several different schools believed religious-based schools have fewer problems with violence. 'I have two faith-based schools that I find I'm not called there even a fraction of the time I am for the other schools,' said the officer, who was not personally religious. 'I'm trying to figure out why that is.'"
> (Jonny Wakefield, Time for training, The Calgary Sun, April 28, 2020).

Perhaps belief in Jesus Christ does offer an antidote to the appeals to personal animosity, hatred and violence all too common today in education, the media and political arenas. That is why communism hates it so.

CHAPTER 5: SOCIALISM & COMMUNISM FULFILLED

Ernest Manning wrote in The Face of the Sky – Part 1, 1971:

> "What a price society pays because of the inclinations to wrong-doing (sin) inherent in human nature. Human nature despite education, science, sociology and religion without Christ, inclines deeper and deeper into the swamps of immorality. Genuine Christianity is the most potent force in the world to change human nature through the miracle of a spiritual new birth. Men born again are not likely to steal or destroy or embezzle. How different is the attitude and inclination of men who have been made into new creatures through a spiritual new birth by receiving Jesus Christ into their lives. This is the one effective antidote to the moral poison that is spreading through all stratum of society today. Isn't it time we gave Christianity the recognition it deserves?"

If the Reader can gain anything from this book, it would be to compare the fruit (life and words) of a leader like Ernest Manning to that of Karl Marx and his followers. Chapters 1-3 (Manning) and Chapter 7 (Karl Marx et al) will allow a ready comparison between good leadership in a free democracy and inherently evil leadership in a variety of socialist regimes. Citizens in a free democracy should not fear Christian leadership, for Christ's teachings are the basis for real freedom.

CHAPTER 6

ALBERTA'S RECENT EXPERIMENTS WITH SOCIALISM

Mrs. Rachel Notley
Premier of Alberta
2015-2019

"Federalism is a valuable tool which permits dynamic parties to plant socialist governments in

CHAPTER 6: ALBERTA'S EXPERIMENTS WITH SOCIALISM

> certain provinces from which the seed of radicalism can slowly spread."
>
> **Pierre Elliott Trudeau**

The picture below was chosen to convey the seriousness of electing the right people to run our governments.

"For years Notley has been walking into Alberta's legislature – the seat of the province's democracy – wearing a wristwatch with the face of Che Guevara, the Marxist who helped lead the Cuban communist revolution and served as a minister to Fidel Castro. Like communists everywhere, he was also a brutal murderer of anyone who he thought was an enemy of the cause. **Thomas Lukaszuk**, a former MLA whose family defected from Communist Poland, once told Notley how 'hurtful it is' for her to glorify one of the darlings of a system that brutally oppressed and murdered so many millions of people. '**She didn't seem to care.**'" (Sheila Gunn Reid, Stop Notley: The Case for Throwing Out the NDP, 2019)

The Province of Alberta has largely escaped the negative effects of provincial socialist government, until recently. It has not escaped federally. In both cases anti-capitalist environmental policies and a gender/race-based human rights agenda was aggressively pushed on Albertans. Environmentalism and globalism will be discussed as socialist attacks on free democracy later in this chapter.

Ernest Manning, in the early years of his administration wanted to determine how much of a threat the socialist CCF Party (Cooperative Commonwealth Federation) posed to his Social Credit rule. Voters rejected it as too close to the pre-Socred, scandal-ridden UFA (United Farmers Association) government. During his term in office Manning never saw the Conservative Party as a threat, as they were "so similar to Social Credit philosophically." He ascribed the Progressive Conservative victory under Peter Lougheed in 1971 as a "triumph of personality and political organization rather than one of ideological difference." (Brian Brennan, 2008).

Historically, Alberta enjoyed a Conservative-style of government for 82 years, beginning in 1933 with William Aberhart, until it ended temporarily in 2015. The once strong conservative leadership of Lougheed and Klein deteriorated in the years following with weak leaders and corrupt dealings that undermined the Progressive Conservative Party's popularity.

Ernest C. Manning's Social Credit government was fiscally conservative. Below is a short excerpt from a Manning era tract on economics and government debt entitled, "Your Questions on Social Credit," by Roger Kirk and Joe Irving (1959):

> "When the Social Credit party took up the reins of government in 1935, the province had a debt of $167 million. By 1946, a full year before substantial oil revenues became available, the debt was reduced by

CHAPTER 6: ALBERTA'S EXPERIMENTS WITH SOCIALISM

> $21 million. Now, after 22 years of Social Credit administration, the province is really debt-free. In 1935, it took 51 cents of every dollar collected by the government to pay the interest on the provincial debt. It is true that the widespread discovery of oil in Alberta has been a real advantage, but if the Social Credit government had not been wise in the administration of these natural resources, *The People* of the province would have gained practically nothing even as the people of Manitoba, Ontario and Quebec have gained practically nothing from their natural resources."

This quotation is a glimpse into a mindset of economic management that is sorely lacking in today's governments, whether they be conservative or liberal in their financial policies. It is time to look back at the Manning legacy to try and learn what he did to make Alberta so prosperous and – according to its provincial Coat of Arms, "Strong and Free." He sought God and prayed for his people, whether Christians or not. He loved his fellow man and had their best interests at heart. That is what it means to be a true leader of a free democracy.

Conservative Socialism (1982-1987)

The following account is based upon the writer's personal experience. He joined an independent Baptist church in Calgary in 1982. Shortly after that the Alberta government with a new legislative bill, changed the Education Act, requiring Christian schools to submit to government licensing. Our Baptist church refused to license its school, claiming that the children belonged to the parents and the school was a ministry of the church and, therefore, not subject to government control. In order to prove competency of its education program, the church had its students tested academically. The results

"FORTRESS AMERICA" UNDER SIEGE

proved that the quality of their education was a good as, or better than, students in the public system.

Peter Lougheed's Progressive Conservative government, in 1983, took Western Baptist Church to court. The Family Court judge ruled in favor of the church. The Alberta government appealed, and the case went back to court. In the Traffic Court the judge ruled against the church. The church appealed and the case went before the same court again, and lost again. Finally, the Alberta government took the church to the Court of Queen's Bench where the judge again ruled against the church. The church's final appeal went before the Supreme Court of Canada which ruled against the church. With that result the church had no further recourse but to wait to see what the Alberta Government would do.

During this whole episode the church held rallies, responded in writing to the government legislation, lobbied churches and held town hall meetings to try and show the infringement on personal freedoms that the Lougheed government action represented. Although we had their verbal support no other churches were willing to go to court or risk jail time by taking a stand.

In October, 1987, a police cruiser drove secretly up the alley behind the church and two officers entered the rear door of the parsonage to arrest the pastor in the presence of his wife and eldest daughter. He was led out of his home chained hands and feet. We captured the arrest from a video camera, with a church member hidden in the church building next door. The look of anguish on the faces of the pastor's wife and daughter is hard to describe. The video was immediately taken to CTV News where Pastor Jones' arrest was made public. Without that footage the result of the legal outcome for the church could have been much different.

CHAPTER 6: ALBERTA'S EXPERIMENTS WITH SOCIALISM

While the pastor was in the Spy Hill Correctional Center serving his sentence, the writer took his place as temporary School Administrator. He received a phone call from the government asking him to attend a meeting at the MacDougall center in downtown Calgary. He complied. The meeting was between the writer and Mrs. Nancy Betkowski, the Minister of Education. No other persons were present in the large conference room. She began by telling me that the government wanted to resolve the case but that the church would have to comply with the legislation, or further government action would be taken. I told her that the government could arrest the whole church but we would not comply. She looked infuriated and said our meeting was over. Our communication abruptly ended. She and I both left the room. The government took no further action and Pastor Jones was released from jail after serving his sentence.

Pastor Jones told me personally that the prosecution of the church and 5 years of court cases devastated his family. His eldest daughter and wife had to attend court proceedings, then witness their husband and father's eventual arrest and jailing. The government would not leave the church alone, repeatedly appealing the verdict and continuing its legal action to force submission. In the process, the church finances were depleted.

Attacking God's people is a mistake. The Attorney General who initiated the prosecution died a few years later of an incurable disease. Also, late in the summer of 1987, as the Alberta government was planning to arrest the pastor, three F3/F4 tornados passed through the provincial capital, Edmonton, tragically taking 27 lives. The tornados were up to 1 km in width, and unprecedented in their public display and damage. God was speaking.

Mrs. Betkowski shortly afterward ran for the leadership of the Progressive Conservative Party of Alberta but was defeated in a near miraculous victory by Ralph Klein who went on to become Premier of Alberta for over a decade. Mr. Klein left the church alone during his administration.

Red Tories in the bureaucracy and the government were responsible for this shameful misuse of government authority. Premier Don Getty was in power when the pastor was sent to jail. He did nothing to intervene. Government bullying and intimidation can come from any bureaucracy or political party in which radical socialists are present to force mandatory compliance. If the true conservatives had taken a stand this case could have been resolved.

The education act contained sections exerting government control where we did not believe it belonged. It was devised by socialist educators with little sympathy for non-compliance. The Education Minister was inflexible and demanding. She was a Progressive Conservative 'Red Tory;' a socialist and a feminist in "progressive" political attire. She was enforcing a socialist document. Her predecessor, Dr. Neil Webber, was much easier to talk to and more understanding of the church's situation. He was given another portfolio before things came to a head. The government had Western Baptist Church in its sights and it wasn't going to back off. This protracted struggle was a taste of Christian persecution. Future opposition is coming as socialism enacts more legislation against Christians who obey God's commands in the Bible.

CHAPTER 6: ALBERTA'S EXPERIMENTS WITH SOCIALISM

A temporary alternative to the Progressive Conservatives

As time went on many Alberta provincial conservatives became disillusioned with their party. It had become listless and lost its vision after Ralph Klein retired. Spending increases and patronage became the norm within its ranks. A change was needed before something far worse would happen – a socialist government.

The promising, new Wildrose Party seemed the natural alternative to the Progressive Conservatives. However, it succumbed at the last moment before the 2012 provincial election to alarmism created by the left-wing media against social conservatives in the party. Following that defeat the Wildrose leader and a number of MLAs betrayed the voters and crossed the floor to join with the Progressive Conservatives. That opened the door for disillusioned Albertans to elect a radical socialist NDP government under Rachel Notley. The success of the socialists can be attributed to the failure of the conservative Wildrose and PC parties who 'split' the conservative vote in the 2015 election. Albertans paid a heavy price for electing the NDP, which was defeated after one term in office by Jason Kenny's UCP (United Conservative Party) in 2019.

The New Democratic Party remains a threat as Notley is waiting in the wings to see if Kenny's government loses public support. COVID-19 has made the UCP's task much harder due to federal interference in the Energy Industry and spiraling provincial debt caused by the loss of energy revenues. The NDP would like nothing better than to finish its job of destroying Alberta's entrepreneurial spirit and remaining free enterprise (capitalist) economy. That means destroying **the middle class**. Manning's legacy is all the more important for freedom-loving citizens to examine in light of these ongoing developments.

NDP Radical Socialism (2015-2019):
"The NDP are Liberals in a hurry." (Political proverb)

The following paragraphs will describe the nature and policy of the socialist NDP Alberta government between 2015 and 2019. Notley's socialist government was more radical than other NDP provincial governments of the past. It seems that the NDP is becoming more radical, as demonstrated in the U.S. by the Democratic Party. Excerpts from the 2019 book, "Stop Notley," written by Sheila Gunn Reid are quoted by permission. It was written to warn Albertans against re-electing the NDP to a second term. That would have been fatal to the future of Alberta.

> "A democracy cannot exist as a permanent form of government. It can only exist until the voters discover that they can vote themselves largess from the public treasury. From that time on, the majority always votes for the candidate promising the most benefits from the public treasury, with the results that a democracy always collapses over loose fiscal policy, always followed by a dictatorship." (The Epoch Times, "How the Spectre of Communism is Ruling Our World," Infiltrating the West – Part 1, Chapter 5, 2020).

A timely warning concerning the NDP ideology was given by Candace Malcolm, in "Beware – NDP is more radical than ever," in the June 2, 2018, Calgary Sun newspaper. It was in reference to NDP Leader, Andrea Horwath, whose party was a contender against Doug Ford's conservatives in the 2018 Ontario provincial election.

> "Even in Canada, a country dedicated to the rule of law, quasi-socialist governments get greedy, confiscate too

CHAPTER 6: ALBERTA'S EXPERIMENTS WITH SOCIALISM

> much and lose sight of the fundamentals. **The hallmarks of an NDP government** – whether it's today in Western Canada, or in the past in Ontario under Premier Bob Rae – are 1. Higher taxes, 2. Out-of-control spending, 3. Sky-rocketing debt, and 4. A business environment that chases away private investment."

All of these hallmarks of socialism characterized the Notley socialist government during its four year rule in Alberta. Ms. Malcolm mentioned her experience of the "lost decade" in the 1990s in B.C. during an NDP government. Many young families fled the province to find good blue collar jobs in neighboring Alberta. She stated further,

> "Families were torn apart just so NDP politicians could pursue their socialist utopia. **And today's New Democrats are even more radical.** They've taken the Marxist doctrine of economic oppression – the core philosophy of socialism – and applied it to our social structure...making a hierarchy of victimhood creating divisive identity politics that the far-left embraces.
>
> For example, meet the Ontario NDP caucus...1. Laura Kaminker said wearing a poppy on Remembrance Day was "collective brainwashing" and "war glorification." 2. Tasleem Riaz compared Canadian soldiers in Afghanistan to "war criminals." 3. Jill Andrew said Toronto's black police chief deserves a "coon award." 4. Jagmeet Singh's brother Gurratan, held a sign saying, "F-K the Police." 5. Jessica Bell wrote a pamphlet for activists calling for "economic shutdown," "seizure of assets," and "property destruction." 6. Chandra Pasma said having a job is "dehumanizing. 7. Ramsey Hart has devoted his life to shutting down mining jobs in the North. 7. Erica Kelly said she hopes "gun nuts" would be bombed by drones. 8. Dwayne Morgan believes 9/11 terrorist attacks were orchestrated by the U.S. government. These people don't deserve a place in polite society, yet Horwath defended these extremists, saying, "people do radical things for change." But what

"FORTRESS AMERICA" UNDER SIEGE

kind of change would these radicals bring about? A vote for the NDP is a vote to double down on identity politics and go all-in on spiraling government debt. Replacing the Ontario Liberals with the NDP is like going from a frying pan into the socialist hellfire." (Ibid)

Reading the Ontario NDP's resume is like describing the Alberta NDP and its radical policies, only with a different set of names.

Here is a recent remark made by a NDP MLA in Rachel Notley's Opposition in the Alberta Legislature about the late Margaret Thatcher, one of the greatest leaders of a Western democracy in the last century:

> "Marlin Schmidt was a 'somebody' in the not-in-power anymore Notley NDP government. He said, "Just let me say I am no fan of Margaret Thatcher. If nothing else goes right for me in a day, I can at least count on enjoying the fact that Margaret Thatcher is still dead. The only thing I regret about Margaret Thatcher's death is that it happened probably 30 years too late." (Rick Bell, Dead Wrong – NDP sinks to new low with MLA's slimy Margaret Thatcher comments, The Calgary Sun, July 10, 2020).

Columnist Rick Bell went on to write:

> "Now we get the attitude, people who are positively unhinged, out of touch, unquenchable bitterness oozing out of every pore. It's hatred. I'd run-over-you-in-a-blizzard **hatred**. I'd like-to-see-your-life-destroyed hatred. I'd-dance-on-your-grave hatred. You aren't wrong, you're a worthless human being. You're scum. You're evil."

Vladimir Lenin's modus operandi for socialism-communism was, in his own words **"hatred."** Albertans made a tragic mistake when they elected real haters to

CHAPTER 6: ALBERTA'S EXPERIMENTS WITH SOCIALISM

be in charge of their province. They hate Alberta and Albertans.

Alberta has been endowed with among the largest oil reserves in the world. With these assets the province has prospered and become a powerhouse in the Canadian economy. Sheila Gunn Reid wrote the book, "The Destroyers," to show how the NDP determined to destroy the Alberta Advantage, "the proud, economically strong and free Alberta that generations had worked so hard to build."

> "I described in detail the anti-oil, anti-capitalist radical extremism of Premier Rachel Notley and the NDP. The book made Rachel Notley furious. She would spend the next four years attacking me and The Rebel Media where I work. They are worse than anyone imagined."

Notley gave the impression that her government would be "business friendly" after her surprising election win. Nothing could be further from the truth, and Albertans soon found that out. The integrity and honesty shown by Ernest Manning over 25 years as Premier of Alberta was shown to be completely lacking in Rachel Notley after only 4 years as Premier of Alberta. Things were not going to be A-OK –

> "Not for businesses. Not for the oil patch. Not for investors. Not for workers. Not for taxpayers. The NDP did not turn out to be "business friendly" in the least. They handed unprecedented powers to unions, attacked family farms, ratcheted up minimum wages to record highs, cranked up taxes and even nationalized assets that previous governments had left to the private sector. The NDP oversaw a period of turmoil worse than anything Alberta has seen since the National Energy Program: massive layoffs, dried up foreign investment, and businesses, workers and families fleeing the province."

"FORTRESS AMERICA" UNDER SIEGE

It seems like we're reading Candace Malcolm's article all over again, doesn't it?

Shortly after being elected and declaring her government "business friendly," Notley –

> "raised business taxes, personal taxes and announced – **a carbon tax** – which she never once mentioned during her election campaign.
>
> In four years under Rachel Notley, Alberta went from being one of the most stable, investment-friendly jurisdictions in the world, to being **the most toxic province in the country** for investors and business. Another four years under Notley's radically anti-oil, anti-business and anti-Albertan socialists, and this province may never recover."

We can get the 'temperature' of Alberta's 2015-19 NDP government by meeting **Rachel Notley and her Inner Circle**, of reckless radical socialists:

> "**Albertans literally elected a hostile power to run the province, an enemy of our industry, of our workers, of investors and of the Alberta we and our families have built and love.**" (Sheila Gunn Reid, Stop Notley, 2019)

Rachel Notley

> "She's an **old-school international socialist**...a lefty – a paid up member of the climate cult...a crusader from the international labor movement...for years wearing a wristwatch with the face of Che Guevara, a Marxist who helped lead the Cuban communist revolution under Fidel Castro."

> "Che Guevara, a hero of the left, was a horrific racist. He wrote in his 1952 memoir, *The Motorcycle Diaries:* "The Negro is indolent and lazy and spends his money on frivolities, whereas the European is forward-looking,

CHAPTER 6: ALBERTA'S EXPERIMENTS WITH SOCIALISM

> organized and intelligent." (Walter Williams, Are today's leftists truly Marxists? The Calgary Sun, August 11, 2020).

Mrs. Notley should do her homework before she makes a hero and unashamedly wears his face on her wristwatch in the Alberta Legislature.

> "Condescension for Alberta and the dismissal of any justifiable pride in this province would set the tone for Notley's next four years.
>
> Notley tore into those who dared oppose her party's plan, saying "our government caucus looked the anger machine in the eye and said, 'this is one government you are not going to shout down.' She meant the Opposition (anger machine) supported by 60% of Albertans in the 2015 election.
>
> She is historically anti-pipeline. In 2015 was against **Northern Gateway** saying, "There's too much environmental sensitivity there and there's genuine concern by the Indigenous communities." Despite most "Indigenous communities" affected by Northern Gateway actually supported the plan. Indigenous groups are actually mad because they wanted those tankers and pipeline. She admitted she helped nudge Trudeau toward just the Trans Mountain expansion. She was interested in winnowing down the options to the fewest possible. **Keystone XL** – She said, "We're against it," she had said that over and over again. "The Premier's first directive...stop all KXL lobbying" in Washington, D.C.
>
> When Quebec began to push back on the **Energy East pipeline** using highly exaggerated claims about environmental damage to block Alberta's oil, **Notley supported them**." (Ibid)

So, Rachel Notley, as Alberta's Premier fought against these key pipelines which would have hugely benefitted the province and its citizens. That's not working for your province. Albertans beware! She's trying to get back in.

> "Notley has literally gone along with every single anti-pipeline and anti-oil policy that the Trudeau Liberals have come up with. There are already numerous pipelines in Alberta, in Notley's "backyard." They're safe. They have a far better safety record than any shipping alternative."

Sarah Hoffman (NDP Deputy Premier)

> "They're "**sewer rats**." So that's what she thinks of the Wildrose or today's Conservatives, or just people who disagree with her. They're angry. They're brutal. They're violent."

Shaye Anderson (NDP MLA)

He called one peaceful rally of farmers who opposed her attacks attempting to unionize their home businesses, as "extremely violent and brutal." It wasn't.

Lou Arab (Rachel Notley's husband)

> "the communications officer for CUPE, the union that campaigned against Canada's fight against the Islamic State...that accuses Israel of "unjust and disproportionate violence" against rocket attacks from Gaza; and most recently **supported Venezuela's socialist tyrant Nicholas Maduro** despite the Canadian government refusing to recognize his rigged election and corrupt rule."

Brian Topp (Original Chief of Staff)

> "Once ran for leadership of federal NDP, but was considered too radical.

CHAPTER 6: ALBERTA'S EXPERIMENTS WITH SOCIALISM

One of Notley's most important advisors shortly after her election win, a union leader from Ontario, was unabashedly anti-pipeline, anti-oil sands, vehemently anti-coal...anti-every fossil fuel...said, "Canada should produce a great deal less hydrocarbon energy,"...supported the anti-capitalist Occupy movement...said pro-energy policies are "blighting the rest of our economy," argued for a "legally binding ban on oil tankers" off NW B.C. coast which Liberal government acted on blocking any pipeline to tidewater up there...Dead set against Keystone XL pipeline calling it economic "madness," and "should be stopped;" once said, "force fossil-fueled cars out of our cities."

Topp has represented the NDP at **Socialist International meetings** in Europe.

"Helped B.C.'s NDP get elected in 2017 on an anti-oil platform...and they've been blocking Alberta's pipeline efforts ever since.

Vowed to "Develop a national energy strategy to transition Canada to a low-carbon economy and limit the impacts of the oil sands development during the transition"...compared Canada's oil industry to the arms industry.

In 2016, Topp left Notley's office and headed back to Toronto, but he left behind his plan for emission caps, carbon prices and coal shutdowns that had indeed become the heart of the NDP's government policy."

Shannon Phillips (Environment Minister)

"She helped write a 2004 book with environmental Greenpeace extremist Mike Hudema on how to fight capitalism. Its title, "An Action a Day Keeps Global Capitalism Away." Any actions to stop capitalists such as

"FORTRESS AMERICA" UNDER SIEGE

blockades, climbing buildings, breaking into worksites, hanging from a bridge to protest Alberta's oil sector and hurt Alberta's working families.

She succeeded in a campaign to stop a natural gas production project in Lethbridge...argued in 2012 against expansion of oil sands saying – "The benefits of slowing development far outweigh the risks." In 2008 she travelled to Fort Mc Murray with terror-promoting Al Jazeera to film an unflattering documentary on the oil sands. On a media panel in 2013 argued the oil sands are "the source of the country's fastest-growing carbon emissions, and are having a significant impact on democracy, human and treaty rights, and the social fabric." Argued that the oil sands "hurts women," complained about Alberta's "antiquated approach to the environment and climate change" and called Alberta "a province that pays the bills by pumping CO^2 into the atmosphere."

Rod Loyolla (President of Alberta NDP)

"Long live Hugo Chavez. Long live the values that he stood for," – on his You Tube channel. When Chavez died in 2013, Loyolla organized a vigil for him, calling it "an opportunity to express solidarity with the Venezuelan people and support for the Bolivarian Revolution. Charaterized Alberta's oil and gas industry as colonial oppressors...told VUE magazine in 2014 First Nations need to "defend themselves from these (capitalist) economic systems and the oppression that they have created." Wrote that Canada could learn a lot "regarding democracy and social and economic justice" from Chavez's authoritarian communist leadership. A Venezuela where political opponents are being locked up or killed. Used to be the richest country in SA but now people can't get food or medicine because the maniacal Marxist-Leninist ideology of Chavez and his successors have destroyed the economy."

CHAPTER 6: ALBERTA'S EXPERIMENTS WITH SOCIALISM

Graham Mitchell (Chief of Staff in Alberta energy ministry)

"From Brian Topp's far-left drum-circle in Toronto. Used to run a hard-core left-wing anti-resource group called LeadNow – ran TV ads denouncing the Conservative government's support for the oil industry saying, "The Harper government has stripped our environmental protections…and damaged our international reputation. They've taken our country backwards." He trained other lefty activists to campaign against Alberta's oil and gas."

Colin Piquette (NDP MLA)

"Attacks Canadian resource industries – we were "The Republic of Greedolia," alongside a defaced Canadian flag: Turned upside-down, it had the words "No Justice on Stolen Land" scrawled on it. He said he can't be proud of Alberta…"How can you?" he asked a protest rally where people carried signs that read "Genocide in Our Backyards" and "No Blood for Oil" and another inverted, defaced Maple Leaf flag that read "Canada Stop Denying Your Holocaust.""

Dave Mowatt (Ran NDP royalty review)

"Trained as a disciple of Al Gore to become an "environmental warrior" to spread the anti-oil message of Gore's propaganda film, An Inconvenient Truth. Enthusiastic backer of Tides Foundation devoted to shutting down Alberta's oil industry, with campaigns like "Week to End Enbridge" and "Tanker-Free Coast campaign.""

Brian Mason (NDP MLA, former leader)

"Called the "tar sands an environmental embarrassment.""

"FORTRESS AMERICA" UNDER SIEGE

Notley's well-oiled political machine did not like negative press. No socialist regime likes to have its blatant failures made public, though the public already knows it. Dictatorships always attack freedom of speech. Notley also banned the Rebel Media from the Alberta Legislature. Only recently has it been allowed back in by a Conservative government.

> "Attacks on the Calgary Sun from one of Rachel Notley's most senior advisors...desperate attacks on a newspaper that dared to publish a column critical of the Notley NDP government...if reporting on poll numbers from a credible pollster is deemed to be "weaponizing" and "a danger to a democracy" as the NDP claims, perhaps they can share their own data and their own numbers." (Ric McIver, Selective comments from the NDP not unexpected, The Calgary Sun, December 5, 2018).

Radical Environmentalism – Federally and Provincially

Rachel Notley and the NDP were co-conspirators with the federal Liberal government of Justin Trudeau against Alberta and the oil industry, costing Canada at least $60 billion in energy investment since 2015. No premier stood more solidly with Trudeau on this file than Notley. Her vehement opposition to oil and gas, and pipelines long pre-dated Trudeau.

> "Notley's whole career in the legislature before being premier was the voice for the anti-oil activists...attended a rally where signs read, "no tar sands, no tankers, no pipelines." In opposition one of her staffers was a Greenpeace activist. She's more hardcore anti-pipeline than Justin Trudeau.
>
> She never liked or supported Alberta's oil calling the oil sands "tar sands," warning against "unfettered

CHAPTER 6: ALBERTA'S EXPERIMENTS WITH SOCIALISM

> development" and "expansion...wants to put the brakes on fracking shale, which we've been doing in Alberta for decades.
> She was the first premier ever elected who actually opposed more export capacity for Alberta oil...because she's really against Alberta continuing to produce oil...2015 article in U.K. left-wing Guardian newspaper said, 'No long-term future in tar sands,' says Alberta's premier and forecast an eventual future beyond fossil fuels." (Sheila Gunn Reid, Stop Notley, 2019).

The Carbon Tax was one of Notley's pet projects. She failed to mention it during her election campaign. It's a matter of NDP Big Government knows best; the Alberta voters do not know what's good for them...typical socialism, in Rachel Notley's own words:

> "Once it (carbon tax) comes into play, they'll see that it actually is a tremendous opportunity for them to make better choices. It's not just a question of having a more fuel-efficient vehicle, it could sometimes be a question of taking a bus, walking, **you know**, those kinds of things in terms of the patterns of fuel use that people engage in." (Ibid)

Talk about a low regard for the individual person. It's all about the masses, "you know." Socialism at its best. The NDP knows it's best for us ordinary slobs to walk, but it's OK for them to drive or fly anywhere they like, any time they like.

> "Shannon Phillips, appearing on CBC radio on a frosty winter day – the interviewer asked her how she made her way to the studio that day. Did she take the tremendous opportunity to make better choice for action on climate change with credibility? Phillips admitted she drove in (so) fighting climate change 'isn't about one person's commute.' Meaning it's not about *her* commute; it's about *your* commute, as Notley said, and you 'taking a bus (or) walking.'"

"FORTRESS AMERICA" UNDER SIEGE

> The NDP has a thing for big cars. Service Alberta Minister Stephanie MacLean said, "Any minister and deputy minister needs to have a vehicle that is safe and can contend with the treacherous road conditions that we have in the winter." But think about that. Ministers think they're more important...and want to tax you into a smaller more dangerous car, while they swan around in their fat, all-wheel-drive SUVs. **Could they be more elitist?**"

When the NDP should have been working tirelessly on behalf of the main driver of Alberta's economy it was working tirelessly against it, concurring with the anti-oil federal government every step of the way. "The NDP is embarrassed by people who don't believe in their radical, socialist, big-labor, big government, anti-oil, climate crazy agenda." (Sheila Gunn Reid, Stop Notley: The Case for Throwing Out the NDP, 2019). That's not working for the voters who elected her; it's hurting them, and utterly selfish.

In all of her leftist agenda to destroy Alberta she found a willing partner in Justin Trudeau. Together they developed a socialist synergy in attacking the Prairie work ethic. They despise that hard entrepreneurial self-reliance and strong sense of community that characterized Albertans in building their prosperous and generous province through richly-endowed resources like oil and gas to become a major driver of the Canadian economy.

> "Far from "standing up" for pipelines, Notley has gone along with every single anti-pipeline and anti-oil policy that the Trudeau Liberals have come up with. That includes the Northern Gateway, Energy East, Keystone and Trans-Mountain pipelines. She said all but one were not in the "national interest.

CHAPTER 6: ALBERTA'S EXPERIMENTS WITH SOCIALISM

> When the federal Liberals came up with their carbon-taxing, Notley was first in line to sign up. 'We'll be a willing partner,' she said in 2016."

She was also a willing partner in Trudeau's federal legislation aimed directly against Alberta and its oil industry. She supported ruinous Bill C-69, the so-called Impact Assessment Act, dubbed "the no more pipelines bill, and one of the most dangerous pieces of legislation ever to threaten Alberta's economic future," documented by Sheila Gunn Reid.

> "Trudeau, a trust-fund baby and part time drama teacher turned politician, with no business experience, tore down the NEB (The National Energy Board), "widely admired internationally" for its excellent regulatory policies and scientific record, to create a "progressive" regulator focused on subjective global climate change, identity and gender issues rather than on Canada's economic interests."

Trudeau's anti-pipeline legislation is so radical, that even anti-oil sands radicals can't even understand it. Even an environmental law lawyer confessed, "I don't really know what it (C-69's Impact Assessment) means." The reason is that Trudeau wants to kill energy projects by any available means, no matter how bizarre, impractical or illogical. It is Marxist, and intended to cripple major project approvals in Canada's resource sector.

> "Gender and identity intersectionality is the kind of neo-Marxist social justice theory they teach in Women's Studies and Queer Studies courses at second-rate liberal arts colleges. It is the polar opposite of science, facts and evidence. It is literally stuff people have made up."

Rachel Notley's NDP helped the Liberals all along with C-69. She "agrees with the goals" of Trudeau's pipeline-killing bill. That's not working for Alberta. Furthermore, she allowed the Trudeau government to renew the federal equalization formula for Alberta for another 6 years without fighting Ottawa to stop it, since the province is hurting and struggling. Notley's ideology is too close to Trudeau's for her to fight against him on behalf of Albertans. They are both "progressives," international socialists working toward a globalist "new order," a totalitarian one-world government.

> "Notley's NDP set out to change Alberta, permanently, from a freedom-loving, pro-business, capitalist province to a beachhead for the NDP's globalist socialist vision for Canada." (Sheila Gunn Reid, Stop Notley: The Case for Throwing Out the NDP, 2019).

Notley's anti-capitalist government was big, and like Big Brother, it strong-armed and demeaned anyone in its way. Between 2015 and 2018, 78,000 unionized public service jobs had been added, while those in the private sector fell by 44,000. In 4 years the wealth-consuming public sector ballooned by 21.5%, one in four jobs in Alberta while the wealth-generating private sector was starved of investment. That is socialism on steroids.

Pierre Trudeau, Justin's father, was an international socialist. The federal government increased its bit of the economic activity of the nation by 42% during his tenure. Socialism = Big Government; Big Government = misery for the people it rules. During the 15 ½ years of Trudeau's administration the Misery Index (UI rate + Interest rate) for Canadians was 30. Prior to Trudeau it was 10. After 8 years of Stephen Harper it was 7.8. (Bob Plamondon, The Truth About Trudeau, 2013). The fallout from Justin Trudeau is yet to be seen. It won't be good.

> "The Trudeau government's damaging energy policies have contributed to substantial job loss and a 35% decline oil and gas investment over the last five years

CHAPTER 6: ALBERTA'S EXPERIMENTS WITH SOCIALISM

> (2015-2019) – and that's just the beginning of the bad news. Investment in the oil and gas industry – an important contributor to the Canadian economy – this year could shrink by 40% and see up to 220,000 more jobs lost (Statistics Canada). The Oil Tanker Moratorium Act (Bill C-48) restricts tankers carrying oil off the northern B.C. coast, shutting down access to new markers. To access emergency aid program (LEEFF), oil companies must sign on to Canada's Paris Climate Accord – with zero emissions by 2050 (increasing costs by 25%), diminishing competitiveness." (Ashley Stedman and Elmira Aliakbari, Trudeau energy policies making jobs and investment disappear, The Calgary Sun, July 15, 2020).

> "Enbridge Line 3 is beset by legal hurdles in the U.S. Loss of Line 3, Keystone and Trans Mountain expansion would sap $5/bbl. Of Western Canadian Select oil. Some 5% of government revenue is required to service Alberta's provincial debt, and that number will grow – especially without adequate pipeline access. **Alberta is in a dire fiscal situation**." (Steve Lafleur, Latest pipeline setback another blow to Alberta, The Calgary Sun, 2020).

In "Taxpayers losing billions without pipelines," Aaron Wudrick and Franco Terrazzano of the Canadian Taxpayer's Federation write the following:

> "Governments are getting in the way of pipeline development. The feds : 1. Blocked Northern Gateway; 2. Bill C-48 banned oil tankers off the B.C. coast, but not Saudi oil off the East Coast; 3. Destroyed Energy East with "upstream and downstream emissions reviews," which eastern imported oil is not subject to; 4. Bill C-69 – Impact Assessment Act – "No More Pipelines Act;" 5. Showered B.C. with infrastructure money to block Trans Mountain while tankers carry B.C.'s LNG are allowed. All Canadians lost $6.2 billion between 2013 and 2018 without additional pipeline capacity. **No other province**

> or region gets targeted for similar abuse." (The Calgary Sun, May 25, 2019).

> "In 2018, the feds killed Bill S-245 declaring Trans Mountain to be in the national interest." (Dwight Newman and Joseph Quesnel, The Trans Mountain battle is actually just beginning." (The Calgary Sun, June 25, 2019).

"The Trudeau Liberals just keep on coming against Alberta and the industry that still fuels and greases the wheels of the Canadian economy. They continue to ignore the calls of those premiers, of the Senate and of the industry. **That's what happens when you have radicals running our federal government.**" (Licia Corbella, 'We should be concerned' – Energy industry alarmed at rejection of amendments to federal Bill C-69), The Calgary Sun, June 14, 2019).

Politicians, journalists and industry opposed to Notley's and Trudeau's war against Alberta and the petroleum industry need to cast off their state of 'denial,' that this war is as real as WW II, yet being fought within our borders by radical socialist-communist forces hostile to our free democracy.

> "Notley's NDP is more of a Socialist International solidarity society, with its students, public sector workers and union activists. How does a party get elected in a substantially rural Prairie province with not one single solitary farmer or rancher among its 55 MLAs?" (Sheila Gunn Reid: The Case for Throwing Out the NDP, 2019).

The dictatorial behavior of the NDP was on full display in only four short years in power. It was all based on ideology – socialist ideology. In "No Faith in NDP:

CHAPTER 6: ALBERTA'S EXPERIMENTS WITH SOCIALISM

Province's attack on religious schools violates the Charter," Licia Corbella writes:

> "Alberta's NDP government is threatening to pull funding and accreditation from private religious schools in Alberta for including statements of faith in their anti-bullying policies stating, "language which suggests alternative viewpoints are not equally legitimate, which is disrespectful of diversity." Bill 24 makes it illegal for teachers to tell parents that their child, even as young as 5 years old, has joined a Gay Straight Alliance Group – assuming parents are the enemy of their own children, rather than their best advocates. Minister of Education, David Eggen won't tolerate schools off message saying, 'I have been perfectly clear that all school boards that receive public funding will follow the law.' No choice, no diversity. Just NDP party beliefs taught in Alberta." (The Calgary Sun, October 3, 2018).

This example of **'mandatory'** is as clear a warning as can be made; all socialist governments have within their DNA, the tendency to rule with rigor and authority, not with consensus or concern for the individual. It's the Party-line, or no line at all.

Notley's NDP nationalized the government laundry service of all things. She even tried to silence the Rebel media from exposing her government's dirty laundry. She nationalized 153 Alberta driver's license testing businesses, demeaning the private business owners in the process, taking their livelihoods away. She interfered with the petroleum industry, curtailing production and planning a costly government-controlled crude oil transportation by railway.

> "From laundry to driver testing to the oil and gas industry, unionization of the family farms (Bill 6), and anti-

democratic creation of new eco-parks, the NDP lied, slandered and vilified those who opposed their rule by force as "extremely violent and brutal extremists."

This long four years of radical socialist rule should cause every thinking Albertan and Canadian to examine where we are headed as a nation with a party and a prime minister very much like Rachel Notley's NDP. Remember, the NDP are "Liberals in a hurry." Trudeau's Liberals are making the NDP run faster than ever. Their agenda is not Canadian, not free enterprise and definitely not that of a democracy.

Albertans got a small taste of what is ahead if the international socialist movement attains its globalist agenda.

Communism behind Environmentalism and Globalism

Tom Harris, Executive Director of the Ottawa-based International Climate Science Coalition writes in the July 27, 2020, Calgary Sun:

> "Climate alarmism threatens to ruin the Canada previous generations fought and died to preserve. Researchers have demonstrated that the stated opinions of politicians and other "elites" in society is the primary factor influencing public opinion. Thousands of studies from peer-reviewed scientific journals either refute or cast serious doubt on the climate scare. The idea that we detrimentally affect climate through our use of fossil fuels is **one of the worst deceptions ever perpetrated**. The primary result of the climate crusade will not be enhanced environmental protection but expanded government power, reduced individual freedom, and huge profits for alternative energy companies."

CHAPTER 6: ALBERTA'S EXPERIMENTS WITH SOCIALISM

Notley and her NDP fed on the manufactured climate 'crisis.' The Epoch Times, "How the Spectre of Communism is Ruling our World," The Communism Behind Environmentalism – Part 1, Chapter 16, 2020) details the radical socialist-communist origins and agenda of global warming and the current climate scare. Following are some excerpts from this material:

> "In order to create a tightly-controlled global government, communism must create or use an "enemy" that threatens all of mankind and intimidates the public around the world into handing over both individual liberty and state sovereignty. Creating a global panic about looming environmental and ecological disasters attributed to global warming are the inevitable route to achieving this goal."

Using Marxist atheism and materialism to co-opt environmentalism, communism made free enterprise the "enemy" of nature. This is why NDP governments and the federal Liberals shut down Alberta's proposed pipelines. This radical environmentalism came to view global warming as the main threat to mankind, and viewed fossil fuels as the main culprit.

> "After the end of the Cold War, former communists of the Soviet Union such a Gorbachev, as well as the communists and their "fellow travelers" in the West, all started afresh to join the environmental protection movement in order to limit and fight against the free societies in the West.
>
> Marx regarded any effort to create wealth by using natural resources a vicious cycle, concluding rational agriculture is incompatible with the capitalist system – therefore, all private property must be public. Lenin nationalized land, forest, water, mineral animal, and plant resources in the U.S.S.R. to prevent the public from using them without authorization...because the quest for personal profit is immoral."

"FORTRESS AMERICA" UNDER SIEGE

Tarek Fatah, in a column titled, "Carry on Greta, but beware the millionaire Marxists," the young climate crusader Greta Thunberg's message was put in perspective:

> "For the first time I could see her anger was contrived. I could see the fingerprints of a speech-writer trying to make an autistic child reject what her forefathers had accomplished in the last 200 years, and reject it as the rape of Mother Earth. Her donors include heiress Aileen Getty, American philanthropist Trevor Neilson, and filmmaker Rory Kennedy, a member of the political Kennedy clan." (The Calgary Sun, September 26, 2019)

Canadian Maurice Strong, founder of the UN Environment Program, organized UN conferences on the Environment in 1972 and 1992. His UN agency bears his Marxist views inherited from his aunt, Anna Louise Strong, a pro-communist journalist. Both settled in Communist China and died there. He is called the **"father of modern environmentalism."**

> "Natalie Grant Wraga, an expert on the Soviet Union, conducted an in-depth study on the issue and wrote, 'Protection of the environment may be used as a **pretext** to adopt a series of measures designed to **undermine** the industrial base of developed nations. It may also serve to introduce **malaise** by lowering their standard of living and implanting **communist values**.'"

The Liberal anti-oil Bills (C-69, C-48, etc.) do this exact thing, all the while the politicians and media miss the real agenda behind the legislation...**destroy the middle class**. Fabian socialists, influenced by Karl Marx, started the idea of the "ecosystem," leading to Ecological Marxism and the concepts of economic and ecological crises and conflicts – ecological socialism – in opposition to free enterprise and capitalism. "Canada is largely closed for business in our energy sector despite the fact

CHAPTER 6: ALBERTA'S EXPERIMENTS WITH SOCIALISM

that pipelines are 2.5 times safer than rail transport," according to Elmira Aliakbari and Ashley Stedman of the Fraser Institute. (The Calgary Sun, September 2, 2108). The result of Ecological Marxism would be irreversible economic decline.

There is an indisputable consensus dogma that humans cause global warming according to today's environmental narrative in academia, government and international agencies. The voices of those who oppose the so-called consensus seldom appear in the media or academic journals. They are labeled "deniers," forced to apologize, and silenced. Thus the real debate has been kept from the public. (The Epoch Times, "How the Spectre of Communism is Ruling Our World," The Communism Behind Environmentalism – Part 1, Chapter 16, 2020).

> "Physicist Michael Griffin, a former NASA administrator said in an interview in 2007, "I personally think people have gone overboard in the discussion of climate change. It has almost acquired religious status, which I find deplorable.
>
> Professor Lennart Bengtsson, an eminent meteorologist, joined a think tank that challenges global warming. He faced intense scrutiny and pressure, forcing him to resign. He said, "I would never have expected anything similar in such a peaceful community as meteorology. **Apparently it has been transformed in recent years**." It has, as a result of communist ideology and political struggle tactics such as deception, mobbing, public shaming, loss of tenure, call-outs and open conflict toward "deniers," thus hijacking the field of meteorology. Man-made global warming is now a **consensus dogma**, with scientists, media, environmental activists and politicians working together to spread fear of an imminent disaster – to frighten the public into obeying a political agenda."

Columnist Lorne Gunter in, "Leading voice apologizes for the 'climate scare,' publicized the testimony of one of the world's leading environmentalists over the past three decades on this climate change issue. Michael Schellenberger, an expert reviewer on the UN IPCC (Intergovernmental Panel on Climate Change) – the bible of climate change alarmism, wrote in Forbes Magazine,

> "I would like to formally apologize for the climate scare we created over the last 30 years. Climate change is happening. It's just not the end of the world. It's not even our most serious environmental problem. **I feel an obligation to apologize for how badly we environmentalists have misled the public**. Humans are not causing a 'sixth mass extinction.' Climate change is not making natural disasters worse. The Amazon is not 'the lungs of the world.' Air pollution and carbon emissions have been declining in rich nations for 50 years. **Climate change is not an "existential threat" to civilization.**" (The Calgary Sun, July 5, 2020)

Schellenberger admitted that he remained silent and said nothing out of fear – "he was scared" – of losing friends and funding. He has just written a new book, "Apocalypse Never." He must have gotten sick of the IPCC culture.

> "Because the existing research contains so many different views, in order to 'reach consensus' as it set out to do, the IPCC simply got rid of the opposing views. World-renowned physicist, Frederick Seitz, noted an IPCC report was largely altered after peer review, removing doubts about the human effect on climate change. 'I have never witnessed a more disturbing corruption of the peer-review process than the events that led to this IPCC report.'"

> "Such consensus is the stuff of politics, not of science." (Paul Reiter, Professor, Pasteur Institute, Paris, France).

CHAPTER 6: ALBERTA'S EXPERIMENTS WITH SOCIALISM

> "The IPCC has used 'disaster consensus, motivated by preconceived agendas that are scientifically unsound,' said Christopher Landsea, a hurricane researcher at the U.S. Oceanic and Atmospheric Administration, and one of the leading authors of the 4th IPCC assessment report. He resigned."

Columnist Barbara Kay recently wrote, "in George Orwell's "1984," "the principle of Crimestop is the abrupt, instinctual, fear-driven self-silencing that precluded (prevents) utterance of politically incorrect words that may invoke shaming or worse." She indicated that mainstream publishing houses are following Crimestop concerning gender and identity issues, among many others. The pressure is also on small publishing houses to do the same quenching of free speech. (The Epoch Times, Orwell's 'Crimestop' Alive and Well in 2020).

Society's elite writers comprising *The Authors Guild*, who should value freedom of speech, are aiding and abetting this travesty; their most common response being –

> "'Free speech is the ability to speak. Not the ability to speak without consequences.' Also, 'The last few years there seems to have developed a strange idea – that the First Amendment entitles everyone to express their opinion, in a public forum, with no consequences or even criticism, no matter **how noxious or dangerous or abusive**, and even get paid for it.'" (Bob Zeidman, When the Gatekeepers Abandon Their Posts, The Epoch Times, p. B6, July 23-29, 2020).

Unless freedom-loving men and women are willing to risk their necks and 'stick to their guns,' this Marxist-inspired juggernaut will steamroll onward into a global, international socialist totalitarian state. What will they have to say to their enslaved grandchildren when this tragedy comes to pass?

> "Christopher Horner, senior American researcher at the Competitive Enterprise Institute wrote a book, **"Red Hot Lies, How Global Warming Alarmists Use Threats, Fraud, and Deception to Keep You Misinformed."**

In "Conservative candidates need to push back against the climate scare," Columnist Tom Harris addressed the only political party in Canada that can do something about this globalist, climate deception, and that is, call it out.

> "'Carbon pollution' that the government tells us we must reduce, is really carbon dioxide (CO_2), a colorless, odorless gas essential for plant photosynthesis and so needed for life. It is the very opposite of pollution. It is not worth spending anything at all trying to reduce CO^2 emissions.
>
> Any Conservative leadership candidate so frightened by political correctness that they stand idly by while our nation is sucked further into the **black hole of climate alarmism** is not worthy of leading any party, let alone becoming prime minister.'" (The Calgary Sun, July 22, 2020).

Erin O'Toole, the new Conservative leader, elected yesterday, has no plans to withdraw Canada from the Paris Climate Accord should he become prime minister. If he wise, he will change his mind. Hopefully, he will avoid the leftist 'baited traps' and go on to form a Conservative federal government after the next election.

CHAPTER 6: ALBERTA'S EXPERIMENTS WITH SOCIALISM

Creating a 'crisis mentality' is being used to strip affluent individuals and countries of their wealth and redistribute it on a global scale to the 'poor.' Making people afraid to use fossil fuels is designed to destroy the economies of energy producing provinces such as Alberta, thereby damaging Canada's economy as well. Rectifying their loss by alternative measures such as costly solar panels and emission standards for cars is a sham. (The Epoch Times, "How the Spectre of Communism is Ruling Our World," The Communism Behind Environmentalism – Part 2, Chapter 16, 2020).

Here are a few of many experts who were punished or intimidated into silence for questioning the manmade global warming consensus dogma. Silencing people of this caliber means that the UN, politicians and environmental groups have something to hide, and that they don't want made known.

> "Late David Bellamy: well-known British botanist; late William Gray: renowned professor, pioneer of hurricane research; Patrick J. Michaels: former president of the American Association of State Climatologists; Mark Albright: Washington state assistant climatologist; Judith Curry: climatologist and former chair of the School of Earth and Atmospheric Sciences at Georgia Institute of Technology; Roger Pielke Jr.: professor at the University of Colorado; Joanne Simpson: award-winning NASA atmospheric scientist.
>
> Meteorologist Joseph D'Aleo, former chairman of the American Meteorological Society's Committee on Weather Analysis and Forecasting believed there was 'very likely a **silent majority** of scientists in climatology, meteorology, and allied sciences who do not endorse what is said to be the consensus position.'" (Ibid)

"FORTRESS AMERICA" UNDER SIEGE

Jacqui Tam, a 21st Century university vice-president recently lost her job for inadvertently crossing the global warming consensus dogma line. How shameful for University of Alberta President David Turpin to throw Ms. Tam under the bus of political correctness for something as innocuous as supporting the ad below. It is **intellectual insanity**.

> "Jacqui Tam was forced to resign last Sunday because – get this – she approved a billboard campaign that implied very, very indirectly that global warming might not be 100% evil and destructive. The ad reads, "Beefier barley: climate change will boost Alberta's barley yield with less water, feeding more cattle." These days universities are just about the last place to look for free expression." (Lorne Gunter, Even barley yield data can upset the politically correct mob, The Calgary Sun, October 2, 2019).

All of these professionals experienced or saw firsthand the extreme methods being used to silence those who opposed the global warming consensus dogma. Joanne Simpson, an award-winning NASA scientist said,

> "As a scientist I remain skeptical...The main basis of the claim that man's release of greenhouse gases is the cause of the warming is based almost entirely upon climate models. We all know the frailty of models concerning the air-surface system." (Ibid)

The writer, a retired geologist, specialized in sedimentary depositional environments in the rock record around the world for over thirty years. He has recognized numerous examples of global warming, wet and dry periods and major sea level fluctuations preserved in sedimentary strata. Human civilization had nothing to do with these changes in the natural environment, and he is certain that it is presumptuous to say that it is today. Mankind is reaching a pinnacle of pride to claim that it can avert

CHAPTER 6: ALBERTA'S EXPERIMENTS WITH SOCIALISM

an eco-catastrophe by its own means, if such should come. The Bible makes it perfectly clear that God is in control of the climate, and not man. **The devil is the author of this deception. Man in his pride is the unwitting victim.**

> *Sing unto the LORD with thanksgiving; sing praise upon the harp unto our God: Who covereth the heavens with clouds, who prepareth rain for the earth, who maketh grass to grow upon the mountains." (Psalm 147:7-8).*

> *"And also I have withholden the rain from you, when there were yet three months to the harvest: and I caused it to rain upon one city, and caused it not to rain upon another city: one piece was rained upon, and the piece whereupon it rained not withered." (Amos 4:7).*

God can create adverse climate and weather events to discipline man or chastise man for sin. Yet, modern man continues to revolt and pretend that God has nothing to do with climate change and the earth's temperature.

Propaganda techniques used by environmentalists to perpetuate the manmade global warming "consensus dogma" include:

> "causing panic, appealing to authority, encouraging a herd mentality, resorting to personal attacks, stereotyping, sensationalism, and falsifying records."

Restricting the right to think is a communist tactic that divorces people from a concept of good and evil based on universal values. So virulent are the attacks that some have tried to use legal means to quench freedom of speech on the issue while others have equated "deniers" to terrorists or morally-depraved accomplices to a coming eco-Holocaust, who may someday face Nuremburg-style criminal trials.

> "British journalist Brendan O'Neil wrote that it's a short step from demonizing a group of people, and describing their arguments as toxic and dangerous, to demanding more and harsher censorship." (Ibid)

Environmentalism has degenerated in recent years to become "a worldwide secular religion." (Michael Crichton, author of "Jurassic Park") –

> "There's an initial Eden, a paradise, a state of grace and unity with nature; there's a fall from grace into a state of pollution as a result of eating from the tree of knowledge (free enterprise-capitalism); and as a result of our actions, there is a judgment day coming for us all (eco-Holocaust). We are all energy sinners (carbon footprint), doomed to die, unless we seek salvation, which is now called sustainability. Sustainability is salvation in the church of the environment." (Ibid)

Many others are sounding the same alarm and yet society proceeds along the anti-God course that Ernest Manning long ago predicted would lead to certain destruction.

> "Religious fervor, enforced dogma, anti-capitalist action, and debasing humanity before the environment will not lead to a healthier natural environment, much less a fairer or more just human society. **Should radical environmentalism succeed in its aims**, we would only need to look at the disasters of communist rule over the previous century to predict the end result." (Ibid)

The Vatican, the undisputed leader of the ecumenical movement is jumping on board the global-warming bandwagon. The Holy See has also made recent overtures to the Chinese Communist Government. The Catholic Church is positioning herself to engage the impending international socialist one-world government. Thus, a 'universal,' one-world ecumenical religion will unite with an

CHAPTER 6: ALBERTA'S EXPERIMENTS WITH SOCIALISM

atheistic one-world totalitarian government. A seemingly unequal yoke, one would say? People involved in these faiths need to ask themselves, "How can this be?" The answer, "They are not of God; none of them."

> "On June 18, 2020, the Vatican urged Catholics to disinvest from the armament and fossil fuels industries warning against climate change, and in order to contain global warming. One action point in the encyclical called on Catholics to "shun companies that are harmful to human or social ecology, and to the environment." Last month, more than 40 faith organizations, more than half of them Catholic, pledged to divest from fossil fuel companies. The Vatican bank has said that it does not invest in fossil fuels and many Catholic dioceses and educational institutions around the world have taken similar positions." (Philip Pullella, 'Shun' Harmful, Reuters, in the Calgary Sun, June 19, 2020).

The Roman Church is openly allying with radical environmentalism...which is nothing other than camouflaged communism. Both consider capitalism no longer relevant. Together they will whip up panic and fear of ecological catastrophe, and then use the power of an authoritarian or totalitarian government to gain supreme control over peoples' assets, property, and religious freedoms; taking away their middle and upper class comforts and conveniences, as well as their spiritual hope.

Author Janet Biehl wrote: "the ecological crisis is resolvable only through totalitarian means" and an "eco-dictatorship" is needed. (The Epoch Times, "How the Spectre of Communism is Ruling Our World," The Communism Behind Environmentalism – Part 2, Chapter 16, 2020).

"FORTRESS AMERICA" UNDER SIEGE

Free enterprise will be destroyed and the world economy totally collectivized. The middle class will be gone. The Bible describes this dictatorship and its supreme ruler, "the beast." The religious leader, the false prophet, causes the world to worship the beast, the political leader. They are in collusion.

> "and power was given him over all kindreds, and tongues, and nations. And all that dwell upon the earth shall worship him. And he (the religious leader) causeth all, both small and great, rich and poor, free and bond, to receive a mark in their right hand, or in their foreheads: And that no man might buy or sell, save he that had the mark, or the name of the beast, or the number of his name...and his number is Six hundred three score and six." (Revelation 13:7, 16-18)

Former Czech president Vaclav Klaus wrote in his 2008 book, "Blue Planet in Green Shackles,"

> "Environmentalism is a movement that intends to radically change the world regardless of the consequences (at the cost of human lives and severe restrictions on individual freedom). It intends to change humankind, human behavior, the structure of society, the system of values – simply everything! A small, elitist minority will rule over and overwhelming majority to produce their utopia (perfect society) by the Marxist approach to economics. The results would be completely different from the intended ones." (Ibid)

> **"And he (false prophet) had power to give life unto the image of the beast, that the image of the beast should both speak, and cause that as many as would not worship the image of the beast should be killed." (Revelation 13:15)**

The climate scare is aimed directly at school children around the world, to convert the next generation to international Marxism. Young Greta Thunberg is a

CHAPTER 6: ALBERTA'S EXPERIMENTS WITH SOCIALISM

celebrated example of this socialist brainwashing aimed at vulnerable and malleable minds. Schools are actively promoting the deception. Parents beware! Get your children out of the government school system.

> "On Friday, many thousands of Canadian schoolchildren will be exposed to ideological alarmist rhetoric at Global Climate Strike rallies taking part across the country. University classes are being cancelled and school boards are sending permission slips home asking parents to allow their kids to attend one of these rallies. "Our planet is on fire. We have to act now." Climate Justice Toronto posted signs it intends to wave during the supposed child-friendly rally. One of them, in all capitals reads **FUCK CAPITALISM**." (Anthony Furey, Parents need to keep a close eye on what the climate strike tells their kids, The Calgary Sun, September 27, 2019). <u>Note</u>: Mr. Furey used only F_ _ K CAPITALISM in his article.

Human life will count for little in the future totalitarian dictatorship. The U.S.S.R., Communist China and Pol Pot's Cambodia, though possibly comparable, may underestimate the last bloody regime before the Lord's return. It will be worse than anything mankind has previously known.

Total economic control and tracing such as the CCP is using in China today will be worldwide and no individual will escape scrutiny in the future communist eco-dictatorship. The Bible describes the Beast or Antichrist as being focused on the Marxist interpretation of materialistic, natural laws – and not on a supernatural Biblical God.

> "Neither shall he (the beast) *regard the God of his fathers, nor the desire of women, nor regard any god: for he shall magnify himself above all. But in his estate shall he* **honor the God of forces**: *and a god whom his fathers knew not shall he honor with gold, and silver, and*

> with precious stones, and pleasant things." (Daniel 11:37-38)

The Antichrist will revel in material wealth while his subjects will be in total subjection and poverty, and under his every whim and desire.

Communism and globalization

Marx and Engels wrote that a communist revolution would have to be a global movement. A former national chairman of Communist Party USA wrote:

> "A Communist world will be a unified, organized world. The economic system will be one great organization, based on the principles of planning now dawning in the USSR. The American Soviet government will be an important section in this world government." (The Epoch Times, "How the Spectre of Communism is Ruling Our World," Globalization and Communism, Chapter 17, 2020).

Joseph Stalin in his book, "Marxism and the National Question," summarized several goals of the communist global revolution. Pierre Trudeau, a Fabian socialist, sympathized with these goals. We do not know whether he had read Stalin's book though he had visited the Soviet Union in 1951, before Stalin died. The late Pierre Trudeau's comments and beliefs are in bold print from the book, "The Truth About Trudeau," Bob Plamondon, 2013). They are compared with Stalin's beliefs. Stalin, by the way, patterned his rule after Vladimir Lenin's example.

1. "Confuse, disorganize, and destroy the forces of capitalism around the world. **Trudeau was anti-capitalist; posited that capitalism was flawed because it had not produced equal sharing of wealth among the population.**

CHAPTER 6: ALBERTA'S EXPERIMENTS WITH SOCIALISM

2. Bring all nations together into a single world system of economy. **"I want a classless society…The very idea of the nation-state is absurd…the party of the people – socialism, communism – will eventually come out the winner."**
3. Force the advanced countries to pour prolonged financial aid into the under-developed countries. **At 1981, G-7 in Canada, Trudeau restated that the world failed to share its wealth more equitably and that the world's richest nations should contribute more money to developing ones.**
4. Divide the world into regional groups as a transitional stage toward total world government. **Trudeau said he was a "citizen of the world. I am opposed to any political system based on race and religion. All such politics are reactionary."** Populations will more readily abandon their national loyalties to a vague regional loyalty than they will to a world authority. Later, the regionals (NATO, OAS, etc.) can be brought all the way into a single world dictatorship of the proletariat. **In 1971 as Prime Minister visited U.S.S.R. saying, "Those of your countrymen now in Canada, Mr. Chairman, find themselves living within a constitutional framework with a formal structure similar to that in the Soviet Union. We have a great deal to learn from the Soviet Union."**

"This is the "paradise on earth," or Orwell's '1984 utopia' promised in communism, a supposed collective society without class, nations, or government, based on the principle that follows: "from each according to his ability and to each according to his need." (The Epoch Times, "How the Spectre of Communism is Ruling Our World," Introduction, 2020).

Fabian socialism, of which Pierre Trudeau belonged since his days at the London School of Economics, is a socialist society with the same objectives as Marxism-Leninism. Lenin stressed again and again that the communists must hide their real intentions.

"FORTRESS AMERICA" UNDER SIEGE

"**The Fabian logo depicts a wolf in sheep's clothing**. To gradually bring about socialism, the British Fabian Society, founded in 1884, invented the policy of "permeation," to take advantage of available openings in politics, business, and civil society – encouraging its members, usually young intellectuals – to ingratiate themselves with important figures such as cabinet ministers, senior administrative officials, industrialists, university deans and church officials.

Bernard Shaw, a Fabian socialist, wrote: 'I also made it quite clear that Socialism means equality of income or nothing, and that under socialism you would not be allowed to be poor. You would be forcibly fed, clothed, lodged, taught, and employed whether you like it or not. If it were discovered that you had not character enough to be worth all this trouble, **you might possibly be executed in a kindly manner**.'" (The Epoch Times, "How The Spectre of Communism is Ruling Our World," Infiltrating the West – Part 1, Chapter 5, 2020).

An unholy trinity has turned Canada to leftist socialism starting with Pierre Trudeau, his understudy Jean Chretien and finally, Justin Trudeau – Pierre's son. They know what is really going on in the socialist takeover of Canada today. That is why Chretien was so close to Jiang Zemin, the Chinese Communist tyrant responsible for the Tiananmen Square massacre in 1989, and the persecution of Falun Gong and other persons of conscience starting in 1999, until the present.

It is reasonable to assume that Prime Minister Justin Trudeau has similar beliefs to his father. His admiration for Communist China seems to mirror that of his father. Pierre Trudeau admired the Soviet Union far more than the United States. Amazingly, our Prime Minister turns a blind eye to our enemy, Communist China, as if capitulating to its detestable program to infiltrate, demoralize and destroy our country in a covert war of espionage, intimidation and bullying.

CHAPTER 6: ALBERTA'S EXPERIMENTS WITH SOCIALISM

For example, two opposite pages in the September 24, 2020, Calgary Sun read: **"Opioid Deaths Surge,"** by Jason Herring and **"Hospital Outbreak Grows,"** by Stephanie Babych. Both of these destabilizing effects are taking place today as deliberate attacks by China on Canadian society, as real as if that country sent troops or missiles to destroy us. Yet, our politicians say, and do, NOTHING! Cowards! The federal Liberal government ignores the same kind of bold Chinese Communist infiltration in Canada – In, "The long tentacles of China's United Front Network," in the February 1-7, 2019, Epoch Times, p. A6, Rahul Vaidyanath writes:

> "Clive Hamilton, an author and professor at Charles Sturt University in Canberra, Australia, has done an in-depth investigation of China's influence and interference operations in **Australia** and published his findings in the 2018 book, "Silent Invasion." Beijing has been working to sway elite opinion in Western countries to conform with the CCP's agenda…to act in ways approved by Beijing. The techniques have been refined over decades and are far more extensive, intrusive, and secretive than those used by other nations.
>
> Thirteen China Party Agencies integrated with five Chinese State Agencies co-ordinate through the Chinese Embassy and Consulates in Australia (and **Canada**) in a **United Front Network** working through the following 5 sectors in Australia (and Canada): Overseas Chinese Media – Australian Council for the Promotion of Peaceful Reunification of China (Targeting Taiwan) – Other Overseas Chinese Associations – Chinese Students and Scholars Associations – Confucius Institutes.
>
> **The United Front** tries to target every aspect of society, from business and cultural organizations to educational institutions and politics. It works to influence the choices, direction, and loyalties of its targets by overcoming negative perceptions and promoting favorable perceptions of CCP rule in China. OC Associations

include hometown, business, ethnic Chinese professional and scientific, cultural/heritage, friendship and alumni associations. It tries to suppress groups in other countries such as democracy advocates, Taiwan supporters, and Falun Dafa adherents, among others."

The word, "Front" seems so innocuous, and yet both Mao Zedong and Xi Jinping called China's "United Front" one of the Party's (Chinese Communist Party) **"magic weapons."** (Ibid) By definition, "front" in this context means,

> "A political party or movement uniting several groups, usually in opposition to conservatives." (Winston College Dictionary)

China knows no limits, and has 'no holds-barred' methods of degrading and destroying her opponents, working in their lands or in China to bias every action, every thought and every word to steal what it can, and to present the CCP and China in a favorable light – and where that does not work she will resort to bullying and intimidation. Canada is part of a "full court press of influence operations," according to Hamilton. And our Liberal government loves to have it so.

Globalization has hollowed out U.S. industry, shrunk the middle class, caused incomes to stagnate, polarized the rich and the poor, and driven rifts through society. Western financial powers shifted wealth to China and Third World countries for economic gains. China, the leader of the Communist world, was accepted into the WTO with former American President Clinton's help. But China did not play by the rules. How could it?

Ernest Manning said it was impossible to negotiate in good faith with a communist regime (Brian Brennan, 2008). CCP operatives have stolen American key

CHAPTER 6: ALBERTA'S EXPERIMENTS WITH SOCIALISM

technologies that have helped in the modernization of their armed forces, including stealth technology for state-of-the-art fighter aircraft. Much of this secret information was stolen during the current era of globalization and 'economic cooperation.'

Canada's crown jewel corporation, Nortel Networks, was taken out by Chinese technology theft when that company expanded into China and opened its research and development secrets to CCP-subsidized businesses. The information was stolen, copied, reproduced and sold for a fraction of cost, putting Nortel out of business. The Canadian government hardly peeped in protest, though tens of thousands of Nortel staff lost their jobs and careers.

> "Brian Shields, a former senior security adviser at Nortel, became aware of IP (Intellectual Property) theft by Chinese hackers between 2004 and 2009, when he left the company. Based on the level of sophistication of the hacking operation, it was clear to Shields that it was the Chinese state that was behind the hackings. Mark Anderson, a tech guru and CEO of U.S.-based Strategic News Service, said it was **no coincidence that Huawei was rising at the same time that Nortel was going down**. In Anderson's assessment, Nortel was Canada's best company but IP theft by China, 'absolutely destroyed the company.'" (Omid Ghoreishi, How Huawei's Rise Coincided With Telecom Giant Nortel's Demise, The Epoch Times, Special Edition – How the Chinese Communist Party Is Endangering Canada and the World, May/June, 2020).

Kenneth Goff became a communist and later recanted, becoming a genuine Bible-believing Christian in the 1940s. His story contains material confirming the communist strategy for gaining control of a democratic nation. See below.

"3. To promote pacifist groups and have them cry out against war in order to keep America disarmed while Russia prepared for world conquest;

4. **To create unemployment in the United States by "dumping" products produced by slave labor on the markets of the world.**" (E. J. Daniels, The Red Devil of Communism, 1954)

China's centralized economy under the CCP manipulated its currency, stole technology, subsidized its industries, infiltrated academia and every other institution it considered useful to the goal of building itself into the world's second largest economy with the sole objective of supplanting the United States militarily and economically in the near future. The risk of war is very real if hostilities break out, especially in Southeast Asia.

"Christian Brose, in his new book, "The Kill Chain: Defending America in the Future of High Tech Warfare," bluntly maintains that in a conventional force-on-force war with China, America would lose. "Over the past decade, in U.S. war games against China, the United States has a nearly perfect record: we have lost almost every single time." The Department of Defense understands the gravity of these game losses. When Jim Mattis became acting defense secretary, his first words to the press were, "China, China, China." (Barbara Kay, Could Push Come to Shove in US Effort to Rein in Beijing? The Epoch Times, p. B4, July 23-29, 2020).

China hates any example of success that could challenge its monopoly on tyrannical power; and especially among its nearby successful democratic neighbors, namely Hong Kong and Taiwan. These successful free enterprise democracies have flourished without stealing technology or manipulating currencies, unlike the CCP. So the corrupt CCP, out of envy, is seeking to destroy them.

CHAPTER 6: ALBERTA'S EXPERIMENTS WITH SOCIALISM

"Just days after China gave the green light to proceed with its national security law, Hong Kong passed a bill on Thursday that would criminalize disrespect of China's national anthem...ordering primary and secondary school students be taught to sing the March of the Volunteers along with its history and etiquette. The law carries penalties of up to 3 years in prison as well as fines of up to $6,450 for those who insult it." (Reuters, Hong Kong passes China national anthem bill, The Calgary Sun, June 5, 2020)

"For years, China has bullied and waged a virtual commercial war against Asian democracies such as Japan, South Korea, India and Australia. It has subverted almost all international trading norms. Japan and South Korea worried that China might move on Taiwan. While America tears itself apart with endless internal quarreling and media psychodramas, while a weak Europe appeases its enemies, and while the rest of Asia stays mute, waiting to see who wins. China is now on the move – without apologies." (Victor Davis Hansen, China isn't letting a pandemic go to waste, The Calgary Sun, June 5, 2020)

America faces a myriad of challenges dealing with the military threat from Beijing. From hyper-sonic anti-ship ballistic missiles to satellites.

"The fact that the Chinese are obviously targeting the global positioning system should give the entire world pause. They are preparing to take that out, said Greg Autry, space expert and co-author of "Death By China."

"'If I can interfere with your GPS signal, I not only can have your missiles be redirected, but I could also really impose strategic costs on you in your homeland without my ever launching a single ICBM,' said Deng Chang, a senior research fellow at the Heritage Foundation." (Simon Veazey, Infrastructure Warfare: GPS Satellites Face Growing Threat From China, The Epoch Times, p. A1, August 13-19, 2020).

"FORTRESS AMERICA" UNDER SIEGE

In the book, "The Hundred Year Marathon: China's Secret Strategy to Replace America as the Global Superpower," national security expert Michael Pillsbury wrote:

> "**China has a long term strategy to subvert the U.S.-led economic and political order and <u>to replace it with communism by 2049</u>, the 100th anniversary of the Party's rise to power in 1949**." (The Epoch Times, "How the Spectre of Communism is Ruling Our World," The Chinese Communist Party's Global Ambitions – Part 1, Chapter 18, 2020)

China's carefully-timed release of COVID-19 at a critical time in U.S. affairs, together with the death of George Floyd and ensuing BLM violence, have eroded President Donald Trump's popularity and polls before the November, 2020, election. The assurance of a certain Trump victory in November is less certain now than before COVID-19. If Trump is defeated China would be in a much better position to achieve supremacy over the U.S. in the years ahead. A leftist Democratic administration would fatally try to appease China.

> "Gradually, or perhaps immediately, the left would get their way in Biden's and Harris's administration should they be elected. And then it will keep going further...and further...as such things do. Nor will I belabor, as Frederick Hayek explained almost a century ago now, that **socialism leads inexorably to totalitarian communism**. We have had a world full of examples since then.
>
> What it comes to is this: Whether we like him or not, whether we see him as ironic or heroic, or both, **Donald Trump is now the defender of Adam Smith over Karl Marx. He's our last, best hope**." (Roger Simon, Biden-

CHAPTER 6: ALBERTA'S EXPERIMENTS WITH SOCIALISM

> Harris Too Weak to Resist Socialist Wing of Their Party, The Epoch Times, p. B5, August 20-26, 2020).

An election victory by the left in America would be perilous at the least. Trump's accomplishments would be negated and China would continue undermining America's economy and jeopardizing its allies and international supremacy.

> "Since 2000, leftist ideology has grown increasingly influential in the United States, with youth shifting increasingly to the left on social, economic, and political issues. By the 2016 election, a rising demand for socialism was evident, along with increasing political polarization. To a great extent, globalization lay behind these shifts. At the same time, the greater the economic and social strife Western democratic societies appeared to be suffering from, the more triumphant the force of communism appeared on the world stage." (The Epoch Times, "How the Spectre of Communism is Ruling Our World," Globalization and Communism, Chapter 17, 2020).

News channels for September 2, 2020, reported that President Trump has come down with COVID-19, and will have to quarantine. It is suspicious that he should be infected so near the November election. Left-wing sympathizers, operatives and "fellow travelers" have long infested American institutions and would be in-place for causing this kind of obstacle near the end of his presidential campaign – though it cannot be proven. James Comey's (Commie's) latest accusation against the President fits the same category of timed interference in the conservative leader's bid for re-election. It was reported on the same news broadcast.

> "In the 1990s, the U.S. government declassified the "Venona Files," decoded by American intelligence during the 1940s, and up to the end of the war (WW II). These documents show that at least 300 Soviet spies were

working in the U.S. government, including high-ranking officials in the Roosevelt administration who had access to top-secret information. Other agents used their positions to influence American policymaking and statecraft. Among those found to be Soviet spies were U.S. Treasury official Harry Dexter White, State Department official Alger Hiss, and Julius and Ethel Rosenberg, the couple who were executed by electric chair for transmitting military secrets and atomic technologies to the Soviet Union." (The Epoch Times, "How the Spectre of Communism is Ruling Our World," Infiltrating the West – Part 1, Chapter 5, 2020)

Long before the "Venona Files" were made public an American military Liason Officer to the Russian Air Force, Major George Racey Jordan USAF, involved in Lend Lease shipments from Montana to the USSR from 1942 to 1944, wrote in his diaries, published as "How America was Betrayed to Russia: "We Gave the Reds Everything." E.J. Daniels, author of "The Red Devil of Communism," 1954, stated, "It is one of the most revealing books ever written on the subject." The relevant authorities did not act on Major Jordan's warnings but rather reproved him for making them.

> "The stream of "diplomatic suitcases" passing without inspection through Great Falls weighed ever more heavily on my conscience. In January, 1944, I went to Washington in the hope of stirring up interest in what seemed treacherous violations of security. The State Department had no idea how flagrant abuses were at Great Falls – crowds of Russians coming in unrecorded; planeloads of confidential data passing under the guise of "diplomatic immunity. Under the Lend-Lease law the President had full power to decide just what defense assistance the Russians were to get. **He delegated that power to the former social worker Harry Hopkins,** with the result, that in addition to defense supplies, we now learn, the Russians got atomic materials and non-military supplies and whatever they asked for. Hopkins stated at a Russian Aid Rally in Madison Sq. Garden in

CHAPTER 6: ALBERTA'S EXPERIMENTS WITH SOCIALISM

> June, 1942: "We are determined that nothing shall stop us from sharing with you all that we have.." demonstrating the arrogant way the executive branch of our government during the war took unto themselves the construing of the law **to circumvent Congress, and by deception, further their own socialist schemes to aid World Revolution.**" (E. J. Daniels, The Red Devil of Communism, 1954 – Ch. 5, re-printed from "Major Jordan's Diaries")

To a great extent America has already been corrupted by generations of Marxist infiltration and educational brainwashing of the nation's youth. This corruption and materialism has dragged down the Christian churches and they are largely powerless to meet the nation's spiritual needs.

> "Globally, the U.S. leads in the political, economic, and military arenas. After infiltrating and corrupting the family unit, politics, the economy, law, arts, the media, and popular culture across all aspects of daily life in the United States, communism made use of cultural globalization to export this corrupt culture to all part of the world.
>
> Willi Munzenberg, the German communist activist and one of the founders of the Frankfurt School, said, **"[We must] organize the intellectuals and use them to make Western civilization stink. Only then, after they have corrupted all its values and made life impossible, can we impose the dictatorship of the proletariat.**" (Ibid)

By infiltrating and subverting academics, entertainment, the media, political and judicial institutions, and even churches across the U.S. the left has produced corruption that rivals the condition of Sodom and Gomorrah in the Bible. God's swift judgment could come on the U.S., and Canada, if the genuine Christians don't wake up and call upon God for deliverance. Such an outcome would be a tragic indeed; a result of Biblical unbelief and communist influence. This point was emphasized time and again by Ernest C. Manning in his preaching. God warns,

> "At what instant I shall speak concerning a nation, and concerning a kingdom, to pluck up, and to pull down, and to destroy it; If that nation, against whom I have pronounced, turn from their evil, I will repent of the evil that I thought to do unto them." (Jeremiah 18:7-8)

No amount of military might can save a nation that God intends to destroy. Even the greatest of nations are as *"a drop of a bucket"* or *"the small dust of the balances"* in the eyes of God despite the size of their armaments *(Isaiah 40:15)*. Adopting a Marxist-Leninist federal government would be a judgment on America for her sin, and it would destroy the leader of the Free World in only a few short years.

Leftists came to victory in a democratic election in Venezuela in 1998. The writer was there at that time. During his 2 years working there as an advisor in the oil industry he learned that 80% of the people were impoverished, that 250 families controlled the nation's wealth and much of it was in overseas bank accounts. He was told that up to 7 'Marshall Plans'-equivalent wealth had been generated from the oil wealth, yet the country's corruption had kept the people poor and the infrastructure inadequate in many places. The writer witnessed this condition first hand. Hence, the nation was ripe for a socialist-communist takeover, and Hugo Chavez was the man for the occasion in 1998.

The socialists under Chavez held onto power after that by changing the constitution, voter fraud and outright force. By 2013, Venezuela's economy was totally ruined and people began fleeing by the millions. Chavez's successor, Nicholas Maduro, espouses Marxism-Leninism

CHAPTER 6: ALBERTA'S EXPERIMENTS WITH SOCIALISM

as his regime's model of government. God forbid, if America should ever suffer the same fate.

> "Of the experts, scholars, and government officials who actively advocate a world government, the majority are atheists or those who hold progressive views on religious faith. A world government would have atheism as its core value...and oppose concepts of nation states and patriotism or localism. To maintain its rule, this world government would forcibly and violently implement ideological re-education. It would greatly strengthen its military and police forces to prevent fragmentation and independence movements. The result would be the loss of individual freedom." (The Epoch Times, "How the Spectre of Communism is Ruling Our World," Globalization and Communism, Chapter 17, 2020)

Communism 'uses' the U.N. The heads of many important U.N. agencies are communists or their 'fellow travelers.' Of the 14 under-secretary-generals for political and peacebuilding affairs from 1946 to 1992, 13 were Soviet citizens. Dore Gold, former Israeli ambassador to the U.N. said,

> "The UN has actually accelerated and spread global chaos...by value neutrality, moral equivalence, moral relativism, writing that it was "dominated by anti-Western forces, dictatorships, state sponsors of terrorism and America's worst enemies." (Ibid)

Ernest Manning described the U.N. in these same terms only a few years after it was formed.

> "Leaders and statesmen are searching frantically for ways and means to restore a world that is reeling and plunging towards self-annihilation. They establish an elaborate international organization to strive for world security and peace, but they bar the Prince of Peace from its councils for fear of offending ungodly men." (Appendix III).

CHAPTER 7

KARL MARX AND HIS PREDECESSORS, DISCIPLES AND "FELLOW TRAVELERS:"

THE DEVIL'S ADVOCATES

Karl Marx (1818-1883)

"Terrorism does not constitute political violence if it is absolutely needed
to attain the accepted political end of a given nation."

Pierre Elliott Trudeau

CHAPTER 7: KARL MARX AND ASSOCIATES

Communism represents the apex or pinnacle of man's rebellion against God. It is purely satanic to its core. Karl Marx, the patriarch of communism hated God, so he tried to usurp God as the earth's supreme ruler. He hated Christ, so he tried to become the savior of mankind. He hated God's Word, so he tried to replace it with his own writings. This kind of rebellion against God follows Lucifer's attempt to replace God in heaven. So, Marx became Satan's instrument on earth to try and destroy mankind, particularly in the twentieth and twenty-first centuries. Karl Marx and communism represent the world system moving toward its final totalitarian development before the return of the Lord Jesus Christ to this earth to destroy the Antichrist's world government and set up His millennial kingdom. C.I. Scofield defined this world system in his 1909 Old Scofield Study Bible as:

> "**Kosmos,** Summary: In the sense of the present world-system, the ethically bad sense of the word, refers to the "order," "arrangement," under which Satan has organized the world of unbelieving mankind upon his cosmic principles of force, greed, selfishness, ambition, and pleasure. This world-system is imposing and powerful with armies and fleets; is often outwardly religious, scientific, cultured, and elegant; but, seething with national and commercial rivalries and ambitions, is upheld in any real crisis only by armed force, and is dominated by Satanic principles."

As we emphasize: Communism is a spectre (spirit) of supernatural power. It is operating in so many ways that integrate together to bring about a one-world, destructive totalitarian government. Only the Biblical, evil spiritual being, Satan, could author such a movement for his own personal ends – the destruction of humanity.

WWs I and II were fought for these reasons. At the end of WW II, Winston Churchill said,

> "A shadow has fallen upon the scenes so lately lighted by the Allied victory. Nobody knows what Soviet Russia and its communist international organization intend to do in the immediate future, or what are the limits, if any, to their expansive and proselytizing tendencies." (The Epoch Times, "How the Spectre of Communism is Ruling Our World," European Beginnings, Chapter 2, 2020).

The world system, in 2020, is getting worse and worse with socialism-communism in ascendance in the Western democracies which fought so hard to defend our freedoms against it. The proselytizing tendencies of leftist faculties in our universities have trained younger generations in Marxist socialism-communism principles. They did not, however, explain who Marx really was, and what he represented. If they had done so, many of their students would have rejected Marx and Marxism. This chapter presents some of the material which is not taught by those who proselytize the younger generations in our schools and colleges.

> "The anti-communist activists in the West – the older generations who have a deeper understanding of communism – are gradually dying out, while members of the newer generations lack a sufficient understanding of, and the will to understand, communism's evil, murderous and deceptive nature. Consequently, communists have been able to continue their radical or progressive movements to destroy the existing ideologies and social structures and even seize power through violence." (The Epoch Times, "How the Spectre of Communism is Ruling Our World," Exporting Revolution, Chapter 4, 2020).

Concerning the 200th anniversary of Karl Marx's birthday on May 5th, 1818, "none other than the Commissioner of the European Union, Jean Claude Juncker declared, Marx was the **"man whose writings Das Kapital (3 vols.; 1867-94) and The Communist Manifesto (1848) changed the world we live in today."**

CHAPTER 7: KARL MARX AND ASSOCIATES

Bakunin: an anarchist and friend of Karl Marx, said:

> "He (Marx) appeared to be God to people. He cannot tolerate anyone else as God except himself. He wanted people to worship him as they would God, and pay homage to him as their idol. Otherwise, he would subject them to verbal attack or persecution." (The Epoch Times, "Nine Commentaries on the Communist Party," On How the Communist Party is an Anti-Universe Force – Part 4, p.9, 2004),

Many people today espouse socialist and communist sympathies that derive from Karl Marx's teachings. They are typically members of the younger generations. Unfortunately, they do not know the real history of these movements or the men who led them. They do not know much about Karl Marx, whose writings formed the blueprint for 20th Century socialist-communist regimes. They do not know much about Vladimir Lenin or Joseph Stalin and other leaders and advocates of socialism-communism. Jesus Christ said,

> "A good man out of the good treasure of his heart bringeth forth that which is good; and an evil man out of the evil treasure of his heart bringeth forth that which is evil: **for of the abundance of the heart the mouth speaketh**." (Luke 6:45).

A casual reading of the New Testament will reveal that The Lord Jesus Christ, the Son of God, was a good man, and God manifested in the flesh, wholly righteous, holy and true – and without sin. Though we have not seen Him we have the written record of Him in person in the four New Testament gospels, and throughout the whole Bible. The Scriptures declare:

> "Which is the first commandment of all? And Jesus answered him, The first of all the commandments is, Hear, O Israel; The Lord our God is one Lord: And thou

shalt love the Lord thy God with all thy heart, and with all thy soul, and with all thy mind, and with all thy strength: this is the first commandment. And the second is like, namely this, Thou shalt love thy neighbor as thyself. There is none other commandment greater than these." (Mark 11:28-30)

Similarly, we cannot meet Karl Marx or his associates in person. They are all dead. But we have their writings to tell what kind of men they were. We can know their hearts from what they wrote and what was written of them...a sort of "out of the abundance of the heart the pen writeth."

> "English philosopher Francis Bacon once wrote: "One foul sentence doth more hurt than many foul examples. For these do but corrupt the stream, the other corrupteth the fountain." (The Epoch Times, "How the Spectre of Communism is Ruling Our World," Using the Law for Evil, Chapter 10, 2020)

The writer has taken quotes from, and about, these men to inform the reader of their heart's attitude toward God and their fellow man. They are corrupted fountains from which streams of hate have flowed. Such an exercise could occupy many, many pages; so the writer though trying to be brief and concise, has been compelled somewhat to excess. Yet, though much more could be written, a further lengthy dissertation is not needed; the men speak for themselves. Their words are frightening to any person with common sense. Those who advocate MARXISM, take heed!

Karl Marx (1818-1883): the 'father' of socialism-communism; wrote *The Communist Manifesto* (1848) with Engels. "Most people who call themselves Marxists know very little of Karl Marx's life and have never read this three-volume *Das Kapital*. It is easy to be a Marxist if you know little of his life." Marx, a Jew, was a racist

CHAPTER 7: KARL MARX AND ASSOCIATES

and an anti-Semite, is described in a book, "Karl Marx, Racist," by Nathaniel Weyl, a former member of U.S. Communist Party. (Walter Williams, Are today's leftists truly Marxists? The Calgary Sun, August 11, 2020)

The writer tried to obtain a hard copy of Marx's "Communist Manifesto" from a Calgary Public Library as part of his research. The librarian told me there was only one copy available, at the Central Library downtown, and that it could not be taken out of that library, or lent out through another library. So, it was essentially unavailable. I had to order a copy digitally for my Kindle e-reader. The powers that be seem to want this material kept as inaccessible as possible.

Karl Marx's personal war with God

Marx did not mince words in expressing his desire to doom himself to ruin and bring the world down with him. He said: **"With contempt shall I fling my glove in the world's face, then shall I stride through the wreckage a creator!"**

> The **"Communist Manifesto"** begins with, **"A spectre is haunting Europe – the spectre of communism."** Spectre is defined as **"as a spirit, a ghost, a phantom,"** in the Winston College Dictionary. Marx intended that this spectre would destroy civilization.
>
> "All the powers of old Europe have entered into a holy alliance to exorcise this spectre." (Communist Manifesto)
>
> "The Communists disdain to conceal their views and aims. They openly declare their ends can be attained only by the forcible overthrow of all existing social conditions. Let the ruling classes tremble at a Communistic revolution. The proletarians have nothing to lose but their chains. They have a world to win."

(Communist Manifesto in The Epoch Times, "Nine Commentaries on the Communist Party," How the Chinese Communist Party is an Evil Cult – Part 8, p.20, 2004)

"The Communist revolution is the most radical rupture with traditional relations; no wonder that its development involved the most radical rupture with traditional ideas." (Communist Manifesto)

"The history of all hitherto existing society is the history of class struggle." (Communist Manifesto)

The Communist Manifesto promulgates the abolition of the family, the end of nationality and the elimination of nations.

"Law, morality, religion are to him (the proletarian) so many bourgeois prejudices, behind which lurk in ambush just as many bourgeois interests." (E. J. Daniels, The Red Devil of Communism, 1954, from The Communist Manifesto)

Pierre Trudeau and his son, Justin, wanted and want Canada to be part of a worldwide Marxist dictatorship.

"It was **Karl Marx** who created an ideology to encompass the deception of humanity in all its permutations, and it was **Vladimir Lenin** who put the theory into brutal practice." (The Epoch Times, "How the Spectre of Communism is Ruling Our World," Communism's European Beginnings, Chapter 2, 2020).

Marx wrote many books and poems over his lifetime. In these works are revealed his heart and mind toward spiritual matters, specifically toward God and the afterlife. He was at war with God, and deliberately allied with the powers of darkness to accomplish his goals. In

CHAPTER 7: KARL MARX AND ASSOCIATES

the 200 years since his birth his philosophy has reshaped the world for evil and not for good. The Epoch Times ("How the Spectre of Communism is Ruling Our World," Communism's European Beginnings, Chapter 2, 2020) reviews Karl Marx's life below:

> "In his youth Marx was enthusiastic about God before being overcome by his demonic transformation. Marx's soul turned to evil. In his early poem, **"Invocation of One in Despair,"** he wrote of his intention to take revenge on God:
>
> > "So a god has snatched from me my all
> > In the curse and rack of destiny.
> > All his worlds are gone beyond recall!
> > Nothing but revenge is left to me!
> > On myself revenge I'll proudly wreak,
> > On that being, that enthroned Lord,
> > Make my strength a patchwork of what's weak,
> > Leave my better self without reward!
> > I shall build my throne high overhead,
> > Cold, tremendous shall its summit be.
> > For its bulwark – superstitious dread,
> > For its Marshall – blackest agony."
>
> In his poem, **"The Pale Maiden,"** he writes,
>
> > "Thus heaven I've forfeited, I know it full well.
> > My soul, once true to God, is chosen for hell."
>
> Marx's young daughter said her favorite fairy tale from her dad was Hans Rockle, a wizard who was short of cash and sold his lovely puppets to the devil.
>
> In his poem, **"The Fiddler,"** Marx writes,
>
> > "How so! I plunge, plunge without fail
> > My blood-black saber into your soul.
> > That art God neither wants nor wists,
> > It leaps to the brain from Hell's black mists.
> > Till heart's bewitched, till senses reel:

> With Satan I have struck my deal.
> He chalks the signs, beats time for me,
> I play the death march fast and free."

"Robert Payne, in the biography, "Marx," says Marx used allegories for his own life and that he seemed to be knowingly acting on the devil's behalf."

"In his rage against God, Marx joined the devil's cult. Eric Voegelin, an American political philosopher, wrote: **"Marx knew that he was a god creating a world, he did not want to be the creature…he wanted to see the world from the position of God."**

In his poem, *"Human Pride,"* Marx wrote:

> "Then the gauntlet do I fling
> Scornful in the World's wide open face.
> Down the giant She-Dwarf, whimpering,
> Plunges, cannot crush my happiness.
> Like unto a God I dare
> Through that ruined realm in triumph roam
> Every word is Deed and Fire,
> And my bosom like the Maker's own."

Marx actively rebelled against the divine –

"I long to take vengeance on the One Who rules from above." "The idea of God is the keystone of a perverted civilization. It must be destroyed."

"Religion is the opium of the people. Communism begins at the outset with atheism." (The Epoch Times, "How the Spectre of Communism is Ruling Our World," The Revolt Against God, Chapter 6, 2020).

Marx's theories referenced previous intellectuals, but ultimately came from Satan. He wrote in the poem, **"On Hegel,"**

CHAPTER 7: KARL MARX AND ASSOCIATES

> "Since I have found the Highest of things and the
> Depths of them also,
> Rude am I as a God, cloaked by the dark like a God."

Anyone with a sympathy for Marx and his teachings, reading these poems, would have to ask themselves, "What am I doing? Why am I following this man? He has given himself over to Satan and hates God and his fellow man. He knows he is going to hell. Why should I follow him? Do I really want hell-fire with Satan and Karl Marx?"

> "Marx entered the human world and established the cult of communism to corrupt human morality, with the intention that mankind would turn on God and doom themselves to eternal torment in Hell." (The Epoch Times, "How the Spectre of Communism is Ruling Our World," Communism's European Beginnings, Chapter 2, 2020).

The Bible speaks concerning Karl Marx's war against God as originating from Satan; and it shows by prophecy how it will end.

> "How art thou fallen from heaven, O Lucifer, son of the morning! how art thou cut down to the ground, which didst weaken the nations! For thou hast said in thine heart, I will ascend into heaven, I will exalt my throne above the stars of God: I will sit also upon the mount of the congregation, in the sides of the north: I will ascend above the heights of the clouds; **I will be like the Most High**. Yet thou shalt be brought down to hell, to the sides of the pit. They that see thee shall narrowly look upon thee, and consider thee, saying, Is this the man that made the earth to tremble, that did shake the kingdoms; That made the world as a wilderness, and destroyed the cities thereof; that opened not the house of his prisoners?" (Isaiah 14:12-17).

"FORTRESS AMERICA" UNDER SIEGE

The Bible goes on to say that a final Gentile world ruler will sit in the Jewish Third Temple in Jerusalem, in a final act of rebellion against God, before the Second Coming of Jesus Christ. This totalitarian socialist ruler will be a follower of Marx, and fully possessed by Satan. He will be destroyed by Jesus Christ at His Second Coming.

> "Let no man deceive you by any means: for that day shall not come, except there be a falling away first, and that man of sin be revealed, the son of perdition; Who opposeth and exalteth himself above all that is worshipped; so that he as God sitteth in the temple of God, shewing himself that he is God. Even him, whose coming is after the working of Satan with all power and signs and lying wonders...whom the Lord shall consume with the spirit of his mouth, and shall destroy with the brightness of his coming:" (II Thessalonians 2:3-4, 8-9)

These two scripture passages must be read to show what will happen to those who follow Marx's teachings, both in this life and in the hereafter. Marx was a devil, a deceiver, an antichrist. He is the archetype of the final world ruler who will destroy the lives of countless millions, even billions, during the coming Great Tribulation, which immediately follows the rapture of the true Christian Church. Meanwhile mankind follows the wide road to certain destruction paved by the philosophy of Karl Marx and his successors.

> Marx and Engels wrote in <u>The Communist Manifesto</u>, that under their system, "the bourgeois family will vanish as a matter of course." They stated clearly their goal that "communism abolishes eternal truths, it abolishes all religion, and all morality."
>
> "The Communists disdain to conceal their views and aims. They openly declare that their ends can be attained only by the forcible overthrow of all existing social institutions." (The Epoch Times, "How the Spectre of

CHAPTER 7: KARL MARX AND ASSOCIATES

Communism is Ruling Our World," Infiltrating the West – Part 1, Chapter 5, 2020).

"The class making a revolution appears from the very start, merely because it is opposed to a class, not as a class but as the representative of the whole of society; it appears as the whole mass of society confronting the one ruling class."

"Working men have no country. Workers of all countries, unite!" (Ibid)

"Without violence nothing is ever accomplished in history. Is it a misfortune that magnificent California was seized from the lazy Mexicans who did not know what to do with it?" (Walter Williams, Are today's leftists truly Marxists? The Calgary Sun, August 11, 2020).

"His, 'On the Jewish Question' (1844): Jew's religion was 'huckstering' (tricky peddlers) and their god, 'money.' They could only become an emancipated ethnicity when they no longer exist. Marx said, "The classes and the races, too weak to master the new conditions of life, must give way.'" **Just one step short of calling for genocide.** (Ibid)

"Marx's philosophical successors shared ugly thoughts on blacks and other minorities. British socialist Beatrice Webb complained of 'a new social order' created 'by one or other of the colored races, the Negro, the Kaffir or the Chinese, to replace declining birth rates among the higher races.'" (Ibid)

Academics who preach Marxism to their classes fail to tell their students that his ideology has led to the deaths of tens of millions of people. (Ibid)

"Karl Marx was a hater, too. He exultantly boasted that he was 'the greatest hater of the so-called positive.'" (Ibid)

In "The Civil War in France," Marx described the 1871 Paris Commune as a **"communist state."** What followed was killing and destruction on a massive scale as the rebels laid waste to the exquisite relics, monuments, and art of Paris." (The Epoch Times, "How the Spectre of Communism is Ruling Our World," Communism's European Beginnings, Chapter 2, 2020).

"Darwin's book (The Origin of Species, 1859) is very important and serves as a natural-scientific basis for the class struggle in history." (Marx's 1862 letter to socialist philosopher, Ferdinand Lassalle)

Friedrich Engels:

Marx's close associate, and co-author of *The Communist Manifesto*, was also a racist and an advocate for complete moral relativism (against the traditional family)

"Concerning Marx's son-in-law who lived near a Paris zoo, Engels wrote that Paul had, 'one eighth or one twelfth n----blood.' Later to Paul's wife a letter, 'Being in his quality as a n----, a degree nearer to the rest of the animal kingdom than the rest of us, he is undoubtedly the most appropriate representative of that district.'" (Walter Williams, Are today's leftists truly Marxists? The Calgary Sun, August 11, 2020).

"In 'Origin of the Family,' Engels writes: "With the transformation of the means of production into collective property (the sexual organs becoming common property, is his meaning), the monogamous family ceases to be the unit of society...This removes the care about consequences;...hindering the girl to surrender unconditionally to the beloved man. Will this not be sufficient cause for gradual rise of a more unconventional intercourse of the sexes, and a more lenient public opinion regarding virgin honor and female shame."

CHAPTER 7: KARL MARX AND ASSOCIATES

> "And as society has hitherto moved in class antagonisms, morality was always a class morality. But we have not yet passed beyond class morality. A really human morality which transcends class antagonisms and their legacies in thought becomes possible only at a stage of society which has not only overcome class contradictions but has even forgotten them in practical life." (John Bennett, Christianity and Communism Today, 1960)

To those men who espouse Marxism, are you willing to state categorically that your wife or daughter is common property to any other man? Well...

Eugiene Pottier:

Wrote the Communist anthem, "The Internationale," after the failed Paris Commune (1871). Here are a few lines:

> "There has never been any savior of the world, nor deities, on which to depend." It threatened, "The old world shall be destroyed." (The Epoch Times, "How the Spectre of Communism is Ruling Our World," Desecrating the Arts, Chapter 11, 2020)

Jim Jones:

Leader of the People's Temple cult in the 1960s and 1970s; responsible for murdering (by cyanide-laced Kool-Aid) more than 900 of his 'flock' and a U.S. Congressman and reporters in Guyana, November 18, 1978.

> "If you're born in socialism, you're not born in sin. Stop these hysterics. This is not the way for people who are socialists or communists to die committing revolutionary suicide." (Brad Hunter, Followed leader into death, The Calgary Sun, November 11, 2018)

Nothing can show more clearly than this example that socialism-communism, when carried to its end, is **a death cult.**

The Guyana government in 1978 was leftist. The writer worked on an oil exploration project there in 1980-82 and was told that about the country. That was the reason Jim Jones was permitted to move Jonestown there. Therefore, the Guyanese leadership at that time shares guilt for the Jonestown tragedy.

Ella Reeve Bloor:

American female communist leader who taught young women and men.

> "She spoke in glowing terms about becoming 'whores of the revolution. Your body belongs to the Party,' she would shout. Girls were instructed to 'become prostitutes for the advancement of Communism.'" (E. J. Daniels, The Red Devil of Communism, 1954, from Kenneth Goff – Confessions of Stalin's Agent)

> "Evenings found the students in dimly lit rooms at national headquarters, engaging in the basest practices that the human mind can imagine." (Ibid)

Vladimir Lenin (1870-1924):

The 'father' of the U.S.S.R. – author of violent socialist revolution, his corpse is still lying for all to see in Red Square in Moscow. His goal: promote division and hate simultaneously in society to effect violent revolution.

> Winston Churchill re: Germany's role in Lenin's return to Russia in 1917: "They used the most lethal weapon in Russia. They shipped Lenin back in a tightly sealed truck as if shipping a type of plague virus to Russia." (The

CHAPTER 7: KARL MARX AND ASSOCIATES

Epoch Times, "How the Spectre of Communism is Ruling Our World," Mass Killing in the East, Chapter 3, 2020).

"Dictatorship is rule based directly upon force and unrestricted by any laws. The revolutionary dictatorship of the proletariat is rule won and maintained by the use of violence by the proletariat against the bourgeoisie, rule that is unrestricted by any laws." (The Epoch Times, "How the Spectre of Communism is Ruling Our World," Using the Law for Evil, Chapter 10, 2020)

"The easiest way to take a fortress is from within." That's how the Bolsheviks took Russia. That is how they are winning the U.S.A. in 2020.

"The theory of Marx and Engels of the inevitability of a violent revolution refers to the bourgeois state. The latter cannot be superseded by the proletariat state (the dictatorship of the proletariat) through the process of "withering away," but as a general rule, only through a violent revolution." (The Epoch Times, "How the Spectre of Communism is Ruling Our World," Communism Sows Chaos in Politics – Part 2, Chapter 8, 2020)

"The services rendered by Marx and Engels to the working class may be expressed in a few words thus: They taught the working class to know itself and be conscious of itself, and they substituted science for dreams." (Ibid, Communism's European Beginnings, Chapter 2, 2020),

"We can and we must write in the language which sows among the masses hate, revulsion, scorn, and the like, toward those who disagree with us. Outbreaks – demonstrations – street fighting – units of a revolutionary army – such are the stages in the development of the popular uprising." (The Epoch Times, "How the Spectre of Communism is Ruling Our World," Communism Sows Chaos in Politics, Chapter 8, 2020)

Terror was a feature in Lenin's system. "When we are reproached with cruelty," he said, "we wonder how people can forget the most elementary Marxism." (Barbara Kay, The Epoch Times, Human Wreckage: Pondering Lenin's Legacy on 150th Anniversary of His Birth, p. B1, April 23-29, 2020)

"Lenin wrote explicitly in his tract, "Left-Wing Communism," that hatred was "the basis of any socialist and communist movement. (Ibid)

We must teach our children to hate. Hatred is the basis of communism." (Ibid)

Exhorted his favorites to kill people, "without pity, exterminate mercilessly." (Ibid)

"For Lenin, all interactions are a zero-sum game, symbolized by his famous "Who, Whom?" question. Who has the power? Who annihilates whom?" (Ibid)

Lenin approvingly defined dictatorship as "nothing other than power which is totally unlimited by any laws, totally unrestrained by absolutely any rules, and based directly on force." (Ibid)

1908 – Recommended "real, nationwide terror, which invigorates the country and through which the Great French Revolution achieved glory." (Ibid)

"**A good communist is a good Checkist**." (Soviet government secret police up to 1922; later, the Ogpu.) (Ibid)

"In the month following the Bolshevik overthrow of the Russian government in 1917, hundreds of thousands of people were killed in the course of political struggle. The Bolsheviks established the All-Russian Extraordinary Commission, abbreviated **Cheka**, and endowed it with powers of summary execution. From 1918 to 1922, the **Chekists killed no less than 2 million people without trial**." (The Epoch Times, "How the Spectre of

CHAPTER 7: KARL MARX AND ASSOCIATES

Communism is Ruling Our World," Using the Law for Evil, Chapter 10, 2020)

According to Pierre Trudeau, Lenin's Chekists' actions were justified because they were absolutely needed to establish the Soviet state. Pol Pot's actions in Cambodia could be excused for the same perverted thinking.

> Soviet legal code: "The law should not abolish terror. It should be substantiated and legalized in principle, clearly, without evasion or embellishment." (Ibid)

> As Lenin pointed out in "What is to be Done," there is a spectrum. A few people at the top understand what is going on. Then there are those who "just practice the appropriate responses." Finally, there are the entirely innocent, but supremely gullible "foot-soldiers." (Ibid)

> "They stop killing because they have no ideology." (Alexander Solzhenitsyn) Lenin had ideology, so he would not stop his killing. (Ibid)

> "The roots of modern religion are deeply embedded in the social oppression of the working masses, and in their complete helplessness before the blind forces of capitalism." (Lenin in John Bennett, Christianity and Communism Today, 1960)

> In 1922, Lenin declared, "The greater the number of representatives of the reactionary clergy and the reactionary bourgeoisie that we succeed in shooting on this occasion, the better because this 'audience' must precisely now be taught a lesson in such a way that they will not dare to think about any resistance whatsoever for several decades." (The Epoch Times, "How the Spectre of Communism is Ruling Our World," The Revolt Against God, Chapter 6, 2020).

> "Just after (Lenin's) Communists overthrew the Russian government in 1917, Dr. W. A. Wilson wrote: "The Scriptures are being banished from the libraries; their

reading aloud, especially by children, inflicts a death sentence." (E. J. Daniels, The Red Devil of Communism, 1954).

Lenin once said, "Labor unions are the transmission belts from the Communist Party to the masses." Communists seek to gain control of labor unions, thereby controlling a large number of parliamentarians and elected officials turning them to left-wing politics...to capture one or both political parties in the United States. (The Epoch Times, "How the Spectre of Communism is Ruling Our World," Infiltrating the West – Part 2, Chapter 5, 2020).

"The **kulaks** are the most brutal, callous, and savage exploiters. These bloodsuckers have grown rich on the want suffered by the people in the war (WW I). These spiders have grown fat at the expense of the peasants who have been ruined by the war, at the expense of the hungry workers. These leeches sucked the blood of the toilers. These vampires have been gathering the landed estates into their hands; they keep on enslaving the poor peasant." (John Bennett, Christianity and Communism Today, 1960).

Sergy Gennadiyevich Nechayev (1847-1882):

Lenin's hero – while Karl Marx laid out the theoretical basis of communism, Nechayev laid out the method for achieving and maintaining it: infiltration and terror. Lenin applied it.

Excerpts from Nechayev's most famous work, the 1869 dark masterpiece, "Catechism of a Revolutionary." Pure evil in the pursuit of an ill-defined working class utopia. His writing is shown in more detail, because it influenced Lenin, and Lenin influenced Stalin – and, worst of all, Leninism is still alive and well today. Those of you who admire Lenin, could you live like Nechayev? Aspiring Marxist; could you believe and behave as they did??

CHAPTER 7: KARL MARX AND ASSOCIATES

The material below was taken from, "Lenin's Hero Nechayev: The Most Evil Communist Who Ever Lived? (Trevor Loudon, The Epoch Times, p. B6, July 5-11, 2019).

"The revolutionary is a doomed man. He has no personal interests, no business affairs, no emotions, no attachments, no property, and no name. Everything in him is wholly absorbed in the single thought and the single passion for revolution.

The revolutionary knows that in the very depths of his being, not only in words but also in deeds, he has broken all the bonds which tie him to the social order and the civilized world with all its laws, moralities, and customs, and with all its generally accepted conventions. He is their implacable enemy, and if he continues to live with them it is only in order to destroy them more speedily.

The revolutionary despises all doctrines and refuses to accept the mundane sciences, leaving them to future generations. He knows only one science: **the science of destruction**. For this reason, but only for this reason, he will study mechanics, physics, chemistry, and perhaps medicine. But all day and all night, he studies the vital science of human beings, their characteristics and circumstances, and all the phenomena of the present social order. The object is perpetually the same: the surest and quickest way of destroying the whole filthy order.

The revolutionary is a dedicated man, merciless toward the State and toward the educated classes; and he can expect no mercy from them. Between him and them there exists, declared or concealed, a relentless and irreconcilable war to the death. He must accustom himself to torture. Tyrannical toward himself, he must be tyrannical toward others. All the gentle and enervating sentiments of kinship, love, friendship, gratitude, and even honor, must be suppressed in him and give place to the cold and single-minded passion for revolution. Night and day he must have but one thought, one aim –

merciless destruction. He must be prepared to destroy himself and to destroy with his own hands everything that stands in the path of the revolution.

The revolutionary can have no friendship or attachment, except for those who have proved by their actions their usefulness to the cause of revolutionary destruction. He enters the world of the State, of the privileged classes, of the so-called civilization only for the purpose of bringing about its speedy and total destruction. He must hate everyone and everything in it with equal hatred. All the worse for him if he has any relations with parents, friends, or lovers: he is no longer a revolutionary if he is swayed by these relationships. No mercy must be shown to counter-revolutionaries. Those not immediately murdered must be exploited to the hilt.

Aiming at implacable revolution, the revolutionary may and frequently must live within society while pretending to be completely different from what he really is, for he must **penetrate everywhere, into all the higher and middle-classes, into the houses of commerce, the churches, and the palaces of the aristocracy, and into the worlds of the bureaucracy and literature and the military, and also into the Third Division [secret police] and the Winter Palace of the Czar.**"

Joseph Stalin:

Leader of the U.S.S.R. from 1924 to 1954; patterned his regime after Lenin's example...responsible for some 62 million deaths of innocent civilians. The history of the Soviet Union was simply this: a protracted, total engineering application of power to demolish and then rebuild all social institutions – to create on earth **the Marxist Utopia** (Rudolf Rummel, Death by Government, 1987).

"How long will you keep killing people?" asked Lady Astor of Stalin in 1931. Replied Stalin, **"The process would continue as long as was necessary"** to

CHAPTER 7: KARL MARX AND ASSOCIATES

establish a communist society. (Rudolf Rummel, Death by Government, 1987 – 61,911,000 Murdered in The Soviet Gulag State)

"This war is not as in the past, whoever occupies territory also imposes on it his own social system." (The Epoch Times, "How the Spectre of Communism is Ruling Our World," Communism's European Beginnings, Chapter 2, 2020)

"The death of one man is a tragedy. The death of one million is a statistic."

"The **kulak** (a peasant who <u>opposed</u> Soviet economic policy – <u>collectivization of land</u>) is an enemy of the Soviet government. There is not and cannot be peace between him and us. Our policy toward the kulaks is to eliminate them as a class. That, of course, does not mean that we can eliminate them at one stroke. But it does mean that we shall proceed in such a way as to surround them and eliminate them." (John Bennett, Christianity and Communism Today, 1960). <u>Note</u>: Pierre Trudeau's comment on collectivization in this section.

Eva Konopacki's 1939 remembrance on the Russian invasion of E. Poland as a 13-year old: "None of us could guess that Stalin had ordered the total destruction of the Polish upper class – not just officers and their wives and families, but thousands of policemen, judges, intellectuals, businessmen, or anyone with an education who held a civil or religious position. Although these people had never fought against the Soviets, they were all accused of espionage. A year later, 25,000 would be shot and buried in mass graves." (Susan Korah, 'Poland was Like a Burning House:' Polish Canadians Remember Nazi-Soviet Invasion of 1930, The Epoch Times, p. A5, September 3-9, 2020)

E. Kardelj:

A Communist in the Yugoslavian Ministry of Foreign Affairs

> "Between us and America there is an unbridgeable chasm. We are *two worlds*. They cannot be united. When we are victorious over the American world, the world will be one." (Cyril Hutchinson, Prelude to War"" or "Shall We Have One World or Two?" The Prophetic Voice, October, 1946, taken from October Reader's Digest)

Benito Mussolini:

Italian fascist leader allied with Adolf Hitler in WW II:

> "The citizen in the Fascist State is no longer a selfish individual who has the anti-social right of rebelling against any law of the Collectivity." (Joshua Philipp, Nazism, fascism, and socialism are all rooted in communism, The Epoch Times, p. A9, June 8-14, 2018)

> "No prominent European socialist before WW I resembled Lenin more closely than Benito Mussolini. Like Lenin, he headed the anti-revisionist wing of the country's Socialist Party; like him, he believed that the worker was not by nature a revolutionary and had to be prodded to radical action by an intellectual elite." (Ibid, from Richard Pipes, "Russia Under the Bolshevik Regime")

> "Mussolini and Hitler both identified socialism as the core of the fascist and Nazi way of life." (Ibid, from Dinesh D'Souza, "The Big Lie: Exposing the Nazi Roots of the American Left")

Adolf Hitler:

CHAPTER 7: KARL MARX AND ASSOCIATES

Tyrannical leader of the Third Reich from 1933 to 1945, and the author if WW II. Marx's fingerprints were found again in Hitler's National Socialist (Nazi) regime.

"To salve their consciences, the Germans have invented comforting philosophies: the **philosophy of Marxism**, that all politics are but an immaterial reflexion of social relations, and the philosophy of the technocrats, that politics are quite irrelevant." (H. R. Trevor-Roper, The Last Days of Hitler, p. 231, 1947)

"Christianity has poisoned my people; it is a Jewish invention, a slave morality. I will put an end to the period of Christianity, and will begin a new period, that of Hitler." (Cyril Hutchinson, The Downfall of the Dictators, The Prophetic Voice, May, 1945)

Louis P. Lochner (American correspondent in Germany prior to WW II) in the Introduction to The Goebbels Diaries (1948) wrote: "National Socialism stands forth as absolutely amoral and immoral, as ready to cheat friend, foe, and neutral alike. Hitler's and Goebbels's contempt for other nations and their public men was abysmal. **Goebbels gloatingly planned the extermination of all the Jews, and the reduction of the Christian churches to impotence.**" Lochner had interviewed Goebbels prior to the war.

"In the early days of Nazism, Hitler showed a political genius which we are in danger now of forgetting, but which it is very important that we should remember. His ultimate purpose was the destruction of European civilization by a barbarian empire in central Europe – the terrible hegemony of a new, more permanent Genghiz Khan: "a new Dark Age," as Mr. Churchill called it, "made more sinister, and perhaps more protracted, by the lights of perverted science." (H. R. Trevor-Roper, The Last Days of Hitler, p. 231, 1947)

"In his last days, in the days of Radio Werewolf and suicidal strategy, Hitler seems like some cannibal god, rejoicing in the ruin of his own temples. Almost his last orders were for execution: prisoners were to be slaughtered, his old surgeon was to be murdered, his own brother-in-law was executed, all traitors, without further specification, were to die. Like an ancient hero, Hitler wished to be sent with human sacrifices to his grave; and the burning of his own body, which had never ceased to be the center and totam of the Nazi state, was the logical and symbolical conclusion of the Revolution of Destruction." (Ibid, pp. 72-73)

Reichskommissar Eric Koch:

National Socialist Germany military commander in WW II

> "If I should find a Ukrainian who is worthy to sit with me at the table I must let him be shot." (Rudolf Rummel, Death by Government, 1987)

WW II Japanese Rulers:

The military rulers of Japan were also ardent **national socialists,** in the sense of believing in total national control over the country's economy and resources and centralized direction of the people's welfare. One military officer is quoted in 1936, followed by an excerpt from a Language Reader showing the national mindset at that time as the following:

> "We desire a community in which all people are able to work to the fullest degree, accepting 20% of the results of their labor as their private income and turning the rest over to the government as national income." (Rudolf Rummel, "Death by Government," Ch. 5, Japan's Savage Military, 1987)

> "All Japanese must awaken to their duty to execute the divine punishment. By attacking or by punitive treatment, the powers of the world must be broken down in order to fulfill the divine mission of Japan. Someday, when, having swept away all rottenness and subjugated all arrogant and impolite countries of the world, Japan shall

be king of the world and lord over the whole universe." (Japanese New National Language Reader, re-printed in The Prophetic Voice, June, 1943, article "Top Dog of the Nations," by Cyril Hutchinson)

Professor Frederick Schuman:

Described the war against the kulaks in connection with the Soviet-engineered "Great Famine" in the Ukraine in 1932-33:

> "Most of the victims were kulaks who had refused to sow their fields or had destroyed their crops. This portion of the peasantry was left to starve by the authorities and the collective farmers as a more or less deliberate policy. Large numbers were deported to labor camps. The human cost of "class war in the villages" was horrible and heavy. **The Party appeared less disturbed by dead kulaks than by dead cows**. The former were "class enemies." (E. J. Daniels, The Red Devil of Communism, 1954)

Dallin and Nicolaevsky:

Wrote book, Forced Labor in Soviet Russia concerning the 7 to 12 million victims in Stalin's forced labor camps.

> "Each day in a labor camp is a struggle for bare existence, and those win out who have no moral scruples. This produces a general view among the prisoners that there is room in life for those who are not troubled by virtue." (John Bennett, Christianity and Communism Today, 1960)

Alexander Yakovlev:

Former Soviet Politburo member and secretariat of the Communist Party of the Soviet Union, propaganda minister of the Central Committee (from The Epic Times,

"How the Spectre of Communism is Ruling Our World," Using the Law for Evil, Chapter 10, 2020)

> "This century alone, 60 million people in Russia died as a result of war, hunger and repression." Using public archives he estimated the number of people killed in Soviet campaigns of persecution to be 20 to 30 million."
>
> "There's a feeling that I've long been unable to shake. It seems that the perpetrators of these atrocities are a group of people who are mentally deranged, but I fear that such an explanation runs the risk of oversimplifying the problem."

Yakovlev saw the atrocities were carefully planned. They stemmed from IDEOLOGY, MARXIST IDEOLOGY – inherited from Marx's deep **hatred** of life itself and his desire to doom himself and mankind. Therefore, the drivers of communism commit atrocities not out of ignorance, but out of malice. The writer thinks **envy** is behind this malice as it was for those who delivered Jesus Christ to be crucified.

William Foster:

"Blood and thunder" former Leader of the American Communist Party.

> Speech made in May, 1928: "The working class must shatter the capitalist state. It must build a new state, a new government, a worker's and farmer's government – the Soviet government in the United States. When a Communist heads a government of the United States – and that day will come as surely as the sun rises, that government will not be a capitalist government but a Soviet government." (E. J. Daniels, The Red Devil of Communism, 1954).

CHAPTER 7: KARL MARX AND ASSOCIATES

Mao Zedong (1893-1976):

Leader of Communist China from 1949 to 1976; treated like a god. He was set up as the "red sun" and "big liberator," with "One sentence (of Mao) carries the weight of ten thousand sentences. Each one is the truth." (The Epoch Times, "Nine Commentaries on the Communist Party," How the Chinese Communist Party is an Evil Cult – Part 8, p. 19, 2004).

> "Apart from their other characteristics, China's 600 million people have two remarkable peculiarities; they are, first of all, poor, and secondly blank. That may seem like a bad thing, but it is really a good thing. Poor people want change, want to do things, want revolution. A clean sheet of paper has no blotches, and so the newest and most beautiful words can be written on it, the newest and most beautiful pictures can be painted on it." (Rudolf Rummel, Death by Government, 1987)
>
> "Marxist philosophy is a philosophy of struggle."
>
> "Who are our enemies? Who are our friends? This question is the number one question in the revolution."
>
> The Soviet Union (U.S.S.R.) was the backbone and patron of the early CCP. "With the report of the first cannon during the (Russian) October Revolution, it brought us Marxism and Leninism." (The Epoch Times, "Nine Commentaries on the Communist Party," On the Beginnings of the Chinese Communist Party – Part 2, p.4, 2004).
>
> "If we want to overthrow an authority, we must first make propaganda, and do work in the area of **ideology**."
>
> "A revolution is not a dinner party, or writing an essay, or painting a picture, or doing embroidery; it cannot be so refined, so leisurely and gentle, so temperate, kind, courteous, restrained and magnanimous. **A revolution**

is an insurrection, an act of violence by which one class overthrows another."

"We must also have a cultural army, which is absolutely indispensable for uniting our own ranks and defeating the enemy." (i.e., destroying traditional music, literature and the arts) (The Epoch Times, "How the Spectre of Communism is Ruling Our World," Desecrating the Arts, Chapter 11, 2020)

"The intellectuals ought to be aware of the truth…the workers and peasants are the cleanest people, even though their hands were dirty and their feet smeared with cow's dung." Mao was responsible for the famine deaths of some 40 million Chinese peasants during the Great Leap Forward (1959-1962).

"Casualties are inevitable for any struggle. Death happens often." **This is the atheistic Communist's view of life.**

"We definitely do not apply a policy of benevolence to the reactionaries and toward the reactionary activities of the reactionary classes. There are still many places where people are intimidated and dare not to kill the reactionaries openly in large scale." (See Pierre Trudeau's use of the word, **reactionary** below)

"In rural areas, to kill the reactionaries, there should be an average of 1/1000 of the total population killed…in the cities it should be less than that."

"The social scum and hoodlums have always been spurned by the society, but they are actually the bravest, the most thorough and firmest in the revolution in the rural areas."

"The main targets of peasants' attack are local tyrants, the evil gentry and lawless landlords, but in passing they also struck out against all kinds of patriarchal ideas and institutions, against the corrupt officials in the cities and

CHAPTER 7: KARL MARX AND ASSOCIATES

against the bad practices and customs in the rural areas."

"After the chaos (murderous Cultural Revolution: 1966-1976) and the world reaches peace again; 7 or 8 years after that, the chaos needs to happen again."

"What can Emperor Qin brag about? He only killed 460 Confucian scholars, but we killed 46,000 intellectuals. In our suppression of counter-revolutionaries, didn't we kill some counter-revolutionary intellectuals as well? I argued with the pro-democratic people who accused us as acting like Emperor Qin. I said they were wrong. We surpassed him by a hundred times."

"An army of literary arts should serve politics...the literary arts of the proletariat class...are the 'gears and screws' of the revolution machine."

Mao Zedong's teaching inspired and guided Pol Pot's Communist Party to slaughter 2 million Cambodians to "eliminate the system of private ownership," including more than 200,000 ethnic Chinese...1/4 of Cambodia's population in only $3^{2/3}$ years.

Zhou Enlai:

Chinese Premier under Mao Zedong; in 1965, promised Soviet Union and other communist countries:

"There are so many overseas Chinese in Southeast Asia, the Chinese government has the ability to export communism through these overseas Chinese, and make Southeast Asia change color overnight."

'The Party:'

The Chinese Communist Party (CCP) – 1949-2020+; the most devilish regime in human history, a Leninist authoritarian regime – responsible for some 60-80 million deaths of innocent civilians. Taken from The Epoch Times Special Edition, "Nine Commentaries on the Communist Party," On the Chinese Communist Party's History of Killing – Part 7, 2004. It is the current most deadly menace in the world, an anti-humanity death cult.

> The Constitution, as revised in 2004, states: "Chinese people of various ethnicities will continue adhering to the people's democratic dictatorship and socialist path under the leadership of the Chinese Communist Party and the guidance of Marxism-Leninism, Mao Zedong's ideology, Deng Xiaoping's theory and the important thought of (Zemin's) the 'Three Represents'…"
>
> The CCP enshrines Marx as its spiritual 'Lord,' and takes Marxism as "the unbreakable and universal truth." ("How the Spectre of Communism is Ruling Our World," How Communism Sows Chaos in Politics – Part 1, Chapter 8, 2020)
>
> "Chairman Mao is the great savior of the people…only the CCP can save China."
>
> "In China, the CCP exerts total control over every part of society."
>
> Xinhua News Agency is the Party dog: "It is a dog raised by the Party, guarding the Party's gate. It would bite anyone the Party wants it to bite, and bite however many times the Party wants it to." (Sounds like America's 'fake news')
>
> Concerning 9-11, the people said: "Good job!" "We strongly support acts of justice against the U.S.;" "the best is yet to come." (Ibid, The Communist Roots of Terrorism, Chapter 15, 2020)
>
> "Party policy is like the moon; it changes every 15 minutes."

CHAPTER 7: KARL MARX AND ASSOCIATES

> CCP has always advocated, "brutal struggle and merciless crackdown."
>
> CCP's ruling principle: "battle with nature," in an effort to "alter heaven and earth."..."Never more traditions chains shall bind us, arise ye toilers no more in thrall. The earth shall rise on new foundations; we are but naught; **we shall be all**."
>
> "Nothing significant can be accomplished without lying."

"The methods the Chinese regime uses to expand its influence are pervasive and legion. They include acquiring high-tech companies, controlling the shares of important ports, bribing retired politicians to praise the CCP's platform; coaxing sinologists to sing the praises of the CCP, penetrating universities, think tanks, and research institutes, and so on." (The Epoch Times, "How the Spectre of Communism is Ruling our World," The Chinese Communist Party's Global Ambitions – Part 1, Chapter 18, 2020)

This CCP mindset centers on rebellion against the God of the Bible, and is center stage in the so-called human 'battle' against global warming and climate change: man fighting what is God's jurisdiction (see Psalm 2). The Western democracies are developing the same mindset.

> Central CCP: "Other areas which are not killing enough (reactionaries), especially in the large and mid-sized cities, should continue to kill as many as possible and should not stop too soon."
>
> The CCP musical dance, "The East is Red's" entire theme: "killing, killing, and more killing."
>
> Modern opera against class enemies: "Biting into your hatred, chew it and swallow it down. The hatred that enters your heart will sprout."

> "Killing the counter-revolutionaries is an even greater compassion."
> CCP vowed: "to fight beyond the limits,...the atomic bomb is simply a tiger on paper...even if half the population died, the remaining half would still reconstruct our homeland from the ruins."

The last quote is revealing coming from Mao's days – indicating that the Party would do anything to retain power, even sacrifice half the country's population to survive. Xi Jinping is apparently much like Mao in his Marxist-Leninist leadership policies. Would he release COVID-19 on the world to save the CCP in the face of America's resurgence? If the history of the CCP is any indication the answer would be, **yes**, he would.

> Those who join the Chinese Communist Party must swear: "I wish to join the Chinese Communist Party, to support the Party's constitution, follow the Party's regulations, fulfill the member's obligations, execute the Party's decisions, strictly follow the Party's disciplines, keep the Party's secrets, be loyal to the Party, work diligently, dedicate my whole life to Communism, stand ready to sacrifice everything for the Party and the people, and never betray the Party." (CCP Constitution, Chapter 1, Article 6).

> From childhood – "listen to the Party; behave like good children of the Party; I consider the Party as my mother; Oh, Party, my dear mother; The saving grace of the Party is deeper than the ocean; There would be no new China without the CCP; The extinction of the Party and the country; Love for my father and mother cannot surpass love for the Party; the Party commands the gun; What would China do without the CCP? We owe all our achievements to the Party; Heaven and earth are great but greater still is the kindness of the Party; I use my own life to safeguard the Central Committee of the Party; No one was killed on Tiananmen Square; The CCP...the great, glorious, correct and undefeatable party, etc., etc."

CHAPTER 7: KARL MARX AND ASSOCIATES

> "Carry out the party's command if you understand it. Even if you do not understand, carry it out anyway and your understanding should deepen while carrying out the orders."

> "One should be the first to worry for the future of the state and the last to claim his share of happiness."

> Chinese modern ballad: "In the 50's people helped one another; In the 60's people strove with one another; In the 70's people swindled one another; In the 80's people cared only for themselves; In the 90's people took advantage of anyone they ran into."

Today's China is itself a victim of Marxism: "Government officials' profiteering and corruption in real estate and the stock market have run wild. Illegal second wives and smuggling are everywhere. Pornography, gambling and drugs have become rampant all over China." (The Epoch Times, "Nine Commentaries on the Communist Party," On the Collusion of Jiang Zemin and the CCP to Persecute Falun Gong – Part 5, p. 10, 2004).

Dr. Nguyen Manh Tuong:

Speech to the National Congress of the Fatherland Front, Hanoi, October, 1956 –

> "It is better to kill ten innocent people than to let one enemy escape." (Rudolf Rummel, Death by Government, 1987)

Communist Party U.S.A.:

1956 directive to its members – in 1956 Congressional report:

> "Members and front organizations must continually embarrass, discredit, and degrade our critics. When obstructionists become too irritating, label them as fascist, or Nazi or anti-Semitic (or homophobic or racist in 2020). Constantly associate those who oppose us with those names that already have a bad smell. The association will, after enough repetition, become 'fact' in the public mind." ("How the Spectre of Communism is Ruling Our World," Communism Sows Chaos in Politics, Chapter 8, 2020)

Western radical left:

Concerning 9/11, Italian Nobel laureate said,

> "The great speculators wallow in an economy that every year kills tens of millions of people with poverty – so what is 20,000 dead in New York?" (The Epoch Times, "How the Spectre of Communism is Ruling Our World," The Communist Roots of Terrorism, Chapter 15, 2020)

Bernd Langer:

Former German Antifa member said,

> "Communists in Germany **use the phrase "anti-fascism" to mean "anti-capitalism**." He said **these labels are "battle concepts"** that are **part of a "political vocabulary."** (Matthew Vadum, Antifa: The Network of Violent Revolutionaries Behind Much of Today's Rioting, The Epoch Times, p. A2, June 4-10, 2020)

Leibenecht:

World communist and socialist, says in *The Other Side of Socialism*: "The Socialist party is against the worship of Christ. Socialists do not believe in any God. The church will find us its mortal enemy." (E. J. Daniels, The Red Devil of Communism, 1954).

CHAPTER 7: KARL MARX AND ASSOCIATES

Saul Alinsky:

A 1960s radical Marxist activist and professor who worshipped Lenin and Castro, and led his followers into moral bankruptcy to subvert and destroy existing society – called 'the Lenin of the post-communist Left;' originally in a gang before he joined the left and wrote, "Rules for Radicals," 1971.

> "Lest we forget at least an over-the-shoulder acknowledgment to the very first radical: from all our legends, mythology, and history, the first radical known to man who rebelled against the establishment and did it so effectively that he at least won his own kingdom – **Lucifer**." (The Epoch Times, "How the Spectre of Communism is Ruling Our World," Infiltrating the West – Part 2, Chapter 5, 2020).
>
> "Keep the pressure on. Ridicule is a man's most potent weapon, Pick the target, freeze it, personalize it and polarize it." (Ibid – Rules for Radicals, 1971).
>
> "We are not virtuous by not wanting power…We are really cowards for not wanting power…Power is good…Powerlessness is evil." (Ibid).
>
> "Remember: once you organize people around something as commonly agreed upon as pollution, then an organized people is on the move. From there it is a short and natural step to political pollution, to Pentagon pollution." (Ibid).
>
> **"The issue is never the issue; the issue is always the revolution."**
>
> In an interview with Playboy magazine, shortly before his death, he said that when he died he would **"unreservedly choose to go to hell…because they're my kind of people."** (Ibid)

"FORTRESS AMERICA" UNDER SIEGE

Herbert Marcuse:
Frankfurt School of **Critical Theory** (Marxist) radical political theorist who morally corrupted generations of American youth to be anti-tradition, anti-authority, and anti-morality; to indulge in sex, drugs and rock-and-roll without restraint. A guru to 60s and 70s American college radicals; "Make love, not war," came from Marcuse. His book, "Eros and Civilization," 1966, helped corrupt a generation.

> Critical Theory "holds that there is no received tenet of civilization that should not either be questioned or attacked. Critical Theory is the very essence of Satanism: rebellion for the sake of rebellion against an established order that has prevailed for eons, and with no greater promise for the future than destruction." (Michael Walsh, Critical Theory is Bringing Chaos to America's Streets, The Epoch Times, p. B1, September 10-16, 2020)

> A critical mass of journalists in mainstream media seem to believe, "that any writer not actively committed to critical theory in questions of race, gender, sexual orientation, and gender identity is actively, physically harming co-workers merely by existing in the same virtual space," said Andrew Sullivan in his "Farewell Letter" to New York Magazine in July, 2020. (Bruce Pardy, In Critical Race Theory, White Self-Flagellation Is the Only Choice, The Epoch Times, p. B2, July 30-August 5, 2020)

> Preached the doctrine of **"repressive tolerance,"** which means: **"tolerance for me, but not for thee."** (Ibid — defined below)

> "This means that the ways should not be blocked on which a subversive majority could develop, and if they are blocked by organized repression and indoctrination, their reopening may require apparently undemocratic means. This would **include the withdrawal of toleration of speech and assembly from groups and**

CHAPTER 7: KARL MARX AND ASSOCIATES

movements which promote <u>aggressive policies, armament, chauvinism, discrimination on the grounds of race and religion, or which oppose the extension of public services, social security, medical care, etc</u>....Liberating tolerance, then, would mean intolerance against movements from the Right (Conservatives) and tolerance of movements from the Left." (Socialists Liberals, Progressives) (Ibid)

He was regarded as a "spiritual godfather" by rebellious Western students, the "love children."

"Polymorphous sexuality" was the term which I used to indicate that the new direction of progress would depend completely on the opportunity to activate repressed or arrested *organic*, biological needs: to make the human body an instrument of pleasure rather than labor. The Marxian concept stipulated that only those who were free from the blessings of capitalism could possibly change it into a free society: those whose existence was the very negation of capitalist property could become the historical agents of liberation." (Herbert Marcuse, Eros and Civilization, 1966).

"The (1960s) counterculture movement can be called a cultural revolution, since the protest is directed toward the whole cultural establishment, including the morality of existing society. There is one thing which we can say with complete assurance: the traditional idea of revolution and the traditional strategy of revolution has ended. These ideas are old-fashioned. **What we must undertake is a type of diffuse and dispersed disintegration of the system**." (The Epoch Times, "How the Spectre of Communism is Ruling Our World," Infiltrating the West – Part 1, Chapter 5, 2020)

"Art both protests these [given social] relations, and at the same time transcends them. Thereby **art subverts** the dominant consciousness, the ordinary experience." (The Epoch Times, "How the Spectre of Communism is

Ruling Our World," Desecrating the Arts, Chapter 11, 2020)

"Since the 1960s, the United States has been like a patient with an affliction who cannot identify the cause. Para-Marxist ideas have seeped deep into American society and have been metastasizing." (The Epoch Times, How the Spectre of Communism is Ruling Our World, Infiltrating the West – Part2, Chapter 5, 2020). Men like Saul Alinsky and Herbert Marcuse were the cause of America's affliction and their products, men like Stephen Philipps. What we're seeing today on the streets of Portland, Kenosha, Seattle, and elsewhere is Critical Theory in practice. Only the church and the American people can recover themselves by utterly rejecting Marxism-Leninism and getting back to God. That is, if it isn't too late.

Karl Kautsky:

A leading Socialist states Marxist doctrine against marriage and the family.

> "As under Socialism, all other property should be held in common, so property in any particular woman must naturally cease."

This Marxist doctrine points to the abolition of private property, in this case the normal, heterosexual marriage relationship. It will lead to a collective, Orwellian sexual promiscuity as in **George Orwell's book, "1984."**

Stephen Phillips:

Present day, very influential and far-left Democratic Party power player; mega-wealthy San Francisco attorney.

CHAPTER 7: KARL MARX AND ASSOCIATES

> "It's really exciting to see to see the principles of Marxism-Leninism being successful and making a difference. First, let me be clear that I come out of the Left. I've studied Marx, Mao, and Lenin. I organized solidarity efforts for freedom struggles in South Africa and Nicaragua, and I palled around with folks who considered themselves communists and revolutionaries." (Trevor Loudon, Meet the mega-wealthy 'Marxist-Leninist' behind four potential US governors, The Epoch Times, p. A7, September 7-13, 2018)

Ronald Radosh:

Former Marxist and anti-Vietnam War activist

> "Our intention was never so much to end the war as to use anti-war sentiment to create a new revolutionary socialist movement at home." (The Epoch Times, "How the Spectre of Communism is Ruling Our World," Infiltrating the West – Part 1, Chapter 5, 2020).

Ion Mihai Pacepa:

Former two-star general in communist Romania, chief of the country's foreign intelligence service, and state secretary of the Ministry of the Interior, defected to the U.S. in 1978

> Quoting Aleksandr Sakharovsky, head of the Soviet foreign intelligence service: "In today's world, when nuclear arms have made military force obsolete, terrorism should become our main weapon." (The Epoch Times, "How the Spectre of Communism is Ruling Our World," The Communist Roots of Terrorism, Chapter 15, 2020)

"FORTRESS AMERICA" UNDER SIEGE

Anonymous author:

"The real enemy confronting the free world remains Communism, and radical Islam is nothing more than Communism cloaked in the traditional garments of Islam." (Ibid)

Lavrentiy Beria:

Stalin's secret police chief

> "Show me the man and I'll find you the crime."
>
> "The real law underlying the arrests of those years was the assignment of quotas, the norms set, the planned allocations. Every city, every district, every military unit was assigned a specific quota of arrests to be carried out by a stipulated time. From then on everything else depended on the ingenuity of the Security operations personnel." (Solzhenitsyn regarding the Great Terror in 1936-1938 in Rudolf Rummel, Death by Government, 1987)

Pierre Elliott Trudeau (1919-2000):

Former Prime Minister of Canada (1968-1984); and a far-left international Fabian Socialist – Marxist intellectual; mentor of Jean Chretien and Fidel Castro. Quotes from (Bob Plamondon, The Truth About Trudeau, 2013). Many other quotes throughout this book show the man to be a full-fledged communist intent upon creating a global socialist-communist Utopia.

"I want a classless society. The party of the people – socialism-communism – will

CHAPTER 7: KARL MARX AND ASSOCIATES

eventually come out the winner." (from Bob Plamondon, The Truth About Trudeau, 2013)

> Said Tanzania's radical socialist Nyerare's expulsion of 10 million peasants from their land, and imposing a one-party state, was for "the collective good."
> "The very idea of the nation-state is absurd. For the past 150 years nationalism has been an anachronistic notion."
>
> "Was overheard by reporters saying how much easier governing would be if things were run "the Cuban way." That is, like Fidel Castro's communist dictatorship.

Trudeau wanted poly-ethnic pluralism in a multinational state with entrenched individual rights to thwart "the tyranny of the majority." He ended up producing the "tyranny of the minority;" a 'one-world Canada' – his "citizens of the world" concept.

> "Globalism is a postmodern cultural Marxist ideology that seeks a world where biological and cultural distinctions no longer exist...and attacks any sense of identity on a national scale...Society thus becomes atomized, rootless, and completely vulnerable to globalist convergence." (i.e., a one-world government) (Cid Lazarou, Globalism: Hybrid ideology of the 21st century, The Epoch Times, October 19-25, 2018)

Jean Chretien:

Former Prime Minister of Canada (1993-2003) and protégé of Pierre Trudeau. Ottawa took a "distinct pro-Beijing left turn" under Chretien. His ten-year tenure was involved in many cases of patronage and corruption.

> "For the 10 years as the prime minister, I met the president of China (Jiang Zemin) 17 times, so I was close to China."

Sought to immortalize Trudeau after his death...rename highest peak in the Rockies, Mt. Pierre Elliott Trudeau –

rejected by Canadians! Established Pierre Elliott Trudeau Foundation, assisted with $125 million of taxpayer's money – a Chretien government-sponsored charity established by Trudeau's family, friends and colleagues as a living memorial – **aligned to Trudeau's major political, social and economic philosophy**, which we know was unapologetically socialism-communism. (Bob Plamondon, The Truth about Trudeau, 2013). This effort, and his China ties, qualified Chretien as unapologetically socialist-communist like his mentor. It also showed both men's agenda for the future of Canada.

No such government-sponsored luxury was ever accorded any other Canadian prime minister, though Trudeau rated 5th out of 9 as the best two-term prime ministers in Canadian history...in the middle of the pack. (Ibid)

Hillary Clinton:

U.S. Secretary of State during Barak Obama's administration. Her characterization of her opponents qualifies her being put in this section. After all, what do you do with "deplorable people," liquidate them?

> "She described those who would vote for a conservative Republican candidate as "**a basket of deplorables**."
>
> Deplorable is defined as "grievous"...meaning people who are "atrocious, painful, hard to be borne and burdensome." (The Winston College Dictionary)

Barak Obama:

Democrat U.S. President from 2008 to 2016.

> "In June, 2016, the U.S. Supreme Court ruled that same-sex marriage is a right guaranteed by the Constitution.

CHAPTER 7: KARL MARX AND ASSOCIATES

The president changed the banner on the White House's official Twitter account to the **rainbow flag** in support of LGBT rights." (The Epoch Times, "How the Spectre of Communism is Ruling Our World," Using the Law for Evil, Chapter 10, 2020)

Yasser Arafat:

Head of the terrorist PLO (FATAH), visited China 14 times meeting Mao Zedong, Zhou Enlai, Deng Xiaoping and Jiang Zemin. Close to China and other communist countries; member of the Socialist International; FATAH an observer in the Party of European Socialists. Died in 2004. (The Epoch Times, "How the Spectre of Communism is Ruling Our World," The Communist Roots of Terrorism, Chapter 15, 2020)

Osama bin Laden:

Terrorist leader of Al Queida. In February, 2003, released an audio through Al Jazeera saying:

> "The interests of Muslims and the interests of the socialists coincide in the war against the crusaders."

Justin Trudeau:

Prime Minister of Canada from 2015 to ??; a spending fanatic, global warming, anti-oil/anti-pipeline green energy/gender/identity, virtue-signaling pro-Beijing activist groomed by Pierre Trudeau and coached by Jean Chretien toward a near future Marxist dictatorial takeover of Canada's government. Below are a few comments on the man.

> "Beijing is no friend of Canada." (David Mulroney, former Canadian ambassador to China – 2009-2012).

"It's obvious that Canada needs to distance itself from the authoritarian Communist government in Beijing. Polls show this is what Canadians want. **It appears the only hold out is the Liberal government of Prime Minister Justin Trudeau.**" (The Calgary Sun editorial, August 10, 2020).

"Nine out of 10 Liberal voters approve of Trudeau's job along with six out of 10 in the NDP camp. Those two groups don't think corruption is one of the top issues. Help! "I don't know what people in eastern Canada are waiting for," says Barlow (Conservative MP, southern Alberta). "Sooner or later you have to say, Geez, the prime minister is corrupt. **This is corruption.**"

M. Stanton Evans:

Defected Soviet spy concerning socialist infiltration into influential positions in the American government during the 1940s:

"The agents of an enemy power were in a position to do much more than purloin documents. They were in a position to influence the nation's foreign policy in the interest of the nation's chief enemy, and not only on exceptional occasions...but in what must have been the staggering sum of day to day operations."

Jiang Zemin:

Former Chinese Communist Leader; coordinated 1989 Tiananmen Square Massacre and brutal suppression of Falun Gong. Friend of Jean Chretien.

At Central Committee's working conference to suppress Falun Gong: "I just don't believe that the CCP can't beat Falun Gong."

Jiang's 1999 directive toward Falun Gong who believe in Truthfulness, Compassion and Tolerance: "Kill them physically, bankrupt them financially, and ruin their reputations."

"Bloody Harvest: The Killing of Falun Gong for Their Organs,"..."a disgusting form of evil...new to this planet."

"No one is guilty of killing Falun Gong practitioners."
Mike Wallace asked Zemin in 2000 why China did not conduct popular elections? Zemin's answer: "The Chinese people are way too low in education." In 1939 the CCP's Xinhua Daily wrote: "The Kuomintang think that democratic politics in China are not to be realized today, but some years later. They hope that democratic politics should wait until the knowledge and education of the Chinese people reach those of bourgeois democratic countries in Europe and America...but, only under the democratic system will it become easier to educate and train the people." (The Epoch Times, Nine Commentaries on the Communist Party – Part 9, The Scoundrel Nature of the Communist Party, p. 22).

Berdyaev:

Writer of *Origin of Russian Communism*

> "But there is a domain in which Communism is changeless, pitiless, fanatical, and in which it will grant no concessions whatever. That is the domain of 'world outlook,' of philosophy and consequently of religion also." (John Bennett, Christianity and Communism Today, 1960)

Deng Xiaoping:

Former Chinese Communist Leader

> Asked in 1980 interview, "How many people died in the 1966-1976 Cultural Revolution?" Deng replied: "How many people really died in the Cultural Revolution? The figure is astronomical and can never be estimated."

> He justified "Killing 200,000 people in exchange for 20 years stability."

Arthur Koestler:

Ex-communist and writer of the novel, "Darkness at Noon." See how his character, the old Communist Ivanov's mindset fits Deng Xiaoping's comment above. (John Bennett, Christianity and Communism Today, 1960)

> "Every year several million people are killed quite pointlessly by epidemics and other natural catastrophies. And we (communists) should shrink from sacrificing a few hundred thousand for the most promising experiment in history (communist utopia)?"

All communist leaders were tyrants – arrogant, lewd, and completely unethical. To expect their followers to be vastly improved in moral standards runs counter to reason. To put it simply: radical socialist excrement fills the septic tank of communism...the leaders themselves being the witnesses.

Joseph Goebbels:

National Socialist propaganda minister for Hitler's Third Reich, wrote:

> "He **(Adolph Hitler)** is the German miracle. Everything else in our country can be explained – he alone is our mystery and the myth of the German people. Hitler has a sixth sense – that is the gift to see what is hidden from the human eye. He knows about things to come. He is truth personified. If only the world knew how much his love extends beyond his own people toward the universe, they would forswear their false gods and turn to WORSHIP HIM, the greatest personality history has

CHAPTER 7: KARL MARX AND ASSOCIATES

> known." (Cyril Hutchinson, The Downfall of the Dictators, The Prophetic Voice, May, 1945)

> "The above article went on to state: The strange thing about these above creatures is the peculiar power that they were able to exert over their followers. They had beyond any doubt an influence that was mesmeric, compelling and almost irresistible in its overpowering qualities. Hitler had diabolical cunning and a fascinating hold over the minds and lives of so many millions. So mighty was this uncanny power that the dictators became as gods in the eyes of their blind devotees, and the actual worship of these self-exalted blasphemers was carried on the gullible and deluded multitudes."

A fitting tribute to the end of the Jew-hater Joseph Goebbels is recorded in the April, 1945, issue of "The Prophetic Voice," by Cyril Hutchinson. It is titled, "The Sure Law of Retribution."

> "A recent article published on the front page of many newspapers carried with it an implication that is one of the most significant and far-reaching that we have seen in modern times. It was date-lined March 31st, 1945, and dispatched from Muenchen Gladbach, Germany. It said in part: "The scene was Propaganda Minister Joseph Goebbels's home here – and the ceremony was the traditional Passover festival. About 300 American soldiers made the ancient Jewish holiday a doubly important occasion Friday by joining in the festival in the home of one of Naziland's most rabid Jewish persecutors." "It is retribution come home," said Lieut. Joseph Shubow of Boston, Mass., who gave the Passover service."

Shortly thereafter in Berlin, Joseph Goebbels committed suicide, and prevailed upon his wife to poison herself and their six children. God's Word was fulfilled again toward those who attack the Jews. Long before that, the LORD said to Abram:

> "And **I will** bless them that bless thee, and **curse him that curseth thee:** and in thee shall all families of the earth be blessed." (Genesis 12:3)

As if sent as a warning from heaven, this last excerpt from a message preached by William Aberhart at the Grand Theatre in Calgary, Alberta, in about 1923, pre-dated WW II, and carries us into the twenty-first century – and much nearer to the prophesied one-world totalitarian dictatorship. The Antichrist's destruction of humanity and cruelty will exceed all present and pre-existing murderous dictators. He will be the ultimate Marxist. "Antichrist" means 'in the place of Christ,' and that is exactly what Marx wanted.

> "Let us not forget that the present world trend to Socialism will eventually produce another great dictator, the prophesied Antichrist! And then individual freedom will be taken away. In Revelation 13:1 he is pictured as a beast rising from a turbulent sea. Out of the restless nations of the last days, borne on a strong tide of Socialism, he will be swept up to become the World Dictator (Revelation 13:15-17). **He is coming!** Surely freedom-loving people *everywhere* must breast that tide, and resist as long as possible the coming of that awful dictatorship." (William Aberhart, God's Great Divisions of the World's History, reprinted in The Prophetic Voice, November, 1945)

The essence of Marxism is an insatiable lust for power, and that, of supernatural origin. It is Satanic, and is a product of spiritual forces working in human beings in the temporal realm. The Bible makes this abundantly clear. Jesus Christ said so.

If you desire to be a leader of men Karl Marx is not the man to follow. The writer would recommend William Aberhart and Ernest Manning as examples to follow. But in order to do so you must first be saved. (see Appendix 1)

CHAPTER 8

THE LEGACY OF THE HON. WILLIAM ABERHART:

THE VOICE OF REASON

"His character has been above question or suspicion and no unworthy act has marred his administration."

Pastor Harrison Villett

*Funeral Service for William Aberhart (May 30, 1943)
Forest Lawn Memorial Gardens, Burnaby, British Columbia*

William Aberhart accomplished much in his life, despite it being shortened by illness and his untimely death in Vancouver, British Columbia, on May 23, 1943, at the age of 64. Prior to his travelling west to Calgary in 1910, at about 31 years of age, little is known of Mr. Aberhart's life. His legacy, therefore, concerns his time in the west, and particularly in Calgary, Alberta, where he founded **The Prophetic Bible Institute**. His evangelical radio ministry began in 1925 and touched many thousands of lives across Western Canada and the northwestern U.S. in the years following.

Details of Mr. Aberhart's career as a teacher and principal, and his work in Christian ministry in Calgary prior to entering politics are given in Chapter 1 and Appendix 5. Mr. Manning's writings and legacy were the outcome of William Aberhart's faithful service for God. Specific information on Mr. Albehart's involvement in politics as Premier of Alberta from 1935 to 1943 are given in Brian Brennan's book, "The Good Steward: The Ernest C. Manning Story," 2008.

The writer was loaned a number of copies of **"The Prophetic Voice,"** the monthly bulletin of Mr. Aberhart's Prophetic Bible Institute in Calgary. Many of Mr. Aberhart's vintage messages from the 1920s were re-printed in these issues, mostly dating from the Second World War years, and shortly thereafter. They also contain articles on contemporary events written by young people who were converted to Jesus Christ under Mr. Aberhart's ministry. Together with Mr. Manning's Christian ministry and Social Credit administration they comprise a valuable resource for understanding political and social developments in today's world from a Christian standpoint. This view is needed especially in our present day when most people, including politicians, are trying to apologize for their faith and solve social and

CHAPTER 8: THE LEGACY OF ABERHART

economic problems without any reference to spiritual matters, especially concerning the Judeo-Christian faith. Excerpts from these writings and some of Mr. Aberhart's preaching messages are compiled below as part of his invaluable legacy.

In the May, 1944, Gospel Chimes bulletin for the Bible Institute Baptist Church, Calgary, the Editorial said:

> "It was just one year ago this month that our beloved Bro. W. Aberhart was called home to meet his Savior. He often told us he never expected to die, but to be translated (i.e. in the Rapture). However, he will come with his Savior at the Appearing of Christ for His saints. What a grand reunion that will be when we can see our Savior face to face, and also see our beloved Bro. Aberhart once again. We have sorely missed him in many ways, missed his friendly smile and handshake, missed his counsel, missed his teaching of the Word, missed his sympathy and also his love for his fellow-men."

Mr. Aberhart was affectionately called, "Bible Bill Aberhart," for those who knew and respected him. He had to deal with the Bible-deniers in his university education, but overcame that stumbling block through studying the Word himself. The following three excerpts re-printed in "The Prophetic Voice," in the October and December, 1945, issues were taken from messages Mr. Aberhart preached in the Grand Theatre, Calgary, in about 1923.

> "About 20 years ago (at about age 23) I was in this position. While in my university course I had listened to the vaporing of modern theology. I heard them say that the first twelve chapters of Genesis was an allegory; that the story of the Flood was an Eastern Exaggeration, for the water had not covered the whole earth; that the crossing of the Red Sea was Eastern Imagery, and that it was the natural result of an East wind; that the yarn of

Joshua and the Sun standing still was merely National legend, and not by any means scientifically accurate; that the story of Jonah and the whale was picturesque and figurative, and not meant to be taken in any literal fashion; that the first chapter of Matthew, which describes the virgin birth was unscientific and fanciful. I heard them say these things, and for a time I hardly knew where I was at. Then one day I came across 2 Timothy 3:16-17."

"All scripture is given by inspiration of God, and is profitable for doctrine, for reproof, for correction, for instruction in righteousness: That the man of God may be perfect, thoroughly furnished unto all good works."

"This blessed old Book from first to last is one harmonious whole. There are no contradictions in it, and neither could there be since it is God's Inspired Word. This fact has become like a great wedge driven into humanity at the present time, separating us into two great camps; 1) Those who find harmony and unity in the Word of God and who, therefore, are able to accept its statements as authoritative and inerrant, and 2) Those who claim that there are contradictions and errors in the Bible, and who hold a creed out of harmony with its plain statements."

"I claim, my brother, that if God is to hold you and me responsible, he surely must reveal himself in a way that we can understand. We must read the Bible for ourselves." (William Aberhart, God's Great Divisions of the World's History, The Prophetic Voice, December, 1945)

"I am persuaded that no one is using good judgment who criticizes and finds fault with the Bible before he has studied it carefully." (Ibid)

Mr. Aberhart preached the gospel of Jesus Christ, his passion. At the end of a message given in the Grand Theatre, Calgary, 1923, he again lifted up the Savour to

CHAPTER 8: THE LEGACY OF ABERHART

those present. Seventeen-year-old Ernest Manning probably heard something like this in 1925/26 when he was saved listening to William Aberhart preaching over Calgary's CFCN radio on his dad's farm near Rosetown, Saskatchewan.

> "We should remember that every age has had its end. It came suddenly; it came quickly, so may the end of this dispensation come. The Lord Jesus Himself, while on earth, tried to impress upon the minds of His hearers this very important fact. He reminded them of the days of Noah, calling their attention to the apparent indifference and ignorance of the people at large to the impending judgment, and urged them to beware of similar conditions that would come upon us."

> *"But as the days of Noe were, so shall also the coming of the Son of man be. For as in the days that were before the flood they were eating and drinking, marrying and giving in marriage, until the day that Noe entered into the ark, And knew not until the flood came, and took them all away; so shall also the coming of the Son of man be."* (Matthew 24:37-39)

> "My friend, you do well to consider your ways as you see events gathering upon us, which point unmistakably to the preparation that comes before the end. Are you ready to be called to account? Have you settled the sin question? Do you know the efficacy of the Blood, and the purpose of the Cross of Calvary? If you do not, take up your Bible at once, and slowly and carefully ponder the following passages."

> *"But he was wounded for our transgressions, he was bruised for our iniquities: the chastisement of our peace was upon him; and with his stripes we are healed. All we like sheep have gone astray; we have turned everyone to his own way; and the LORD hath laid on him the iniquity of us all."* (Isaiah 53:5-6)

"Who his own self bare our sins in his own body on the tree, that we, being dead to sins, should live unto righteousness: by whose stripes ye were healed. (1 Peter 2:24)

"For he hath made him to be sin for us, who knew no sin; that we might be made the righteousness of God in him." (2 Corinthians 5:21)

"For God so loved the world, that he gave his only begotten Son, that whosoever believeth in him should not perish, but have everlasting life." (John 3:16)

"Be it known unto you therefore, men and brethren, that through this man is preached unto you the forgiveness of sins: And by him all that believe are justified from all things, from which ye could not be justified by the law of Moses." (Acts 13:38-39)

"But as many as received him, to them gave he power to become the sons of God, even to them that believe on his name:" (John 1:12)

"**Why not receive Him now? For –**

It may be at morn, when the day is awaking,
When the sunlight through darkness and shadow is breaking,
That Jesus will come in the fullness of glory
To receive from the world His own.
O, Lord Jesus, how long?
How long, ere we shout the glad song?
– Christ returneth –
Hallelujah!   Hallelujah!
Amen."

Nearing the end of WW II this article appeared in The Prophetic Voice, asking a timely question, **"V-E Day – Then What?"** If we look ahead 75 years to 2020, the world is in exactly the same peril as it was in the 1930s, just before the onset of WW II. The greatest refuge for

CHAPTER 8: THE LEGACY OF ABERHART

the individual today is not the government, but the Lord Jesus Christ.

> "News broadcasts lately have enkindled our hopes that V-E Day may be near at hand. Radio announcers tell of the almost unbelievable exploits of Allied troops. The world listens breathlessly. Germany, that nation which has ruthlessly overrun so many countries, now knows how it feels to have a foreign foe advancing within her own territories. Nevertheless, she is not ready to surrender. But her fate is sealed. Defeat is imminent. A year ago the world was waiting, expectantly, for D-Day. Today the world is waiting no less expectantly for V-E Day. A national holiday is to be declared. It seems most fitting that in the hour of victory, the work of the nation should stop; that there should be something akin to "the holy day" of old; that thanks should be poured out from grateful hearts to God Almighty.
>
> The question now on countless lips is: "After V-E Day, then what?" And behind that question lurks the fear that the same selfishness which ruled in the world before this titanic conflict, may stalk through the land once again. Governments are tackling the problems of the Post-War period. Legislation covering Rehabilitation is being discussed everywhere. But mere legislation can never make the kind of world being envisaged today. And why? **Because the human heart can never be changed by enacting laws. There is only one thing which will transform the world after V-E Day.** It is the winning of a battle by individuals, the enthroning of Jesus Christ in the human heart. **When multitudes within a nation will turn to Jesus Christ, then, and only then, can that nation experience a real transformation.**" (Mabel C. Ethes, V-E Day – Then What? The Prophetic Voice, April, 1945)

Mr. Henry Mc Culloch preached a highly-instructive sermon, "Two W's of Victory," at the Bible Institute Baptist Church evening service on August 19th, 1945, one week after Japan surrendered to end the Second World

"FORTRESS AMERICA" UNDER SIEGE

War. The euphoria of the Allied victory over Germany and Japan was still fresh in people's hearts and minds. But this success needed some serious introspection on the part of the victors. The great triumph, as seen through Christian eyes, differed from the eyes of those who had not been enlightened by the gospel of Jesus Christ. The Western world needs statesmen, leaders and citizens in general with that kind of faith and insight today. For our Western nations are again in great peril. For that reason Mr. Mc Culloch's message is reprinted in almost its entirety from the September, 1945, Gospel Chimes Bulletin, of the Bible Institute Baptist Church, Calgary.

> "On Tuesday of last week you and I heard the proclamation that the war in the Far East had come to a close. We rejoice that peace has once more returned to a war-shattered world, but in our hearts is a prayer of thanks not only that peace has come, but that victory over our enemies has been given to us. Because of the events of the past week, two questions came to my mind for this message, **"Two W's of Victory."** The first question: **"Whence came victory?"** From what source has come this victory which has put rejoicing and thankfulness in our hearts? The thought may come to us that we gained the victory because of our armed strength; the determination and bravery of our fighting forces; the deeds of valor displayed in active service. And I am willing to say that as far as that statement will go, it is true, but it does not give us a complete explanation, as it does not, for example tell us why, in the early days of the war, the army that landed in France was evacuated without engaging the enemy, while the army that landed in France on D-Day swept the enemy before it. We cannot claim that they were braver men. **There must be some other reason**.
>
> Could it be that by the time D-Day had arrived the wheels of industry had turned out guns, tanks, planes ships to equip our men for victory? Now again, as far as that statement will reach, that is true; but it also falls short of an explanation. When France fell, our industries had

CHAPTER 8: THE LEGACY OF ABERHART

hardly begun to function. **What power held back the enemy when he seemed to hold all the advantages, and give our staggering people a chance to recover, and through our industries, turn out the equipment for warfare?"**

"We hear that it was Hitler's blunder; he failed to attack Britain when he might gained an easy victory. I ask, "Why did he blunder?" I am not ready to accept that Hitler was a man who lacked the ability to reason and plan; or that he was a type of imbecile. He was the same man who occupied the Rhineland, Austria and Norway without fighting a battle. He met the leading statesmen of France and Great Britain in conference at the same time, won their confidence by his treachery and deceit, and then before they knew it, occupied Czechoslovakia. How much better to realize how dangerous our enemy is, than to underestimate his abilities. And that same man turned from tottering Britain to attack a nation with whom he had just previously formed a friendship pact. Now to explain all this is to answer my first question, **"Whence came victory?" Whence came the power that, contrary to all military possibilities, saved the army that was evacuated from Dunkirk? Whence came the power that upheld the stout hearts of the British people in their affliction, or that preserved Malta from being bombed off the face of the earth?** Whence came the power that confounded the plans of our enemies, or kept from them the secrets of the atomic bomb for which they sought, and failed to get? Surely, in the light of all these things, you and I can say with the psalmist of old:

"I will lift up mine eyes unto the hills from whence cometh my help. My help cometh from the LORD, which made heaven and earth." (Psalm 121:1-2)

"While we honor the men and women for whose services we are so indebted, today we must, in all humility give thanks to Almighty God, Who, by His grace and mercy, gave us the victory.

The second question I want to ask next is **"Wherefore came victory?"** Why did God give us victory over our enemies? Sometimes we hear such reasoning as this, "Hitler was a Jew-hating pagan; Mussolini repudiated the Church, and was considered by many to be an antichrist; the Japanese are a heathen race; while we are a CHRISTIAN nation. For that reason God couldn't very well do anything else but give us victory. Do we mean that we had God at a disadvantage? Or do we mean that we in ourselves merit something from Him. Granted the truth of the statements against our enemies, BUT, can we honestly say that even in our war effort, the things we did were pleasing to a holy God? Is God pleased with the sin and immorality in our society, even in a so-called Christian nation? Can we claim that we merit something from Him? The Bible helps us put this question in perspective.

In Genesis 18 the great man of God, Abraham, interceded with God over His plans to destroy the wicked cities, Sodom and Gomorrah, but to no avail because there were no spiritual God-fearing persons there. Lot was backslidden and his family lost and worldly. His warnings went unheeded. Abraham was a righteous man, justified by faith, and he came before God to intercede based on that authority. What was the basis for Abraham's intercession? Was it to justify those sinful people? No. It was only the mercy of God on their behalf. How did WW II fit into this picture?

In the days of peril through which we passed there were men and women who believed in God who were on their knees before Him, pleading not how good we are as a Christian nation, but rather the mercy of God upon us as sinful creatures. Think of the national days of prayer proclaimed by our gracious King; the prayers of individuals who could meet God at the throne of grace through His Son; and there were men and women in the services who were not ashamed to pray. **"Wherefore came the victory? Because of the mercy of God."**

CHAPTER 8: THE LEGACY OF ABERHART

Someone may say, "I don't believe it. I never prayed." That may be true. I know that on the first Lord's Day after D-Day, while many were on their knees before God others were knocking a little white ball around the prairies. But I turn again to Sodom. Suppose Lot had warned the people of the danger that was coming, and let us suppose that ten righteous people had been found, the city would have been spared. Wouldn't the scoffers have had a field day afterwards? They might well have said, "Lot, you didn't know what you were talking about. You told us about fire and brimstone. You're getting to be one of those hell-fire preachers, aren't you? But we don't believe in that stuff. We are educated; we know better than that." **And the poor, deluded people would never know how close destruction had been.** The people of Sodom, however, were not that fortunate. With us in Canada, there are those who scoff at prayer; who are celebrating victory, and don't know why. The only way they know how to celebrate is by drunkenness and revelry. **But there are those of us who know how to say, "Thanks be to God who giveth us the victory."**

But don't make any mistake. Just as sure as fire fell on Sodom, someday this Christ-rejecting world will have its way. Jesus said in John 5:43: *"I am come in my Father's name, and ye receive me not; if another shall come in his own name, him ye will receive."* Someday the world will have its antichrist (meaning 'in the place of Christ'), and tribulation will fall. How will it be with you in that day? Will it be victory, or will it be defeat?

I am interested in Abraham's question in Genesis 18:23; "Wilt thou also destroy the righteous with the wicked?" What did happen? There were four delivered. Before the judgment fell they were called out of the city. In the same way, before the coming Great Tribulation the redeemed will be called out in the Rapture.

"In a moment, in the twinkling of the eye, at the last trump:" (1 Corinthians 15:52)

> *"For the Lord himself shall descend from heaven with a shout, with the voice of the archangel, and with the trump of God, and the dead in Christ shall rise first: then we which are alive and remain shall be caught up together with them in the clouds, to meet the Lord in the air: and so shall we ever be with the Lord." (1 Thessalonians 4:16-17)*
>
> Have you prepared yourself that in that day you will have the victory through Christ? **"Whence cometh that victory?"** (I Corinthians 15:57) *"But thanks be to God, which giveth us the victory through our Lord Jesus Christ."* **"Wherefore comes that victory?"** *"He (God) loved us and sent his Son to be the propitiation for our sin."*

While WW II was raging on, and D-Day was nearing, Cyril Hutchinson wrote an article titled, "A King's Responsibility" or "What Must the Nations Do?" in the April, 1944, Prophetic Voice. Here are some excerpts:

> "May I ask this pertinent question? Is there ONE who is above all kings and nations, to whom all men are responsible, or is human power and human wisdom the final directing authority? Do we believe that the Dictators are right in gathering all power to themselves, and in refusing to be held accountable to God or men? When Napoleon was approached by a number of his officers with the question as to whether there is a God or not, he pointed to the starry heavens and said, "Gentlemen, who made all these stars?"
>
> The Bible plainly declares that God is a Person, able to create, to give life, to speak, to hear, to act, to love, capable of anger, and able to judge the hearts of men. It stands to reason that since God gives life and intelligence to men, they are all inescapably responsible to Him. The solemn truth of Romans 14:12 declares: *"So then, every one of us shall give account of himself to God."* Every individual is a moral agent. A KING is accountable to God! A NATION must heed His commands, or suffer the consequences!

CHAPTER 8: THE LEGACY OF ABERHART

It is true that God exercises great patience and forbearance with mankind. If He did not, no nation could escape immediate judgment. Britain is not without sin. Canada is not all that God would have her to be. No nation or race is righteous before God, only His love and patience postpones the awful reckoning. God has been most patient with men, even with the graft and greed, the dishonesty and truce-breaking, the lust and immorality, the violence and aggression that are everywhere in the world today. How long will God's patience last?

Unfortunately, there is growing surely and steadily, a fearful, threatening, swelling tide of **SACRILEGE**! (i.e., the sin of desecrating or profaning sacred persons or things) Leaders and nations are forgetting their responsibility to God, and are plunging recklessly into this world's awful crime. (read Pierre Trudeau's sacrilege on pp. 296-297). What is the sacrilege they are committing today? Do they recognize anything to be holy today? Is nothing sacred to them?

Take heed to this! God is holy! His name is holy! The Scriptures are holy (Romans 1:2)! The Christian faith is holy (Jude 20)! The Christian's body is holy (1 Cor. 3:17)! **Jesus Christ, and His name, are both HOLY!**

Do you realize how much sacrilege is in the world today? How often are these HOLY things reviled or cursed? How long then will it be before the patience of God will be completely exhausted? **Is it any wonder that the scourge of war, suffering and bloodshed is on the nations today?** Have they, as the Psalmist said, cast off God completely? There is nothing more important today than that we should recognize our RESPONSIBILITY TO GOD.

May I ask you this solemn question; what is your relationship to Jesus Christ? How do YOU treat God's Holy Son? Every man or woman must either meet Christ now, and acknowledge Him as Savior, the One Who bore all our sins, and Who washes us white in His own blood, or else, through scoffing or sacrilege, meet the judgment which is due to him. Let me call upon every one of you to heed the warning and turn back to God, back to the Bible, back to the old-fashioned faith in Christ."

In May, 1945, the war in Europe had just ended. The Prophetic Voice for that month carried an article in its Monthly Meditation titled, "Prayer after Peace," giving a solemn reminder and sober warning to the Allied victors. This simple message is poignant for Canada, the United States and Britain today, seventy-five years later. The writer remembers a saying he read – **"War is God's judgment on sin here; Hell is God's judgment on sin hereafter."**

> "When hostilities ceased in Europe, there were scenes of great rejoicing all over the world. Many people were careful to take time to return thanks to Almighty God for the deliverance that He had granted to us; deliverance from war and fear from bondage and oppression, from death and destruction. **Now the excitement has subsided, the prayers have been said, and the world is rapidly resuming its self-satisfied complacency, and pursuing its self-gratifying tasks.** What is ahead now? Will mankind have truly learned the great lessons of the terrible days that are now behind us? Or will we again forget, and repeat the same tragic mistakes?"

Post-WW II Western society did indeed return to self-satisfied complacency and self-gratifying materialism. God was left out of the picture as the victorious nations became enamored with their newfound wealth and prosperity. This trend has continued to the present day, even with the economic turmoil of 2008 and the present day COVID-19 crisis. Leaders continue to govern as though there was no danger of imminent demise, such as occurred in 1939/40 at the beginning of WW II. In this light, the Monthly Meditation above went on to describe the condition of Great Britain at the apex of its power near the end of Queen Victoria's reign. It is a lesson in

CHAPTER 8: THE LEGACY OF ABERHART

humility for the Western democracies in 2020, particularly the United States.

"In 1897 England saw a gorgeous celebration, far greater than any brought about by the victory of the past week or so. It was Queen Victoria's Diamond Jubilee, when representatives came from the remotest parts of the British Empire to take part in the triumphal procession through the streets of London. A great naval review provided an imposing display of British strength upon the seas. **The great poet Kipling was asked to write something suitable to this great occasion, but for some time he could find no fitting subject or words.** At last, after the celebrations were finished, **he wrote his famous "Recessional,"** and thereby created a great stir in England, some congratulating him, others indignant over what he wrote. Here is –

"Recessional"

"God of our fathers, known of old –
Lord of our far-flung battle line –
Beneath whose awful hand we hold
Dominion over palm and pine –
Lord of Hosts be with us yet,
Lest we forget – lest we forget!

The tumult and the shouting dies –
The Captains and the Kings depart –
Still stands Thine ancient sacrifice,
An humble and a contrite heart.
Lord God of Hosts, be with us yet,
Lest we forget – lest we forget!

Far-called, our navies melt away –
On dune and headline sinks the fire –
Lo, all our pomp of yesterday
Is one with Nineveh and Tyre!
Judge of the Nations, spare us yet,
Lest we forget – lest we forget!

If, drunk with sight of power, we loose
Wild tongues that have not Thee in awe –
Such boasting as the Gentiles use,

> Or lesser breeds without the Law –
> Lord God of Hosts, be with us yet,
> Lest we forget – lest we forget!
>
> For heathen heart that puts her trust
> In reeking tube and iron shard –
> All valiant dust that builds on dust,
> And guarding calls not Thee to guard –
> For frantic boast and foolish word,
> Thy Mercy and Thy People, Lord!"
>
> "Amen."
>
> "Rudyard Kipling wrote that thrilling and stirring poem to remind Britons everywhere that they held a vast Empire, a vaster Empire than has ever been, not by their own prowess of arms nor because of their own merit, **but by the Grace of Almighty God!** (Kipling knew the Bible and may have gotten his idea of "Lest we forget" from God's warning to Israel in Deuteronomy 4:9)
>
> Should not the same truth come home to our hearts today (in 1945)? Lest we forget – lest we forget! Let our "Prayer after Peace" be that our nation, our Empire, may not forget that our times, our lives, our all in in God's hands. We owe Him an eternal debt of gratitude that cannot be repaid by a few moments of muttered prayers. Surely His manifest grace demands our lives, our worship, our devotion, our service for evermore!"

In the November, 1946, issue of The Prophetic Voice Mr. Cyril Hutchinson in his article, "Slime and Bricks in '46,' exposed the fallacy of the newly formed United Nations and the failure it would end up being as an instrument for world peace. Like Ernest Manning, his understanding of God's Word gave an insight that the world's leaders lacked.

> "No statesman or diplomat has ever been able to arrange lasting peace. Within the United Nations organization there are two distinct and diametrically opposed brands of social order, the democratic way of life as we know it,

CHAPTER 8: THE LEGACY OF ABERHART

involving the complete freedom of the citizens of our land, and maintaining the four freedoms of the Atlantic Charter; and the totalitarian way of life, involving a dictatorship, and denying individual freedom of thought or action or even word. **How can a unified world "city" be built out of that conflict? Someday the Antichrist will try to do it by force.**

Examining the story of the Tower of Babel in Genesis 11:5-6 a little more closely, we find The Resolution they passed in Council was filled with the personal pronouns "Us, us, us, we, we the people, and NO MENTION OF GOD AT ALL! They tried to build a permanent but Godless civilization and society, to obtain security upon the basis of secular authority, and at the same time shutting God out completely. They reckoned themselves quite able to run their own affairs. Thus the very materials of that Tower (slime and mortar) symbolized the attempts of MAN, apart from God's help, trying to gain world unity and security, **relying on sinful human nature to bind the whole thing together**!

When will men learn that to leave God out always spells tragedy? He alone can bind men together in love and fellowship. No one else can do it. That means war again someday, when these things again come to a head. This is the secret of all our present troubles."

Mr. Hutchinson, in October, 1944, wrote in The Prophetic Voice, "The Startling Revelations of Germany's Latest Secret Document," that that nation would one day ally with Russia and other nations to war again – in Palestine. The author does not name Israel, for it was not re-established as a nation until May 14, 1948. Bible prophecy was the evidence for his article.

"Despite the herculean efforts of well-meaning men, the evil forces of this world cannot be long restrained. They lie deep in the sinful hearts of men, in their passions and lusts, and no government can control or eradicate them.

> In the last days there is to be a MIGHTY RUSSIA (Gog and Magog), ruling the entire north of Europe and Asia. And when she moves toward Palestine (now The State of Israel) GOMER (root name for Germany) AND ALL HIS BANDS will join with her. Germany will fight again!"

The ancient nation of Russia, the Biblical land of Magog with its 'race names,' Meshech and Tubal, will one day figure prominently geo-politically in world affairs, particularly in the Middle East. Immediately after the end of WW II several articles came out in The Prophetic Voice concerning Russia. They are worthy of note because of that nation's prominent mention in the Bible as an enemy of Israel and therefore, the Judeo-Christian faith represented in the Western democracies. These excerpts follow chronologically:

> **"Will Canada be the Next Battlefield?"** (Cyril Hutchinson, October, 1945) – "The Bible does not make specific reference to Canada, but only in a general sense as one of the nations. The critical battles of the world will NOT be fought in Canada, for we are NOT THE CENTRE of national destiny. The focal point where the course of nations will be determined is PALESTINE, the centre of the world's greatest land area! It is the centre of the past world empires, for two were on the east and two on the west. Ezekiel 38 tells us that Russia will seek to seize that strategic land. The antichrist will set up his image and throne there. And, finally, the Lord Jesus Christ will make Palestine the centre of His world government (Micah 4:1-2), when He returns to reign. Palestine (now the State of Israel) is the storm-centre, the prophetic key-place of all the earth!
>
> The Bible clearly points to Russia as the King of the North, sweeping down as a Godless aggressor down upon the lands of the Mediterranean and Palestine."

But what other plans does Russia have? To conquer North America with its fertile Midwest and Western plains, and

CHAPTER 8: THE LEGACY OF ABERHART

wealth? Most wars are fought for these fundamental reasons, ideology notwithstanding...in the destruction of the leader of the world's free democracies.

"During the conflict just ended, Canada was perhaps one of the safest places on earth, far removed from the world's great battlefields. **The other day, however, one of the best-known of news commentators made a most remarkable statement.** He declared, in substance, that the NEXT WAR will be fought between Russia and the United States of America on CANADIAN SOIL! That is the solemn judgment of one who has proved to be a sober analyst of human affairs throughout the past years. It is not some fantastic dream of an irresponsible scare-monger, and thus we do well to give earnest heed to what he says. Of course, he may be mistaken, but he gave some very striking and potent reasons for this statement.

He pointed out that Russia and America are controlled by diametrically opposed policies, and imbued with ideologies that are in sharp contrast and conflict. He believes that the attempts of Communism to undermine and usurp our democratic principles, working even here on the American continent, will inevitably and finally lead to open warfare. Moreover, if that war comes, it will be of a new nature to what we have ever seen before. It will consist of mobile, fast-moving armies, necessarily deployed over great areas. There will be vast aerial coverage, armed with atomic bombs that will demand wide dispersal of ground forces. They will need plenty of room. Where then would such a war be fought out between Russia (and now China) and the U.S.A.? **Russia and Alaska lie only 36 miles apart, and Canada is just east of Alaska, with its vast plains where that space is to be found. Russia and Canada lie just across the North Pole from each other, an easy flight for modern airplanes.** Moreover, Russia once owned American soil, and must have bitterly regretted her loss of the fabulous wealth of Alaska. For these reasons this news analyst believes that someday Russia (and China) will strike into Canada, and deploy

"FORTRESS AMERICA" UNDER SIEGE

her (their) forces here for a titanic struggle with the United States of America."

We are at War "*The Declaration*" (J. Henry Mc Culloch, December, 1945) – "In 1914, Germany, in her desire to make a quick attack on France, failed to respect the boundaries of Belgium; the result – over four years of war. In 1939, the same aggressor nation refused to respect the borders of its neighbors, among them Poland; this time, nearly six years of brutal war. **So when the borders of an established domain are crossed by an opposing power, whose intentions are malicious and destructive, war is inevitably the result.**

Today, as the world quakes with wars and rumors of wars, as society is marred by sin and the degradation that it brings, we see that the old struggle still goes on, and whether we like it or not, the devil, with his legions, is our enemy with whom WE ARE AT WAR!"

It is 75 years since Mr. Hutchinson referenced this news commentator. The Cold War ended and yet, communism's demise did not occur. China has taken the leadership of the communist world, and Russia, though not in the front is still sympathetic to the cause and far from non-involved. The danger to North America has not diminished; it has increased. If this continent is ever invaded the writer concurs with this news commentator's prediction that it will be from the north with China and Russia both involved along with some smaller nations.

The real possibility of an attack on North America is now emerging in the Twenty-first Century. "Fortress America" is no longer protected by its isolation and geography. Experts stated that renewed Russian bomber patrols in 2007-08 have started up the Cold War once more. Both China and Russia have a keen eye on the Arctic. In an article entitled, "Canada Unprepared for Military Aggression Via Arctic, Say Defence Experts," in the

CHAPTER 8: THE LEGACY OF ABERHART

February 6-12, 2020, Epoch Times, Raul Vaidyanath writes,

"The Canadian Global Affairs Institute (CGAI) hosted a major defence conference in Ottawa – "They [the Russians and Chinese] have the weapons systems and we are increasingly seeing the intent. This government (Liberals) has shown no willingness to deal with military security (in the north)," said U. of Calgary political science professor Rob Huebert. The protection of the North American continent requires a change of mindset given the advanced capabilities of the Russians and Chinese and their imperialist goals. Experts say the government can no longer ignore the military threat from Russia and China. **"Russia wants to destroy us and China wants to own us,"** said John Sanford of the U.S.'s National Maritime Intelligence Integration Office.

A power play is shaping up between the United States, China and Russia, **and the Arctic is the epicentre of the military conflict**. That makes it Canada's business. Norad's deputy director of strategy, Commodore Jamie Clarke said, "There is a real threat. We are defending our entire way of life." At risk is Canada's economy and infrastructure, not to mention that of the U.S. **There is an outdated 1980s Cold War-style defence system with no comprehensive replacement in the works.** "We can't miss generations of technology the way we have been since WW II ended," said Jody Thomas, Deputy Minister of National Defence. She added, **"We are no longer protected by our geography."**

"The Arctic is strategically located where distances between Canada and Russia are much shorter. Russia's hypersonic missile threat is a game-changer and the North Warning System (NWS) simply can't defend against it. Integrated detection capabilities from air, ground and space are a must for tracking such cruise missiles. **"The number one defence priority for Canada as well as the United States – that's homeland defence,"** said James Fergusson, director of

U. of Manitoba's Centre for Defence and Security Studies."

It has been said that America is impregnable – it cannot be invaded and conquered. That it is, "Fortress America." But it isn't a fortress anymore. And, if God withdraws His hand of protection, as Manning warned could happen, Canada and the U.S. could fall prey to invasion, destruction and occupation by hostile foreign powers.

In 595 B.C., Babylon was the world's greatest power. Jeremiah prophesied it would be destroyed. In 536 B.C., Babylon fell under God's judgment and was destroyed. God's judgment came because of Babylon's great sin.

> "The word that the LORD spake against Babylon and against the land of the Chaldeans by Jeremiah the prophet. For, lo, I will raise and cause to come against Babylon an assembly of great nations from the north country: and they shall set themselves in array against her; from thence she shall be taken: their arrows shall be of a mighty expert man; none shall return in vain...which shall make her land desolate... Behold, a people shall come from the north, and a great nation, and many kings shall be raised up from the coasts of the earth. At the noise of the taking of Babylon the earth is moved, and the cry is heard among the nations." (Jeremiah 50:1, 3, 9, 41, 46)

Mao in his "Little Red Book," 1964, stated, with the help of Lin Biao that conventional ground warfare will still be the final decisive determinant in any conflict between China and the free democracies of the West, principally the United States. China's 2020 communist leadership, including Xi Jinping, were indoctrinated in Mao's Thought, and though his book was not published in China since 1979, still carry his strategic advice at heart. Their deliberate creation of the hate-America "Wolf culture" among the younger generations will prime the Chinese

CHAPTER 8: THE LEGACY OF ABERHART

population for any future conflict according to Mao's philosophy of war.

> "In the final analysis the outcome of a war will be decided by the sustained fighting of the ground forces, by the fighting at close quarters on battlefields, by the political consciousness of the men, by their courage and spirit of sacrifice. Here the weak points of US imperialism will be completely laid bare, while **the superiority of the revolutionary people will be brought into full play.** The reactionary troops of US imperialism cannot possibly be endowed with the courage and the spirit of sacrifice possessed by the revolutionary people. The greatest military force is people, armed with Mao Zedong Thought; its courage and fearlessness of death.
>
> We have no experience in atomic war. So, how many will be killed cannot be known. The best outcome may be that only half of the population [of the world] is left and the second best may be only one-third. When 900 million are left out of 2.9 billion, several 5-year plans can be developed for the total elimination of capitalism and for permanent peace. **It is not a bad thing**.
>
> We always maintain that the significant human factor and the policy of turning the whole people into fighting men constitute a powerful spiritual atom bomb which we have long had in our possession." **Mao argued that nuclear weapons could destroy the world, but still they could not *win* it.**
>
> Mao Zedong's thought is Marxism-Leninism of the era in which imperialism is headed for total collapse and socialism is advancing to world-wide victory, Once Marxism-Leninism-Mao Zedong Thought is integrated with the revolutionary practice of the people of all countries, *the entire old world* will be smashed to smithereens." (Lin Bao) **Lin Bao drew up grand visions of people's war on a global scale, with the world's hinterland (Third World nations) surrounding and destroying its cities (First World capitalist states).**

"FORTRESS AMERICA" UNDER SIEGE

> The Little Red Book, as a flexible and dynamic script for revolution, travelled easily from its contingent and specific origins in China to a great many different kinds of places."

In "Battlefield Notes," 2003, Dr. Peter S. Ruckman, a former U.S. marine from a distinguished military family wrote from a vast knowledge of historical wars and battles over time the following:

> "All wars and battles are over *real estate*. Therefore, the deciding factor (as the *Queen* in chess, since she can move as a bishop or a castle) is GROUND TROOPS (*pawns*) conquering DIRT and holding it. We lost two wars (Korea and Vietnam) because we pretended *history* had never taken place. In the news media's fantastic world of virtual "reality," you can win a "war" by bombing or shelling a country or by harassing it. **No such thing ever happened in history, any time, any place, anywhere.** It is the *Infantry* (on their FEET) who is the decisive factor in the end. You did NOT whip Germany by "imposing casualties." You won it by marching into Berlin, Hamburg, et cetera, and **taking over the country.** Ditto Japan; and ditto anything else. That is *"WAR."* It always has been and always will be, and there is no substitute for it."

The great danger is that China not only has developed ground warfare capabilities but has also advanced its military capabilities and global strategy in Maoist fashion, to gradually isolate U.S. forces to a defense of North America. By increasing its bio-warfare, 5G - IT, cyber, space and laser capabilities it is rapidly seeking to gain worldwide military dominance for the sole purpose of creating a global socialist-communist state based on the "China model."

> "The CCP's military strategy is to move from being a land power to being a maritime superpower and eventually establishing hegemony over both. Lawrence Sellin,

CHAPTER 8: THE LEGACY OF ABERHART

retired U.S. Army colonel and military commentator wrote in 2018, "China is now attempting to extend its international influence beyond the South China Sea by linking to a similar framework for dominance in the northern Indian Ocean. If permitted to complete the link, **China could be in an unassailable position to exert authority over roughly one-half of the global GDP**.

The Chinese regime maintains the largest army in the world. The PLA has the largest ground force in the world, the largest number of warships, the third-most naval tonnage and a massive air force. It has a nuclear strike capability with intercontinental ballistic missiles, ballistic-missile submarines, and strategic bombers. The CCP uses a broad range of espionage to catch up with the U.S. in technology. In 2018, it revealed its land-based, supersonic YJ-12B anti-ship cruise missile – known as the **"aircraft-carrier killer."** It is also making advances in the realms of space and electromagnetic warfare.

Adm. Philip Davidson, commander of the U.S. Indo-Pacific Command, said that China is building critical asymmetric capabilities, including the use of anti-ship missiles and capabilities in submarine warfare. Because of this, **he warned that "that there is no guarantee that the United States would win a future conflict with China**." (The Epoch Times, "How the Spectre of Communism is Ruling Our World," The Chinese Communist Party's Global Ambitions – Part 1, Chapter 18, 2020)

In order to degrade its enemies' capabilities it will take risks itself, causing casualties among its own people to advance its long term military objectives. This principle follows Mao Thought outlined in "The Little Red Book."

China's Xi Jinping is upping his country's jingoism as the U.S. election nears. With this kind of rhetoric it is only a matter of time before a mistake or deliberate act, likely on China's part, leads to a terrible conflict. Residents from various cities were told to prepare emergency

"FORTRESS AMERICA" UNDER SIEGE

supplies. Xi said to marine troops stationed in Chaozhou city:

> "Put all your thoughts and energies on preparing for war, and remain on high alert." U.S.-based China affairs commentator Tang Jingyuan said it was likely part of a propaganda strategy to intimidate Taiwan. U.S.-based Chinese democracy activist and scholar Wang Juntao told the Epoch Times that he believes Xi would not start a conflict in the Taiwan Strait in the near future, but could do it before 2027." (Nicole Hao, As Xi Calls on Troops to Prepare for War, Chinese City Orders Residents to Prepare Emergency Supplies, The Epoch Times, p. A9, October 23-28, 2020)

Based upon Mao Zedong's philosophy, Xi's actions are prepping the Chinese for a war with the U.S., whether sooner or later. It seems likely to start over Taiwan. And after that who knows? When she perceives America to be at its weakest she could strike militarily. A Biden presidency would be to her advantage.

President Trump's lawyer, Rudi Giuliani, in a definite indictment of China, accused the communist regime of conducting an "act of war" on the U.S. in unleashing the COVID-19 pandemic.

> "China knew about it for a month to a month and a half before they told us. They closed down China, and for months after they allowed thousands and hundreds of thousands of Chinese to travel all over Europe, and all over the United States. They wanted to make sure that the rest of the world was damaged as much as China was." (Ivan Pentchoukov, Giuliani: Chinese Regime Let CCP Virus Escape to Damage the World in 'Act of War,' The Epoch Times, p. A10, October 8-14, 2020)

The war against the Free World is multi-faceted involving every imaginable device. As Yuri Bezmenov, the defected KGB spy, warned; the **demoralization** of a target nation

CHAPTER 8: THE LEGACY OF ABERHART

is a primary objective of a communist state for eventual defeat and occupation (see Appendix 4). COVID-19 (the CCP virus) is achieving that goal spectacularly. Experts argue against further lockdowns except in hotspots and say that the effects of the lockdowns are worse than the disease itself. Suicides are burgeoning.

> "Dr. Roger McIntyre, a professor of psychiatry and pharmacology at the U. of Toronto said, "This is not just about managing a virus. It's also an economic as well as a mental health crisis. And that triple threat is surrounded by malignant uncertainty (leading to a volatile situation) that's beyond belief. Human beings can't live with malignant uncertainty – it leads to anxiety, insomnia, post-traumatic stress, drug and alcohol abuse and depression. What I've heard from a majority of patients is the **demoralization, the disconnection, the loneliness**, with the added disconnection stemming from social distancing measures." (Justina Wheale, Pandemic's 'Triple Threat' Devastating to Mental Health, Says Professor of Psychiatry," The Epoch Times, p. A1, 3, October 22-28, 2020)

COVID-19 is being used as a weapon against Trump in the American election, now only one week away. Without a doubt China planned it this way.

America's national security is coming under greater threat as Russia and China both ramp up their "weaponization of space." Is it a coincidence that both of these countries have come out with hypersonic missiles while the U.S., bound by earlier treaties, deferred from the same objectives? It is racing to catch up. In "Trillion-Dollar Push Needed by US to Avoid 'Space Pearl Harbor:' Expert Warns," in the October 8-14, 2020, Epoch Times. Brandon Weichert is quoted by journalist Simon Veazey:

> "Instead of being a 'safe haven,' space is becoming a potential warfighting domain. China views space as it

views the South China Sea. "They're sort of showing us what they're going to do in space. As the history of warfare has proven, if you control the high ground, you control the whole dynamic on the lower planes of battle. The idea that space is a sanctuary like Antarctica is insane and dangerous, and **will lead to an attack on us in space from either China or Russia.**" In the meantime, the U.S. needs "stalker satellites" as bodyguards around America's vulnerable satellites to knock out rival satellites. China is also racing to get to Mars first and has land-based anti-satellite lasers."

Russian and Chinese interests still coincide in one important respect and that is the overthrow of the leader of the "Free World," the United States. Though they seem ambivalent toward one another they still are working together. They presently support a Marxist-Leninist leader in Venezuela.

Another key observation is Ethiopia, recently called "Africa's China." Ethiopia is named among the nations allied with Russia when it invades Israel during the Great Tribulation (Ezekiel 38:5). This union brings Beijing and Moscow together, showing both socialist regimes have a common purpose in destroying the only democratic state in the Middle East and an ally of the U.S. Western leaders, particularly the American administration, would do well to consider that these two countries are still working together in their effort to destroy the free democracies and control the world in 2020 in the interests of the Comintern – as planned by the Soviets long ago.

The writer dearly loves the U.S. as Canada's good neighbor but he fears greatly for that country today. Her sin is great, like Canada's. She is slowly being encircled by China's OBOR (One Belt One Road) and international strategy, devised by Mao Zedong, to take the country and surround the cities, then defeat them. That is how

CHAPTER 8: THE LEGACY OF ABERHART

the communists conquered China in 1949. Today, China, with Russia's tacit approval, is taking the weaker countries under its control economically, and bribing the stronger ones, to isolate America in that same fashion. In the event that an invasion of America from the north through Canada ever takes place, the enemy will occupy the countryside – the plains and Midwest – and then take the densely-populated urban areas along America's coastlines to the east and west, and south. This sounds far-fetched but is a real future danger, given the geo-politics of 2020.

ONLY GOD'S HAND CAN DELIVER THE U.S. IN THE DAYS AHEAD. THAT IS WHY THE COUNTRY <u>MUST</u> TURN BACK TO GOD AND FULFILL "IN GOD WE TRUST" WITH A NATIONAL REVIVAL.

> **"Russian Path Through Persia"** (Cyril Hutchinson, January, 1946) – "Russia is going to have Persia, for her path to PALESTINE (now the State of Israel) lies through PERSIA! Russia will come upon Palestine from the northeast, and that means through Persia (modern day Iran). Persia lies under the domination of Mohammedanism, a dark, bitter land, Christ rejecting and Christ hating. In Daniel's day it was a country dominated by terrible evil powers, the wicked spiritual powers of darkness (Daniel 10:10-13). It will not be too surprising, then, if she eventually throws in her lot with an evil-thinking Russia, to help destroy the hated Jew. It will be well to keep an eye on Persia for we shall soon see strange things there!
>
> Surely these things indicate that we are nearing the last days! Evil powers are seeking to control the nations. Wicked spiritual powers are seeking to control the lives and wills of men and women everywhere."
>
> **"The Power Behind the Kremlin"** or **"How are Dictators Born?"** (Cyril Hutchinson, February, 1947) – "Russia is a great nation. She is perhaps even greater than we know. Certainly her might and power has been

demonstrated to a large degree in past days. Hitler underestimated her powers of resistance, and even her allies felt that she would collapse under the mighty pressure of the Nazi armies. Yet she emerged from the war with mighty, conquering power, and **today she remains largely an unknown quantity because she is still strangely incomprehensible, reticent and mysterious. Her policies are hidden and undeclared: she takes no one into her confidence. We must therefore be most careful in seeking to estimate her proper position and future courses of action**.

Russia is today isolating herself more and more in her own political world, and is fast becoming the enigma (a riddle, anything that puzzles or baffles) of the nations. She pursues her own course utterly regardless of the desires, and even the rights, of others. She likes to keep the other nations guessing, while she pursues her own way ruthlessly, seemingly unrestrained by any ethics or moral principles. She seems to be opposed to everything that is not completely Soviet, whether it be her former allies, or her enemies, or the Vatican, or whatever it may be. **And so the statesmen of the world run to Moscow to see if they can make some agreement with a state that is ONLY self-interested.** What do the powers behind the Kremlin really desire?"

"The Seething Pot of the Earth" (Cyril Hutchinson, June, 1946) – "The news in almost every paper tells us of the seething. The Arab newspaper "Falestin" has published a severe attack on President Truman for his request that 100,000 Jews be admitted into Palestine. Openly insulting him, the paper said: "The rawness with which Truman tackles the Palestine question is the best example of his boyish mentality...This man Truman has a raw mentality and behaves like a schoolboy. Such a man will annoy England, but cannot influence her." From other sources: "To prevent the existence of a Jewish State in Palestine we Arabs will fight until they are exterminated;" crowds of Arabs marched in Damascus shouting, "The Curse of God be upon the Zionists." The Arabs promised there would be 100,000 corpses in Palestine if this quota of Jews is allowed to come in.

CHAPTER 8: THE LEGACY OF ABERHART

The New York Times quoted this: "Should violence be used to prevent Jewish immigration into Palestine, Jewish forces, well-armed and organized will themselves resort to violence in retaliation."

The prelude to the terrible Battle of Armageddon will be when the ruler (Gog) of the great northern Empire of Russia (Magog) will descend upon Palestine with Muslim allies, determined to utterly wipe out the remnant of Judah."

"The Impossibility of Peace" or "Will Russia Sponsor the Arabs?" (Cyril Hutchinson, July, 1947) – "Almost everywhere, we hear of RUSSIA. Russian influence is in China. Russia is heard in the United Nations Assemblies. Russia is in Germany, in the Balkans, in Hungary, and penetrating into Austria. Russia is everywhere, in belligerent mood, determined to have her own way regardless of the wishes and rights of others, breaking the peace plans, obstructing everything she does not want, boycotting her critics, bullying where she can, threatening where she can't.

A recent newspaper headline read thus: "RUSSIA READY TO BACK ARABS." Dated at Damascus the article went on to say: "The Soviet minister to Syria has told the Syrian government that the Soviet government has decided to back the Arab case if the Arab League brings the Palestine problem before the United Nations." It seems strange to see a great nation like Russia seeking to join with the Arab cause. Why? May we suggest two reasons? **Firstly**, these two people are in the same class in many ways. We can hardly class the Russians as uncivilized "wild men," but more and more the hands of Russians are "against every man, and every man's hand against them." Russia is turning more and more to the outlaw position. Then, too, in the latter days both Russia and the Arabs are to be the enemies of God, away from the truth, and thus under his displeasure. Finally, both Russia and Arabia are at enmity with Israel. In Ezekiel 38:3 we read,

"FORTRESS AMERICA" UNDER SIEGE

"Thus saith the Lord GOD; Behold, I am against thee, O Gog, the chief prince of Meshech and Tubal:"

Secondly, Russia wants to USE THE ARABS! Russia does not love the Arabs, but she would like to use them as her pawns, her unsuspecting tool, to further her nefarious schemes, opposing the forces of the Democratic nations...including Britain's immigration quota of Jews into Palestine...and to seek an outlet on the Mediterranean Sea to control the Middle East. An ARABIAN ALLIANCE WILL BE A POWERFUL WEAPON TO USE in obtaining these coveted advantages. A reliable observer in the Middle East reports, **"The situation is almost like that which existed in Europe in 1939, with Russia replacing Germany.** Russians are training a considerable number of RELIGIOUS EXPERTS FOR PROPAGANDA IN THE MIDDLE EAST." So we may well expect a Russian-Arabian alliance in spite of the strange circumstances.

First backing the Arabs, then turning pro-Jewish, Russia will end up bitterly anti-Semitic, once more turning violently against Israel. Why? Why? Let us learn this fact, and beware of it: Russia WILL USE ANYTHING TO FURTHER HER OWN ENDS! "What," you may say, "Has she no principle at all?" Let me quote something that the famous columnist, Dorothy Thompson recently wrote: **"No one will ever understand the Soviets who has not known the Communists. It is NOT A BREACH OF PRINCIPLE to lie, cheat, deceive, forge, make fools of 'rotten liberals,' betray friendships, make 'united fronts' only to subvert them, or indulge in any means whatsoever to defeat non-Communist policies...If necessary, through blood and slime – the exploitation of every vice, the assassination of every opponent, the wily deception of the tolerant, the mobilization of every passion of envy, frustration and hatred; the exacerbation of every injustice; the promotion of every Utopia, the temporary flattering of the capitalist; the harsh disciplining of the worker; the debunking of traditional heroes; the subversion of the law – <u>through all these the Communist faithful press toward the great redemption, in a generation</u>**

<u>**or in a century, but with unswerving conviction of the final unconditional surrender of the their enemies."**</u>

Strong words – but TRUE! That is what we face today, what the Democracies face. Let the nations beware of trusting Russia in the slightest degree!

Peace is impossible UNTIL JESUS COMES! And when He comes, He will bring peace. Dear reader, has He come into your heart and life? Have you asked Him to? He waits to cleanse men from all sin, to bring peace and joy to your heart. How good to have a Savior that you can trust, wholly and personally, when all others fail! He never fails. He will see any man or woman through this life, and into the home beyond! Lean upon Him; trust Him; believe on Him; and you will possess His gift of "everlasting life."

William Aberhart's Prophetic Bible Institute and the False 'Man of Peace' – the Antichrist or Beast of Biblical Prophecy

In the June, 1946, issue of The Prophetic Voice, Mr. J. Henry Mc Culloch of the Bible Institute Baptist Church in Calgary wrote, "The Great Withdrawal and Enemy Occupation," describing from Biblical prophecy the events unfolding at the end of the present Church age.

> "We are at war. Our enemy is the devil with all his legions, seeking the destruction of the souls of men. Someday this enemy will occupy the earth. As a great world dictator the Antichrist, the beast of Revelation 13, the incarnation of the devil himself, will rule with great power. What will his occupational role be like? Matthew 24:21 tells us of that time:
>
> *"For then shall be great tribulation, such as was not since the beginning of the world to this time, no, nor ever shall be."*

Men, women and children shall be required to worship the image of this ruthless dictator or suffer death. His rationing system will be unique, but thoroughly effective. The word of a man who knows no mercy will be the law.

"He causeth all, both small and great, rich and poor, free and bond to receive a mark in their right hand, or in their foreheads; and that no man might buy or sell, save he that had the mark, or the name of the beast, or the number of his name." (Revelation 13:16-17)

Tribulation far exceeding the atrocities of war will be let loose upon the earth such as has never been known before. How terrible will be that day of enemy occupation."

Mr. Hutchinson wrote an article titled, "The Radio Voice of the Antichrist," in the May, 1948, Prophetic Voice. Radio then, could cover vast areas but not the whole world at one instant. Today, TV, the internet – with Facebook, LinkedIn, Instagram, smartphones, etc.; – the soon appearing 5G networks, as well as radio, all make the entire world one integrated whole, ready for the Antichrist's appearing. But, it is still the Age of Grace and you, who do not know the Lord Jesus Christ as your personal Savior, can still be saved (see Appendix 1).

"It almost seems as though God is making possible one last call to the whole world. And then, the Day of Grace is over, when God calls no more as He does today, the voice of **Antichrist** (Anti means 'in place of') will certainly be heard in the world, and undoubtedly through the use of the radio. When he gets control, he will be able to speak to the world, to issue his edicts, and everybody will be compelled to hear, and to obey. The dictators of our day insist on controlling the radio, and insist that their people listen only to them.

The other day President Truman made this remarkable statement: "The thing you have to be careful of is that someday a fine-voiced, good looking

CHAPTER 8: THE LEGACY OF ABERHART

demagogue (an insincere political leader who appeals to the masses for his own advantage) doesn't GET CONTROL OF THE AIR and do what Alicibades did to Greece." Alicibades was a charming, unprincipled soldier who kept Athens and her neighbors in an uproar in the days of Socrates, four centuries before Christ."

Those who refuse the Savior will certainly hear and heed the voice of the Antichrist. There is no alternative; it is either Jesus Christ or the Antichrist. And the time is drawing very near. May God turn our hearts, every one of us, to the Savior of Calvary!

In this May, 1948, issue of The Prophetic Voice was an "In Memorium" stating, "We remember at this time that it was five years ago we were all plunged into great sorrow as we learned of the passing of that great leader and beloved Christian, William Aberhart, who died on May 23rd, 1943. His works follow after him, today many thousands can say, "Thank God for the ministry of William Aberhart." We add our heartfelt "AMEN."

Mr. Aberhart did in fact speak much about the coming Antichrist. He preached a series of messages in the Grand Theatre in Calgary in 1923 about this subject, entitled, **"The Present Eastern Question in the Light of Prophecy or What the Bible Says about Turkey."** They were reprinted in eight issues of the Prophetic Voice after his death. These messages have great relevance to twenty-first century geo-politics. Extracts from them follow in order from the start:

FOREWORD – WHAT DOES IT ALL MEAN?

"That the human race is gradually approaching a supreme crisis is obvious to the dullest intelligence. Nothing like the events of today has ever marked the long life of humanity on the earth. It is impossible to restrain an honest effort to find the meaning of it all. Ernest men

"FORTRESS AMERICA" UNDER SIEGE

and women are beginning to believe that somehow, somewhere in the inspired writings of the prophets and the authoritative statements of the Lord Jesus Christ, is to be found an explanation. This lecture is a sincere attempt to call attention to some plain and explicit declarations from the Bible regarding the trend of events leading up to the end of time."

Part I (November, 1944) – "The recent developments in the Near East have drawn the attention of the world to the most hated of all nations – Turkey. The threatening clouds of war, that have overshadowed our nations (WW I), have turned our faces to a history that is filled with horrible atrocities and cruelties to helpless women and children, heathenish brutalities to Christians, and Demonic manifestations that have brought Turkey to the inevitable position that she now holds. About a century ago Turkey's control extended over a vast area surrounding the Black Sea. In 1821, the Greeks revolted under her oppression, and after a war of frightful atrocities gained their independence in 1829. On January 9, 1853, the Russian Czar said to the British Ambassador regarding Turkey, "We have on our hands a sick man – a very sick man. It will be a great misfortune if one of these days he should slip away from us before the necessary arrangements have been made." But Turkey later pounced upon the Bulgarian peasants in a dreadful massacre. In the late 1870s Romania, Serbia and Montenegro were set free from Turkish control. After that she carried out the Armenian Genocide during WW I. Turkey has never been under Jewish domination.

The Hon. W. E. Gladstone, that grand old man of England, once said of Turkey, "It is not a question of Mohammedanism simply, but of a race. They (the Ottoman Turks) are not the mild Mohammedans of India, nor the chivalrous Saladins of Syria, nor the cultured Moors of Spain. **They were upon the whole, when they first entered Europe, the one great Anti-human specimen of humanity.** Wherever they went a broad line of blood marked the trace behind them and as far as their dominion reached civilization disappeared from view. **This advancing curse menaced the whole of**

CHAPTER 8: THE LEGACY OF ABERHART

Europe." **In 1895, the Marquis of Salisbury,** Prime Minister of Great Britain said, "Turkey is in that remarkable condition that it has now stood for half a century merely because the Great Powers of the world have resolved that for the peace of Christendom it is necessary that the Ottoman Empire should stand. That was a danger that was present in the minds of our fathers, when they resolved to make the integrity and independence of **the Ottoman Empire** a matter of European treaty and that **is a danger that has not passed away.**" Note: **Part II (December, 1945)** – is missing.

Part III (January, 1945) – "Let us then get out of our heads the idea that Turkey is being "dried up." Be on your guard, lest some of these proclamations concerning the "Sick Man" dying since General Allenby drove them out of Palestine in 1919, sweep you off your feet. It seems to me that the present conditions would indicate if this were true, it is not the cat this time, but the Turkey, that has the proverbial nine lives. In discussing this matter with some people they have a great big (?) in their minds. They say, "The idea of thinking that the Bible speaks about Turkey! Surely if this were so, our statesmen would read and know exactly what to expect." Note: February and March, 1945, Issues **(Parts IV & V)** did not contain information essential to the identification of the Antichrist.

Part V (April, 1945) – "We will attempt to trace out the ancestry of the Turk. One Bible truth we can set down as self-evident; all our present day nations may be traced back to the sons or grandsons of Noah. These were the only survivors of the flood. Their names are carefully recorded in the 10th chapter of Genesis. The sons of Noah were Shem, Ham and Japheth. Japheth had seven sons, namely, Gomer, Magog, Madai, Javan, Meshech and **Tiras**, and these sons produced ten grandsons, as follows: Gomer had three, Ashkenaz (Saxon); Riphath (Danes); Togarmah (Austria). Magog, Tubal and Meshech combined to form one (Russia). Javan had four grandsons, Elishah (Spain); Tarshish (Great Britain); Kittim (Italy); Dodanim (France) and **Tiras**. It is to this last one, **Tiras**, that I call your attention at this time. I would

"FORTRESS AMERICA" UNDER SIEGE

have you note that these ten grandsons point unmistakably to the great and terrible World Empire composed of ten kingdoms (Daniel 2), or as Nebuchadnezzar's image signifies, ten toes.

The early location of **Tiras** became the Biblical strong city of Tyre. Joshua mentions this city as a boundary line mark, with Israel's ten tribes to the south. Very early in their history they came in contact with the Zidonians (Sidon). Jesus always associated Tyre and Sidon as if one. Now, turning back to Genesis 10:6 & 15, we find that Ham begat Canaan, and Canaan begat Sidon, his firstborn. Hence the union of Tyre and Sidon is a union of Japheth and Ham, and here again we have a daughter of Babylon. In the 12th century B.C., the Philistines persecuted the Zidonians and many of them were forced into Tyre. After this, Tyre's population compelled the people to search many coasts for colonization purposes. Many drifted to North Africa, India and Spain. In the days of King Solomon Hiram, King of Tyre, formed an alliance with Israel, and aided him in building the temple. In the eighth century B.C. Shalmaneser, King of Assyria cut off the water supply and besieged the city for 5 years but was unsuccessful in taking it.

It was against this great city so situated, and to all appearances so invulnerable, that several prophets, particularly Isaiah and Ezekiel, fulminate the denunciations which Jehovah dictated. Before a generation had passed away, according to Philostratus, Josephus and Sedar Olam, the declaration predicted in Ezekiel 26:7-9 had come to pass. Babylon's Nebuchadnezzar came upon Tyre, and at the end of 13 years took the part of the city on the mainland, and Tyre was forgotten 70 years just as Isaiah 23:15 declared it would be. In 332 B.C., Tyre had again become a flourishing and prosperous emporium for all the kingdoms of the world. Then Alexander the Great in his Oriental career of conquest took the island city by means of a mole (massive breakwater at the mouth of a harbor) after a 7 month siege through which it was turned into a peninsula rendered accessible to land forces. God's final

CHAPTER 8: THE LEGACY OF ABERHART

verdict on Tyre was given in Ezekiel 26:12 & 14, 256 years before it was completed in full."

"And they shall break down thy walls, and destroy thy pleasant houses; and they shall lay thy stones and thy timbers in the midst of the water. And I will make thee like the top of a rock: thou shalt be a place to spread nets upon; thou shalt be built no more: for I the LORD have spoken it, saith the LORD God."

Part VI (May, 1945) – "Some of the inhabitants of Tyre escaped and tried to settle in Chittim (Italy), where they were called **Etruscans** (inhabitants out of Tyras-E-out of). Others passed over to Tarshish (Great Britain). A third group sought a place of settlement in Thrace (SE Balkan Peninsula – the site of Constantinople; now Istanbul, Turkey). Isaiah 23:1-3, 12, prophesied of this disaster and what was to happen to each of these three groups. The inhabitants of the Isles of Tarshish refused to allow them to settle there, and the people of Chittim allowed them to rest in their land. Finally the **Etruscans** settled by the great waters where the mart of the nations (Constantinople) was established. Hence, the **Tyruscans**, after leaving their original city, were called **Etruscans**. Then, after settlement in their new home, by the "great waters," were called **Thracians**, which became abbreviated to **Thraks**. This, in turn, by a natural language change, became **Turks**."

Part VII (June, 1945) – "AN OBJECTION RAISED: Someone may say, "Do we not understand that the Turks came across from Central Asia?" I reply, that Osmanli, or Ottomans, or as the Chinese call them, Huing-Nu, did come across from Central Asia, but not till long after this. In 433 A.D., a Huing-Nu clan, called Asena, on account of their dislike of Emperor Wei, moved westward, and in the sixth century had reached the Ural Mts., and the country south of the Caspian Sea. But not until the thirteenth century, when the Mongols drove them out – three millions of them – did they drift toward the land of the Turks, and having taken Byzantium, south of the Black Sea, crossed the straits, and in 1453 A.D., took

Constantinople (the last stronghold of the Eastern Holy Roman Empire).

You may say, "If Osmanli, or Ottomans, conquered the Thracians, or Tyruscans, why not abandon that line of descendancy?" In reply, I submit that the conquerors did not overwhelm the conquered but merely assumed the governing power. A similar state of affairs occurred in England in 1066 A.D., when William of Normandy, with his numerous barons obtained the ruling power there. Still, we maintain that the inhabitants of Britain are British, and not French, though our language and customs were greatly changed. In this, and similar cases, the permanency of the race is maintained by the persistency and doggedness of the character of the conquered, and their immensely greater numbers. **Thus, we maintain, that the Turks are early descendants of the former inhabitants of Tyre,** who were a mixture through intermarriage of the descendants of Tyras – seventh son of Japheth, and those of Sidon, the first-born of Canaan, the fourth son of Ham.

The student of prophecy, therefore, must bear this in mind when understanding the prophecies that are yet to be fulfilled in connection with Tyre. **If he reads of a future Prince of Tyre, he may know at once, it is referring to the Prince of Turkey.**"

PROPHECY CONCERNING TYRE YET TO BE FULFILLED

CHAPTER 8: THE LEGACY OF ABERHART

Erdogan's Ottoman Guard from 16 past Ottoman Empires in 2015

The age of Gentile world power from the time of Babylon to its destruction at the Battle of Armageddon was described in Daniel chapter 2 in relation to its effect on the Jewish nation. The following four quotes are from the Old Scofield Reference Bible (1909) notes:

> "The latter power, Rome, is seen divided, first into two (the legs) fulfilled in the Eastern and Western Roman empires, and then into ten kingdoms (the toes), partly weak and partly strong. **This is precisely what has come to pass in the constitutional monarchies which, with the Republic of France <u>and the despotism of Turkey, cover the sphere of ancient Roman rule</u>**. (C. I. Scofield, Old Scofield Reference Bible, p. 901)

The former Roman Empire at the end of Gentile world-domination will have ten horns (10 nation powers). There rises up among the ten kings a "little horn" (king), who subdues three of the ten kings so completely that the separate identity of their kingdoms is destroyed. Seven kings of the ten are left, and the "little horn." He is the "king of fierce countenance;" "the prince that shall come," (Daniel 9:26); the "king" of Daniel 11:36-45; "the man of sin," of 2 Thessalonians 2:4-8; and the "Beast" of Revelation 13:4-8. (Ibid, p. 910)

Fragments of the ancient Roman empire have never ceased to exist as separate kingdoms. It was the imperial form of government which ceased; the one head wounded to death. What we have prophetically in Revelation 13:3 is the restoration of the imperial form as such, though over a federated empire of ten kingdoms; the "head" is "healed," i.e. restored; there is an emperor again – the **Beast**. (Ibid, p. 1342) The "**false prophet**" of Revelation 16:13 and 19:20 is the last (one-world) ecclesiastical head, as the **Beast** of Revelation 13:1-8 is the last (one-world) civil head. For the purpose of persecution the "false prophet" is permitted to exercise the autocratic power of the emperor-Beast. (Ibid, pp. 1342-43)

The Beast is the earth's last and most awful tyrant, Satan's fell (cruel, destructive, powerful, barbarous) instrument of wrath and hatred against God, mankind and the Jewish saints. He begins by the conquest of three of the ten kingdoms into which the former Roman Empire will then be divided, but soon establishes the ecclesiastical and governmental tyranny described in Daniel chapters 7, 9 and 11. Satan gives the Beast the power which he offered to Christ during his temptation, and which Christ refused."

"Again, the devil taketh him into an exceeding high mountain, and shewed him all the kingdoms of the world, and the glory of them; And saith unto him, All these things will I give thee, if thou wilt fall down and worship me. Then saith Jesus unto him, Get thee hence, Satan: for it is

CHAPTER 8: THE LEGACY OF ABERHART

> written, Thou shalt worship the Lord thy God, and him only shalt thou serve." (Matthew 4:8-10)

Karl Marx accepted the devil's offer and set out to lay the groundwork for Satan's kingdom on earth. The Beast and the false prophet will both bring to fruition the "The Communist Manifesto," in which Marx proclaimed, "A spectre (spirit) is haunting Europe, the spectre of Communism." Anyone and everyone who has taken up Marx's cause, has come under the power of this spirit, who is Satan. Communist China and its regime has come under its blinding power. The last world ruler will be fully possessed by Satan, the fallen heavenly being (cherubim), next in power to God. No earthly ruler or Christ-rejecting individual can withstand his diabolical cunning and persuasion. Those who have rejected Christ will accept the Beast. Period. That is the "strong delusion" that God will send on the Christ-rejecting world at the end of the church age of grace. Their end, according to the Scriptures, will be "the lake of fire."

> "Then shall he say also to unto them on the left hand, Depart from me, ye cursed, into everlasting fire, prepared for the devil and his angels:" (Matthew 25:41)

William Aberhart unequivocally stated his conclusions about the Beast, using the scriptures:

> "One of the nations under the Antichrist (the Beast) at the Battle of Armageddon, will be Turkey...one of the 10 kingdoms (of the revived Roman Empire). The king of Tyrus will be there. We are plainly warned that the Antichrist to come is to be **a Turkish prince** (ruler), wiser than Daniel, and rebellious to all that is called God."

> "Let no man deceive you by any means: for that day shall not come, except there come a falling away first, and **the man of sin** be revealed, **the son of perdition**; Who opposeth and exalteth himself above all that is called

God, or that is worshipped; so that he as God sitteth in the Temple of God, shewing himself that he is God. Even him, whose coming is after the working of Satan will all power and signs and lying wonders. And for this cause God shall send them strong delusion, that they should believe a lie:" (2 Thessalonians 2:3-4, 9, 11)

"Turning to the Book of Ezekiel, we find that the same description is given to one who is spoken of as the Prince of Tyre. It is evident, therefore, the Antichrist (the Beast) is to be a Turkish Prince."

"Son of man, say unto the prince of Tyrus, thus saith the Lord GOD; Because thine heart is lifted up, and thou hast said, I am a God, I sit in the seat of God, in the midst of the seas; yet thou art a man, and not God, though thou set thine heart as the heart of God: Behold, thou art wiser than Daniel; there is no secret that they can hide from thee: Son of man, take up a lamentation upon king of Tyrus, and say unto him, Thus saith the Lord GOD; **Thou sealest up the sum, full of wisdom, and perfect in beauty. Thou hast been in Eden the garden of God; every precious stone was thy covering, the sardius, topaz, and the diamond, the beryl, the onyx, and the jasper, the sapphire, the emerald, and the carbuncle, and gold:** the workmanship of thy tabrets and of thy pipes was prepared in thee in the day that thou wast created. **Thou art the anointed cherub that covereth;** and I have set thee so: thou wast upon the mountain of God; thou hast walked up and down in the midst of the stones of fire. Thou was perfect in thy ways from the day that thou wast created, till iniquity was found in thee. By the multitude of thy merchandise they have filled thee with violence, and thou has sinned.: **therefore I will cast thee as profane out of the mountain of God: and I will destroy thee, O covering cherub, from the midst of the stones of fire**...and I will bring thee to ashes upon the earth in the sight of all them that behold thee." (Ezekiel 28:2-3, 12-16, 18)

So, the Beast is a man, possessed of the devil (Satan) and a Prince of Turkey. Today, nearly 100 years after Mr.

CHAPTER 8: THE LEGACY OF ABERHART

Aberhart's messages on the Antichrist, the world scene is rapidly moving toward the fulfillment of these Biblical prophecies. WW II was a pre-fulfillment of the socialist effort to win control of the world under Adolf Hitler and his '1000 year' Third Reich. In his ambition, Hitler, fulfilled the ambition of the Antichrist. In "The Last Days of Hitler," by H. R. Trevor Roper, 1947, we learn of that man, as he writes "a self-portrait," while in prison in his own words:

> "At long intervals in human history," Hitler wrote, "it may occasionally happen that the practical politician and the political philosopher are one. The more intimate the union, the greater his political difficulties. Such a man does not labor to satisfy the demands that are obvious to every philistine; he reaches out towards ends that are comprehensible only to the few. Therefore his life is torn between hatred and love. The protest of the present generation, which does not understand him, wrestles with the recognition of posterity, for whom he also works." (pp. 40-41)

Roper goes on to add concerning Hitler's mesmeric power; a foreshadowing of what the Antichrist will be like:

> "His own firm belief in his **messianic mission** was perhaps the most important element in the extraordinary power of his personality, which lasted long after the external reasons for its survival had disappeared; and the acceptance of this myth even by the intelligent Speer is the best evidence of its power." (Ibid, p. 41)

General Halder, the ablest of Hitler's generals wrote concerning the man:

> "When I was working with him, I was always looking for signs of genius in him. I tried hard to be honest and impartial, and not to be blinded by my antipathy to the

man. **I *never* found genius in him, <u>only the diabolical</u>**." (Ibid, p.40)

Who in the modern geo-political world best fits the description of the Beast in Biblical prophecy, considering the example of the National Socialist, Adolf Hitler, whose aggressions brought on WW II? Brad Johnson, a retired CIA senior operations officer and a former chief of station, provides a careful glimpse into one who may be closest to being the best candidate for the end-times Beast currently present on the world stage. In two recent articles in the Epoch Times Johnson writes:

> "**Erdogan is far more advanced in re-establishing the Ottoman Empire with himself as caliph** (supreme Muslim leader) **than anyone in the West is willing to admit. <u>He's a budding new Hitler, our implacable foe, and an enemy to the free world</u>**. He will have to be stopped sooner or later, one way or another. We have to set aside politics and deal with the reality that faces us. <u>**Removing Turkey from NATO and containing its expansionist efforts would be a good start, but only the beginning.**</u>" (Brad Johnson, Turkish President Erdogan: Friend or Foe? The Epoch Times, p. A8, August 15-21, 2019)

Erdogan rose to power from being a soccer player to becoming mayor of Istanbul in 1994. He was banned from politics and spent a short time in jail for his Islamic extremist politics. Later he formed his own political party, falsely describing himself as a conservative democrat to become prime minister of Turkey, and then President in 2014. He rapidly acted to move Turkey away from its secular base to Islamic extremism. He carefully avoided being truthful about his real position and agenda to establish his current extremist government.

Hitler and Erdogan both consolidated their power before becoming more and more dictatorial, proving the old

CHAPTER 8: THE LEGACY OF ABERHART

proverb, "Absolute power corrupts absolutely." In Joseph Goebbels' own words;

> "The reconstruction of the Egyptian Government has brought no sensational changes. Nahas Pasha declared that he intended to carry out the treaty with England without any reservation. He was clever enough, however, to dissolve Parliament. That, undoubtedly, is right. He must get parliamentary backing before he can bring about fundamental changes. **We did the same thing in February, 1933.**" Lochner notes: [**The dissolution of the German Reichstag early in February, 1933, enabled the Nazis to terrorize the population during the campaign for new elections, start the Reichstag fire, and use alleged Communist incendiarism as an excuse for outlawing the Communist party and fully entrenching themselves.**]" (Louis P. Lochner, The Goebbels Diaries, 1948, p. 73)

Erdogan soon devised a ruse, a fake coup, to discredit his enemies and drive them from any position of power or influence in Turkey's secular society. Having removed them he installed his own loyalists in the resulting vacuum, becoming a dictator intent on creating an extremist Islamic state.

> "In mid-2016 the Turkish military reportedly attempted a coup in order to oust Erdogan from power. The coup was put down immediately under **extraordinarily suspicious circumstances**, leading some to suggest that the coup was, in fact, staged by Erdogan. Even more suspicious was that within days, the regime arrested more than 200 journalists, closed more than 120 media outlets, and fired approximately 160,000 government employees from every Turkish government agency, including judges. In all cases, those arrested or fired were those not loyal to Erdogan, and they were quickly replaced with loyalists. The sheer magnitude of (these actions) would have required many months of preparation in order to put together such comprehensive lists, so much so that **it's almost impossible for the so-**

"FORTRESS AMERICA" UNDER SIEGE

called coup to have been anything other than a blatant power grab by Erdogan. He used the event to consolidate his power in the entire country, including the media, <u>and now holds complete dictatorial power in Turkey</u>. (Brad Johnson, Turkish President Erdogan: Friend or Foe? The Epoch Times, p. A8, August 15-21, 2019)

Following the coup, the mass arrests included tens of thousands of soldiers, judges, teachers, and every government ministry. Several hundred thousand Turks fled the country in fear and are spread around the world in exile. Erdogan claimed that all of these people were linked to the Gulen movement – a social movement based on moral values, education, civil society, tolerance, and peace. Gulen and his followers have suggested the coup attempt was a ruse carried out by Erdogan himself." (Brad Johnson, The Math of Long Term Strategic Threats to the US," The Epoch Times, p. B1, July 26-August 1, 2019)

Erdogan is fixated on re-establishing the glory of the past Ottoman Empire that formally ended after WW I. He has a **messianic mindset** about accomplishing this feat, and going further with plans to bring Europe under the unfinished Ottoman conquests of the past centuries. In this sense he is like Hitler, with his vision of a 1000 year Reich.

> "Erdogan has worked to re-establish a number of Ottoman customs and traditions, including a reintroduction of Ottoman terms not used in nearly 100 years. For example, when meeting with foreign leaders, he reportedly uses an Ottoman-style reception with guards dressed in period costumes based on 16 Great Turkish Empires of the past (see preceding Picture). Worth noting, as a backdrop to those receptions, Erdogan built a lavish 1,150 – room presidential palace, **the largest in the world**, at the cost of well over a half-billion dollars. While Erdogan hasn't said so publicly, some of his close associates and other regime loyalists

CHAPTER 8: THE LEGACY OF ABERHART

have done so, and **there is no doubt of his intentions nor of his actions to return to the Ottoman caliphate**." (Ibid)

"Since consolidating his power, Erdogan has been quite clear that he intends to reestablish unquestioned Turkish influence in the areas that were previously under Ottoman Empire rule, **which means the re-conquest of parts of Europe, at a minimum**. The world has changed once again and in ways not beneficial to U.S. national security. Enter Turkey. The math of long-term strategic threats that face the United States have shifted again and **we need to pay attention**. It's now one (China) plus four (Russia, Iran, North Korea, terrorism) plus one (**Turkey**). **If my calculations are correct, that equals six**." (Brad Johnson, The Math of Long Term Strategic Threats to the US," The Epoch Times, p. B1, July 26-August 1, 2019)

In only a few short years under Erdogan, Turkey has openly gone over to the dark side, allying with extremist Muslim elements in the Middle East, North Africa and Europe and also extending into the United States and beyond. Erdogan allies with both Sunni and Shiite Muslims and even uses any and every faction that will suit his diabolical purposes, even including mafia-style crime boss, Sedat Peker. He is moving quickly in his dark plans as Hitler did in the 1930s.

"The regime has openly supported the Muslim Brotherhood for nearly a decade, and has been a sanctuary for their exiled leadership and is now their largest benefactor. Erdogan has also aligned himself with Islamic extremists in Iran, Libya, and Syria, as well as the terror group al-Qaeda. The regime is able to use the Muslim Brotherhood as leverage against Saudi Arabia, Egypt, and other countries in the Middle East, including Syria. **Erdogan is absorbing Muslim Brotherhood infrastructure in Europe and the United States, which allows him to control and influence the flow of information. He has absorbed the Grey Wolves,** which are similar to the Brownshirts of Nazi Germany and are large, organized and active in Europe. The Muslim Brotherhood shares the goal of establishing a Caliphate. <u>Turkey is a member of NATO and has negotiated in the past to become a member of the European Union. Turkey is perfectly positioned to become a serious problem</u>." (Brad Johnson – The Epoch Times – both above articles)

The Turkish prince mentioned by William Aberhart in his 1923 series of messages given at the Palace Theatre in Calgary could be coming to reality under the administration of Recep Tayyip Erdogan, the current President of Turkey. His rapid rise to power, deceptive ability and ambitions are Hitleresque and a threat to Europe, the United States and the world at large. If the Antichrist, the Biblical Beast, should arise from Turkey, and this nation be accepted into the European Union then the stage will be set for the last world dictator to take control and form the final, brutal, totalitarian dictatorship before the return of Christ to establish His millennial kingdom. While Erdogan himself may not be the final dictator, because he has been married and has a son, one of his offspring could likely take over the dictatorship from his father and carry his ambition to fruition in typical Middle Eastern tribal tradition.

> "The Turkish International Defense and Consulting Company's (SADAT) stated goal is to create an Islamic army in the Middle East, so that **the Islamic world can take its rightful place as a world super-power. This can mean only one thing: the re-conquest of Europe and beyond**." (Brad Johnson, Turkish President Erdogan: Friend or Foe?, The Epoch Times, p. A8, August 15-21, 2019)

The Rapture of the Christian Church and the Revealing of the Beast

CHAPTER 8: THE LEGACY OF ABERHART

The removal (Rapture) of the genuine Bible-believing Christians (the true Church) will occur before the Antichrist takes control and establishes his Satanic one-world government. He will use the apostate church as his instrument to garner worship for himself, and persecute those who are saved during his seven year-long reign described in the Book of Revelation Chapters 4 through 19. Aberhart's younger men, including Ernest Manning, preached often concerning these prophetic events. Mr. J. Henry Mc Culloch writes in his article, "We are at War: The Great Withdrawal and Enemy Occupation," in June, 1946, in The Prophetic Voice:

> "So the great withdrawal – the rapture is coming. Christians will be caught away to be with the Lord. The hindering power of the Holy Spirit will be taken out of the way as described in 2 Thessalonians 2:6-7.
>
> *"For the Lord himself shall descend from heaven with a shout, with the voice of the archangel and with the trump of God: and the dead in Christ shall rise first: then we which are alive and remain shall be caught up together with them to meet the Lord in the air: and so shall we ever be with the Lord." (1 Thessalonians 4:16-17)*
>
> So, a blinded world, having rejected Christ, will receive the enemy – the devil in the person of the Antichrist. Before the time of enemy occupation comes the great withdrawal. At that time all who are trusting in Christ, whether having died in Him or living in faith in Him at that time shall be caught away from this world to be with the Savior as described in 1 Corinthians 15:51-52.
>
> Tribulation (severe affliction, distress, trouble) far exceeding the atrocities of war will be let loose upon the earth such as has never been known before. How terrible will be that day of enemy occupation. The enemy (the Beast/Antichrist) will occupy the territory and bring with his rule suffering and privation beyond description. Hungry, homeless, persecuted, branded like cattle,

human beings who rejected the Savor will wait release by death, and then only to go out into a lost eternity."

But the rapture comes first. Are you ready to go? Have you received Jesus Christ as your Savior? If you have, you can say with the Apostle Paul, *"I have a desire to depart, and to be with Christ; which is far better:"* **(Philippians 1:23)** <u>To be ready when He appears, get ready now</u>."

Remember W. E. Gladstone's comment concerning Turkey, given in William Aberhart's 1923 message, "The Present Eastern Question in the Light of Prophecy or What the Bible Says About Turkey," – Part 1, re-printed in the November, 1944, Prophetic Voice:

> "They were upon the whole, when they first entered Europe, the one great Anti-human specimen of humanity. Wherever they went a broad line of blood marked the trace behind them and as far as their dominion reached civilization disappeared from view. **This advancing curse menaced the whole of Europe.**"

Turkey has made headlines recently becoming involved in a war between Moslem Azerbaijan and Christian Armenia. The impact of this involvement goes far beyond that conflict. It has alarmed the European Union as a potential indicator of trouble ahead for the 27 nation body. It is as if Aberhart's and Gladstone's words are becoming prophetic, as one EU delegate worried that Turkey's rise threatened European civilization.

> "Many pressed for harsher measures against Erdogan's government. A Croatian member of the European parliament said, **"It seems that many if not most of our foreign policy challenges have Turkey as a common denominator and cause.** Its latest actions are yet another clear sign of Ankara's departure from EU values and international law standards." A French delegate added: "It is unacceptable Europe has not put an end to

CHAPTER 8: THE LEGACY OF ABERHART

> Turkey's accession (increase, augment – as coming to a throne) procedure. Europe is not a toy. Our values, our principles, **the heart of our civilization is not negotiable**." (Nick Gutteridge, EU Lawmakers Urge Bloc to Follow Canada's Example to Embargo Arms Sales to Turkey," The Epoch Times, pp. A1, 10, October 8-14, 2020)

Though Turkey was known as the "Sick Man" in the late eighteenth and early nineteenth centuries, she has had nine lives and now is positioned to become a real problem for the Western democracies, and the world at large. The Antichrist is to rise up as a "little horn,' (horn means power) out of a small people to gain worldwide power. Turkey is not a major power, but she is a major threat, as Brad Johnson reports in his two 2019 Epoch Times articles. Her extremist Islamic government and terrorist network described in Johnson's articles are aligned with International Socialism-Communism's agenda to overthrow the Western democracies. They are both rooted in the same Marxist-Leninist doctrines and have the same agenda, making Turkey a greater threat than political analysts imagine. The Epoch Times discussed this danger in "How the Spectre of Communism is Ruling Our World," The Communist Roots of Terrorism – Chapter 15, 2020:

> "The arguments made here are that the real enemy confronting the free world remains Communism and that radical Islam is nothing more than Communism cloaked in the traditional garments of Islam. The ideological source of bin Laden's Islamic extremism can be traced back to Sayyid Qutb, the Egyptian pioneer of Islamic terrorism, a man who could be described as the Marx of Islamic jihad and who is often referred to as the "godfather of modern jihad." **Qutb was a member of the Communist Party in his youth, and his ideas were steeped in the rhetoric of Marxism-Leninism. Robert R. Reilly, a senior fellow at the U.S. Foreign Policy Committee, has said that <u>Qutb was actually a</u>**

Communist International (Comintern) liason for the Egyptian Muslim Brotherhood and the Communist Party of Egypt."

Erdogan has harnessed the power of Islamic extremism and integrated it with the radical socialist-communist movement in Europe, the United States and other nations around the world to become a terrorist super-power – the restored Roman Empire, fully able to cause catastrophic destruction given the right circumstances. That the **Beast** will have extraordinary power is attested to in the Scriptures.

> "And I saw one of his heads as it were wounded to death; and his deadly wound was healed (Roman Empire restored): and all the world wondered after the beast. And they worshipped the dragon (the Devil) which gave power unto the beast: and they worshipped the beast, saying, **who is like unto the beast? Who is able to make war with him?**" (Revelation 13:3-4)

Apparently, no nation is able to overcome the Beast in warfare. Satanic power best explains this phenomenon. It may be that Saddam Hussein's apparently non-existent 'weapons of mass destruction' existed after all, and ended up in Turkey which borders Iraq, and still remain there ready to be used clandestinely by the Prince of Turkey, the Beast, at the right moment. This is pure speculation, but not inconceivable.

That Erdogan is ruthless is beyond question. His own words testify to that fact. Concerning the Christian Armenian Genocide committed by Muslim Turkey during WW I, Erdogan's response and statement was thus:

> "Erdogan took a deeply revealing public position in late 2008, when he came out in opposition to the Armenian Genocide. In WW I, Turkey rounded up all the Armenians (men, women and children) that it could get its hands on

CHAPTER 8: THE LEGACY OF ABERHART

and marched them off into the desert without supplies, where they died of thirst and the elements."

Erdogan stated, "We did not commit a crime and therefore, we do not need to apologize. **It is not possible for those who belong to the Muslim faith to carry out genocide**."

Brad Johnson's response: "To be absolutely clear, this represents the radical Islamic view that killing non-Muslims by definition can neither be genocide or a crime. **There can be no doubt that Erdogan will happily slaughter people by the thousands to achieve his goals**. That's not the kind of person who will ever be a friend to the United States or the world."

Rudolf Rummel, a professor at the University of Hawaii described this genocide, his 'democide,' in detail in his book, Death by Government (1987):

"In 1922 only about 100,000 Armenians – 5% of the probable 1914 population – were left alive in Turkey, mainly in a few major cities. Simply consider the moral message communicated to the world (by the Western democracies, including the U.S.) by purposely ignoring the Young Turk genocide of nearly 1,500,000 Armenians."

"It has been previously communicated that the government by the order of the Assembly (Jemiet) has decided to exterminate entirely all the Armenians living in Turkey. Those who oppose this order can no longer function as part of the government. Without regard to women, children and invalids, however tragic may be the means of transportation, an end must be put to their existence. (Telegram from Minister of the Interior, Talaat – in Rudolf Rummel, Death by Government, 1987)

This kind of communication and Erdogan's response to the genocide show the darkened heart of the Turkish regime, both in the past and in the present. Brad

Johnson's warning should be taken very seriously concerning this man and this nation – TURKEY.

Destruction of the final remnants of apostate Christendom in Europe and the annihilation of the State of Israel will be the primary goals of the Beast. Through his diabolical rule over the European Union, the re-constituted Eastern and Western Holy Roman Empire, he will persuade Israel to sign a counterfeit peace pact with the Muslim world, in order to destroy the Jewish people.

Biblical prophecy identifies the final world dictatorship as one in which the leader, the **Beast**, uses craft (i.e., cunning, guile and deceit) to reach the pinnacle of power, changes times and laws, and has no interest in a natural female sexual relationship. That seems to exclude Recep Erdogan who is married and has a rich, married businessman son, Ahmet Burak, and a married daughter. Evidently his son is as corrupt as his father and, some years ago killed a young woman with his automobile. His father sent him abroad and the files and charges disappeared. Ahmet then became known as Erdogan's "ghost son," as so little is known about him. Whether Erdogan's son or son-in-law succeeds him, or someone else in that administration or family could well arise to fulfill Biblical prophecy and be the future Beast or Antichrist of Ottoman mold or character who will not be revealed until after the Rapture of the genuine, Bible-believing saved children of God, the true Christian Church.

> "Widely reported audio recordings surfaced in 2013-14 of Erdogan and his son allegedly discussing how to hide very large sums of money. The regime instituted full control over the internet in Turkey, allowing the government to block any sites reporting the corruption, and yet gave the government full access to everyone's private information." (Brad Johnson, Turkish President

CHAPTER 8: THE LEGACY OF ABERHART

Erdogan: Friend or Foe? The Epoch Times, p. A8, August 15-21, 2019)

"And the king shall do according to his will, and he shall exalt himself, and magnify himself above every god, and shall speak marvelous things against the God of gods, and shall prosper till the indignation (the Great Tribulation) *be accomplished: Neither shall he regard the God of his fathers, <u>nor the desire of women</u>, nor regard any god: for he shall magnify himself above all. But in his estate shall he honor the God of forces:* (natural force, materialism) *and a god whom his fathers knew not shall he honor with gold, and silver, and with precious stones, and pleasant things."* (Daniel 11:34-36)

A similar example of son succeeding father in politics exists in Canada where Pierre Trudeau ruled as Prime Minister for 15 ½ years and was succeeded 31 years later by his son, Justin, who is even more politically dangerous to Canada's free democracy than his father. The son also has a colored past and a narcissistic character.

If the Turkish prince (leader) is allowed into the European Union, he will take control through supernatural power, destroy three nations in the process and leverage himself to the pinnacle of power through diplomatic craft and deceit to gain world-wide dictatorial control. This seems impossible to contemplate, but it is the clear teaching of Scripture. Turkey's ascendancy is beginning to emerge in our times as foretold in the Scriptures through Erdogan's rise to power in Turkey. That Erdogan or one of his successors could accomplish such amazing political and military feats would mean that God has sent His long-promised **strong delusion** to mankind and given over unbelieving humanity into the hand of Satan – as God pours out His wrath on a Christ-rejecting world during the Great Tribulation.

"FORTRESS AMERICA" UNDER SIEGE

> *"And the ten horns* (powers) *out of this kingdom* (revived Roman Empire) *are ten kings that shall arise: and another shall arise after them* (the little horn – the Beast); *and he shall be diverse from the first, and he shall subdue three kings. And he shall speak great words against the most High, and shall wear out the saints of the most High* (Tribulation believers), *and **think to change times and laws**: and they shall be given into his hand until a time and times and the dividing of time – 3 ½ years."* (Daniel 7:24-25)

Scofield, in his notes, states that the Antichrist is an apostate from Christianity, not Judaism. Turkey was once dominated by New Testament Christianity, before being conquered by Islam which destroyed the Christian faith. Therefore, it would not be surprising for a Turkish prince to become the Antichrist and *"think to change times and laws,"* as mentioned in Daniel 7:25, to accord with the Muslim faith.

God's final judgment on the Beast and his kingdom will be catastrophic and final. The Bible explains it in detail in many places in the Bible, most notably in the books of Daniel, Joel, Zechariah, Matthew, Mark, Luke, 2 Thessalonians and Revelation 6-19.

> *"And then shall that Wicked* (the Beast/Antichrist) *be revealed, whom the Lord shall consume with the spirit of his mouth, and destroy with the brightness of his coming: Even him, whose coming is after the working of Satan with all power and signs and lying wonders,"* (2 Thessalonians 2:8-9)

William Aberhart wrote in his final message on Turkey in 1923, re-printed in the July, 1945, issue of The Prophetic Voice that God's judgment at the end of the Great Tribulation comes when Jesus Christ returns to this earth. It will fall on the Prince of Turkey's historical capitol, Istanbul, which was Constantinople, the modern-

CHAPTER 8: THE LEGACY OF ABERHART

day Tyre, and the final stronghold of the Eastern Holy Roman Empire, conquered by the Ottomans in 1453 A.D. The regional Anatolian fault zone runs through this part of Turkey and could be the future crustal weak spot through which God brings the final destruction of the Beast's seat of proud influence and affection.

> "The present situation (1922) with Kemal Pasha attempting to secure Constantinople will make the next prophecy concerned of intense interest to Bible readers. The prophecy in Ezekiel 26:19-20 and 27:27, 32-34 indicates that the city of Constantinople will be destroyed by subsidence into the midst of the Black Sea."

William Aberhart preached on Christ's Second Coming; both the first phase, the Rapture, and the second phase, the Revelation, Christ's return to this earth at the Battle of Armageddon. Below are some excerpts from a message titled, "Is Christ's Coming Again a Reality of a Mere Fancy?" by Dean Aberhart, B.A., at the Opening of the Prophetic Conference in Calgary, in the Fall of 1924, re-printed in The Prophetic Voice, May, 1947.

> "It is time for our church people to arouse themselves. I am persuaded that many of our church people are being hoodwinked by those of Modernist tendencies who sneer and jeer at this doctrine as fanciful and fanatical. You cannot go far in these days before your meet them. They are found in the Colleges, in the pulpits, in the pews. I met one of these modernists a few years ago and he was a bird (a real fowl of the air in the Scriptural sense), **a religious Bolshevist**. After he had delivered a suave, smoothly-finished tirade regarding the fanaticism and foolishness of this doctrine and all who believed in it, I ventured a question: "Will you kindly explain to me – 1 Thessalonians 4:16-17 and John 14:1-3?"
>
> "Well," he said, as a dark scowl crept over his face, "I speak with reverence (?) when I say, Jesus Himself shared the same delusion. He, of course, did not know

his statement was false." I looked at him for a moment in dumbfounded amazement, then I ventured again, "But what about the declaration of the two messengers from heaven in Acts 1:11?" He replied, "The trouble with you, and others like you, is that you treat the Bible as literal and final. The majority of scholars (?) have long since discovered the fallacy of that." Then I said to him, "What would you say to your people, as a pastor, if they asked you what these passages meant?" He answered, "I would simply warn them to leave this matter alone."

"That was exactly the attitude of the priests and scribes at the First Coming of Christ. Some of the members of our **Evangelical Churches** today have assumed this attitude, and are being governed by these men. Listen, men and women! Hearken unto me! The next time any of these fellows come along with doctrines such as that, take the creed of your church and ask them if they said they believed this creed to be in harmony with the Scriptures of the Old and New Testaments, and would preach it faithfully? You **Anglicans**, take your Book of Common Prayer and turn to the Collect for the third Sunday in Advent, and read it to them. Then turn to the Articles of Religion, Clause 8, and read this also. No good Anglican doubts the reality of the Second Coming of Christ. You **Presbyterians**, take your Westminster Confession of Faith, and turn to Chapter 33, Section 3, and show it to them. Surely a Presbyterian must renounce his established creed who doubts the reality of the Second Coming of Christ. And you **Baptists**, tell them, will you? that as early as 1660, the Baptist Confession of Faith declared...Acts 1:3, 11; Colossians 3:4, etc," That surely is plain. **The Baptist Church loses its authority for its existence immediately when it departs from the literalness of God's Word."** And lastly, you **Methodists** should know that John Wesley, that glorious saint of God, is responsible for the following – "Perhaps He will appear as the day-spring from on high before the morning light. Oh, do not set Him a time. Expect Him every hour. Now He is nigh, even at the door." Charles Wesley, his brother, was known as the Millennial Poet.

CHAPTER 8: THE LEGACY OF ABERHART

It strikes me that a man who can boldly proclaim that all the Bible declarations, and all the utterances of the great reformers, and all the statements of the Evangelical Church Creeds are foolish and fanatical and not worthy of a Christian's attention, has really a very high opinion of himself. Does he not? Hear me, men and women, as long as you will continue to listen to these proud, presumptuous boasters you will never get anywhere. You will be of no use to God or man. **What a difference it would make to your life if you actually believed, down in the depths of your heart, that Jesus was really coming again?**" There is no use saying you believe Jesus is coming again unless the effect is seen in your life. It is all very well to say you give assent to it mentally. Do you love His appearing? Are you willing to live truly for Him? I call you to a higher life. Will you come?"

In the final analysis, Mr. Aberhart is calling people in the churches back to God – back to faith in God's Word and living for God. To fight back against the apostasy of the churches. That was nearly 100 years ago. In 2020, it is ten times worse. That is the whole problem in Western society today and why socialism-communism has made such inroads into our families and churches and society, and our nation as a whole. Continuing along the path we are on will bring disaster. We must find our way back, as Mr. Aberhart beckoned so long ago. **Revival in the Christian churches is the only way out of the crisis we face today in Canada and the United States of America. Only this can prevent "Fortress America" from certain defeat by the forces of Marxist socialism-communism.**

A future invasion of "Fortress America" is a distinct possibility. Storm clouds are surrounding the North American continent on all sides, with a particular concentration along the northeastern and western coastlines, and in the north on both the Alaskan and

"FORTRESS AMERICA" UNDER SIEGE

Canadian Arctic regions. The ancient 'superpower' Babylon's destruction came from the north as shown earlier in the chapter. This picture portrays the writer's view that the American continent is vulnerable to invasion from the north through Alaska and the western plains of Canada and from there down into the U.S. heartland. God's judgment in the Bible almost always came from the north upon nations that He was punishing for their sin. He chooses the north because the Bible describes Mt. Zion as God's center of power, where He dwells, "on the sides of the North." (Psalm 48:2)

> "Beautiful for situation, the joy of the whole earth, is mount Zion, **on the sides of the north**, the city of the great King."

Egypt's judgment came from the north. God judged the wealthy sea-faring city of Tyre for its sin. Tyre's destruction came from the north. Babylon was God's instrument of judgment in both cases. God's Tribulation judgment on Israel is yet future but will also come from the north. A Russian-led confederacy will invade Israel from the north during the Great Tribulation. God's Tribulation judgments and miraculous deliverance of His chosen people, Israel, will bring that nation to repentance and acceptance of their Messiah, Jesus Christ.

> "Egypt is like a very fair heifer, but destruction cometh **out of the north**...she shall be delivered into the hand of **the people of the north**." (Jeremiah 46:20, 24)

> "For thus saith the Lord GOD; Behold, I will bring upon Tyrus Nebuchadrezzar king of Babylon, a king of kings, **from the north**, with horses, and with chariots, and with horsemen, and companies, and much people." (Ezekiel 26:7)

> "For a nation is come up upon my land (Israel), strong, and without number, whose teeth are the teeth of a lion,

CHAPTER 8: THE LEGACY OF ABERHART

*and he hath the cheek teeth of a great lion...Then will the LORD be jealous for his land, and pity his people...I will remove from you **the northern army**, and will drive him into a land barren and desolate, with has face toward the east sea, and his hinder part toward the utmost sea," (Joel 1:6 & 2:18, 20)*

Canada and the United States cannot expect any less severe punishment for our manifold sins and backslidden churches in the twenty-first century – <u>if we will not repent</u>? China and Russia are the two nations that would be sent by God from the north to judge us for our sins.

CHAPTER 9

THE WAY BACK: A RETURN TO FREE DEMOCRACY

CHAPTER 9: THE WAY BACK

> **"In America, we don't worship government, we worship God."**
> President Donald Trump

THE POLITICAL ISSUES INVOLVED

Judeo-Christian culture formed the bedrock of Western society for hundreds of years since the Reformation. Those of us who have grown up in democratically-free Western society take it for granted. Our forefathers fought to preserve it in World Wars I and II, but now we are in peril and WW III is being fought within our own borders.

> "The democratic civilization of the West owes its success to the Judeo-Christian ethic that formed its roots. Societal cohesion in times of strife depends on a solid foundation of time-tested values and virtuous principles of which the Marxist postmodern school of thought is thoroughly devoid. For centuries these principles have enabled people to persevere with hope and purpose through the darkest of times. **They are the bedrock that has built greatness and encouraged the fragile human spirit to become more than itself.**" (Ryan Moffatt, On Traditional Values and Weathering the COVID-19 Storm, The Epoch Times, p. B1, March 26-April 1, 2020)

Alexis de Tocqueville, a great 19th century French thinker and philosopher, visited America and verbalized what the saw, and the same could also be said for Canada, America's northern neighbor.

> "He came to a great appreciation for the society. He was impressed with American's ability for introspection, their understanding of evil, their willingness to solve problems with patience, and the general lack of violence in solving social problems. He thought that the greatness of the United States lay in its ability to correct its own mistakes." (The Epoch Times, "How the Spectre of Communism is

Ruling Our World," How Communism Sows Chaos in Politics – Part 2, Chapter 8, 2020)

William Aberhart and Ernest Manning were two genuine Christian leaders who came out of Western civilization. Their combined 33 years in office exhibited the kind of greatness described by Mr. de Tocqueville. Mr. Manning, mentored by Mr. Aberhart, came from a farm boy's background to become perhaps the greatest provincial premier in Canadian history.

William Gairdner delved into the roots and accomplishments of this great Western civilization in his article, "Celebrating the West," in the April 9-15, 2020, Epoch Times.

> **"Western citizens must stand proudly in defence of their liberty-based laws and rights.** Compared to all other systems – ours is quite amazing. Its focus is the flourishing of free individual initiative under the same rules for all. It is a system that supplies the ordinary individual with largely unrestricted free choice in daily commercial life with respect to how to spend the fruits of personal labor and invention.
>
> At the root of all cultural/moral systems a distinct theology may always be discovered. Despite many faults and wrong turns...the theology of love and moral self-examination at the heart of Christendom seems quite fundamental as the basis for a sound national culture and morality. Because Christianity is uniquely rooted in a belief of absolutes – in the existence of discoverable universal truth – we have been culturally gifted the belief that we live in a universe of profound (and discoverable) meaning. This belief has unleashed a cornucopia of near-miraculous scientific and technological development – copied by other cultures, but never exceeded. In terms of worldwide patents issued on a per-capita national basis, the nations of Judeo-Christian origin dominate.

CHAPTER 9: THE WAY BACK

> The Christian communities and citizens of the West tend to be universally more freely-charitable than their secular counterparts in the West. Christendom was responsible for the creation of the world's first true universities, and for many of the world's great hospitals, and of course for countless national and global charitable organizations. They have given "freely" because they give of their own free will and are not commanded to do this by state or church. A great many of the private international organizations that help the poor and less developed world are also of Christian origin. **In these, as in so many things, the West, my deep culture, has never had an equal – and it still doesn't. This is a truth of which to be proud, and to defend.**"

Many great scientists and politicians were genuine Christians, as well as a myriad of persons from all walks of life. Their faith lifted the moral authority of society as a whole out of paganism and hedonism to produce progress in everything from the arts and literature to education, social justice, law and government. Free democracy grew out of this Bible-based culture. Below is one of many examples of human greatness mixed with humility characteristic of that age.

> "The renowned scientist Isaac Newton, in his book "Principles of Mathematics," published in 1678, explained in detail the principles of mechanics, tidal formation, and planetary movement, and calculated the movements of the solar system. Newton, who was so eminently accomplished, said repeatedly that his book was a mere description of surface phenomena, and that he absolutely did not dare to talk about the real meaning of the ultimate God in creating the universe. In the second edition of the "Principles of Mathematics," in expressing his faith, Newton wrote, "This most beautiful system of the sun, planets, and comets could only proceed from the counsel and dominion of an intelligent and powerful being...As a blind man has no idea of colors, so we have no idea of the manner by which the all-wise God

"FORTRESS AMERICA" UNDER SIEGE

> perceives and understands all things." (The Epoch Times, "Nine Commentaries on the Communist Party," On How the Communist Party is an Anti-Universe Force – Part 4, p.9, 2004).

The Chinese Communist Party set itself up to contend with heaven and earth, instead of submitting to God and His Word as Isaac Newton did. During the disastrous Great Leap Forward its pride and arrogance was displayed in folk songs:

> "Let the mountains bow and let the rivers step aside."
> "There's no Jade Emperor in the heaven and there's no King of Dragons on earth. I am the Jade Emperor and I am the King of Dragons. I order the three mountains and five gorges to step aside, and here I come!" (Ibid).

Below is the essence of a quote taken from Alexander Solzhenitsyn, author of "The Gulag Archipelago," the story of Stalin's socialist-communist concentration camps in the U.S.S.R.

> "We saw what was happening, only we did nothing to stop it. If we had tried, and lost, at least we would have tried; and maybe we would have succeeded."

The Hon. Ernest C. Manning once began a speech to a secular audience, that all Albertans acknowledged the –

> "sovereignty (supreme power or dominion) of Almighty God, whose omnipotent arm is our strongest defense and whose Divine Providence affords security and peace to all who will put their trust in Him." (B. Brennan, The Good Steward – The Ernest C. Manning Story, 2008)

In its effort to supplant God's sovereign authority, Communism has trumpeted its cause as a promise of a more just order of society. Pierre Trudeau believed that lie (page 296). While Canadian Prime Minister he told Mr.

CHAPTER 9: THE WAY BACK

Manning that he would rather have him in the Canadian Senate than out on the street talking to people. He feared the genuine Christianity of Ernest C. Manning. Trudeau then coached his son, Justin, to have the same left-wing mindset and to reject genuine Biblical Christianity of which Manning was a prime example. It was a tragic error in judgment, because the trail of blood left behind by communist regimes until the present day bears witness to the evil of totalitarian leadership. Justin already has blood on his hands.

The Lord Jesus Christ said in reference to wolves in sheep's clothing:

> "Wherefore by their fruits ye shall know them." (Matthew 7:20)

SOCIALISM-COMMUNISM'S FRUIT – HATRED: Lenin's violent revolution and murders, Stalin's and accomplice's 62 million killed, Mao's and accomplice's 76 million killed, Zemin's and Xi's hundreds of thousands, or more, killed – many for their organs to be sold, Pol Pot's murder of 1 out of 4 Cambodians, Fidel Castro's killings, North Korea's mass killings, Venezuela's Chavez's and Maduro's killings and driving 1 out of 6 citizens out of the country, et cetera. Not to mention the families and lives ruined forever by the tyranny of these totalitarian regimes everywhere they have taken power.

North America is currently experiencing the beginning of an overt socialist revolution and most people are unaware of what is happening.

> "It is only fair to realize that Communists are at war with the enemies of their class or cause (race/gender/environment in 2020) and that they expect that out of the struggle will come better results than have ever been promised to Christian citizens who sought

victory in war. They have more effective methods than atomic attacks that are better calculated to leave something more than a desert over which to rule." (John Bennett, Christianity and Communism, 1960).

The influence of radical socialists on the Democratic Party is described by Paul Adams in The Epoch Times, p. B4, October 8-14, 2020, in "Judge Barrett and the Bigotry of the Democrats." He wrote:

"The Democratic Party of 2020 is out of step with the beliefs of most Americans and most of those who are inclined to vote for it. It has moved in a more and more extreme direction (with) **endemic and extreme hostility, bias and bigotry to Christians who adhere to the teaching of the faith.** Republican Senator Hawley reminded Minority Leader Schumer about Feinstein's "egregious personal attacks on Judge Barrett's (Catholic) Christian faith...and to abstain from that anti-Catholic, anti-Christian anti-faith vitriol (biting, caustic, sarcastic) in the hearings to come." The ideologically-driven core of younger, angry, secular, cosmopolitan, more affluent and highly-educated "progressive activists" represent the "politically-correct," "Hidden Tribes" white wing (and) 8% of the party. Like Pierre Trudeau in Canada in the 1960s they are using the Democratic Party as their vehicle to impose radical socialism on a naïve and unsuspecting U.S. citizenry. The power of this affluent elite in society lies in its hegemony (powerful or predominating influence) in big business, the academy, entertainment, professional sport, the civil service bureaucracy, and the media. To win elections it needs to persuade enough of the 66% of unideological liberals and moderates to vote Democrat. The challenge for the Democrats, now the party of the affluent and woke, is to hang on to what it can of its traditional working-class, culturally Catholic, family-oriented, patriotic base **while moving ever leftward in its identity politics.**

Now it's time for the Democrats to be held accountable for the terrorist groups and actions of the left, the mayhem, rioting, and violence they've

CHAPTER 9: THE WAY BACK

been unwilling or unable to control, or even acknowledge, much less denounce, in cities they govern."

Dennis Prager said that radical socialism would destroy Liberalism. Kenneth Goff's 1940s statement – "He (a young communist lecturer) called us Liberals, and said we were like armies without generals, or plans to carry out our campaign" – and only by developing trained leadership could we attain to goal of a new world order, or **international Communism**!" The radical leftists or progressives plan to provide one or more of these "generals" to the Democratic Party at some time in the near future, if they can. This is the current state of the Democrats in the U.S.A. and the Liberal Party in Canada. Ideological Marxists will triumph over liberals and moderates who lack an ideologically-driven agenda. It will happen in only a matter of time.

As the American election looms, Democratic Party Speaker of the House, Nancy Pelosi, is intimating that she could take the presidency of the U.S. if a majority doesn't emerge for either President Trump or Joe Biden. Since the Democrats have been trying to oust Trump from the beginning of his mandate it is no surprise that they are planning to do so again in any way possible. Pelosi is vehemently anti-Trump. The leftist forces are preparing themselves to take over the United States of America. The leader of the "Free World" is under siege:

> "Congress hasn't been used to intervene in a presidential election since 1877." (Jack Phillips, Pelosi Raises Possibility of Becoming Acting President in Election Chaos, The Epoch Times, p. A5, October 8-14, 2020)

AMERICAN DEMOCRACY WILL BE SAVED OR LOST BY THE AMERICAN VOTER IN NOVEMBER, 2020.

"FORTRESS AMERICA" UNDER SIEGE

In "Values at the Heart of the Fight for Canada, writer Brad Bird, states with realism and deep concern that –

> "Liberty is in retreat. Today, we do things that 50 years ago would have raised eyebrows. We hire those who check the affirmative action boxes, as per government rules. We kill unborn children in the name of women's rights, with hardly a qualm or second thought. We discourage traditional family roles to appease feminists. (Even in 1959 my mother's doctor recommended I be aborted, given her age of 40. One-parent homes produce confused, and dysfunctional children. We house seniors in care facilities instead of blending them into our families, where tasks, values, wisdom and love were once shared. The new values are discouraging personal initiative, creating social cleavages and adding billions of dollars yearly to the national debt.
>
> Most of us sit idly by as successive Liberal and Conservative governments strengthen state power and promote egalitarianism (classless society), and discourage individualism and debate – actions which characterized Nazism (National Socialism), and communism. **It is a painful irony – and a huge red flag – that the values we defeated in 1945 and with the fall of the Soviet Union in 1991 are now endangering us**."
> (Brad Bird, Values at the Heart of the Fight for Canada, The Epoch Times, p. B1, August 6-12, 2020)

Mr. Bird's assessment of both main political parties as guilty in this decline, is correct. Those Conservatives hoping in Mr. O' Toole's leadership must realize that he has publicly endorsed the LGBTQ2S+ and the Paris Climate accord, both key parts of the global socialist agenda. A Conservative government might slow down the drift to the far left, but it will not stop it.

John Robson wrote in Taking Stock of Canada's Decades-Long Veer to the Left, that according to Andrew Coyne, the Left has been "running the table" on every

CHAPTER 9: THE WAY BACK

imaginable public issue in Canada for decades, from economic to social to foreign policy. (The Epoch Times, p. B4, September 17-24, 2020) This does not bode well for the future of our free democracy. Coyne wrote further:

> "**The energy, the impetus, the advantage today is all on the left.** On issue after issue the left has been orthodoxies long considered invincible, like the taboo on deficits, or opening new territory for the expanding state, from pensions to Pharmacare to a guaranteed annual income. **Perhaps the most startling advances have come in the social issues.** From same-sex marriage to legalized marijuana to assisted suicide, public opinion and legislation seem in a headlong race to see which can undo centuries of custom and precedent the fastest, while across the multiplying fronts on the wars on identity – racial, sexual and the rest – one famous victory follows another." (Ibid)

As the Left gains more and more power and wins legitimacy in the public's eyes, it becomes less and less tolerant of dissenting views, particularly those of conservatives. The leftist momentum has pushed the Conservative Party of Canada into a corner. In the recent leadership race, social conservative Derek Sloan won only 8% of the vote, coming a distant fourth to Erin O'Toole, who won. The new leader did little to contest the table that the left is running.

> "He campaigned for his party's leadership as a true conservative against his supposedly, and actually, "Red Tory" main rival Peter MacKay. But **as soon as he won O'Toole emphasized his pro-choice views, embraced the Paris Climate Accord, and endorsed managed trade**. Perhaps he does not know that the left is running the table. Or perhaps he approves. If so he doesn't need to do anything including run for office. As former world chess champion Garry Kasparov really did say, about

> Russian politics, **There is no good move in a lost position**.
>
> Undeterred by looming public insolvency, private economic collapse, or increasing regional tensions, **the prime minister already has a plan...to move rapidly leftward** if he can locate any files on which it wasn't already done years ago." (Ibid)

A friend of the writer has a 95 year-old father who fought in WW II as a commando in the British SAS, and then in another similar unit before the end of the war. The man told his son recently, concerning Canada's situation:

> "Everything I fought for in WW II was a waste of time."

In discussing the present state of judicial decisions in the arena of human rights, Bob Plamondon in his book, "The Truth About Trudeau, mentioned that in today's Canada, judges rule according to the prevailing public view on issues.

> "As Trudeau hoped, the Charter of Rights and Freedoms provides a check on parliamentarians, which equates to a check on democratic will. The Constitution and Charter are here to stay – without amendments. **If social conservatives or social progressives want to influence the court's interpretation of the Charter, they must first change the views of society.**"

A good example is the **mandatory** Medicare policy established during Trudeau's regime, ensconced in the Charter of Rights. Canadians currently support mandatory Medicare. The past president of the Ontario Medical Association writes:

> "Seventy-three percent of Canadians still find personal or collective pride in universal health care. (BUT) study after study ranks Canadian health care below most other OECD countries. The provincial insurance system that

CHAPTER 9: THE WAY BACK

birthed Medicare in the early 1970s is nothing like the centrally controlled, rationed, managed care entitlement program that politicians play football with today. Canada could have universal health care without having government-run health care. Only fear prevents us from improving our system – fear sold by ideologues, collectivists, and all the rent-seekers who currently get fat at the single-payer (government) trough." (Shawn Whatley, Is Canadians' Pride in Universal Health Care Misplaced? The Epoch Times, p. B2, July 5-11, 2020)

Trudeau's **"mandatory"** is what makes Canada almost unique in this regard. All other OECD countries have successful, alternative private care within their Medicare systems. Canada does not, limiting individual Canadian's freedom of choice.

"Albertans are effectively denied any alternative to government-run health care. Last week, the B.C. Supreme Court dismissed a court challenge by Dr. Brian Day, former head of the Canadian Medical Association, whose surgical clinic in Vancouver provided medical services to patients failed by the public system, in violation of B.C. law. British Columbians remain locked within government-run health care and jeopardizes the few alternatives that currently exist in Canada.

Canadian health care is more costly, has fewer medical resources and reports mediocre outcomes compared to other wealthy countries with universal health care. We also have some of the longest wait times in the world. More than one million patients waited almost 20 weeks on average for medically-necessary care last year – with their subsequent pain, suffering, mental anguish, lost productivity at work and lost leisure time. Delayed access can lead to poorer outcomes, or even death. **Unlike citizens of every other developed country we're stuck with two options – wait for our turn for health care here (and suffer the consequences) or cross the border for treatment elsewhere.**" (Nadeem Esmail and Bacchus Barua, Ruling locks patients into government-run health care only, The Calgary Sun, September 16, 2020)

Socialism translates to **"mandatory"** in every area that it formulates public policy. Trudeau's mandatory adoption of the metric system took 10 years and a billion dollars to implement across the country. He wanted to "go European" following many social democratic and communist countries – while ignoring our closest allies, the U.S. and U.K. that continued successfully with the Imperial system – whom he termed "dinosaurs." (Bob Plamondon, The Truth About Trudeau, 2008)

Through the progressives systematic re-programing of society through co-opting the educational system most of the judicial rulings now go against society's former Judeo-Christian values, and rule according to leftist dictates. If those who value our past cultural traditions wish to see a return to former cultural and moral standards then society will have to change. The only thing that could cause such a catastrophic sea change in moral outlook nationally would be a nationwide revival of the Christian churches; a Great Awakening among God's people and a renewed evangelistic movement from the churches. There seems to be no indication to the present that such a revival is imminent, only further spiritual decline. COVID-19 has done much to fragment and scatter the already weakened local churches, preventing Christians from meeting together in person, thereby weakening individual lives and exacerbating the spiritual decline.

COVID-19 seems to be fulfilling the goals of the left-wing agenda. It has raised Trudeau in the polls through his massive money handouts. It has caused Donald Trump the possibility of defeat in the November U.S. election through damage to the economy, BLM riots and the

CHAPTER 9: THE WAY BACK

surge in coronavirus infections in many states. America is in great jeopardy in July, 2020.

Aberhart's and Manning's governments lasted 33 years (1935-1968) and left no bodies in the streets, no hatred to their fellow man, no bloody repression and communist tactics to enforce their rule, and eliminate opposition. Their motivation? Love for their God first, and then love toward their fellow man; in Mr. Aberhart's case, love for the disenfranchised students he taught in high school, and wanted to help regain their lives during the Great Depression.

Albertans and Canadians would be wise to consider their options in 2020 and beyond. We are in WW III for our future and freedom. Will we opt for socialism-communism in the years to come or return to "God's Government," as the Aberhart-Manning years were called? It will require taking a stand that is extremely unpopular with the left-wing media, politicians and special interest groups. But it is the only way back to our traditional Judeo-Christian cultural foundation for Canada. It is our only hope and it will take sacrifice.

Communism does not work! Not in Russia, not in China or in any other countries where it has been tried. There is not one communist country that has allowed everyone to have an equal share of all property. Every communist country has made the government the OWNER and the BOSS. Citizens are deprived of their property and become slaves..."the communist proletariat," to the leaders, dictators, office holders, and hoodlums of the regime...the "genuine communist bourgeoisie," if you like.

> "There is no true Communism – that is, a community of goods. The term is a wrong name to lead poor people in

the hope of "sharing the wealth" of the rich. The tragic result is that all end up sharing poverty, heartache, disappointment, drudgery and slavery."

Witness Venezuela, North Korea, the Eastern bloc countries, etc. Read a real life account under communism in Appendix 4. If Communist China had not 'used' the Western democracies, and sucked their technology like a vampire, manipulating their trust and good will in the process, its state-controlled economy would have long since crumbled and the CCP would be history.

Some socialists appeal to the parable of the Good Samaritan in the Bible as a model for giving. Kamala Harris, Joe Biden's VP nomination uses the parable often in her campaigning, an oxymoron called Christian Socialism. It is a farce. She's a committed leftist.

> "Let us suppose that the Samaritan is a big, strong man capable of intimidating others. He sees several prosperous travelers walking by. He accosts the travelers and threatens them with his staff unless they give money for the wounded man's care. Would we hold that Samaritan in high regard today? Not likely. And why? Because of his use of force. **That is the crucial difference between socialism and Christianity. Socialist "giving" is compulsory. Christian giving is voluntary.** The former relies on force imposed from without. The latter acts from grace within. **Christian socialism is literally an oxymoron** (contradictory ideas): **There is no such thing as "compulsory charity."** When politicians use the powers of the state to give financial assistance to others, they are proposing to do so using other people's money, not their own. That's a false, counterfeit charity, quite the opposite of the good Samaritan's genuine (i.e., voluntary) charity." (Mark Hendrickson, Kamala Harris, the Good Samaritan, and the Christian Socialism Oxymoron, The Epoch Times, p. B5, September 3-9. 2020)

CHAPTER 9: THE WAY BACK

As a system of thought socialism-communism is a compound of half-truth and positive error, and is an essential threat to personal and political freedom, as illustrated by the "Christian socialism" oxymoron above. It cannot be defeated by negative propaganda accompanied by religious hostility or inspired by those who benefit from Western capitalism. And it cannot be overcome by military power alone.

Genuine Bible Christianity is the only weapon that can effectively oppose and defeat left-wing progressive socialism-communism in today's world. A revival of the Christian Church would defeat Marxism. It is either Christ or Marx. God back and read Chapter 7 if you have any difficulty deciding.

> "It can be prevented only by those who have a sounder faith and a better program to meet human needs and unsolved problems.
>
> Communism has been strong where Christians and churches have been weak...the errors of Communism are in large part the result of the failure of Christians, and of the Christian churches, to be true to the revolutionary implications of their own faith.
>
> It is a responsibility of Christians to resist its extension in the world." (John Bennett, Christianity and Communism Today, 1960)

Both Aberhart and Manning entered politics during the Great Depression in 1933 through a Christian motivation with a sole desire to help people solve their problems of poverty, unemployment and hopelessness, when no other political parties or leaders would answer their call for help (B. Brennan, 2008).

Manning's goal in Alberta was to show how a society could be established in Alberta that was superior to anything that socialism or communism could produce. He succeeded. (B. Brennan, The Good Steward: The Ernest C. Manning Story, 2008)

> "For Albertans this book by Brian Brennon is a confirmation of identity: for Canadians a genuine revelation."

Aberhart's and Manning's legacies should be publicized for every Albertan and Canadian to read. The schools should teach the younger generation their stories. Their contributions to society should not be buried, as the left-wing progressives would like, but published for all to hear and read. They were both *Good Samaritans* to the people of Alberta and Canada. From Mr. Aberhart's Funeral Message conducted by a pastor friend (Appendix 5) we read the following:

> "When no voice was speaking for them, and no statesman had any solution, when orthodox politics and orthodox finance had utterly failed to shed any ray of hope, Mr. Aberhart was forced by conviction and desperation to launch out into the untried seas of political action.
>
> And every man or woman who recalls the "jungles" of Canada and the roaming desperate, unwanted youth, will recall with gratitude this Friend whom Conservative Leader Graydon yesterday in Ottawa called, "a pioneer in social and economic reform."
>
> Alongside his deep concern for young people was his sympathy for the poor. One of Alberta's best known men said to me in a letter yesterday, "What kept so many people in Alberta loyal to him was the feeling that he was interested in the poor people; and many felt that no matter how dark the situation was, some day Mr.

CHAPTER 9: THE WAY BACK

Aberhart would see that justice was done to them." These people now echo David's words:

> *"Know ye not that a prince and a great man is fallen this day?" (2 Samuel 3:38)*

Mr. Aberhart mentored Ernest Manning as a young man in his own home and later, together with his best friend, left his honored place as Principal of Crescent Heights High School in Calgary to take on the thankless work as Premier of Alberta for 8 years, which eventually wore down his health and cost him a shorter life. William Aberhart's legacy should never be forgotten. He was a Christian leader, and servant of the people, as Mr. Manning would later become also. Both men continued their radio preaching and teaching ministries while they faithfully carried out their political roles.

THE SPIRITUAL ISSUES INVOLVED

Personal salvation is the most important need in life (See Appendix 1). Ernest Manning always emphasized this point in his Christian counsel and preaching. Once asked, "What would he say if his grand-children wanted to enter public life?" He said that he would consent – with one reservation:

> "Your number one concern in life should be your personal relationship to Jesus Christ. He's the Sovereign Lord of everyone. Settle that matter to start with. It'll do more to change your life and stabilize your life than any single thing you can do. Ambition is a wonderful thing. But in the process, don't barge off on your own. Just keep that other factor in mind: is this what God wants me to do?" (Brennan, 2008)

"FORTRESS AMERICA" UNDER SIEGE

Mr. Manning, now home with his Lord and Savior, would address this same urgent appeal to each and every one who has opened even one page of this book to read it. That is, "Are you saved?" "If not; why not?"

There are three attitudes towards one's life goals and possessions illustrated in Jesus' parable of the poor man who was robbed on the Jericho Road.

The first is the materialistic attitude of the robber:

> "What is thine is mine, and I'm going to get it anyway I can." Many people are like that."

The second is the materialistic attitude shown by the Levite and by the Priest, who both passed by the poor man who had been robbed and beaten:

> "What is mine is mine, and I'm going to keep it."

Multitudes of good people let the less fortunate stay "wounded by the roadside." The correct spiritual and material attitude was demonstrated by the *Good Samaritan*:

> "What is mine is thine if thou needest it more than I do."

O, how little place there would be for the "share the wealth" propaganda of the Communists if all of us had this helpful attitude toward our fellow man! May God help us to have it."

William Aberhart did not want to leave his occupation as a Principal to go into the blood sport of politics (Appendix 5). Nor was Ernest Manning's first desire to be in politics. But both men did it out of a concern for

CHAPTER 9: THE WAY BACK

the people of Alberta who were in great distress at that time. In Manning's own words:

> "It was a Christian motivation that put us into politics. I had no desire to go into politics, and I know he didn't. It was a concern for people and a desire to help solve their problems. I'd just as soon be busy with my Bible work.
>
> Our government's basic philosophy was very humanitarian. Our primary emphasis was on the individual, not the masses. If you looked after the individual, the masses would take care of themselves. But our approach to meeting those social needs was through the private enterprise system." (B. Brennan, The Good Steward: The Ernest C. Manning Story, 2008)

Reverend Harrison Villett, a personal friend of Aberhart's for twenty years, gave Premier Aberhart's Funeral Service message on May 30, 1943. Here is an extract confirming the man as a *Good Samaritan*:

> "I saw him sacrificing his place of security, of honor in the neighborhood, his place of influence and service – deliberately taking on a task that would bring heartache, and eventually shorten his days, for a hope that possessed his soul. No responsible man in Canada has ever doubted his sincerity, nor has anyone questioned his motive." (H. Villett, The Prophetic Voice, June, 1943)

Aberhart and Manning can provide Canadians a way back to free democracy if their legacies are promoted and made known to the citizens of our individual provinces and the Canadian public in general.

> *"For the transgression of a land many are the princes thereof: but by a man of understanding and knowledge the state thereof shall be prolonged." (Proverbs 28:2)*

If the more fortunate had always practiced the *Good Samaritan* spirit with the less fortunate, as Manning and Aberhart demonstrated, there would be less cause for dissatisfaction with the democratic and capitalistic way of life and government. Had even those who profess to be Christians done this, it is doubtful if Communism would ever have started. None of us can deny that we need to have more real brotherly love toward others, and more kindness toward all who need our help.

It has often been pointed out that Communism could only have been developed on soil prepared by dead and backslidden Christianity.

> "He asks: "What is the cause of this [the atheism of Communism]?" He answers: "It is, I hold, because it originates, chiefly through the fault of a Christian world unfaithful to its own principles, in a profound sense of resentment, not only against the Christian world, but – and here lies the tragedy – against Christianity itself." (John Bennett, Christianity and Communism Today, 1960)

Nicolas Berdyaev, a victim of Russian Communism's anti-Christian policy and teachings, said in summary;

> "The sins of Christians, the sins of the historical churches, have been very great, and these sins bring with them their just punishment."

That 'just punishment' was socialism-communism in the form of the U.S.S.R., and the resulting persecution of the church and the population as a whole. Everybody suffered as we see in Venezuela today.

Canada is moving in the same direction in 2020.

CHAPTER 9: THE WAY BACK

Ernest Manning agonized over the condition of the Christian churches early in his ministry. Reacting to Prime Minister Pierre Trudeau's public use of Jesus Christ's Name in a sacrilegious answer to a Regina high school student's question, he wrote:

> "Where are our churches, our Christian ministers, our community leaders, our Christian Activists? How long, O God, how long?" (The Face of the Sky – Part 2, 1972, Back to the Bible Hour pamphlet)

He was appalled that the students only laughed at Trudeau's statement.

> "Children and young people reflect the spiritual and moral standards of the homes from which they come. This is a sobering thought." (Ibid)

He gave this same warning in a radio address given in Chicago in 1948:

> "If there is to be a miraculous healing of the mortal wounds from which Christian civilization is dying today, it will not be brought about by governments or by recovery programs, nor by force of arms, or iron curtains and atomic bombs. It will come to pass only when men and women profess the Name of Christ, humble themselves before God and prayerfully seek His face in unconditional surrender to His blessed will." (read Appendix 3 for the full message)

Mr. Manning recognized that the Canadian churches faced a very real danger from materialism in their conflict with Communism:

> "There are more Christians in Russia today than at any time in its history. Persecution has strengthened the believers and caused them to realize that they are

missionaries, they are witnesses. The evangelical faith has increased ten times in the last 50 years. **Christians in Russia are praying for us. They are praying that we might not succumb to our materialism, for our materialism is more dangerous than their materialism."** (E. Manning, The Face of the Sky – Part 2, 1972, Back to the Bible Hour pamphlet)

Solzhenitsyn, the great 20th Century Russian author, was imprisoned in concentration camps after WW II. His expose of communism in "The Gulag Archipelago," laid bare the malicious heart of Marxism-Leninism. A decorated soldier in the Red Army in WW II, he too, experienced the gulag for expressing his concerns. In exile in the U.S.,

> "He also raised a challenge to the West, chastising us for our own loss of spirit and our growing materialism." (Gary Gregg, Remembering Solzhenitsyn and the Brutality of the Gulag, The Epoch Times, December 21-27, 2018)

The material blessings bestowed by God upon our Western democracies has not made us more humble and dependent upon God but more selfish in our pursuit of material wealth, possessions and prestige; and further from God in our churches and spiritual lives.

> "Even *Forbes* magazine, the voice of big business, raised the alarm last week...concern over the economic conditions that give rise to racism. *Forbes* reported, "The bottom 50% (of the U.S. population) saw essentially zero net gain in wealth over those 30 years, driving their already meagre share of total wealth down to just 1% from 4%. Another survey showed the wealthiest 1% of U.S. families held 40% of all wealth and the bottom 90% held less than 25%. (Tarek Fatah, The American Uprising, The Calgary Sun, June 4, 2020)

CHAPTER 9: THE WAY BACK

In the United States, and Canada for that matter, the divide between the rich and poor is increasing while the spiritual life of the churches is becoming weaker and weaker. This is the perfect formula for the rise of socialism-communism.

Manning saw the spiritual decline of Western society in 1971/72, writing this rebuke:

> "The sacrilegious portrayal of Christ in such productions as "Jesus Christ Superstar," and the musical, "Godspell," can only be described as blasphemy, and it is a significant sign of the approaching universal apostasy which will mark the end of this current age." (E. Manning, The Face of the Sky – Part 1, 1971, Back to the Bible Hour pamphlet)

> "Speaking of the future, the scriptures affirm that this present age will terminate in a world-wide state of crisis. The society of the period when the predicted crisis will develop will be characterized by unprecedented material progress, with great emphasis on human self-sufficiency but an abandonment of faith in and respect for God's holiness and divine authority." (E. Manning, The Face of the Sky – Part 2, 1972, Back to the Bible Hour pamphlet)

Signs of the end of the Church age are given in the Bible. Falling away from the Word of God and materialism will be the hallmarks of this decline, and they will debilitate the Western churches which have been God's main instrument for transforming society and evangelizing the world since the Reformation.

> *"Let no man deceive you by any means: for that day shall not come, except there come a falling away first, and that man of sin be revealed, the son of perdition;"* (2 Thessalonians 2:3)

"FORTRESS AMERICA" UNDER SIEGE

In 1923, William Aberhart preached "The Trend of Religion down the Ages," and concluded his message by pointing out the falling away from God's Word in his day. Mr. Manning continued preaching the same message as his mentor did, but the churches continued to move further and further away from sound doctrine and separation from the world.

> "During the last half of the 18th century, and most of the 19th the stage of heresy set in under the guise of <u>higher criticism</u>. Men generally questioned the reliability of the Scriptures, and scoffing began at the preaching of the blood. A new proposal was made by them to solve the world's troubles. They claimed that social evolution and reformation would gradually and finally create conditions in which the human race would find their <u>Utopia</u>. We are now in the midst of other movements, and the final stage of apostasy, into which the world is fast rushing, is yet before us." (reprinted in The Prophetic Voice, November, 1948)

Now, almost 100 years later, the Western church is almost impotent in its effect on society. Under these circumstances socialism has had little opposition in implementing its agenda. It is steamrolling on.

Laodicea, the church at the time of the Lord's return, is described by Jesus Christ in these words:

> *"So then because thou art lukewarm, and neither cold nor hot, I will spue thee out of my mouth. Because thou sayest, I am rich, and increased with goods, and have need of nothing; and knowest not that thou art wretched, and miserable, and poor, and blind, and naked:"* (Revelation 3:16-17)

CHAPTER 9: THE WAY BACK

The Laodicean church is a weak church, a carnal church, a materialistic church and a church unable to combat and resist the growing tide of socialism-communism that is sweeping over the Western world. Most professing Christians in these churches are unsaved or badly backslidden. They will not be able to resist being swept, like Lot or a lost heathen, into an international socialist dictatorship. Jesus Christ will personally intervene to rapture out His Church just prior to the revelation of the Antichrist and his totalitarian government.

Before that happens, Mr. Manning gave advice to those who do not yet know the Lord.

> "There is little hope that society will act on their warning any more than on the far more reliable information and counsel of God, revealed in Holy Writ. Remedial action therefore becomes a matter for individual persons and families. It is something you should think about and discuss with your loved ones. God has been changing the lifestyle of men ever since Christ died and rose again. He will change your life course if you will let Him. He will assure your future for time and eternity if you will receive His Son as your personal Savior and make Him the Lord of your life. This is God's solution for your dilemma." (E. Manning, The Face of the Sky – Part 2, 1972, Back to the Bible Hour pamphlet)

The concerned reader should turn to Appendix 1 and read "The Gospel of Jesus Christ," to deal with their need for Biblical salvation. Backslidden Christians should turn to Christ's warning for the Laodicean Church and act accordingly. We all are in this together.

> "As many as I love, I rebuke and chasten: be zealous therefore, and repent. Behold, I stand at the door, and

> knock: if any man hear my voice, and open the door, I will come in to him, and will sup with him, and he with me." (Revelation 3:19-20)

Meanwhile, those who treasure our free democracy must continue to oppose the encroachment of socialism-communism upon our liberties and our freedoms here in Alberta and Canada as a whole. We must pray for America our neighbor.

We must seek a revival in our own heart, church, community and nation. That is exactly what Ernest C. Manning preached for so many years in Alberta before he went home to be with the Lord in 1996. The one thing that will save the world from Socialism – Communism, and the resulting revolution of anarchy such as we see in the U.S. in June, 2020, is a genuine revival of Christianity. Christians must NOT give up, but fight "the good fight of faith."

> "Genuine Bible Christianity is the greatest force in this world to bring about the transformation of attitude and lifestyle on the part of those who appropriate the salvation of God available in Jesus Christ. Through it spiritual revival has transformed nations." (The Hon. Ernest C. Manning)

SAVED OUT OF SOCIALISM – COMMUNISM

Perhaps it is best to illustrate how a dedicated Communist got saved and became a gospel witness and servant of Jesus Christ. This is the testimony of Kenneth Goff extracted from Chapter 6, Confessions of Stalin's Agent (in E. J. Daniels, The Red Devil of Communism, 1954)

CHAPTER 9: THE WAY BACK

> "My parents were old-fashioned Christians. Sunday mornings always found the entire family in Church. It was a little white frame building. Here we barefooted boys would gather with other youngsters and be taught from the pages of God's Word. After Sunday school we joined our parents for morning worship. Afterward we had a picnic dinner on the Church lawn."

Kenneth's family moved to a new church in town when their old building was sold. The new pastor was a Modernist teaching a Social Gospel. He undermined the young man's faith in the Bible and the fundamental Christian doctrines. This attack continued into high school where evolutionary dogma further contaminated him. In the years following, Kenneth was invited to Communist lectures and rallies, and ended up joining the Communist Party U.S.A.

> "Already in our generation, men are teaching in our Sunday Schools that the Bible is made up largely of myths and fables. Once confidence in the literal infallibility of Holy Writ is undermined, how easy it will be for false teachers to persuade the next generation to accept any false philosophy they choose to advance." (E. Manning, World Conditions in the Last Days, Back to the Bible Hour pamphlet no. 43)

Time passed and he became a hardened and committed atheistic Communist. He married a clever and hardened fellow Communist, Doris Berger.

Then something miraculous happened. In Kenneth Goff's own words:

> "One evening Mrs. Goff and I were together in the kitchen. I have no way of explaining what caused me to start singing a hymn learned at home in my boyhood,

"Rescue the Perishing." It was the farthest thing from my mind to chant such a melody, because I was then taking my Communism very seriously. My back was turned to Mrs. Goff as I sang the words:

> "Down in the human heart,
> Crushed by the tempter;
> Feelings lie buried,
> That grace can restore.
> Touched by a loving heart,
> Wakened by kindness,
> Chords that are broken
> Will vibrate once more."

I heard my hardened Bolshevik wife sobbing.

The entire episode made me mad. Communists are not supposed to cry. I asked what was ailing her any way!

The tears continued to flow. She said that she knew in her heart that Jesus Christ was different than the Communists explained; that He was truly God on our earth; that heaven was real; that Christ could make her life clean; and true Christians were the only truly happy people in the world.

I flew into a rage and told her to forget that nonsense. I promised that I would never again be guilty of singing such bunk in her presence.

She refused to listen to me and was miraculously converted a short time later. It was in the dead of winter and the preacher had to cut a hole in the ice to baptize her.

I tried to make myself believe she had "gone crazy over religion." But I knew better! Childhood memories came vividly before me.

CHAPTER 9: THE WAY BACK

> She continued to pray for me...and before long those prayers were answered. And that is the real reason why I left the Communist Party."

How important it is for young people to be taught God's Word and for their parents to keep them in a good Bible-believing local church. Mr. Goff's life was nearly destroyed by a Modernist minister and a secular education. Christian parents must –

> "Train up a child in the way he should go: and when he is old, he will not depart from it." (Proverbs 22:4)

The greatest weapon against any false religion, including Socialism-Communism is the Gospel of Jesus Christ, genuine Bible Christianity as Ernest Manning put it. See Appendix 1.

> "Genuine Christianity is the most potent force in the world to change human nature through the miracle of a spiritual new birth. Men born again are not likely to steal or destroy or embezzle."

> "Human nature despite education, science, sociology and religion, without Christ, inclines deeper and deeper into the swamps of immorality. How different is the attitude and inclination of men who have been made into new creatures through a spiritual new birth by receiving Jesus Christ into their lives. This is the one effective antidote to the moral poison that is spreading through all strata (layers) of society today. Please help us bring this truth home to the Canadian people." (E. Manning, The Face of the Sky – Part 1, 1971, Canada's National Back to the Bible Hour pamphlet)

MANNING'S ADVICE FOR CONCERNED CANADIANS

Ernest Manning spent nearly his whole working life in politics; 8 years as an Alberta Cabinet Minister, 25 years as Alberta's Premier – occupying several portfolios at the same time, including Attorney General for 13 years – and finally, 13 years as an appointed Member of the Canadian Senate in Ottawa.

Mr. Manning's wise political and spiritual advice to Canadians to preserve their free democracy is of grave importance today, for the present Liberal government of Justin Trudeau is showing a tendency toward totalitarianism. Manning wrote concerning a news article on the run-up to the 1971 U.S. national election between a far-left leaning Democratic Party and the conservative Republicans:

> "When the rhetorical decibel count rises in the fall, neither the Democrats nor the Republicans will supply more light than heat as they work for votes.
>
> This article reflects two things. First, the magnitude of the public issues confronting society and the tendency of political parties to sacrifice a clear, honest approach to major problems in the hope of gaining political advantage over their opponents. The writer points to the disgust and frustration this creates among genuinely concerned citizens, especially those committed to Christian principles of life and conduct.
>
> In the second place, the article points out the danger of Christians failing to assume their responsibilities in the decision making processes of society, leading to moral battles being lost by default. Concerned Christians should make it their business to see that honest, constructive God-fearing men are recruited to stand for election, men whom concerned citizens can

conscientiously support, knowing they will not compromise what is right after they are elected.

Our national political parties as such, command such confidence. The character and the convictions of the individual candidate therefore becomes an important consideration. What we are seeking to do is to recruit and mobilize a mighty national force for good, a force of men and women who respect God and righteousness, and truth; and who are prepared to speak out against that which is destructive and degrading, promoted by men who leave God out of their judgments." (Ernest Manning, The Face of the Sky – Part 2, 1972, Canada's National Back to the Bible Hour pamphlet)

Mr. Manning wrote again on the sanctity of life based upon a Toronto news report in The People's Magazine:

> "Killing a child before birth is as wrong as killing a child shortly after birth. When we get used to killing the not-yet-born because we do not want them, on the excuse that they are not yet fully human, and we have very quickly grown used to it, it will be easier to decide to kill the already born – the old and the senile who are often not wanted.
>
> Concerned men and women can stem the evil tides in our permissive society, and reverse evil trends, if they will speak up and use every legitimate means to make their influence felt in the arenas where social and political decisions are made. I urge all such to look about you in your own community and at the national level. I am certain you can pin-point several major issues of important concern in which you could mobilize constructive concern to actively and vigorously support what is morally right and to oppose any position that is morally wrong."

The writer's brother was recently euthanized in Winnipeg after the Trudeau government legalized MAiD (Medical Assistance in Dying) in 2016. It is trying to loosen the restrictions and make it easier to die in 2020.

As the same government seeks to disarm law-abiding Canadians, the writer received a May, 2020 letter in the mail from The National Firearms Association. In it was the following urgent appeal concerning their up-coming court challenge against the federal government over Trudeau's draconian gun ban.

> "As you know, the NFA was founded to be the voice of law-abiding gun owners and firearms enthusiasts across Canada. We are the last and greatest defence against an overreaching, totalitarian federal government determined to OUTLAW GUNS and STRIP US OF OUR FREEDOMS. If you abandon the NFA today, I fear Justin Trudeau's gun ban will go ahead. And, once we lose our rights as firearms owners, we'll never get them back." (Sheldon Clare, President – Canada's National Firearms Association)

On May 10, 2020, the writer received a letter from the RCMP titled, **Announcement of a Firearms Prohibition**, laying out the terms and conditions of the "newly prohibited firearms." The left-wing is no longer hiding their intentions. They are wide out in the open opposing free democracy and citizens' rights to their private property. There is a flood of news over these issues in the daily conservative newspapers, particularly in The Epoch Times and The Calgary Sun.

The 2019 election of a conservative government in Alberta has brought more freedom to the people in the

CHAPTER 9: THE WAY BACK

sphere of education. Premier Jason Kenny announced, together with the Education Minister, on May 28, 2020:

> "The UCP (United Conservative Party) introduced the new Choice in Education Act (Bill 15) making several changes to the Education Act for the K-12 system. School choice and the freedom of parents to direct their kids' education is not a policy preference, it is a fundamental human right. The legislation enshrines the belief of Albertans in freedom, diversity, pluralism and choice. We believe that parents know better than politicians or bureaucrats about what is in the best interest of their kids. I am proud to say that Alberta is the leader in choice available to families, and provides parents with more opportunities for their children's education than anywhere else in Canada." (Eva Ferguson, Bill Spurs Concerns, Calgary Sun, May 29, 2020)

As expected, the Alberta Teacher's Association (Union) opposed the Bill, as well as advocates against the religious base, who complained about the Premier's talk,

> "Expanding school choice must never come at the expense of public education",...and he's referring to the religious portion of society who may not want to teach their kids about evolution, or gender diversity and many other important things."

Notley's NDP socialist government would never have implemented such legislation. If anything, it would have curtailed more parental choice for their children's education.

GOD IS SPEAKING – BUT WILL WE LISTEN?

While we could go on with more examples of resisting the onslaught of socialism upon our freedoms it is wise to remember in ending, Manning's words in one of his messages:

> "There are entrenched trends in materialistic society that contain the seeds of self-destruction spiritually, morally, socially, economically and politically. Both the Christian minority and the secular majority that dominate society are being swept along by relentless tides towards the ultimate destruction of society itself. Man's best efforts to recover himself from these trends are proving futile, and we are rapidly reaching the point of no return."

A similar assessment of our moral condition is given in the Epoch Times, "How the Spectre of Communism is Ruling Our World," Using the Law for Evil, Chapter 10, 2020). Legal scholar Harold Berman wrote as follows:

> "The law must be believed in; otherwise it exists in name only." The latter option entails a slippery slope of moral decline, creating a downward cycle in which the law and the state of society compete in a race to reach the bottom. In either case, society at large would have no way out of this demonic vortex."

National repentance and a return to God and His Word is the only thing that will spare Canada from God's judgment. Manning's warnings go back many years, and still God in mercy has withheld His judgment, waiting for Albertans and Canadians in general to respond. God continues to speak. COVID-19 is a wake-up call. Will anyone listen and respond?

CHAPTER 9: THE WAY BACK

God spoke to the Western democracies during WW II, with military defeats and setbacks. By miracle after miracle both Britain and Malta escaped invasion and certain defeat in 1940.

Lt.-General Sir William Dobbie, Britain's Governor of Malta during the great blitz in 1940-42 recognized God's hand in the great deliverances and ultimate victory in WW II over Nazi Germany. He was a genuine Bible-believing Christian, like Ernest Manning, saved at 14 years of age.

> "In June, 1940, the siege of Malta began. Our resources both of material and personnel were woefully inadequate...so we turned to Him Who alone is the giver of victory. I was greatly encouraged by a personal telegram from the Chief of the Imperial General Staff. It contained a scriptural reference:
>
> "Ye shall not fear them: for the LORD your God he shall fight for you." (Deuteronomy 3:22)
>
> The help which God gave was very obvious and real. The same help was noticed at the time of the withdrawal from Dunkirk, and during the "Battle of Britain." It certainly was so in the "Battle of Malta." Why did Italy not attempt the invasion we expected? Why did the Germans not invade Britain immediately after Dunkirk? The only reason I can find, is that in each case God's restraining hand kept them from attacking us when we were so weak and ill-prepared to meet such an attack." (Lt.-General Sir William Dobbie, A Very Present Help, 1945)

During the "Battle of Malta," 10 enemy fighter planes were shot down for every British plane lost (Flying Officer George Beurling, Malta Spitfire – The Story of a Fighter Pilot, 1943). Mr. Beurling was a Canadian ace.

William Dobbie testified of his conversion to Jesus Christ when God in His mercy, "caused me to feel the weight and the burden of my sins. It was a heavy burden, a crushing burden, and one which made me feel miserable, and from which I greatly desired relief. On the first Sunday of November, 1893, I realized for the first time, though I had often heard it before, that Jesus Christ, the Son of God, had come to this earth for the express purpose of laying down His life as the Atonement for my sin, in order to deliver me from its penalty and power, so that I might go free. Burdened as I was with the guilt of my sin, I realized that this remedy exactly met my need, and I then and there accepted Jesus Christ as my Saviour, on the grounds that by His death He had settled my sin debt once for all, and that, therefore, I went free. That was the turning point in my life." As a genuine Christian like Ernest C. Manning, British General William Dobbie spoke from experience, and with authority about God's dealings with nations.

> "There is no doubt that during this Second World War God has been speaking to the nations, our own included, just as He did in the previous world war. It is possible that we did not pay attention to what He said to us then, and that may be the reason why He has had to speak again. God's voice surely has been plain. We do well to take heed.
>
> God has been speaking – *"Beware **lest thou forget** the Lord thy God...And that thou say in thine heart, 'My power and the might of mine hand hath gotten me this wealth. For it is He who giveth thee power to get wealth.'"* (Deuteronomy 8:11, 17 and 18)
>
> It is true that our cause is just and righteous. But are we righteous? It must be confessed that we are not...there

CHAPTER 9: THE WAY BACK

is much in our national life which must be displeasing to Him. In spite of the way God has been speaking to us, both in judgment and in mercy, we as a nation have not turned to Him. We have not discarded or turned from many things which we know are abhorrent to Him (if we think at all). He is still largely crowded out of our life, and is ignored and disregarded by us – all this in spite of what He has done for us. May God open the eyes of our nation to see, and open their ears to hear, and may we humbly acknowledge our sin and turn to Him. It is not enough to have a righteous cause. We need righteous people as well.

There is only one Foundation on which our nation can safely build, and that is Christ, the Rock of Ages. God grant that our nation may build on Him." (See Appendix 1)

General Dobbie's advice in 1944 still applies today, notwithstanding the failures of the professing Christian churches and the worldliness of so many of God's saved children.

> "Some years ago I was asked to address an Armistice Day gathering on the subject, "Has Christianity failed?" But in one sense it does not matter very much whether or not Christianity has failed, especially as a number of conflicting views may be held about the subject. **But what does matter is that Christ has not failed, and no one who has any personal experience of Him can doubt that statement. That is a sure and certain fact."**
> (Lt.-General Sir William Dobbie, A Very Present Help, 1945)

Isn't that exactly what the aged Ernest C. Manning told his granddaughter? (p. 80)

"FORTRESS AMERICA" UNDER SIEGE

The Western democracies, including Canada and the United States, are on a much less sure footing in 2020 than they were in 1944/45, when God granted them victory over Germany and Japan. China, Russia and Iran are now boldly opposing the Free World, and the possibility exists of defeat if another military conflict occurs. Canada has utterly rejected God's Word in its institutions and could forfeit His mercy if we continue in our rebellion.

> **"War is God's judgment on sin here; and Hell is God's judgment on sin hereafter."** (author unknown)

The world is rapidly approaching another crisis where God's judgment on sin here will come to pass. It will be much worse than WW II.

Both Canada and the United States have been thoroughly infiltrated and weakened internally by left-wing Marxist ideology which has gradually transformed our societies toward radical socialism and immoral cesspools, en route to a global dictatorship. The U.S. has a larger Christian remnant than Canada but is still being shaken to the core by the socialist juggernaut that is trying to remove Donald Trump from office. Canada has nearly succumbed to the leftist agenda with the far-left Trudeau government in power in Ottawa today. Free elections upon which both of our democracies depend still exist, but can easily be lost, if the communist-inspired destabilization continues unabated. The ballot box is still our only option.

Continental European democracies are in a more advanced stage of socialist decline than the U.S. They are much more openly sympathetic toward the legacy of

CHAPTER 9: THE WAY BACK

Karl Marx, especially within the European Union. Their survival is more in doubt with Russia and China seeking to break them away from their alliance with the United States. Socialism will win out in the end for a brief period. But we must still fight for our freedom, no matter what.

The protracted closure of the U.S. – Canadian border is another way of slowly separating key allies at a time when radical socialists are attempting to overthrow the American president and his conservative Republicans. COVID-19 is a pretext for this socialist strategy of dividing and conquering.

Only a miracle of God can deliver our country and the other Western democracies from an impending totalitarian international socialist take over. Manning saw this coming and warned us. God is still speaking through troubles and calamities afflicting our democracies. The COVID-19 'scamdemic' is a prime, current example. Yet still, very few people are listening. They are blinded by the god of this world, Satan.

Our free democracy, the depository of our own personal freedoms, may soon be lost through internal and/or external conflict if we continue to ignore the warning signs. If we do not start listening to God, the God of Israel, and respond to Him in repentance there will be no deliverance for Canada or the United States.

> *"Righteousness exalteth a nation: but sin is a reproach to any people." (Proverbs 14:34)*

"FORTRESS AMERICA" UNDER SIEGE

"Blessed is the nation whose God is the LORD; and the people whom he hath chosen for his own inheritance." (Psalm 34:12)

The Old Testament Book of Jonah documents how a wicked nation, Assyria, with its capital at Nineveh repented of its sin, from its king downward, through the preaching of the prophet Jonah and saw God's miracle of mercy defer His imminent judgment. We are at that point today. May God have mercy on us all! We need a MIRACLE! Pray, Christian, pray! Amen!

EPILOGUE & PERSONAL TESTIMONY: SOCIALISM-COMMUNISM OR CHRISTIANITY?

That is Our Choice

"Thus saith the LORD, Stand ye in the ways, and see, and ask for the old paths, where is the good way, and walk therein, and ye shall find rest for your souls. But they said, We will not walk therein."

Jeremiah 6:16

"FORTRESS AMERICA" UNDER SIEGE

Christianity and Communism are at war today. Both are revolutionary in nature. So, Communism is against Christianity. They are irreconcilable.

> "The conflict between Christianity and Communism is closely related to the conflict between Democracy and Communism, in so far that Democracy stands for the continued openness of society that keeps the power of old and new regimes alike under criticism and provides the means by which injustices can be corrected. **The institutions of spiritual and cultural freedom on which this "openness" depends have grown in soil prepared by Christianity.** Without them Christians themselves are likely to be driven underground or their religious expression so limited that there can be no public teaching of the faith. Also, without them the rights of expression that Christians regard as essential to the development of persons are consciously and systematically denied." (John Bennett, Christianity and Communism Today, 1960).

"The communist spectre is tied to Satan. It derives its energy from the hatred that wells up in the human heart." (The Epoch Times, "How the Spectre of Communism is Ruling Our World," Introduction, 2020).

"**<u>Power</u> is always the core of Marxist political theory.** The instigation of revolution can be divided into the following steps:

1. Foment hatred and discord among the people;
2. Deceive the public with lies and establish a "revolutionary united front;"
3. Defeat the forces of resistance one at a time;

EPILOGUE

4. Use violence to create an atmosphere of chaos and terror;
5. Launch a coup to seize power;
6. Suppress the "reactionaries," (those in opposition);
7. Build and maintain a "new order" using the terror of revolution (normalization)."

"Everywhere it is at last dawning upon men and women that the Communistic philosophy is absolutely incompatible, nay, bitterly antagonistic to our democratic and Christian way of life. They can never be reconciled, for Communism has declared war to the death against everything we hold dear and right. These articles name the two worlds for us: Anglo-American and Soviet, with their respective spheres of influence and control." (Cyril Hutchinson, "Prelude to War or Shall We Have One World or Two?" The Prophetic Voice, October, 1946)

A three-pronged attack on the Judeo-Christian foundation of the Western democracies took place in the mid-nineteenth century. The 1848 "Communist Manifesto," called for the destruction of the family, the church and the nation-state – which the "new order" will replace. That is why humanity has suffered so terribly under its power. The 1930s importation of cultural Marxists from the Frankfurt School in Germany to prestigious American universities introduced Marxist Critical Theory to question all existing traditions upon which Western society was based, most notably the Judeo-Christian tradition. Shortly after that Darwin published his 1859 "Origin of Species," bringing his theory of evolution to undermine the Judeo-Christian Biblical record of creation. It has since been disproven but is still taught in schools and colleges as fact. Finally, two apostates of the Anglican Church in England, Professor Fenton John Anthony Hort and Bishop B. F. Westcott, devised their false "canons" of Textual Criticism based upon the same German rationalistic Critical Theory to undermine the Traditional Texts (Old

& New Testaments) of the English King James Bible (Frank Crawford, "A Tower of Babble Silenced by the Voice of Reason," 2010). Their 1881 *Critical Greek Text* and resulting English Revised Version of the Bible followed corrupted Old and New Testament Manuscripts. Professor Hort was the primary formulator of these false doctrines. Both Marx and Westcott admired Darwin's work and said it helped them refine their own critical theories. Again, Westcott and Hort sought to supplant the proven Word of God with a Critical Text, based upon corrupt Hebrew and Greek manuscripts. These have since led to multiple Bible translations in English and other languages. All of these critical endeavors weakened, and finally destroyed the Judeo-Christian traditional culture in the West – leading to the apostasy of the churches and today's rise to ascendancy of Marxist socialism-communism across the Free World.

> "Christian faith would be rejected by Communist thinkers who believe that science interpreted by Marxist philosophy is the beginning and end of human wisdom. Its center of history is the Russian Revolution and the Communist movement which will bring redemption from all social evil. It has no understanding of the persistence of human sin – that is, of the corrupting effect of pride and self-centeredness and the will to power – within it. Communism is at its center a gigantic effort at construction – a short cut to an ideal society – to be accomplished by a ruthlessness that is abhorrent." (John Bennett, Christianity and Communism Today, 1960)
>
> The communist's opponent becomes an outcast "fascist," "warmonger," or "reactionary" and that is the end of the matter until the day comes when through numerous purges and liquidations, there is a world in which there are no opponents. But all of the opponents who have stood in the way in the course of this development are lost souls and for them there is no redemption…they are all physically dead, or destroyed in both soul and spirit." (Ibid)

EPILOGUE

With Christianity looking like it's on the losing end of this war, perhaps it is time to claim the attitude of Ferdinand Foch at the First Battle of the Marne in 1914. We have nothing to lose at this point.

> "My center is yielding. My right is retreating. Situation excellent. I am attacking." (John Robson, Leftist Policies Surge When the Centre Yields and the Right Retreats, The Epoch Times, p. B2, September 3-9, 2020)

Christianity prioritizes Christ above all; that is, above the family, the church and the nation-state because they are all institutions established by God in His Word. God's Word is *"the sword of the Spirit,"* an offensive weapon.

> "Christianity affirms belief in a particular revelation and in particular redemptive acts of God in history. The faith that Christ was the center of a series of historical events in which God sought to draw men to himself is so distinctive that it separates Christianity not only from Communism but from all other non-Christian religions and philosophies. A nation or a social order that acknowledges that it stands under God is open to criticism and correction and growth." (John Bennett, Christianity and Communism Today, 1960)

> The Christian gospel stands or falls with the faith in the aggressive love of God for those who do not deserve it on any human basis (grace). *"But God commendeth his love toward us, in that, while we were yet sinners, Christ died for us." (Romans 5:8)*. The individual person is the ultimate unit of moral and religious decision. No one else can repent for him. No one else can respond in faith to the truth in his place. No one else can assume his moral responsibility. It is highly significant that Christians have always seen the supreme revelation of God and the supreme action of God in human life in an individual Person, the Lord Jesus Christ." (Ibid)

Christianity propagates without the sword of violence, and Communism propagates by the sword of violence and oppression. Formal, dead, institutional Christianity has little power against socialism-communism. In fact, it will often compromise and yoke up with statist regimes to enhance its own power and prestige. Uncompromising, genuine Bible Christianity, as exemplified by gospel preachers such as William Aberhart and Ernest Manning are a threat to today's left-wing, collectivist mindset and movements. Genuine revival in the churches and strong Christian leadership in the political arena are the best defense against Marxism and a future socialist-communist take-over of our free democracy. Revival can come only when individual Christians return to God with all their heart, soul and mind.

> "Bible Christianity is the greatest force in this world to bring about a transformation of attitude and lifestyle on the part of those who appropriate the salvation of God available to them only in the Person of Jesus Christ." (Ernest C. Manning, The Concerns of Our Times (#5), Back to the Bible Hour message, late 1980s).

> "The real power of Communism lies in winning its way by propaganda and infiltration. It provides a faith, especially for young people, who have never encountered any faith which put much meaning into life and which adequately related their social aspirations and ideals to an interpretation of the world. It is based especially on the aspirations and resentments of the colored races, and upon the unsolved problems of capitalism, especially the expected catastrophic depression which, according to Communist schedule, will undermine the strength of the West." (John Bennett, Christianity and Communism Today, 1960)

EPILOGUE

William Aberhart and Ernest Manning were both Christian leaders in the secular realm. Their testimony is a strong witness that free democracy works best when leaders have a living relationship with God's Son, the Lord Jesus Christ. Leftists and false religion work fanatically to try to discredit this truth.

> "There is no other faith which can compare with Communism except Christianity. Christianity, when its full meaning is not hidden by one-sided teaching or distorted by alliances between the Church and privileged groups, is a faith that can meet the needs of those who struggle for equal justice in the social order. The first responsibility of the Christian community is not to save any institutions from Communism, but to present its faith by word and life to the people of all conditions and of all lands, that they may find for themselves the essential truth about life." (Ibid).

This book has emphasized the contrast between the Christian beliefs of Ernest Manning and those of Communism as exemplified by Karl Marx and his disciples, one of which was Vladimir Lenin. There is much confusion between Christianity in politics today but little about left-wing socialism and communism in politics. Perhaps a comparison between leaders from the two belief systems would help clear up some of this confusion.

I was referred to the 2015 book, "The Conservative Heart," by Arthur Brooks as a blueprint for Conservative politicians in today's world. Although the book is good from a secular standpoint, it lacks the essential element, Christian conversion and faith. He writes about the "happiness portfolio: faith, family, community, and earned success through work." While all of this is good and true; one thing is missing – spiritual regeneration like that experienced and preached by William Aberhart and Ernest C. Manning.

> *"Happy is that people, that is in such a case: yea, happy is that people, whose God is the LORD." (Psalm 144:15)*
>
> *"Happy is he that hath the God of Jacob for his help, whose hope is in the LORD his God:" (Psalm 146:5)*

There is no lasting hope, no help, no happiness without the God of Jacob, the God of Israel – specifically the Lord Jesus Christ in your life as your personal Lord and Savior. Without Christ in the affairs of the individual, and in the nation, all effort will be in vain hoping for a return to God's blessings, deliverance and prosperity into the future. Ernest Manning repeated this truth in his messages over and over again (Appendix 3).

In comparing and contrasting Communism and Christianity the issue of the individual person and the masses is key. William Aberhart and Ernest Manning believed first in the individual, but did not neglect or ignore the masses;

> "The voters needed to be told how these social programs would differ from what a (socialist) CCF government might have brought in. Manning explained, **"Our basic philosophy first of all was very humanitarian. The whole concept of Social Credit was that the individual was the most important unit in society, NOT society collectively.** Our primary emphasis was on the individual, not the masses. If you looked after the individual, the masses would take care of themselves." Manning would maintain throughout his political life that Social Credit was just as committed to serving the social needs of people as any socialist party. **"But our approach to meeting those social needs was through**

the private enterprise system." (Brian Brennan, The Good Steward: The Ernest C. Manning Story, 2008).

In "Christianity and Communism Today," (1960) John Bennett described the main difference between these two systems:

> "There has been a tendency in Communism to lose interest in the dignity and freedom of the person. The materialistic and deterministic categories of thought have had a depersonalizing effect upon the spirit of (socialism) Communism. The inevitable preoccupation with the problems of the masses and the long years of revolution and dictatorship when the (individual) person is necessarily sacrificed to the community have had the same effect. Communism does not have an adequate frame of reference to provide an understanding of the conditions upon which the dignity of the person depends. **There are depths of personal life that are beyond the comprehension of those who concentrate exclusively on social forces, historical processes and systems of production.**
>
> Christianity combines, in a remarkable way, concern for the uniqueness and ultimate worth of every person with concern for the community of persons. There is a radical individualism in the gospel, with its assurance that *"even the hairs of your head are numbered," (Matthew 10:30)*, with its faith that God cares about the single sheep that is lost (Matthew 18:12-14), with its warning about "despising one of these little ones" (Matthew 18:10). The love that is central to the whole New Testament is love directed toward individual persons, and yet it is love that binds them together in a community. Jacques Maritain expresses the interrelationship between the person and the community: "Man (the individual) finds himself by subordinating himself to the group; the group attains its goal only by serving man and by realizing that man has

secrets which escape the group and a vocation which the group does not encompass.

The Christian gospel stands or falls with the faith in the aggressive love of God for those who do not deserve it on any human basis (i.e., grace). It was an individual Person (the Lord Jesus Christ in John 1:14), *"the Word was made flesh, and dwelt among us,"* (Who came to save sinners). One of the key sentences in the New Testament is Paul's surprising claim in Romans 5:8; *"But God commendeth his love toward us, in that, while we were yet sinners, Christ died for us."* The individual person is the ultimate unit of moral and religious decision. No one else can repent for him. No one else can respond in faith to the truth in his place. No one else can assume his moral responsibility. No external authority can create in him conscience or moral insight of what is good upon which his judgments must depend. (Therefore) Christians must seek the kind of spiritual freedom that leaves air for the person to breathe (free will) and in which it is externally possible for the truth to be accepted or rejected."

Communism knows nothing about such teaching as this. The opponent becomes an outcast "fascist," "warmonger," or "reactionary," and that is the end of the matter until the day comes when through the working out of the historical process, after numerous purges and liquidations, there is a world in which there are no opponents. But all of the opponents who have stood in the way of this development are lost souls and for them there is no redemption."

Bennet illustrated the philosophical differences in governing using Abraham Lincoln as an example. Lincoln was a statesman with strong Biblical beliefs. The stark contrast between the Christian spirit in politics and the Communist spirit in politics is shown in the contrast between Lincoln and Lenin. Both were men of integrity who served causes that could claim high moral sanction. Berdyaev says of Lenin:

> "Lenin was not a vicious man; there was a great deal of good in him; he was unmercenary, absolutely devoted to an idea; he was not even a particularly ambitious man or a great lover of power; he thought but little of himself; but the sole obsession of a single idea led to a dreadful narrowing of thought and to a moral transformation which permitted entirely immoral methods of carrying out the conflict." (Ibid)

Among his "immoral methods," Lenin wrote explicitly in his tract, "Left-Wing Communism," that hatred was "the basis of any socialist and communist movement." (Mark Hendrickson, Ominous signs of Hatred in Politics, The Epoch Times, p. B1, October 17-23, 2019).

> "Abraham Lincoln – was a man of profound biblical faith, and it would be difficult to find in history a better example of a Christian statesman who did not allow his scruples to destroy his sense of responsibility for determined action and who did not allow his sense of responsibility for determined action to destroy his charity or his humility.
>
> **The chief difference** between Lenin and Lincoln was that for Lenin the cause was everything, while for Lincoln the purpose and judgment of God, which in ways beyond human understanding embraced both sides in the conflict, transcended even his cause. As a consequence of this, Lincoln's enemies, whom he had to fight and to whose sufferings he could never become callous, were always the objects of his charity."

The same comparison can be made between the two Christian statesmen William Aberhart and Ernest Manning, representing free democracy, and Vladimir Lenin, representing socialism-communism as well. Aberhart mentored Manning who went on to serve Albertans for 33 years, 25 years as premier, during which time the province of Alberta was blessed abundantly by God, and peace and stability were the norm. Lenin mentored Joseph Stalin who went on to rule the U.S.S.R. for about 30 years during which time over 60 million Russians perished brutally under a totalitarian dictatorship, and God was banished from the life of the nation.

A fitting tribute to our Canadian free democracy and an answer to the vitriol levelled against our society here is a testimony of the opportunities that still exist in our great country.

> "When he first came to Alberta from his native Nigeria in 2005 and was struggling to support his family by washing dishes, Kaycee Madu never dreamt that one day he'd be appointed to one of the most important cabinet posts in that province in his adopted country. But the Edmontonian has come to realize since then that the system in his province is "built in a way that rewards hard work and risk-takers. It doesn't matter where you come from in this province. If you work hard, the sky won't even be a limit," Madu said in an interview." (Omid Ghoreishi, Hard Work & System That Rewards It: Canada's First Black Justice Minister on New Appointment, The Epoch Times, p. A1, September 3-9, 2020)

It is only fitting to conclude this section with Ernest Manning's exhortation to young people, as fitting today as when it was preached many years ago.

EPILOGUE

"Let me say a special word to you young people who are particularly sensitive to the many injustices and inequities of our modern materialistic society. You deserve respect and admiration for your zeal in working for social change and your dedication to causes which have as their objective, righting social wrongs and stopping the exploitation of the poor and the underprivileged. You oppose war and the rape of the earth's resources and you condemn selfishness and material greed, and that is good. But I hope you will not overlook the fact that if a better world free from exploitation and inequities and injustices, and a world at peace, is really your goal, the greatest step you could take to hasten the realization of that goal is to align yourself with the Lord Jesus Christ. And that is precisely what He will do when returns to this earth to set up His universal millennial kingdom.

You have the opportunity to have a place and a part in the ultimate realization of your dream, but remember aligning yourself with Jesus Christ involves much more than merely subscribing to His teachings and precepts and example, and endorsing what He has affirmed to be His ultimate goal for this earth and for mankind. That can be yours only through Jesus Christ and your acceptance of Him into your life as your personal Savior. Open your heart and life to Him and receive Him as your Savior, and enthrone Him as the Lord of your life and know the joy of sins forgiven and the realism of a genuine spiritual new birth. Remember, it was He who said,

"Except a man be born again he cannot see the kingdom of God."

(John 3:3)

MY PERSONAL TESTIMONY FOR WRITING AND COMPILING THIS BOOK

A few years ago I had begun to cut out articles from The Epoch Times and The Calgary Sun on issues pertinent to politics and society in general due to the alarming trends in society that I was observing. These trends contrasted with conditions that were present during my younger years, as I am now an old man. It became evident before long that socialism and communism were coming up over and over again in the newspaper columns. It was in the back of my mind to write on the subject at some future point but I had no idea or motivation of when or how to start such a work.

My methodology for compiling and writing this book followed the advice of my geological mentor, Dr. Herb Teitz, a former German soldier who survived the Battle of Stalingrad in WW II, and later moved to Canada. He advised me to "Observe; Remember; Compare," when performing my exploration projects. That principle of reasoning helps integrate and make sense of widely dispersed and variable information from which to derive meaningful and reasonable conclusions. The reader is invited to judge this approach when reading, "Fortress America Under Siege."

It was in church in 2019 that and older Christian brother, Dennis Snyder, brought me a handful of messages by Ernest C. Manning, the former Premier of Alberta. I had not asked Dennis to do this for I knew little about Mr. Manning. As I read the vintage messages and a short biography of the man my interest grew for he had similar concerns about socialism-communism to myself, only many years before. Soon after, I obtained a biography on Ernest C. Manning from the Library and read through it carefully, taking notes. Again, his life and work encouraged me to write three tracts on the man, his political life and his Christian preaching. It became evident to me that Manning was an extraordinary individual and that his connection to William Aberhart was unique. Both were Bible-believing saved men; both were premiers of Alberta for an overall period of 33 years. Both were conservatives under the Social Credit banner. Both preached the gospel while they carried out their responsibilities as political leaders. Both were unashamed of their Christian faith and warned about the dangers of socialism-communism. Both were deeply concerned for the welfare of the citizens of Alberta and entered politics out of a motivation to help their fellow man during desperately difficult times in the Great Depression of the 1930s. The elder mentored the younger, and through Mr. Aberhart's radio preaching Mr. Manning was saved as a teenage farm boy.

After writing the three tracts I considered my work done concerning Mr. Manning. However, circumstances changed and I was asked to consider publishing the written material. That was the beginning of a more extensive project to write a book on Ernest Manning's warnings concerning collectivism that threatened Canada's free democracy. I had by this time an extensive collection of newspaper articles on the subject. At the same time, Mr. Snyder, brought me many more vintage messages and pamphlets from the Aberhart/Manning years with much information concerning their teaching preaching and messages. The more I read about them the more I was encouraged to go forward with writing a book on their warnings to their contemporary society in the 1920s and onward for Mr. Aberhart, and the 1940s and onward for Mr. Manning. I then began the work in earnest. My main focus at the start was on Mr. Manning, then on Mr. Aberhart toward the end as I learned more about his teachings from the material Mr. Snyder provided me with, and the connection they had to current geo-political trends.

The Calgary Sun and The Epoch Times both provided excellent articles on the subject of socialism-communism. They, and other written material in books and internet sources became available to me as I pursued the work of writing and compiling the material out of a concern for my country and its future. The more that I studied and wrote, the more I became concerned that Canada and the United States, and their citizens, are in a crisis situation that if, left unchallenged will result in our total loss of freedom in the not-too-distant future. It was during the middle of the work that two unexpected, providential events happened that further motivated me to continue the book to completion.

In 2007, long before this book came to mind, my wife and I purchased a plot at Edenbrook Cemetery in southwest Calgary. We did this because of our tragic loss of our nine year-old grandniece in a vehicle accident. We obtained our future grave site next to hers. In the spring of 2020 I learned from my research that Mr. Manning was buried in Edenbrook in 1996, and that he was interred in the Christus section of the cemetery. I decided to look for his site. After driving around the cemetery I could not find it. Then I looked across from our site and saw the Christus Garden sign. When the snow was fully gone I looked for Mr. Manning's grave, and found it and Mrs. Manning's about 60 yards from ours in the adjoining Heritage Garden. I thought, "What a coincidence! The Lord must have arranged this." It was an encouragement.

PERSONAL TESTIMONY

Then, this summer, in 2020, my wife and I and three other couples drove to Vancouver, B.C., about 650 miles west of Calgary. We were invited to go to help out one of the older couples in their driving. Shortly before our trip, when studying The Prophetic Voice bulletins from Mr. Aberhart's Prophetic Bible Institute in Calgary, I came across his funeral service message conducted on May 30, 1943, one week after his death in Vancouver. That message provided the name of the cemetery, Forest Lawn Burial Park (now Forest Lawn Memorial Gardens) in Burnaby, B.C. After arriving in Vancouver I phoned the cemetery and found that it was only about a 20 minute drive from our hotel in downtown Vancouver. On our way home to Calgary at the end of the week we drove there and asked to visit Mr. Aberhart's grave. The staff didn't have it in the computer system but it was found in the old paper files. We then visited it. While we were standing there looking at the beautiful view around to the Vancouver skyline, my wife noticed something I had missed. She said, "Look Dear." Immediately adjoining William and Janet Aberharts' gravestones were two gravestones with the inscriptions as follows: Mrs. Janet Crawford and Mr. Charles Crawford, buried in 1948 and 1950, respectively. I was born in 1947. Again, a most amazing providential circumstance that encouraged me to continue writing.

Both men, the late Mr. William Aberhart and the late Ernest C. Manning, were both close by those with the Crawford name – ourselves at Edenbrook in Calgary, and a husband and wife with our last name in Burnaby, B.C. Janet Crawford and Janet Aberhart had the same first name. I had a cousin named Janet Crawford who lived in the same town as my family. We used to visit. Statistically, this is remarkable. In comparing 10,000 names of Canadian airmen who died in WW II on the marble plaque at Bomber Command Museum in Nanton,

AB, there were three Mannings, 10 Crawfords and no Aberharts listed. These airmen died over widely separated areas in Europe, North Africa and the Far East. Few if any died together in the same place. Some would say that these Aberhart/Manning/Crawford connections are just happenstance, and maybe they're right. But to me it provided encouragement that I was doing something that God wanted me to do, and that I needed to go forward and finish it to the best of my ability.

My past work in the oil industry also was useful in providing material for the subject of this work. I lived and worked in Venezuela for nearly 2 years. I left when Hugo Chavez was elected there. He led that country to socialist ruin. I also lived in Libya when the dictator Ghadaffi was in power and later visited Syria on two occasions where Bashur al Assad was dictator. Long before that I visited Guyana, SA, on an exploration project one year after the Jonestown tragedy. All of these experiences make me value our freedom in Canada, that our soldiers fought and died for in WW II, and which we are now losing without a fight.

Also, while a member in a Baptist church in Calgary in the 1980s I experienced, along with my fellow believer-friends, dictatorial Conservative government policies in the area of education that led, after 5 years of court cases, to our pastor being put in jail, the first incident of its kind to my knowledge in Canada. Again, this experience taught me how fragile our freedoms really are, even in a free democracy, if the wrong people get into power – in the bureaucracy and in politics.

I have tried by the foregoing to try to show the reader why I have gone forward to write and compile this work. Yes; it is too long. Many times my wife said to me, "Dear, it is too long. No one will read it. Keep it short and to the

PERSONAL TESTIMONY

point." I beg you, the reader, for your forgiveness for not following my wife's advice. But I hope somewhere in this lengthy treatise, that you will find something of help and of value to do your part to fight for our remaining freedoms, and develop the motivation to take a stand yourself to help preserve our free democracy for your children and grandchildren. Remember – Christ is the answer!

Yours respectfully,

Frank Crawford

APPENDIX 1
THE GOSPEL OF JESUS CHRIST

By Pastor Travis Alltop & Frank Crawford

"Genuine Christianity is the most potent force in the world to change human nature through the miracle of a spiritual new birth. Men born again are not likely to steal or destroy or embezzle. Isn't it time we gave Christianity the recognition it deserves?" (Ernest C. Manning, The Face of the Sky – Part 1, 1971, Back to the Bible Hour pamphlet)

> "Examine yourselves, whether ye be in the faith; prove your own selves. Know ye not your own selves, how that Jesus Christ is in you, except ye be reprobates?"
> (2 Corinthians 13:5)

According to the Bible, very few people are saved and go to heaven after they die. Jesus said,

APPENDIX 1

> *"Enter ye in at the strait gate: for wide is the gate, and broad is the way, that leadeth to destruction, and many there be which go in thereat: Because strait is the gate, and narrow is the way, which leadeth unto life, and few there be that find it." (Matthew 7:13-14)*

The wide road leads to hell and the lake of fire; while the narrow way leads to heaven.

Jesus Christ alone provided for the salvation of your never-dying soul through his death, burial and resurrection. Much unnecessary confusion exists today over salvation. Paul stated it simply as,

> *"...repentance toward God, and faith toward our Lord Jesus Christ." (Acts 20:21)*

It applies to all men everywhere.

Please take 20 minutes to read this pamphlet carefully. Here is what you need to understand clearly:

1. ALL MEN ARE SINNERS, AND THIS INCLUDES YOU.

> *"For all have sinned, and come short of the glory of God;" (Romans 3:23)*

Men are natural born rebels against the Law of God. God's Law is holy, and pure; and you have broken it repeatedly throughout your life. If you doubt this, why not examine your own heart against the Law, otherwise known as the Ten Commandments found in Exodus 20:1-17?

Have you ever told a lie? Have you honored your parents at all times? Have you ever blasphemed by using the name of God in vain? Have you ever stolen anything? Have you ever committed adultery in your heart by looking with lust? If you have failed in any of these areas, and many more, James 2:10 states plainly,

> "For whosoever shall keep the whole law, and yet offend in one point, he is guilty of all."

> "As it is written, There is none righteous, no, not one:" (Romans 3:10)

That is because each one of us has been born with a sin nature, inherited from our first parents, Adam and Eve. They willfully disobeyed God's single command in the Garden of Eden, not to eat of –

> "the tree of the knowledge of good and evil:...for in the day that thou eatest thereof thou shalt surely die." (Genesis 2:17)

That sin-infected, sin-prone condition makes every person – *"dead in trespasses and sins;"* (Ephesians 2:1) – and in spiritual darkness and alienation from a holy God. We are born, live and die as lost sinners.

2. YOUR PERSONAL SINS HAVE EARNED YOU A WAGE.

The consequences of the fall of man, and SIN are devastating to the never-dying soul. Romans 5:12 says,

> "Wherefore, as by one man (Adam) *sin entered into the world, and death by sin; and so death passed upon all men, for that all have sinned:"* (Romans 5:12)

The first death is physical death; "the second death" is "the lake of fire." Both of them are the result of sin.

"For the wages of sin is death;…" "And death and hell were cast into the lake of fire. This is the second death." (Romans 6:23a; Revelation 20:14)

It is living tormented in fire, and damned for ever, because of your sin.

A righteous, holy and just God will never allow sin into heaven and rebellion to go unpunished, or He would cease to be holy. God will never compromise His righteousness or holiness to allow a guilty sinner to go free! You wouldn't think a judge on this earth was a good judge if he allowed known criminals to go free, would you? No, the Bible promises a due reward for your sins and transgressions. For –

> *"…God shall judge the secrets of men by Jesus Christ…" (Romans 2:16)*

> *"And whosoever was not found written in the book of life was cast into the lake of fire." (Revelation 20:15)*

Hell was made for the devil and his angels, and not for man.

> *"Then shall he say also unto them on the left hand, Depart from me, ye cursed, into everlasting fire, prepared for the devil and his angels." (Matthew 25:41)*

3. GOD, IN HIS LOVE AND MERCY, HAS PROVIDED SALVATION FOR YOU.

The nature and character of God made it possible for man to escape the consequences of his sin and be saved, that is, forgiven his sin.

> *"And the LORD passed by before him (Moses), and proclaimed, The LORD God, merciful and gracious, longsuffering, and abundant in goodness and truth, Keeping mercy for thousands, forgiving iniquity and transgressions and sin, and that will by no means clear the guilty; visiting the iniquity of the fathers upon the children, and upon the children's children, unto the third and to the fourth generation." (Exodus 34:6, 7)*

To bring to an end the Old Testament animal sacrifices, God sent his only begotten Son into the world, to live a sinless life, and do what no other living man could do.

> *"But God commendeth his love toward us, in that, while we were yet sinners, Christ died for us." (Romans 5:8)*

There is nothing you can do to atone for your sins, or to make peace with God. Your good deeds or good intentions cannot take away your sins! Church membership, water baptism and religion cannot take away your sins. But, God sent his only begotten Son, the Lord Jesus Christ, to die condemned in your place and pay for your ungodliness! When John the Baptist first saw the Lord Jesus Christ coming to him, he proclaimed,

> *"...Behold the Lamb of God, which taketh away the sin of the world." (John 1:29)*

This is the good news! Jesus Christ died on the cross for your sins, was buried and rose again the third day. Isaiah prophesied that Jesus Christ would die and rise again, FOR US, seven hundred years before it happened,

> *"But he was wounded for our transgressions, he was bruised for our iniquities: the chastisement of our peace was upon him; and with his stripes we are healed. All we like sheep have gone astray; we have turned every one*

APPENDIX 1

> to his own way; and the LORD hath laid on him the iniquity of us all...it pleased the LORD to bruise him; he hath put him to grief: thou shalt make his soul an offering for sin...He shall see of the travail of his soul, and shall be satisfied..." (Isaiah 53:5-6, 10, 11)

The New Testament presents this great sacrifice in John 3:16.

> "For God so loved the world, that he gave his only begotten Son, that whosoever believeth in him should not perish, but have everlasting life."

The damage done to Jesus' body and face as he bore our sins is described in Isaiah 52:14.

> "As many were astonied (astonished) at thee; his visage (face) was so marred more than any man, and his form (whole body) more than the sons of men:"

Moreover, every sin committed by every living human being over all time was laid on God's willing, sinless Son, as his Father offered Him up on the cross for us all.

> "For he hath made him to be sin for us, who knew no sin; that we might be made the righteousness of God in him." (2 Corinthians 5:21)

He was marred, and broken, and made SIN: FOR you and FOR me.

God Almighty was satisfied with the payment (i.e. atonement) that His Son Jesus Christ made for your sins; and that was why Jesus rose from the dead. His sacrifice is the only thing that will satisfy God's holy wrath. Jesus fulfilled the Law for us, having lived a holy and sinless life for 33 years before He went to the cross. God now has a holy and just way to redeem guilty sinners by His Son's precious blood...

> "and without shedding of blood is no remission…Being justified freely by his grace (i.e., God's unmerited favor) through the redemption that is in Christ Jesus: Whom God hath set forth to be a propitiation (atonement) through faith in his blood…and the blood of Jesus Christ his Son cleanseth us from all sin." (Hebrews 9:22, Romans 3:24, 25, 1 John 1:7)

Only Jesus' blood atones for sin. It was the redemption or price paid by God Himself to deliver guilty sinners from the world's slave market of sin.

No one can keep the Law. The purpose of the Law is to show us that we are guilty sinners, and to plainly point us to Jesus Christ to be saved.

> "Wherefore the law was our schoolmaster (i.e., principal or head teacher) to bring us unto Christ, that we might be justified by faith." (Galatians 3:24)

> "Christ hath redeemed us from the curse of the law, being made a curse for us…" (Galatians 3:13)

> "For Christ also hath once suffered for sins, the just for the unjust, that he might bring us to God…" (1 Peter 3:18)

> "Neither is there salvation in any other: for there is none other name under heaven given among men, whereby we must be saved." (Acts 4:12)

> "How shall we escape, if we neglect so great salvation;" (Hebrews 2:3a, b)

4. YOU CAN BE SAVED AND POSSESS ETERNAL LIFE RIGHT NOW!

You cannot do enough good to merit heaven. One sin will keep you out. God is Holy, and there is no sin in heaven. Sin must be forgiven, or the sinner pay for his own sin in

APPENDIX 1

hell and the lake of fire (the second death). God describes the very best that man can offer Him in the Scriptures.

> "But we are all as an unclean thing, and all our righteousnesses are as filthy rags; we all do fade as a leaf; and our iniquities, like the wind, have taken us away." (Isaiah 64:6)

> "For by grace are ye saved through faith; and that not of yourselves: it is the gift of God: Not of works, lest any man should boast." (Ephesians 2:8, 9)

We cannot be saved by our own efforts. There are no good works that we can do to atone for our sins; only a sinner's dead works, in God's holy eyes.

You must come humbly to Jesus Christ and put your complete faith and trust in Him.

> "Jesus saith unto him, I am the way, the truth, and the life: no man cometh unto the Father, but by me." (John 14:6)

To believe on Him is to trust Him alone for your soul's salvation! Most people will not put their complete faith in the Lord Jesus because they are rebels against God, and would rather continue in their sins, or hold onto the self-righteousness of their own 'good works' or religion. Our pride is our worst enemy.

Without repentance you will perish in the lake of fire. The gospel of Jesus Christ declares, 'turn or burn.' This is why Jesus said twice in one short space of scripture,

> "I tell you, Nay: but, except ye repent, ye shall all likewise perish." (Luke 13:3, 5)

"FORTRESS AMERICA" UNDER SIEGE

The apostle Paul told some superstitious pagans in Acts 17:30 that God used to *"wink at"* (i.e., overlook) their ignorant idolatrous worship,

> *"...but now commandeth all men everywhere to repent."*

Repentance is a change of mind that produces a change of heart and leads to an 180° turn-around in your life. It is an act of the will in which you turn from self and sin to Christ. IT IS LIFE-CHANGING!

Are you sick of your sin? Are you sick of yourself and the way you are living – hurting yourself and others around you; and most of all, angering God by your wickedness?

Then turn from sin to God right now! Put your complete faith and trust in the Lord Jesus Christ, and in Him alone. Call upon Him to save you from your sins – to save your never-dying soul (Romans 10:9-10, 13).

> *"That if thou shalt confess with thy mouth the Lord Jesus, and shalt believe in thine heart that God hath raised him from the dead, thou shalt be saved;*
>
> *For with the heart man believeth unto righteousness; and with the mouth confession is made unto salvation."*
>
> *"For whosoever shall call upon the name of the Lord shall be saved."*

These are God's promises in His Word, and you can rest on, and trust in, God's promises explicitly!

> *..."yea, let God be true, but every man a liar;"* (Romans 3:4)
>
> *"For all the promises of God in him in him are yea, and in him Amen,"* (2 Corinthians 1:20)

APPENDIX 1

I repeat, most solemnly and sincerely; DO YOU REALLY desire to be saved? DO YOU REALLY desire a new life that comes by trusting Jesus Christ as your personal Lord and Savior? Then, why not call on God right now, and receive the Lord Jesus Christ into your heart by faith? His invitation and promise is,

> *"Come now, and let us reason together, saith the LORD: though your sins be as scarlet, they shall be as white as snow; though they be red like crimson, they shall be as wool. (Isaiah 1:18)*
>
> *"Come unto me, all ye that labor and are heavy laden, and I will give you rest. (Matthew 11:28)*
>
> *"...him that cometh to me I will in no wise cast out." (John 6:37)*

It is the Holy Spirit that is drawing you, wooing you, and pleading with you to come to Christ and be saved. Be saved NOW; and don't delay!

> *"Boast nor thyself of tomorrow; for thou knowest not what a day may bring forth." (Proverbs 27:1)*

Many a soul has waited for tomorrow; only to die today. You can't pick and choose the time you want to be saved. If you feel the drawing of the Holy Spirit and want to be saved, now is God's time for you.

> *"Behold, now is the accepted time; behold, now is the day of salvation." (2 Corinthians 6:2)*

You may not get another chance. Jesus said,

> *"No man can come to me, except the Father which hath sent me draw him:" (John 8:44)*

"FORTRESS AMERICA" UNDER SIEGE

Do you want the burden and guilt of your sins removed? Do you want God to save you? Then call on the Lord Jesus Christ, believing that He will hear you, forgive your sin, and save your never-dying soul.

> *"This poor man cried, and the LORD heard him, and saved him out of all his troubles. (Psalm 34:6)*
>
> *"As far as the east is from the west, so far hath he removed our transgressions from us." (Psalm 103:12)*

Praise God! If you have called upon the name of the Lord from an honest and repentant heart, we rejoice with you...

> *"there is joy in the presence of the angels of God over one sinner that repenteth." (Luke 15:10)*

You NOW have eternal salvation and will NEVER come into condemnation. You belong to God now and He will keep you as His own child for ever. That is Jesus' promise:

> *"Verily, verily, I say unto you, He that heareth my word, and believeth on him that sent me, hath everlasting life, and shall not come into condemnation; is passed from death unto life." (John 5:24)*

APPENDIX 2
"CANADA'S CHRISTIAN HERITAGE"
A clarion call to our nation

"He shall have dominion also from sea to sea, and from the river unto the ends of the earth."
Psalms 72:8

By Jim Tuovila & Frank Crawford

The Dominion of Canada:

Canada was born as a sovereign nation out of the British Empire on July 1, 1867. Its name was recommended from Psalm 72:8 (above) by Sir Samuel Tilley, a devoted Christian and New Brunswick's leading Father of Confederation. The society and culture were distinctly Judeo-Christian in origin. The Bible was respected and believed by our forefathers and deeply ingrained into the laws of our society. Churches were respected, and regarded as places to hear God's Word preached to guide the faith and moral practices of the Canadian people. Few would dispute the claim that Canada is one of the best countries in the world in which to live. As a people we enjoy freedom, peace, prosperity and opportunities for advancement that citizens in many other countries only wish to have, but do not. Although we have had our problems our culture has generally sought peaceful and practical methods to solve them. This character has endured in the Canadian identity to modern times. We should be very thankful for Canada and our Christian heritage.

It is well worthwhile to review some of foundational statements left by our founding fathers, both in print and in stone, in the architecture and public records of our great land. This review is an appeal to our leaders and citizenry not to dismiss or forget these important reminders of our Canadian past; and to,

> *"Remove not the ancient landmark, which thy fathers have set." (Proverbs 22:28)*

Thanksgiving Day

The first national Thanksgiving Day was celebrated in Canada in 1859. This holiday was intended for the "public and solemn recognition of God's mercies." It is said that some citizens "objected to this government request, saying it blurred the distinction between church and state that was so important to many Canadians." However, someone in government knew the following verse, Psalm 136:1:

APPENDIX 2

> *"O give thanks unto the LORD; for he is good: for his mercy endureth for ever."*

The first Thanksgiving after Confederation (1867) was observed on April 5, 1872; and became an annual event on November 6, 1879. The holiday occurred as late in the year as December 6 and even coincided several times with American Thanksgiving (November 28), although the third week of October was chosen when the fall weather was generally still amenable for outdoor activities.

Beginning in 1921, Thanksgiving and Armistice Day (introduced in 1919) were celebrated on the same day – the first Monday in the week of November 11. But in order to give more recognition to our veterans, 11 November was set solely as Remembrance Day in 1931. Thanksgiving was again proclaimed annually and typically observed on the second Monday of October until the present day. It was not until January 31, 1957 that the Governor General of Canada, Vincent Massey issued a proclamation stating:

> "A Day of General **Thanksgiving to Almighty God** for the bountiful harvest with which Canada has been blessed."

This proclamation is truly an 'ancient landmark,' and it should not be forgotten or removed by any modern day linguistic tricks or political correctness.

Canada's National Coat of Arms

The testimony of the Scriptures remain preserved in many of our most ancient and revered Canadian landmarks, including our Coat of Arms shown on this tract heading.

The National Coat of Arms bears two inscriptions, both in Latin, from the Holy Bible. "A MARI USQUE AD MARE," is from "**sea to sea**" taken from Psalm 72:8, describing the future rule of God's Son (Jesus Christ):

> "He shall have dominion also from sea to sea, and from the river unto the ends of the earth."

This same verse of Scripture is also inscribed in the East Window of the Peace Tower on Parliament Hill. Prior to 1983 Canada celebrated **Dominion Day** each year on July 1. Prime Minister Pierre Elliot Trudeau changed it to Canada Day in 1982, with only a few Members of Parliament present to vote, at 4 pm on the day before summer recess of Parliament. This deliberate act removed an ancient landmark from Canadian history and memory, and attacked our Christian heritage. The red ribbon at the center of the Coat of Arms bears the inscription, "DESIDERANTES MELIOREM PATRIAM," meaning, **"desiring a better country,"** which is the motto of The Order of Canada, taken from Hebrews 11:16:

> "But now they desire a better country, that is, an heavenly: wherefore God is not ashamed to be called their God: for he hath prepared for them a city."

The reference here is for those who have trusted Jesus Christ as Lord and Savior and have their citizenship in the New Jerusalem, the eternal City of God.

Canada's Parliament Buildings

APPENDIX 2

Canada's Parliament Buildings in Ottawa contain Scriptures carved into the stones. As our nation's leaders have abandoned the Bible, God's Word engraved in the very stones of our legislative buildings bear witness to our nation's roots:

> "And he answered and said unto them, I tell you that, if these should hold their peace, the stones would immediately cry out." (Luke 19:40)

What would they cry out today? Read on.

In the Memorial Chamber is Ephesians 6:13:

> "Wherefore take unto you the whole armor of God, that ye may be able to withstand in the evil day, and having done all, to stand."

Etched in marble on the south wall of the same room is Psalm 139:8-10:

> "If I ascend up into heaven, thou art there: if I make my bed in hell, behold, thou art there. If I take the wings of the morning, and dwell in the uttermost parts of the sea; Even there shall thy hand lead me, and thy right hand shall hold me."

In the Opposition Board Room is the last part of 1 Peter 2:17 –

> "Fear God. Honor the king."

It would do well for all of our MPs to perform the beginning of this verse,

> "Honour all men. Love the brotherhood."

The Cabinet Room in the Parliament Building is inscribed with,

> "Love justice, you that are the rulers of the earth."

This statement is likely taken from King David, who wrote by divine inspiration,

> *"The God of Israel said, the Rock of Israel spake to me, He that ruleth over men must be just, ruling in the fear of God." (2 Samuel 23:3)*

This command contains a promise for national blessing that is given elsewhere in the Bible. Two examples are in Proverbs 14:34 and Psalm 33:12;

> *"Righteousness exalteth a nation: but sin is a reproach to any people."*

> *"Blessed is the nation whose God is the LORD; and the people whom he hath chosen for his own inheritance."*

No amount of man's effort can heal our land; only God can do that, if we are willing to let Him. Turn back to God.

APPENDIX 2

The Parliament Building and Peace Tower

Completed on 11 November, 1928, this edifice is a national treasure and a testimony to the world that God laid the foundation for our country. Psalm 72:8 is inscribed on its entrance. On the South Window is etched Psalm 72:1.

> "Give the king thy judgments O God, and thy righteousness unto the king's son."

The verse is taken from a Messianic Psalm referring to the future millennial reign of Jesus Christ from David's throne over all the earth. On the West Window is the part underlined in Proverbs 29:18.

> "<u>Where there is no vision, the people perish</u>: but he that keepeth the law, happy is he."

"FORTRESS AMERICA" UNDER SIEGE

A nation forgets God when it turns away from His Word.
> *"The wicked shall be turned into hell, and all the nations that forget God." (Psalm 9:17)*

The largest Bell in our Peace Tower belfry has inscribed on it Luke 2:17.

> *"Glory to God in the highest, and on earth peace, good will toward men."*

The peace in this verse refers to the coming of the Son of God, Jesus Christ, to die for the sin of the world. Through Him is real peace for your soul, and the nation.

> *"For God so loved the world, that he gave his only begotten Son, that whosoever believeth in him should not perish, but have everlasting life." (John 3:16)*

APPENDIX 3
ERNEST C. MANNING
RADIO ADDRESS
CHICAGO, APRIL 9, 1948

The Hon. E. C. Manning was a guest speaker at the "America for Christ" rally held recently in Chicago. His sermon was broadcast over WMBI and WDLM radio, and was reprinted in the May, 1948, Prophetic Voice booklet.

"WHATSOEVER HE SAITH UNTO YOU, DO IT"

INTRODUCTION

Good morning friends. I am grateful to you for permitting me, a stranger, to enter your home via the radio to speak to you about a matter of extreme importance.

It would be presumption for me to ask your attention even for a moment if my purpose was to burden you with thoughts and opinions of my own. Let me hasten to assure you that I have no such intention. I am in your great country and city on official business – very, very important business in which you are vitally and personally concerned.

I am speaking to you this morning in an official capacity. No, do not misunderstand me. I am not speaking as the Premier of a Canadian Province or the representative of a neighbor country. It is my privilege to speak to you this morning as an ambassador of One whose Name is above every name, whose throne fills the heavens and whose footstool is the earth – Jesus Christ, the Son of God, the

Prince of Peace, the King of kings, my Savior and my Lord.

I am happy to be one of that great company whose letters patent (lying open to public view) were dictated in the courts of heaven, and inscribed on the sacred pages of an indestructible book by holy men of God who spake as they were moved by the Holy Ghost. They read as follows"

> "And all things are of God, who hath reconciled us to himself by Jesus Christ, and hath given to us the ministry of reconciliation; To wit, that God was in Christ, reconciling the world unto himself, not imputing their trespasses unto them; and hath committed unto us the word of reconciliation. Now then we are ambassadors for Christ, as though God did beseech you by us: we pray you in Christ's stead, be ye reconciled to God." (2 Corinthians 5:18-20)

My friend, listen to me. It is of no importance if you speedily forget my name and the sound of my voice, but it is of supreme importance that you give to Him in whose Name I speak this morning the reverent attention of which He is more than worthy, and the willing obedience which He has a right to expect from every creature under heaven.

ERNEST MANNING'S TESTIMONY OF SALVATION

Perhaps I should tell you briefly how it came about, that I became a lowly subject of His heavenly kingdom and a grateful ambassador for Him. Like millions of others, I knew many things about Jesus Christ before I knew Him personally. His name was a familiar name. In childhood I learned many stories of His wonderful works in the days

APPENDIX 3

when He lived among men. His Word was a familiar book. Like millions of others, I subscribed as a matter of course to the teachings and ethics of what is commonly referred to as the Christian way of life. As a matter of course I often attended His house of worship and sang with those assembled there,

> "When I survey the wondrous cross
> On which the Prince of glory died,
> My richest gain I count but loss,
> And pour contempt on all my pride."

But one day I turned on my radio, just as you did this morning and from a distant city I heard a faithful ambassador of Jesus Christ bearing witness for his Lord. As I listened on that far off Sunday afternoon, I realized for the first time that there is an all – important difference between knowing about Jesus Christ and knowing Jesus Christ personally. It is one thing to be able to say I know about the Man of Galilee, I know about His miraculous birth, His marvelous life among men, His substitutionary death on the Cross of Calvary and His bodily resurrection from the dead. But it is something altogether different to meet Him personally as the Savior who died for you, and bow in His living presence a lost and helpless sinner to receive from Him forgiveness of sins, the gift of eternal life, and a new nature born of God. Then, and not until then, can you rise from your knees and say in truth and with joy,

> "Tis done, the great transaction's done,
> I am my Lord's and He is mine."

"For I know whom I have believed, and am persuaded that he is able to keep that which I have committed unto him against that day." (2 Timothy 1:12)

That was my personal experience now over twenty years ago. The intervening years have been eventful and filled with many interesting experiences. Each passing year and each new experience has strengthened my conviction that mankind's greatest need is not more formal religion, not new creeds and dogmas, not better codes of social and moral ethics, but the greatest and most urgent need of every man and woman today is to know Jesus Christ personally as a real, living, divine Savior and Lord and coming King.

That's why this morning I want to talk to you, not about myself, but about Him, not about my opinions and beliefs, but about His blessed and perfect Will as recorded in the world's one and only infallible Book, the verbally inspired and divinely preserved Word of the living God.

GOD'S UNIVERSAL COMMAND

The message I bring you in His name this morning is contained in one brief sentence of seven words from John 2:7. It is this:

"Whatsoever he saith unto you, do it."

Those words are not mine. They were first spoken by one who knew Jesus Christ more intimately than any other. They are the words which Mary, His mother, spoke at the marriage feast in Cana of Galilee as she pointed to Him, whom she above all others knew to be the Son of God.

"Whatsoever he saith unto you, do it."

APPENDIX 3

No more profound advice and wise counsel ever fell from human lips. We who name the Name of Christ in this day and generation would do well to cry these words from every housetop and whisper them in every listening ear – *"Whatsoever he saith unto you, do it."*

There are many different voices in this world today. Never before in human history has the world scene been more chaotic and confused. On every hand men and nations are groping blindly for acceptable answers to the complex problems on this crucial hour. But in all the conflicting viewpoints and opinions there is little to kindle hope or inspire confidence. One voice cries this, another that. What is confused and frustrated humanity to do? Is there is all the world no eye that can penetrate the gathering darkness? Is there no voice that can speak with certainty and whose counsel men can accept with confidence? I say to you this morning, there is one and only one. Blessed be God, there is One who can see the end of time from the beginning, whose infinite knowledge of all things is perfect and complete, and whose voice still speaks today with divine certainty and authority from the sacred pages of God's infallible book.

> *"God, who at sundry times and in diverse manners spake in time past unto the fathers by the prophets, Hath in these last days spoken unto us by his Son, whom he hath appointed heir of all things, by whom also he made the worlds;" (Hebrews 1:1-2)*

And down the years from the feast in Cana of Galilee comes the echo of Mary's voice,

> *"Whatsoever he saith unto you, do it."*

MANKIND'S RESPONSE TO GOD'S COMMAND

It is a strange and tragic paradox, indeed, that people will listen to almost any other voice in the world except the voice of Jesus Christ. Let a man come forward and proclaim a plan to abolish war and bloodshed, or violence and crime, and all ears will listen eagerly to what he has to propose. If another declares he has devised a way to curb sickness and suffering, how eagerly men listen to his voice. If I could bring to your home this morning someone who professes to know the answer to all sorrow and heartache, how readily you would bid him speak. And so it goes, irrespective of the fact that down the years thousands have proposed so-called solutions to these very same problems without any measure of success.

MANNING'S ADVICE TO HIS LISTENERS

But how different it is with Him whose divine counsel I ask you to accept this morning. He undertook and accomplished that which no other ever has, or ever will be able, to do. He triumphed over the root cause of all the wars and bloodshed, all the violence and crime, all the sickness and suffering and all the sorrow and heartache in the universe, when –

> "once in the end of the world hath he appeared to put away sin by the sacrifice of himself." (Hebrews 9:26)

> "Behold the Lamb of God, which taketh away the sin of the world." (John 1:29)

And you will recognize in Him one more than able to deal with every problem of life and meet your every need.

APPENDIX 3

"Whatsoever he saith unto you, do it."

If still more is needed to make you realize the wisdom of obeying His voice, I ask you to consider the experience of others. You can search this world through but I'll guarantee you won't find one man who obeyed the instructions of Jesus Christ without afterwards being glad he did so, and no man ever refused God's counsel without living to regret his folly. I think of the man born blind, to whom Christ said, *"Go wash in the pool of Siloam."* Blind man, *"whatsoever he saith unto you, do it."* The blind man went to the pool and washed, and returned to his friends shouting for joy, *"whereas once I was blind, now I can see."* Jesus said to Zacchaeus, who had climbed a sycamore tree to watch Him pass by, *"Zacchaeus, make haste and come down; for today I must abide at thy house."* Zacchaeus, *"Whatsoever he saith unto you, do it."* The record says, Zacchaeus made haste, came down and received Him joyfully; and before the sun set he was rejoicing in salvation and the testimony of his new found Lord and Savior. Jesus said,

> *"This day is salvation come to this (Zacchaeus') house."*

Jesus said to the fishermen of Galilee, *"Follow me and I will make you fishers of men."* Fishermen, *"Whatsoever he saith unto you, do it."* Scripture records, *"They forsook their nets and left all and followed him."* And because they obeyed, there is a day coming in Christ's millennial kingdom, when with their fellow apostles, they will sit on twelve thrones judging the twelve tribes of Israel. I repeat, no man ever obeyed the voice of Jesus Christ and afterwards regretted his obedience, and no man ever refused to obey without living to regret his folly.

MANKIND'S REJECTION OF GOD'S COMMAND

There are those who will think me old-fashioned when I say that man's disobedience to God is at the root of all the individual and national and international and world troubles of all ages, past and present. But, old-fashioned or not, it is true, and humanity is only prolonging and intensifying its own misery by shutting its eyes to this basic fact of life.

In all the world there is no more obvious and positively established fact than the inherent and universal depravity (sinfulness) of man. Nor does the irrefutable evidence of the ages, permit any other explanation than that recorded in the holy writ (Bible), namely, that man was created sinless and perfect, but fell from that glorious estate through the willful disobedience to the expressed will of his divine Creator.

> *"Wherefore, as by one man (Adam) sin entered into the world, and death by sin; and so death passed upon all men, for that all have sinned:" (Romans 5:12)*

> *"And even as they did not like to retain God in their knowledge, God gave them over to a reprobate mind to do those things which are not convenient; being filled with all unrighteousness, fornication, wickedness, covetousness, maliciousness; full of envy, murder, debate, deceit, malignity; whisperers, back-biters, haters of God, despiteful, proud, boasters, inventors of evil things, disobedient to parents, without understanding, covenant breakers, without natural affection, implacable, unmerciful: who, knowing the judgment of God that they*

APPENDIX 3

> which commit such things are worthy of death, not only do the same, but have pleasure in them that do them." (Romans 1:28-32)

Such is the testimony of holy writ concerning the tragic consequences of man's willful disobedience to God, and the sordid human record now reaching its climax in the disintegration of a Christ rejecting world. This is the irrefutable evidence that the testimony of scripture is true. But God who is rich in mercy did not leave mankind to endure, without hope, the eternal consequences of willful disobedience to his own Creator.

> "But when the fullness of the time was come, God sent – his only begotten Son into the world that we might live through him." (Galatians 4:4, I John 4:10)

Never forget that Jesus Christ came for the express purpose of paying in full the price necessary to recover mankind from the present and future consequences of his present and future disobedience to God.

> "For God so loved the world, that he gave his only begotten Son, that whosoever believeth in him should not perish, but have everlasting life. For God sent not his Son into the world to condemn the world; but that the world through him might be saved." (John 3:16-17)

Think of it! When Jesus Christ died on the Cross of Calvary, there was gathered into His divine and sinless body all the sin and disobedience of every member of the human family from Adam until the end of time. When He shed His divine blood of atonement, He paid the price sufficient to redeem (purchase) the whole world from the state of sin and misery into which man's sinful disobedience to God had plunged the human race.

When God raised Him from the dead and received Him back into His presence and eternal glory, it was proof positive that the work of atonement and redemption had been completed, and a way of deliverance had been opened for every man willing to obey the gospel of our Lord Jesus Christ and return to God by way of His finished work on Calvary's cross.

I am convinced that we have now reached the place in history where men and women must face and acknowledge three all-important facts:

1. The fact that mankind brought the awful and ever increasing consequences of sin on himself by his willful disobedience to God.

2. The fact that despite man's guilt and unworthiness, God, in His infinite love and mercy, at the cost of the life blood of His divine Son has provided a solution to the problem of sin, and a way of deliverance from its terrible consequences; both in this world and in the world to come. *"And death and hell were cast into the lake of fire. This is the second death. And whosoever was not found written in the book of life* (not saved) *was cast into the lake of fire." (Revelation 20:14-15)*

3. The fact that it now rests with men and nations to decide whether they will go on rejecting God until human depravity precipitates utter chaos and destruction through a succession of world crises already in sight, or whether they will enthrone Jesus Christ in His rightful place and accept and experience deliverance through Him.

ATTITUDE OF THE NATIONS TOWARD GOD

Consider for a moment the present attitude of the nations of this earth. On every side leaders and statesmen are searching

APPENDIX 3

frantically for ways and means to restore the equilibrium of a world that has lost its balance and is reeling and plunging towards self-annihilation. But the tragic fact is they are looking for deliverance in every direction except up. They seek advice and counsel from everyone except the Son of God,

> *"in whom are hid all the treasures of wisdom and knowledge." (Colossians 2:3)*

They pin their hopes on puny men who cannot see one hour into the future, but turn a deaf ear to the Lord of Glory to whom the annals of all time are an open book, and who knows the end from the beginning. They establish an elaborate international organization (the United Nations) to strive for world security and peace, but they bar the Prince of Peace from its councils for fear of offending ungodly men.

Nations today devise countless man-made laws in vain endeavors to legislate righteousness among men, but they ignore God's perfect law of liberty and allow dust to gather on the statutes of the Lord which – *"rejoice the heart and enlighten the eyes, and make men wise unto salvation."*

The following 2 quotes form a parenthesis and are current:

> In, **"Canada and the New Global Order,"** 72 years later,
>
> "The U.N. has drifted from its original mandate of fostering international cooperation to being unduly influenced by totalitarian and communist regimes whose agendas are opposed to democratic values and disproportionately dictate the policies of the U.N. and

"FORTRESS AMERICA" UNDER SIEGE

WHO, setting a very dangerous precedent. The U.N. fails to recognize the universality of basic human rights or a government's responsibility to treat its citizens with a modicum (a small amount) of decency." (Ryan Moffatt, The Epoch Times, p. B5, April 30-May 6, 2020)

"The UN General Assembly and its offshoots, such as the UN Human Rights Council, are vipers' nests of Jew-hatred, dominated by some of the world's most brutal and hate-filled dictatorships…among the world's worst human rights violators." (Lorrie Goldstein, Is Trudeau denouncing of Israel about his UN bid? The Calgary Sun, June 4, 2020)

In, **"How the Spectre of Communism is Ruling Our World,"** Sabotaging Education – Part 2, 2020, we read:

"The first director general of the World Health Organization, Canadian psychologist, Brock Chisholm, **said in a speech in 1946** "In every civilization the only psychological force capable of producing artificially imposed perversions of inferiority, guilt, and fear is morality, the concept of right and wrong…the concept of sin. Morality produces so much of the social maladjustment and unhappiness in the world. Freedom from morality means freedom to observe, to think and behave sensibly…If the race is to be freed of its crippling burden of good and evil it must be psychiatrists who take the original responsibility."

NO WONDER, 74 YEARS AFTER CHISHOLM'S SPEECH IN 1946, THE U.N. REMAINS A CORRUPT ORGANIZATION, AS MR. MANNING OBSERVED IN 1948.

MANNING'S ADVICE ON GOVERNMENT

APPENDIX 3

I have spent a third of my life in legislative halls and the executive offices of government, and I can say without hesitation that the problems that stem from human depravity (sin) cannot be solved by the laws and efforts of men. But I thank God that I can say with equal certainty that –

> *"Jesus Christ* (is) *the same yesterday, and to day, and for ever." (Hebrews 13:8)*

There is no limit to His mighty power, and none can doubt His readiness to recover men and nations from the brink of disaster which humanity has reached by following the paths of Godless materialism (Marx's dialectical) and stubbornly refusing to obey the voice of God. Let me recall to you His promise of old:

> *"If my people, which are called by my name, shall humble themselves, and pray, and seek my face, and turn from their wicked ways; then will I hear from heaven, and will forgive their sin, and will heal their land." (2 Chronicles 7:14)*

Let there be no mistake about this edict of God. If there is to be a miraculous healing of the mortal wounds from which Christian civilization is dying today, it will not be brought about by governments or by recovery programs, nor by force of arms, or iron curtains and atomic bombs. It will come to pass only when men and women profess the Name of Christ, humble themselves before God and prayerfully seek His face in unconditional surrender to His blessed will.

It will come pass when nations stop making a mockery of their Christian profession and restore the Family Altar to their homes, the Bible to their pulpits, and Jesus Christ to His rightful place in their lives and the councils of their land. Then, and not till then,

> "shall the Sun of righteousness arise with healing in his wings;" (Malachi 3:2)

to bind up humanity's wounds and recover men and nations from the horrible pit which they have digged for themselves.

> "Return unto me, and I will return unto you, saith the LORD of hosts" (Malachi 3:7)
>
> "How long halt ye between two opinions? if the LORD be God, follow him:" (1 Kings 18:21)
>
> – And, "Whatsoever he saith unto you, do it."

MANNING CHALLENGES CHRISTIANS

I repeat those words especially for you who know from personal experience, the saving and keeping power of the living Christ. It is a wonderful thing to trust in His finished work on Calvary's Cross and be born again by the Holy Spirit of God. It is a blessed thing to know that all your sins are forgiven and that your name is written forever in the Lamb's Book of Life!

But tell me – have you learned not only to trust, but to obey? Let me remind you of this. There is no limit to what Jesus Christ can do with and through that life of yours provided you will yield it wholly and unreservedly to Him.

APPENDIX 3

Are you prepared now to face the issue before you? Are you willing to confess this morning, that you haven't been living out and out for Christ? Perhaps the Holy Spirit has spoken to your soul as you have listened to this broadcast. If so, remember,

> "Whatsoever he saith unto you, do it."

It may be that He has made you willing to kneel, right now, before your Lord in the quietude of your home and say:

> "Blessed Savior, I have resisted thy will for me, and too often I've failed – or refused to obey thy Word: but this morning Thou hast brought me to the place where I can say –
>
> > Just as I am, thy love unknown
> > Has broken every barrier down:
> > Now to be thine, yea thine alone
> > O Lamb of God, I come!"

MANNING'S INVITATION TO THE UNSAVED

And now let me say a word to those of you who do not know Jesus Christ personally as your own living Savior and Lord. You know His name, - you know something about His life and death, and His resurrection from the dead. But you cannot say –

> "I know Him. I know the literal and glorious reality of the New Birth – I know the blessed peace of sins forgiven."

On the Divine authority of His infallible Word, I tell you this morning that you can know all those things this very hour, if you are prepared to obey His voice.

"FORTRESS AMERICA" UNDER SIEGE

"Come now, and let us reason together, saith the LORD: though your sins be as scarlet, they shall be as white as snow; though they be red like crimson, they shall be as wool." (Isaiah 1:18)

"Come unto me, all ye that labor and are heavy laden, and I will give you rest." (Matthew 11:28)

That is Christ's own invitation – and it is addressed to you – yes, to you! Now tell me, are you willing to accept it? Are you willing to accept it this morning – not tomorrow, not next week or next month, but right now? If you are, will you, too, bow reverently before the Son of God and say from the depths of your soul in obedience to Him...

"Just as I am without one plea
But that thy blood was shed for me,
And that thou bid'st me come to Thee
Oh Lamb of God, I come.

Just as I am thou wilt receive
Wilt welcome, pardon, cleanse, relieve,
Because thy promise I believe
Oh Lamb of God, I come."

"May God bless you!"

And now it's time for me to bid you good morning, and thank you again for the privilege of visiting your home as an Ambassador of Him Whose name rightly is called, *"Wonderful, Counsellor, the mighty God, the everlasting Father, the Prince of Peace." (Isaiah 9:6)*

Many of you may never hear my voice again, but of one thing you may be certain – no matter who you are – or where you go, you can never, never get beyond the

APPENDIX 3

Voice of God, and wherever I am, my prayer for you will be: **"Whatsoever he saith unto you, do it!"**

This message in Chicago was just one of many Mr. Manning preached over a lifetime serving Jesus Christ.

THE PROPHETIC VOICE

Calgary Prophetic Bible Institute
Calling ....
"Send the Light, the Blessed Gospel Light"

Western Canada's Pioneer Gospel Broadcast

C. F. C. N.   1060 Kilocycles
CALGARY — ALBERTA

Conducted By:
HON. ERNEST C. MANNING
Premier of Alberta

EVERY SUNDAY
C. F. C. N.   10.00 A.M.   C. F. C. N.

"The Family Altar"

Gather around your radio with Bible in hand. Have all the family join in. Encourage the children to take their part in this FAMILY BIBLE STUDY HOUR.

EVERY SUNDAY
C.F.C.N.   3.00 P.M.   C.F.C.N.

LISTEN TO PREMIER MANNING'S
Sunday Afternoon Broadcasts
VITAL MESSAGES
on
UP-TO-THE-MINUTE- TOPICS
With the
Old Fashioned Gospel

"Righteousness exalteth a Nation"
LET US ALL GET BACK TO THE BIBLE.

APPENDIX 4
"I SURVIVED COMMUNISM – ARE YOU READY FOR YOUR TURN?"

By Zuzana Janosova Den Boer

2019

The article below was written by Zuzana Janosova Den Boer, who experienced Communist rule in Czechoslovakia before coming to Canada. She said,

"Having recognized all-too familiar signs of the same propaganda in my adopted country of Canada, I felt obligated to write the article below ("**I Survived Communism – Are you Ready for your Turn?**")– because I do not want my adopted country to suffer the same fate as the country from which I emigrated (Czechoslovakia)."

Her warning is something all Canadians need to read.

> "It was scientifically proven that communism is the only social-economic system providing the masses with justice and equality – 100% of scientists agree on this. The topic is not up for debate!"

So proclaimed my professor during one of his lectures on the subject 'scientific communism', while the country of Czechoslovakia was still under communist control. I was reminded of his blustery pronouncement the first time I encountered the spurious claim that –

> "a consensus of 97% of scientists agree global warming is man-made."

Most people don't question scientific statements because they think they are facts. They do not understand that scientific statements must *always* be challenged, because **Science is not about 'consensus'**; *ideology is*.

In March, 2007, the website *WorldNetDaily* published an article entitled *"Environmentalism is new communism."* In it, the former Czech president, Vaclav Klaus, stated:

> "It becomes evident that, while discussing climate, we are not witnessing a clash of views about the environment, but a clash of views about human freedom."

He goes on to describe environmentalism as

> "the biggest threat to freedom, democracy, the market economy and prosperity."

Klaus has also written a book: *"Blue planet in green shackles"*, in which he states –

> "communism and environmentalism have the same roots; they both suppress freedom."

He also warns that any brand of environmentalism calling for centralized planning of the economy under the slogan of 'protecting nature' is nothing less than a reincarnation of communism – *new communism*.

Klaus understands communist propaganda very well – he should. Most of us who lived and suffered under communism can instantly recognize any signs of communist ideology, no matter how slight or subtle. Since I received my own vaccination of communist propaganda, during the first 27 years of my life, I too am immune to this disease. If someone is trying to 'save me' against my will, I'm instantly wary and ready to fight back – if it walks like a duck and quacks like a duck, it's a duck. So try to imagine how I feel, now as a Canadian, when I see the same tactics and hear the same phrases I saw and heard for years under communism, only this time in English! If you think I'm paranoid, or that communism in North America is far-fetched, then good luck to you – I hope you enjoy what's coming your way:

> "You [North] Americans are so gullible. No, you won't accept Communism outright; but we'll keep feeding you small doses of Socialism until you will finally wake up and find that you already have Communism. We won't have to fight you; we'll so weaken your economy, until you fall like overripe fruit into our hands."

- Nikita Khrushchev (1960)

Communism can be characterized by a single word: **deception**. Communists never disclose their real intentions. They are fraudsters who employ different identities, names and slogans, all for one goal: totalitarian enslavement. Since 1970, the goal of the *Communist Party USA* has been to subvert environmentalism and use it to advance their agenda. In 1972, Gus Hall, then chairman of the Communist Party USA, stipulated in his book "*Ecology*":

> "Human society cannot basically stop the destruction of the environment under capitalism. Socialism is the only structure that makes it possible ...This is true in the struggle to save the environment ... We must be the organizers, the leaders of these movements. What is new, is that knowledge of [a] point-of-no-return gives this struggle an unusual urgency."

This idea was incorporated into the US *Green Party* program in 1989 (the same year soviet communism collapsed), in which the fictitious threats of '*global warming*' and '*climate change*' are used to scare

APPENDIX 4

the public into believing humanity must "save the planet":

> "This urgency, along with other Green issues and themes it interrelates, makes confronting the greenhouse [effect] a powerful organizing tool ... Survival is highly motivating, and may help us to build a mass movement that will lead to large-scale political and societal change in a very short time ...
>
> First of all, we [must] inform the public that the crisis is more immediate and severe than [they] are being told, [that] its implications are too great to wait for the universal scientific confirmation that only eco-catastrophe would establish."

Do you think the UN *Intergovernmental Panel on Climate Change* is promoting science rather than socialism? Read the following admission from the co-chair of the UN IPCC Working Group III, during an interview in 2010 with the Swiss newspaper *Neue Zürcher Zeitung*:

> "We must free ourselves from the illusion that international climate policy is environmental policy ... We must state clearly that we use climate policy de facto to redistribute the world's wealth."

Do I have your attention? Then let me describe to you how communist propaganda and methodology work. There are 3 main stages:

1. Polarization

    (*KGB term: "demoralization")

2. Destabilization

3. Revolution

"FORTRESS AMERICA" UNDER SIEGE

* Demoralization: to corrupt; to deprive of spirit or energy to resist; to throw into confusion or disorganization

Stage 1:   Polarization – Divide and Conquer

In order to win power, communists first polarize their target society. The notion of *injustice* is introduced. One group of people – *poor workers* – are made to feel victimized by a second group, to the point that they demand civil discourse. Who are these people that supposedly victimize poor workers? Here's a clue:

> "Communists don't care about poor people, they just hate rich ones."
> **– George Orwell**

The one thing a communist cannot abide is a wealthy person. For communists, the *rich* are owners of private businesses, especially successful ones. They are loathed and demonized as heartless, spiteful monsters who exploit their employees and don't care about their welfare. The rich are public enemy #1 – they don't care about people or the environment; they care only about profit and wealth. Dare to disagree? Then you are a "denier" and "imperialist traitor", and after completion of stage 3, you will be *physically liquidated*.

> "We must hate. Hatred is the basis of communism. Children must be taught to hate their parents if they are not communists."
> **– Vladimir Ilyich Lenin**

During the first stage, communists focus on altruistic (unselfish, benevolent) people – people with big hearts, full of good intentions, who believe in doing good, for goodness' sake. Why? Because idealistic people are usually naïve and easy to manipulate, especially via their emotions. Recognizing how essential these people are to the success of his revolution, Lenin referred to them as *"useful idiots"*.

Stage 2: Destabilization

During the second stage the basic values of society are targeted for change. This always starts with *education*:

> "Give me your child for eight years, and [he or she] will be a communist forever."
> **– Vladimir Ilyich Lenin**

Communism always uses teachers and the education system to impose its ideology and promote its values – through *indoctrination* (see pp. 137-139). My own indoctrination started in elementary school. In grade four, we all had to become *Young Pioneers*. From that day, we were taught about the 'imminent danger' posed by capitalistic countries. The curriculum in school gradually, but firmly, established admiration for communism and loyalty to the communist party. We were constantly reminded of how we live in the –

> "best political system in the world", the "country with the best social justice and equality."

Our teachers participated in this process, either voluntarily or involuntarily. I remember teachers who actively reinforced communist indoctrination in schools. They exploited a child's emotional immaturity, lack of experience and knowledge –*vulnerability* – to impose their communist ideas, beliefs and values. They took advantage of their position of authority, of the natural trust that children place in teachers, to brainwash a young and vulnerable generation – to train the next generation of communists. Scare-mongering was a favorite tactic:

"FORTRESS AMERICA" UNDER SIEGE

> "Embrace communism! Fear capitalism! Otherwise, your country will be overtaken by imperialists and you will be exploited! ... Who is not with us is against us!"

If you think this can't happen in Canada, then I have news for you: it's been happening for some time, in both Canada and the US. The environmental cause was targeted years ago by communists as a catalyst for promoting socialism and paving the way for communism.

New communism is based on all the old communist ideological principles and beliefs, but **uses environmentalism as its agent of change**, to completely alter the core values of western democracy and destabilize (demoralize) society.

As illustrated by the following excerpt from *Captain Eco*, written by Jonathon Porrit-Ellis Nadler and published in 1991, children are being indoctrinated in our schools, being made to believe that it's their responsibility to 'save the planet':

> "Your planet is in serious trouble – from pollution, toxic waste and the loss of forest, farmland and fresh water...
> Your parents and grandparents have made a mess of looking after the earth. They may deny it, but they are little more than thieves. And they are stealing your future from under your noses."

Some more examples:

1. In May 2012, a <u>grade-3 class</u> took to the streets of Toronto with signs, to protest the construction of the *Northern Gateway* pipeline. The protest was organized by their teacher and a local community volunteer. Pure Marxist method. Just like these kids, who marched in protest to "save the planet", we too were

APPENDIX 4

made by our teachers to march with banners and signs to save our country from imperialists.

2.   In 2011, in Laval, Quebec, a six-year-old boy was <u>disqualified</u> from a teddy-bear contest because a Ziploc was found in his lunch instead of a reusable container. How did this boy feel, after being ostracized and excluded from his peers? Maybe he felt punished for his parents' action. What's the next step? Encourage children to report their own parents, who use Ziplocs instead of reusable containers – *denunciation* is common practice during communism.

3.   In April 2018, an Edmonton father went to an elementary school to see his grade-4 daughter's play. In the play, the children sabotaged a factory, in the name of *climate-change*, then went on to save Alberta from its "evil oil industry" and "greedy oil barons". Textbook communist methodology – demonizing the private sector (oil industry) by representing them as "greedy oil barons".

In some university lecture halls, professors are also trying to indoctrinate the new upcoming "proletariat." Every time I see elite university students protesting capitalism and advocating socialism, I wonder if they realize that if they succeed, it will be their very last protest. In an interview recorded in 1984, KGB defector *Yuri Bezmenov* described the consequences of *ideological subversion (indoctrination)*. Here is a short excerpt:

> "A person who is demoralized (indoctrinated) is unable to assess true information, the facts tell nothing to him....even if I shower him with information, with authentic proof, with documents, with pictures ... even if I take him, by force, to the Soviet Union and show him a concentration camp, he will refuse to believe it ... until he

will receive a kick in his fat bottom, by a totalitarian military boot."

- Yuri Bezmenov:

on "Useful Idiots" and the True Face of Communism (1984 Interview)

https://www.youtube.com/watch?v=K4kHiUAjTvQ

Bezmenov said that these leftist intellectuals would also be liquidated themselves if the communists take over. They would not realize their goals of being leaders in the new society.

Now, in 2020, we are coming very close to radical socialism/communism taking over the governments of the United States and Canada. The main threat is coming from within our countries, not from outside. A new socialist generation is arising among our young adults and children. Water Williams, professor of economics at George Mason University, warns in the two articles below:

> "Recall the campus demonstrations of the 1960s, in which campus radicals, often accompanied by their professors, marched around singing the praises of Mao and waving Mao's 'Little Red Book.' That may explain some of the campus mess today. Some of those campus radicals are now tenured professors and administrators at today's universities and colleges, and K-12 school-teachers and principals indoctrinating our youth." (**Leftists remain too soft on communism**, The Calgary Sun, Dec. 19, 2017)

> "A recent Victims of Communism Memorial Foundation survey found 51% of American millennials would rather live in a socialist or communist country than in a capitalist country. Only 42% prefer the latter." (**Young people and troubling views on socialism communism**, The Calgary Sun, Dec. 7, 2018)

APPENDIX 4

The children currently attending our elementary schools will vote in 10-12 years. How many of these children are being (or have already been) brainwashed into believing that in order to "save the planet", they must vote for a government that will stop "destroying the planet", by eliminating private ownership and taking control of production?

> "The philosophy of the classroom in one generation will be the philosophy of government in the next."
> **- Abraham Lincoln**

If you believe warm, cuddly socialism leads to utopian communism, in which equality and social justice prevail, then allow me to impart some insights about the 'social justice' delivered to us by communists. You deserve to know a little about the substance in which you will have to swim, before you dive into the cesspool called communism.

Stage 3: Revolution

After gaining the support of a majority, communists call for a democratic election. If they win it, they seize power and abolish democratic elections altogether. At this point, members of opposition parties, along with all other opponents deemed to be a potential threat, are 'physically liquidated'. (In case you aren't familiar with this quaint communist phrase; it means *executed*). Private businesses are immediately seized and confiscated – *nationalized*. Key supporters who now finally realize how they have been manipulated and exploited (*i.e.* "useful idiots" who are no longer useful) are either jailed or executed, to prevent the formation of any dissident movements. All other useful idiots, having fulfilled their purpose **of bringing communists to power**, are now either enslaved into the new ideology, or disposed of in a variety of prescribed ways. A new privileged elite of communist party leaders is now formed. (No hypocrisy here! After all those angry claims of exploitation by a privileged elite, what's the first thing communists do once they gain power?) Leaders of every key institution or organization: company, hospital, police, school, *etc.* are now replaced by an official member of the communist party. Competence, ability or fitness for the job is no longer relevant or required; the only prerequisite is loyalty to The Party.

Economic Consequences of Communism:

Do you think communism failed because of oppression? No. You can brainwash and threaten people, keep them dangling like puppets, *until the supply of goods starts to disappear*. Economic reality always prevails.

> "The problem with socialism is that you eventually run out of other's people money."
> **– Margaret Thatcher**

The economic consequences of communism are always the same – **poverty**, and this one comes with an ironclad guarantee – a lifetime warranty. People always spend their own money more carefully than someone else's. Capitalism is about efficiency. Private businesses must spend their capital very carefully. They cannot afford to make investments in their business, unless they are sure it will be worth it. A mistake could result in an increased price for their product, reduced cash-flow, loss of competitiveness and eventual bankruptcy.

In a centrally-planned economy, all production is controlled by government. The revenue required to operate the government and the economy is obtained

APPENDIX 4

through taxation. Because a centrally-planned economy is not subject to the laws of supply and demand, financial goals become meaningless, since there are no penalties for not achieving them. Thus, long-term government plans are never fulfilled and financial goals are replaced by imaginary production quotas. The result is profligate waste and inefficiency on a monumental scale. Communism institutes mandatory employment with pre-determined duties and salaries. The problem is lack of goods and services. Even if you have money, you will have few opportunities to spend it for your own benefit.

Both socialism and communism believe in the abolishment of private business; economic resources may be 'publicly owned', but they are *controlled* by government. Communism is implemented in two stages. During the first stage (socialism), wealth is distributed to people according to their productivity. During the second stage (communism), wealth is distributed according to individual need, but **it is the government, not the individual, who decides what those needs are, and if they even matter**. Remember the key word: deception? Socialism equals communism. Any political party or organization that advocates socialism is advocating communism. If you think socialism cares about democracy or freedom, then reread "Stage 3: Revolution" above.

Life under Communism:

What is life like under communism? In the Eastern Bloc countries, shortages of basic goods began in the 1980s. People had to get up at 3 AM in order to stand in line for basic necessities: bread, milk, meat, eggs, toilet paper, oil, *et cetera*. You could stand in line for hours and not even get a chance to buy something, once products ran out.

"FORTRESS AMERICA" UNDER SIEGE

Here are some other 'appealing' aspects:

1. Want an apartment? You can't buy one; real-estate markets don't exist. You'll probably get one (eventually) for free, but the government will decide the size, type, location, as well as your position in the queue, which may take years.

2. Want a car? You must first submit an application, or buy a permit, to buy a car from the government; then wait in line, for years. The wait time might be 2-3 years, or it could be as long as 7-10 years.

3. Want to use some recreational facilities (government built, of course) for your vacation? You need to be approved by a labor union, and wait.

4. Want day-care for your child? Submit an application, and wait.

5. Want a garage for your car? Submit an application, and wait. I submitted an application for a garage in 1988. When I left Slovakia in 1997, I still had not received a response.

Sounds idyllic (pleasantly simple), doesn't it? But here's the best part: there's no guarantee you will *ever* receive an apartment, car, garage, daycare, recreation, or anything else you might want. If there is *any* record (*ever*) of your non-compliance with communist ideology, **you will receive nothing**. As one communist leader informed me, after I refused to become member of a socialist party:

> "Forget about an apartment; forget about day-care; forget about a salary raise; forget about any benefits."

APPENDIX 4

Communism results in the poverty of an entire society. By comparison, free-market capitalism (individual enterprise) has lifted the highest number of people out of poverty of any other form of government in human history.

Corruption under Communism:

Because of lack of goods and services, corruption and bribery become endemic (always found) under communism. Of course, corruption also exists in capitalist countries, but communism elevates it to a completely different (*systemic*) level.

> "It's not **what** you know, but **who** you know."

To function, in order to survive, you must have a network of connections, and pay bribes, for *everything*. For example:

1.   Education may be for free, but there's no guarantee you'll ever get into your desired school's program, even if you have top marks. The state might have different plans for you, or for your child. But with good connections, *and* the timely delivery of a *valuable* gift to the school principal or party leader, anything is possible.

2.   Health care may be for free, but if you want your doctor to be sober for your surgery, better pay up. Paying bribes to doctors in cash or gold was common in the Eastern Bloc. I was even told how much I must pay *by the doctor himself*.

3.   Police are a special case: corrupt, enjoying their power immensely. Did you speed? Your choice is

"FORTRESS AMERICA" UNDER SIEGE

between a lesser bribe and much more expensive ticket. No court, no argument, no place to complain.

4. Need anything from government employees? Good luck. Communists invented stamps of different sizes and shapes. To get your document (or permit) stamped, you must pay a bribe.

5. Want a new book, new clothes, or a better piece of meat? Better know the saleswoman and be *really* nice to her.

6. Your car has broken down and needs repair? Oh dear, now you're in real trouble. Leaving a car in a repair shop entails the risk of good (functioning) components in your car being secretly replaced by inferior (or non-functioning) ones. The good components will be sold or exchanged for other goods. This is how *exchange markets* work under communism.

Due to lack of goods, everyone steals. We used to say:

> "Who is not stealing from the State is robbing his own family."

Without connections, you will remain in a queue for a very long time.

And finally, here's a truly delicious irony for you. Do you think communists care about the environment? I remember hills near chemical plants, laid bare and denuded of vegetation, by polluted air and acid rain; towns where heavy metals were produced became places where aluminum had poisoned the ground-water; cities where the haze from industrial smog was so thick you couldn't see through it, and it hung there for months; places where noxious compounds in the air forced residents to wear face-masks. Naturally, there

APPENDIX 4

were *environmental laws*, all conveniently ignored, in the name of glorious *socialism*.

The worst part is *fear*, of being arrested, of being tortured, of dying as a political prisoner in a prison, labour camp or uranium mine (slow death from radiation poisoning), incarceration in an insane asylum (you have to be crazy to oppose the regime), or of the same thing happening to someone you love. Fear is the primary tool for keeping people silent and obedient. Those who do not comply are interrogated, tortured, intimidated; put under surveillance as *MUKL* (destined for liquidation) by the Secret Police, or just killed (quicker and much easier). Those political prostitutes called *informers* are everywhere, especially in universities. They'll report everything you do or say. Forget about freedom; of action, speech or even thought. The Party controls everything, **and you voted for them, didn't you**?

> "Freedom is a fragile thing and is never more than one generation away from extinction. Those who have known freedom, then lost it, have never known it again."
> **– Ronald Reagan**

How many people have been murdered in capitalist countries for not being supporters of capitalism? How many have been murdered by a capitalist state for being anti-capitalist? If we turn the questions around and ask how many have been murdered in communist countries, the answer is between 80 to 100 million, globally.

<u>We are currently in the second stage (destabilization) of the *new green communism*.</u>

Are we so gullible that we can be taken without one shot, as Khrushchev predicted? Have we all taken our (many) freedoms for granted? Are we prepared to gullibly give up those freedoms to those advocating 'socialism', or are we prepared to resist the tide of radical leftism? Socialism equals communism – and after reading this article, I hope you have no illusions about what it is or where it leads.

Canadians will soon have the chance to demonstrate if, and how much, they treasure their freedom.

Good luck, Canada!

Zuzana Janosova den Boer

Ernest Manning wrote in The Face of the Sky – Part 1, 1971, the following:

News Report: Prague, Czechoslovakia

"Czechs Warned Against Religion"

"Czechoslovak parents have been warned in a series of articles published in the Slovak Communist Party Organ Pravda, that religion constitutes a grave hazard for the mental health of children. Religion interferes with sound, harmonious emotional development of children. It impedes social adaptability by burdening the nervous system. It leads to psychical disorders. It brings up individuals with undermined wills."

Manning commented:

"This wholly false propaganda is directly contradicted by Christ's affirmation to all mankind –

"I am come that they might have life, and that they might have it more abundantly." (John 10:10)

APPENDIX 5
WILLIAM ABERHART

ERNEST C. MANNING'S MENTOR & BEST FRIEND

William Aberhart
(1879-1943)

Pioneer Reformer

"A noble character is more valuable than life, which is yet more valuable than wealth."

Ernest Manning was saved one Sunday afternoon in 1926 through hearing the preaching of William Aberhart over CFCN radio in Calgary. Soon after, he travelled from his father's farm in Rosetown, Saskatchewan, to meet Mr. Aberhart and see his Christian ministry with young people.

After Mr. Aberhart opened his Calgary Prophetic Bible Institute in Calgary in 1927, the young Manning enrolled and soon after moved into the Aberhart's home and continued his studies, completing his formal education and taking Bible courses to begin the Christian ministry.

During that time he assumed responsibilities managing the Institute and co-preaching over the radio with Mr. Aberhart. He became like a son to the 20 year older man of God, and through their long association developed a strong Christian faith and character patterned after his mentor and best friend.

They carried their concern for their fellow man into politics in the early 1930s depression years, and assumed office together as Social Credit MLAs in 1935. They served together in the Alberta Legislature, with Mr. Aberhart as Premier and the younger Manning as Minister of Trade and Commerce, until the untimely death of William Aberhart on May 23, 1943.

Up until that time Ernest Manning was faithful to his friend amid the many bitter struggles the elder man faced in trying to lift an impoverished province out of economic and social despair. This heavy load contributed to Mr. Aberhart's early death, years before it should have come.

After William Aberhart's death Ernest C. Manning became the 8th Premier of Alberta, and carried the torch as Mr. Aberhart would have wished for the next 25 years, retiring in 1968. Mr. Manning realized his mentor's dream of building the Province of Alberta into an economic success, all the while faithfully preaching God's Word and bearing Christ's testimony before all men, as Mr. Aberhart had done all his years in public service as a school principal, pioneer radio preacher and politician.

What follows are two messages on Mr. Aberhart's life; the first is given by Rev. Harrison Villett at Mr. Aberhart's funeral service on May 30, 1943 (in The Prophetic Voice, June, 1943, vol. 1, no. 12), in Vancouver where he died on May 23. The second is Mr. Manning's January 28, 1945, address dedicating the William Aberhart Memorial Organ at the Prophetic Bible Institute in downtown Calgary (in The Prophetic Voice, February, 1945, vol. 3, no. 7). Both of these men's messages give a deep look into this remarkable man who had such a great impact and long-lasting influence for good on the Province of Alberta and places beyond.

In about 1923, shortly after the end of WW I, Mr. Aberhart preached these words in two separate messages in the Grand Theatre, Calgary, Alberta. Brief excerpts were reprinted in the Prophetic Voice in 1945, at the end of WW II.

> "If I judge correctly, there are too many people who treat the Bible as having no bearing on present day life with

all its struggles. No wonder many Bibles are left on the shelf, and the rising generation are beginning to believe that the Bible is of no account. Ah, no, my friend, the Bible does deal with nations, as well as individuals. If our statesmen should ever be able to read the Bible and understand it, I would like to ask if it would not be far better for them to do so than to blunder along in the dark, and sacrifice many valuable lives?" (The Present Eastern Question in the Light of Prophecy, The Prophetic Voice, January, 1945)

"When events so rapid in their succession as they are startling in their magnitude, terribleness and far-reaching consequences, chase each other as waves of the sea, or come upon us like falling stars on a dark winter evening, I think we should be looking to the God of Heaven to make known to us what it all means." (God's Great Divisions of the World's History, The Prophetic Voice, November, 1945)

Funeral Service Message
William Aberhart

by Rev. Harrison Villett

"And the king said unto his servants, Know ye not that there is a prince and a great man fallen this day in Israel?" (2 Samuel 3:38)

So well-known are these words and the historical background from whence they have come that they need no word of explanation from me.

I wish to take them from their context and use them to express what we all feel today.

APPENDIX 5

When David used the words "PRINCE" and "GREAT MAN," in relationship to his friend they had no reference whatever to Royal lineage and kingly ancestry. Rather, he was expressing the gifts of leadership displayed, and the bonds of affection uniting him to his country and to his people.

So, too, I feel that I can use these words today without fear of misrepresentation and misunderstanding.

> *"Know ye not that there is a prince and a great man fallen this day in Israel?"*

My knowledge of Mr. Aberhart goes back some twenty years when he was well known as one of the most capable and most effective school principals in Alberta. Teachers who served on his staff and students who passed through his school, alike held him in high esteem and deep respect.

He was known, too, as an educator who believed in Christianity as fundamental to any stable form of citizenship, and long before I met him I knew his voice as he crusaded by radio for Christian teaching and Christian practice in our everyday mode of life.

He was our pioneer radio preacher and one of the first to recognize the power and influence of the radio in education and religious teaching. Consequently, when our paths met and we became personally acquainted, I already felt we were not strangers, but friends.

And in his later years while serving the people of Alberta in the highest place of responsibility in the province, I have had no reason to change my estimation of his sincerity, ability and genuine character.

Today, I wish to mention several things that must not be overlooked, and without which we shall miss the key that interprets all his career and his rise to Dominion-wide, nay, world-wide prominence.

Mr. Aberhart had a deep love for, and an abiding faith in, young people. Doubtless, in his class room and principal's office there were forged those chains of affection for youth that later determined his career.

His graduates invariably led the Province; and when the depression laid the blight of poverty, unemployment, vice and defeat upon his graduates, Mr. Aberhart suffered in their suffering and prayed for their deliverance. It was this shocking state of affairs that impelled him to seek alleviation of the tragedies of our glorious Canadian youth.

When no voice was speaking for them, and no statesman had any solution, when orthodox politics and orthodox finance had utterly failed to shed any ray of hope, Mr. Aberhart was forced by conviction and desperation to launch out into the untried seas of political action.

And every man or woman who recalls the "jungles" of Canada and the roaming desperate, unwanted youth, will recall with gratitude this Friend whom Conservative Leader Graydon yesterday in Ottawa called, "a pioneer in social and economic reform."

APPENDIX 5

Alongside his deep concern for young people was his sympathy for the poor. One of Alberta's best known men said to me in a letter yesterday, "What kept so many people in Alberta loyal to him was the feeling that he was interested in the poor people; and many felt that no matter how dark the situation was, some day Mr. Aberhart would see that justice was done to them." These people now echo David's words,

> "Know ye not that a prince and a great man is fallen this day?"

It is a trite saying that we stone our prophets, crucify our Saviours and ridicule our reformers. Certain it is that nearly all accepted inventions and discoveries were once the cause of cruel mockery and insults. A pioneer in any realm walks a hard road, but in social and economic adventure the *via dolorous*. This way was taken by Mr. Aberhart because of his deep conviction that a solution of our ills was possible.

I saw him sacrificing his place of security, of honor in the neighborhood, his place of influence and service – deliberately taking on a task that would bring heartache, and eventually shorten his days, for a hope that possessed his soul. No responsible man in Canada has ever doubted his sincerity, nor has anyone questioned his motive.

His character has been above question or suspicion, and no shadow of any unworthy act has marred his administration.

The things I have mentioned as characteristic of this unusual leader had their roots in an abiding faith in

"FORTRESS AMERICA" UNDER SIEGE

Jesus Christ. His love for his fellow man was the product of his love of God. A writer, "Roman Collar," said in one of our national papers,

> "For a Premier to confess Christ constantly is indeed something."

I know nothing of Mr. Aberhart's boyhood and early manhood, but I know that from his arrival in Calgary until the day of his death, his witness for his Lord and Master has been steady, constant and unashamed. His example of Christian discipleship has been a beacon light to many a youth hard-pressed in the battle of life.

Emerson says:

> "Not gold, but only men can make
> A people great and strong,
> Men who for truth and honor's sake
> Stand fast and suffer long.
> Brave men who work while others sleep
> Who dare while others fly—
> They build a nation's pillars deep
> And lift them to the sky."

But it was his own fireside he found his inspiration, and approached the ideal in his domestic life. He and his faithful wife, who was both his helpmate and companion, inhabited as tenants that sacred spot called home, and needed no court to define their relative rights and duties. The invisible walls which shut in that home, and shut out all else, had their foundations upon the earth and their battlements in the skies. No force could break them down, no poisoned arrows could cross their tops, and at the gates Love and Confidence stood ever upon guard.

APPENDIX 5

The sympathy of the country goes out to Mrs. Aberhart and her two daughters, nor would we forget his aged mother in the east, in the hour of their bereavement. Our prayer is that the Lord who comforted the husband and father may comfort them in their sorrow.
And now we must say farewell.

Farewell to a Prince and a great man.

Farewell to a Pioneer who never spared himself, but whose chief concern was for others.

Farewell to a Christian gentleman who by his walk and conversation enriched the lives of countless numbers who with us now mourn his passing.

> "Now the laborer's task is o'er;
> Now the battle day is past;
> Now upon the farther shore
> Lands the voyager at last.
> Father, in Thy gracious keeping
> Leave me now Thy servant sleeping."

The service took place in the Canadian Memorial Church in Vancouver, and Mr. Aberhart was laid to rest at the beautiful Forest Lawn Memorial Gardens in Burnaby, British Columbia. His wife, Janet Aberhart (1878-1966), was laid to rest beside her husband. The setting has a beautiful view of Vancouver to the north.

A Memorial Service was held in Calgary on May 30, 1943. In The Prophetic Voice,

> "Mr. Manning, struggling under the stress of strong emotion, spoke of the splendid qualities of our departed brother, both as his best friend, and in the larger field of public life."

Within a week Mr. Manning assumed the position of Premier of Alberta, an office in which he remained for the next twenty-five years.

Looking back through the last ninety years the impact of Mr. Aberhart is seen in retrospect in the life of Ernest C. Manning. The young farm boy from Saskatchewan was saved and his character transformed through the preaching ministry and mentorship of William Aberhart. Mr. Manning would never have entered politics or become the transformative political power that he was for Albertans' general good had not his life and character been molded under the wings of his predecessor at the Aberhart's home, in the Bible Institute and in the provincial legislature during his formative years as a young adult, politician and Christian leader.

The people of Alberta saw what true, genuine Christian leadership could do for "the benefit of society as a whole" through the lives of these two consecrated men. Their examples should be the best standard for Albertans and Canadians to gauge the direction that our country is heading, and reject the leftist, Marxist socialist direction of our current Parliament and many of our provincial legislatures in the recent past.

APPENDIX 5

Dedication Address
William Aberhart Memorial Organ
The Hon. Ernest C. Manning

This address was made for the William Aberhart Memorial Organ donated to the Prophetic Bible Institute in Calgary in memory of the dearly beloved Dean. Most of the text of Premier Manning's message follows, as printed in the Prophetic Voice, February, 1945:

"Numerous and varied are the memorials which men have erected to those whom they cherished, and whose memory they desired to perpetuate for all time.

This beautiful memorial organ will perpetuate the living memory of William Aberhart in a manner that is in keeping with the life and the spirit of the man himself, for this instrument will perpetuate his memory through the services of this Institute that he himself founded and which work he so dearly loved.

In the hearts and minds of those many thousands who were numbered among his staunchest and closest friends, his memory will always be inseparably bound up with his work and with his ministry from this city, and especially from this Christian Institute.

Some may perhaps recall those distant days of 1910 – 35 years ago, when Mr. Aberhart first came to the City of Calgary to follow his chosen profession as a teacher. Those who knew him in those earlier days will remember how in a few short years he advanced in that chosen profession to the principalship of Crescent Heights High

"FORTRESS AMERICA" UNDER SIEGE

School of this city, the position which he held with such distinction for twenty years.

Many indeed will be the memories of the thousands of young men and young women, the students who graduated from that institution with distinction under his able leadership.

Many listening to this Dedication Service today will be calling to mind the days of 1916 and 1917 when the Calgary Prophetic Bible Conference was organized by the man whose memory we honor today. They will be thinking of how he commenced those early meetings on Sunday afternoons in the Public Library of this city, and how in a very short time the throngs who gathered to hear his expositions of the Bible were so great that he was compelled to seek a larger place.

Some will be thinking of the year 1920 when this Conference work was moved to the Grand Theatre, and I will venture to say there are some listening in today who found Jesus Christ as their own personal Savior in the old Grand Theatre.

Still others will recall most vividly the year 1924 when Mr. Aberhart's Conference work had grown once more to such an extent that again a larger place was necessary. In that year the services were held in the Palace Theatre here in down town Calgary. Many indeed will recall the great services of those days.

I know many of the radio friends will bring to mind more particularly the days of 1925, for that was the year in which Mr. Aberhart first broadcast his Sunday afternoon

APPENDIX 5

services. Those were the days when radio was in its infancy and I venture to say that thousands listening to us this afternoon can well remember, as some of us here can too, the first time we heard that voice over the air waves, declaring the unsearchable riches of Jesus Christ. Some of you have listened regularly these twenty years.

Friends, eternity itself will be required to measure the extent of that vast radio work, carried on so faithfully through all those 20 years – the thousands who were led to Christ, and the thousands who were built up in the Christian faith only eternity will disclose. This worthwhile Christian ministry has influenced, and will continue to influence, the life of this Western country for generations to come. The worthwhile things in life born of those great services which came to our minds, will be revived in our hearts from week to week as the strains of this beautiful memorial organ fall on our ears.

Outstanding in the minds of some will be the year 1926, the year in which Mr. Aberhart proposed the erection of a Christian Bible Institute here in the City of Calgary, for this Western country. With his unbounded zeal he threw himself into the task, until a year later, in the fall of 1927, this fine building, the Calgary Prophetic Bible Institute, was dedicated to the glory of God.

The hundreds of students who have passed through this place since those days will recall many, many cherished memories.

About the same time the Radio Sunday School was organized by the late founder of this Institute. Through this great branch of the work, thousands of boys and

"FORTRESS AMERICA" UNDER SIEGE

girls, many now grown to manhood and womanhood, have been brought into a saving relationship with the Savior and a knowledge of His Word.

Familiar to us all are the more recent years of 1933 to 1935, when in his love for the good and welfare of his fellow men, Mr. Aberhart not only spoke from this platform but travelled back and forth throughout the length and breadth of this Province, talking to men and women of the solutions to the problems of life which concerned them from day to day.

But still more vivid in our minds are the memories of 1935 to 1943, when Mr. Aberhart served with such distinction in the larger field to which his people called him that his name became known around the earth. That field was not a new field, but rather it was an enlargement of a great service to his fellow men which he had rendered for so many years.

And again, there are many who cherish memories of him as a friend, memories too sacred to touch upon, memories of him in his home with his family and his beloved wife, whom it is an honor to have present with us at this service today.

As we now dedicate to the glory of God this instrument which is the tribute of thousands, to a beloved friend, and a great soldier of Jesus Christ, whose work and whose memory it will perpetuate throughout the years to come, from the depths of our hearts we all can say,

"It is right, it is fitting that it should be so."

APPENDIX 5

Ernest C. Manning and his wife, Muriel Manning, are laid to rest together in the *Christus Garden* of Eden Brook Cemetery in the Springbank area of southwest Calgary. They lie on a gentle hillside with a beautiful view of the Rocky Mountains toward the west. Their simple, bronze grave markers each read,

"In God's Loving Care"

When Jesus returns they will both rise together to meet Him in the air and forever be with their Lord and Savior, Jesus Christ, in their resurrected bodies.

> *"O death, where is thy sting? O grave, where is thy victory? (1 Corinthians 15:55)*

> *"For the Lord himself shall descend from heaven with a shout, with the voice of the archangel, and with the trump of God: and the dead in Christ shall rise first: Then we which are alive and remain shall be caught up together with them in the clouds, to meet the Lord in the air: and so shall we ever be with the Lord." (1 Thessalonians 4:16-17)*

Amen, and Amen!

ABOUT THE AUTHOR

Frank Crawford was born in Pine Falls, Manitoba as a Metis "Baby Boomer" in 1947, after his father, David Crawford, a Canadian soldier in the Winnipeg Rifles, returned home from Europe. As a small town Canadian boy he loved the outdoors and the many sports and activities in the close-knit pulp and paper company town. Frank finished High School in Pine Falls and went west to Alberta in 1966 to attend the University of Calgary. In his second year he entered Earth Sciences, majoring in Geology and stayed there to finish his BSc and MSc

ABOUT THE AUTHOR

degrees, graduating in 1972. His special interest was in stratigraphy and sedimentation in ancient depositional environments in the rock record.

Opportunities came to travel across parts of Northwest Territories and adjoining British Columbia as a Junior Geologist prior to graduation. Later Frank worked with oil companies on exploration projects in frontier basins and many international projects, living for a time in Venezuela and Libya, as well as travelling to a number of other countries. His work in exploration spanned the years between 1972 and 2012, in which he developed his skills in analytical work, evaluating and integrating a diversity of technical information in exploration and development geological projects around the world, as well as in Canada. He developed during his travels an interest in foreign countries and cultures in many parts of the world, meeting and working with technical people from some of those places.

In 1981, Frank's interests expanded beyond his career in exploration. Through a variety of circumstances he came into contact with Christians whose testimonies encouraged him to read the Bible on his own, something he had never done before. One night in a Bible study in Calgary he came under the witness of the gospel of Jesus Christ, saw himself as a lost sinner and called on the Lord Jesus Christ to save his soul. That night he was born again, saved and given a new heart and new priorities and affections in life. He then became a Bible reader and witnessing Christian, attending Baptist churches and serving the Lord Jesus Christ until the present day.

Mr. Crawford's main Christian endeavor since his conversion was in spreading the gospel of Jesus Christ. This book contains the salvation message in the main text and appendix for that reason. He became naturally interested in Alberta's William Aberhart and Ernest Manning who both were bold Christian witnesses, even while serving as politicians in public life. When Frank was made aware of their gospel ministries and political accomplishments he decided to bring to public light their Christian contribution to the Province of Alberta and free democracy in general. It is Frank's firm belief that Canada is missing men like this in public office and that more committed Christians should seek to serve their country, first by being unashamed concerning their beliefs, and secondly by offering themselves for public service when led of the Lord and assured of God's calling to run for office. According to Ernest Manning personal salvation should precede public service, for the best outcome.

In the 1980s Frank was in a Baptist Church with a Christian School. The Provincial Government began to force the churches with such schools to be licensed. Frank's Pastor refused to license the church's Christian academy, and a long legal battle began between that church and the provincial government. Five court cases ensued, ending with a decision at the Supreme Court of Canada in 1987. The church won the first case and lost the rest. Subsequently the government acted, arresting the pastor and putting him in jail in October, 1987. Frank witnessed firsthand the whole process as well as the pain and heartache experienced by his pastor's family. This sad episode motivated him to become more interested and active in the political life of Alberta and Canada.

Mr. Crawford became involved in political activities, especially during election time, going door-to-door with candidates and distributing literature. As a Bible-believer he felt obligated to try and ensure Conservative candidates were elected federally and provincially during election cycles beginning in the mid-to-late 1990s at the

ABOUT THE AUTHOR

time the Reform Party of Canada first formed. He became concerned about the direction that his country was taking, especially the moral decline in society and the huge national debt which at that time was around $560 billion. He was very happy to see Stephen Harper elected Prime Minister and remain in that position for 9 ½ years.

Frank Crawford has written and compiled this book out of concern for the future of his country. He believes that Canada is in a major crisis and Canadians are in very real danger of losing their freedom to a dictatorial socialist regime. That is why he has made an effort to analyze and understand how socialism-communism works, what its main beliefs are, and how it manages to undermine and destroy free democracy. Mr. Manning's writings were a great help in making this analysis. He hopes that this book will help those holding public office today and others aspiring to politics to understand better the socialist agenda. Frank has tried to expose the real character of Karl Marx, the patriarch of socialism-communism and his avid followers and fellow travelers. He also hopes that some in the socialist movement will re-evaluate their loyalties and serve the political movement that best assures the preservation of Canada's freedoms, federally, provincially and municipally.

Mr. Crawford has greatly benefitted from Ernest Manning's writings on the subject of socialism-communism and has referenced his material throughout this book. Mr. Manning saw far ahead the dangers Canada was facing from the collectivist movement, that is, socialism-communism. His worst fears are being realized today with a new Liberal Government under Justin Trudeau in power. It is a sad fact that Ernest Manning's, as well as his predecessor William Aberhart's, warnings went unheeded by the general public. Citizen

"FORTRESS AMERICA" UNDER SIEGE

apathy toward the dangers our country faces internally has continued from Manning's time until the present day. It is a sad indictment on Canadians if Canada is defeated from within, as Vladimir Lenin, predicted when he wrote, "The easiest way to take a fortress is from within." Exactly the same thing is happening in the U.S. That is why Frank has entitled this book "Fortress American Under Siege."

The author does not know if it is already too late to reverse the downward trend and preserve our democratic freedom in Canada, or in the U.S. Canada is already the most progressive, leftist 'democracy' in the Western world. How much farther do we have to go for people to open their eyes, before they end up in totalitarian bondage? This book is a serious attempt, hopefully not a futile one, to provide a warning and a way out of our dilemma. I must finally emphasize that politics, though vitally important, is NOT the solution. Secular conservative voters, though important, cannot reverse the slide down the slippery slope to radical socialism that our country is on.

In the final analysis, the solution to our preservation or loss of freedom rests with individual Christians in the Christian churches. The churches are in apostasy or "falling away" from God's Word, meaning His gospel and the commandments in the Holy Writ as Mr. Manning would often preach and write. They have departed from God's Word and His commandments to love and serve the Lord Jesus Christ and their neighbor with all their heart, and with all their soul, and with all their mind and with all their strength. Many church goer's need to check their personal salvation – Is it real?? When were you saved? Do you have a testimony of salvation that is convincing to others and evident in your own life? Mr. Manning emphasized this vital need at the end of every

ABOUT THE AUTHOR

one of his messages. As the great evangelist the Apostle Paul wrote:

> *"God now commandeth all men everywhere to repent: Testifying both to the Jews, and also to the Greeks (Gentiles) repentance toward God, and faith toward our Lord Jesus Christ." (Acts 17:30 & Acts 20:21)*

Frank admits the obvious; socialism-communism is in ascendancy and our Judeo-Christian culture is all but gone from the public arena. He advocates that only a revival of genuine Christians – even beginning with only a few individuals, is what will be needed first to bring the churches and then, hopefully, segments of society back from the abyss – and back to God. Lasting peace and security for our families and fellow citizens can be obtained in no other way. Without a revival of the Christian churches Canada and the United States are doomed, no matter who takes over the reins of power. As Premier Manning said long ago in one of his public addresses – in beginning a speech to a secular audience, as recorded by Brian Brennan in "The Good Steward: The Ernest C. Manning Story," 2008:

> "That all Albertans acknowledged the sovereignty of Almighty God, whose omnipotent arm is our strongest defense and whose Divine Providence affords security and peace to all who will put their trust in Him."

Amen!

IN FLANDERS FIELDS

In Flanders fields the poppies blow
Between the crosses, row on row,
That marks our place; and in the sky
The larks, still bravely singing, fly
Scarce heard amid the guns below.

We are the Dead. Short days ago
We lived, felt dawn, saw sunset glow,
Loved, and were loved, and now we lie
In Flanders fields.

Take up our quarrel with the foe:
To you from failing hands we throw
The torch; be yours to hold it high.
If ye break faith with us who die
We shall not sleep, though poppies grow
In Flanders fields.

                        Lt.-Col. John McCrae
                        (1872-1918)

"Lieutenant Colonel John McCrae, MD was a Canadian poet, physician, author, artist and soldier during World War I, and a surgeon during the Second Battle of Ypres, in Belgium. He is best known for writing the famous war memorial poem "In Flanders Fields". McCrae died of pneumonia near the end of the war.

Born: November 30, 1872, Guelph
Died: January 28, 1918, Boulogne-sur-Mer, France
Place of burial: Commonwealth War Graves Commission Cemetery
Siblings: Thomas McCrae, Geills McCrae
Education: Guelph Collegiate Vocational Institute, University College, University of Toronto" (Wikipedia)

www.ingramcontent.com/pod-product-compliance
Lightning Source LLC
Chambersburg PA
CBHW071429300426
44114CB00013B/1362